HOUSING BOOMS IN GATEWAY CITIES

IJURR-SUSC Published Titles

HOUSING BOOMS IN GATEWAY CITIES

DAVID LEY

WILEY

This edition first published 2023
© 2023 John Wiley & Sons Ltd

The right of David Ley to be identified as the author of this work has been asserted in accordance with law.

Registered Offices
John Wiley & Sons, Inc., 111 River Street, Hoboken, NJ 07030, USA
John Wiley & Sons Ltd, The Atrium, Southern Gate, Chichester, West Sussex, PO19 8SQ, UK

Editorial Offices
9600 Garsington Road, Oxford, OX4 2DQ, UK
The Atrium, Southern Gate, Chichester, West Sussex, PO19 8SQ, UK

For details of our global editorial offices, customer services, and more information about Wiley products visit us at www.wiley.com.

Wiley also publishes its books in a variety of electronic formats and by print-on-demand. Some content that appears in standard print versions of this book may not be available in other formats.

A catalogue record for this book is available from the Library of Congress

Paperback ISBN: 9781119853602; ePub ISBN: 9781119853626; ePDF ISBN: 9781119853633; oBook ISBN: 9781119853619

Cover Images: © Photographs by David Ley
Cover Design: Wiley

Set in 11/13pt AGaramondPro-Regular Integra Software Services Pvt. Ltd, Pondicherry, India
Printed and bound by CPI Group (UK) Ltd, Croydon, CR0 4YY

C9781119853596_230623

Contents

Series Editors' Preface

IJURR Studies in Urban and Social Change Book Series

The International Journal of Urban and Regional Research (IJURR) Studies in Urban and Social Change Book Series shares IJURR's commitments to critical, global, and politically relevant analyses of our urban worlds. Books in this series bring forward innovative theoretical approaches and present rigorous empirical work, deepening understandings of urbanization processes, but also advancing critical insights in support of political action and change. The book series editors appreciate the theoretically eclectic nature of the field of urban studies. It is a strength that we embrace and encourage. The editors are particularly interested in the following issues:

- Comparative urbanism
- Diversity, difference, and neighborhood change
- Environmental sustainability
- Financialization and gentrification
- Governance and politics
- International migration
- Inequalities
- Urban and environmental movements

The series is explicitly interdisciplinary; the editors judge books by their contribution to the field of critical urban studies rather than according to disciplinary origin. We are committed to publishing studies with themes and formats that reflect the many different voices and practices in the field of urban studies. Proposals may be submitted to editor-in-chief, Walter Nicholls (wnicholl@uci.edu), and further information about the series can be found at www.ijurr.org.

Walter Nicholls
Manuel Aalbers
Talja Blokland
Dorothee Brantz
Patrick Le Galès
Jenny Robinson

Acknowledgements

In some places access to housing has become a primary, even the primary, contributor to the meaning of the city. This project began with an ambition to examine housing as a topic that mattered profoundly to people in everyday life. From this phenomenological entrée the book spiralled into consideration of a range of economic, political, and social contexts within which housing markets are embedded. The range of contexts and particularities was expanded by the decision to examine five gateway cities on four continents, and to tease out both local explanations and also broader generalisations within the conceptual framework of housing and wealth accumulation in an asset-based society.

This daunting task could not have been accomplished without the substantial support of colleagues during visits to Singapore, Hong Kong, Sydney, and London. In Singapore I gratefully acknowledge the hospitality of Brenda Yeoh and Elaine Ho at the National University; in Hong Kong, my thanks to George Lin at the University of Hong Kong, and Si-ming Li at the Lam Institute for East-West Studies at Hong Kong Baptist University for their generous assistance; in Sydney, my magnanimous guide was Bill Randolph at the City Futures Research Centre at the University of New South Wales; and in London, Chris Hamnett and Loretta Lees, then at King's College, were knowledgeable interlocutors. These colleagues suggested contacts for me and provided some orientation to local housing markets. Their valuable contributions were continued by the many housing specialists from different sectors who agreed to be interviewed in each city, kindly sharing their specialised knowledge.

My aim to develop a textured interpretation of each city's housing market profited from a critical reading of chapters by local specialists. While I am responsible for interpretations and errors, valuable responses to individual chapters were provided by Elaine Ho and Robbie Goh, George Lin and Leo Shin, Bill Randolph and Dallas Rogers, Josh Gordon, Loretta Lees and Chris Hamnett, and Richard Harris and Elvin Wyly. In Vancouver I have benefitted from conversation with Josh Gordon, Elvin Wyly, and Andy Yan, and from the work of committed investigative journalists including Kerry Gold, Doug Todd, Kathy Tomlinson, and Ian Young. No project of this scale could be conducted without research assistance and I have benefitted from talented researchers, Sin Yih Teo, Idaliya Grigoryeva, and Craig Jones. My thanks to you all.

The Canadian Social Sciences and Humanities Research Council steadfastly provided research support for this study. The Department of Geography at UBC has, throughout my career, offered a stimulating intellectual environment, and once again I am pleased to acknowledge the professional work of Eric Weinberger, departmental cartographer. My thanks to Walter Nicholls, Editor-in-Chief of the Studies in Urban and Social Change series for his encouragement and advice, to the SUSC Editorial Board for endorsement, to two manuscript reviewers for suggestions, and to the editorial and production teams at Wiley for a reassuringly professional publication process. Thanks as always to Sandy for her good humour in allowing another book into the house.

This book is a COVID-19 product. While research began in late 2012, the bulk of the writing occurred between 2019 and 2021, and true to the period was written from the comfort and conviviality of a home office, recovering at least one phenomenological moment in a book about housing which could not be contained within its original frame.

Vancouver, July 2022

List of Figures

List of Tables

CHAPTER 1

Introduction: Housing as Asset

Built Up situates real estate where it belongs, at the very centre of the process of urban development and the broader nature of advanced capitalism today.
(Florida 2022)

Houses are built to be lived in not for speculation.
(Xi Jinping, address to the 19th Party Congress, Beijing, October 2017)

We begin with three propositions:

1. Housing has a new-found centrality in advanced societies due to its expanded role as an investment asset and source of wealth accumulation. Housing matters more both in the macro-economy and in daily life since the financial deregulation of the 1980s and especially following the Global Financial Crisis of 2008–2009, due to an unprecedented low-interest environment and abundant footloose capital. But easy credit also raises the spectre of unstable debt loads and destructive housing bubbles.
2. While the same favourable borrowing terms have been available throughout a nation, housing investment is disproportionately attracted to the property markets of gateway cities, vibrant cosmopolitan portals connected to international flows of trade, capital, and immigrant labour. These cities display exaggerated house price cycles, heightened social inequality, and a political system that typically favours house price inflation as a household asset that offsets declining real wages and welfare expenditures.
3. Heightened investment activity from the globalisation of housing markets decouples an established connection between regional labour markets and housing markets, so that local wage earners are left behind by unaffordable residential prices. Conventional housing market explanations are no longer

adequate in gateway cities where 'fundamentals' must be re-scaled to include immigration, off-shore investors, and the role of the global real estate industry. Financialisation, a growing sophisticated synergy of housing and finance, has up-scaled housing markets.

These three propositions give rise to a series of consequences that define the housing condition of gateway cities. The creation of housing as an asset in a deregulated global economy brings opportunistic capital flows from investors (both national and global) that are commonly willing and able to outbid local end-use buyers. As well-heeled household and institutional investors flood the market, surplus demand, beyond use or need, drives up prices and availability. Affordability becomes a major challenge to local workers. They make adjustments. Displaced from one housing sub-market they occupy another, themselves displacing less well-resourced fellow citizens. They double up or accept smaller units, they rent instead of own, they return to, or do not leave, the parental home, they enter informal housing arrangements, they accept lengthy commutes, they assume heavy mortgage debt, they leave the region, and sometimes they protest politically. They change jobs, take on a second job, become a two-wage earner family, postpone child-rearing, thereby reducing the birth rate.

But their frustrations and stresses contribute to the benefits and satisfactions of better-resourced households who are already property-owners. A broad separation in the distribution of wealth arises between early and late arrivals to the inflating housing market of gateway cities. Indeed, an egregious transfer of wealth occurs as late arrivals – the young, the poor, immigrants – attempt to leave rental units and enter the unaffordable market for a home whose rising cost builds the land-based portfolio of early arrivals. In their life chances early and late arrivals occupy opposing housing classes.

Some justification and expansion are needed of these propositions.

The New Centrality of Housing

During the house price run-up to the Global Financial Crisis (GFC) of 2008–2009, *The Economist* ran a special feature on 'The global housing boom' (The Economist 2005). Its tone was apocalyptic:

> According to estimates by *The Economist*, the total value of residential property in developed economies rose by more than $30 trillion over the past five years, to over $70 trillion, an increase equivalent to 100% of those countries' combined GDPs… it looks like the biggest bubble in history.

With reduced confidence in the stock market, investment energies had turned to property as a favoured asset in many western nations. It was not hard to find evidence for *The Economist's* claim that 'Prices are being driven by speculative demand'. Investment instruments like interest-only and negative-amortisation loans revealed the gambler's stake in the continuing rapid inflation of residential properties; it was estimated that these frothy instruments accounted for 60% of new mortgages in California (The Economist 2005). In 2004, almost a quarter of houses in the United States were purchased for investment purposes, another 13% were second homes. *The Economist* ended its analysis with a doomsday scenario:

> The housing market has played such a big role in propping up America's economy that a sharp slowdown in house prices is likely to have severe consequences. Over the past four years, consumer spending and residential construction have together accounted for 90% of the total growth in GDP. And over two-fifths of all private-sector jobs created since 2001 have been in housing-related sectors, such as construction, real estate and mortgage broking.

Doomsday arrived in short order. The GFC proceeded from the unravelling of toxic home mortgages, extracted from risk-taking and often vulnerable American households, which then passed through an international financial sector short on ethical judgement and due diligence (Wyly et al. 2009; Forrest and Yip 2011; Bardhan et al. 2012; Farlow 2013). When this deck of cards collapsed, housing market failures brought down financial institutions, with knock-on effects through the economy, and unprecedented levels of foreclosure as financial crisis downed the American middle-class. Contagion into the rest of the economy and ensuing policies of harsh austerity in the US and the UK, amongst others, sustained the social misery (Peck 2012; Clark with Heath 2013). Since then, banks have paid over $150 billion in US court-imposed fines for their improprieties. The wider cost of the GFC to the US has been variously estimated from $22 trillion upwards, including lost revenue, incomes, and taxes, and $9.5 trillion in the UK (BBC 2017). Catastrophic though these events were, their inter-connections were not unique. More than two-thirds of banking crises in recent decades followed a boom–bust housing cycle (IMF 2019c, p. 62); consequently, 'House price dynamics and macroeconomic and financial stability are tightly connected' (ibid.). Housing matters!

Housing crises are not limited to western democracies. In East Asia the developmental state has used housing and property development as the front end of its urbanisation mission (Doling and Ronald 2014). In Hong Kong,

Singapore, and China large and energetic property corporations harbour global ambitions. Immense wealth is derived from land development (Lin 2009); seven of the ten wealthiest men in China (including Hong Kong) in 2019 led property development or construction companies (Liu, Yiu and Liu 2020). Real estate has been at the heart of the Chinese economic development model (Wu 2015). Substantial land value gains and high real estate profits in urban China have encouraged excessive leveraging, with heavy overhanging debt loads that threaten both local government and the broader economy. A senior official of the National People's Congress laid out the dilemma:

> The real estate industry's excessive prosperity has not only kidnapped local governments but also kidnapped financial institutions — restraining and even harming the development of the real economy, inflating asset bubbles and accumulating debt risk… The biggest problem facing the country is how to reduce reliance on real estate.
>
> (Yin Zhongqing, cited in Wildau 2017)

The dilemma persisted. In the surprising initial boom during the COVID-19 pandemic, China's top financial regulator warned against the excessive exposure of banks to the property sector as 'the biggest grey rhino'[1] faced by the country's financial sector (Ren 2021) – while the debt crisis among residential developers, led by Evergrande, steadily deepened.

The prominence of the property sector in the macro-economy is matched by its growing salience for private households. A conventional distinction has contrasted the use value from the exchange value of residential property. The former describes the utility and purpose of the home for everyday life, the latter its valuation as a marketable commodity. Together they incorporate the expanded mission of the modern home. As Fiona Allon has written, 'We want our homes to be everything: shelter, identity statement, asset, property investment, a ticket to wealth and riches, and even to function as banks' (Allon 2008, p. 12). As a younger urban Australian, Allon emphasised the economic dimension of the home more than an earlier generation might have done. The increasing cost of entry to homeownership and the potential for significant capital gains have raised its economic stake and sharpened the profile of inequality. In Canada, housing accounted for 34% of household wealth in 1990; in 2015 it crossed the 50% threshold (Statistics Canada 2020). Due largely to house price increases, median family net worth doubled in Canada from 1999 to 2016; in Vancouver, the most expensive city, it almost tripled (Gellatly and Richards 2019). In the pandemic boom, during five quarters following January 2020, household net worth in Canada rose by a substantial

18% to CAD$13.7 trillion, due largely to accelerating house prices; in the final quarter, homeowners absorbed 95% of that growth, leaving the nation's renters with a pittance. Household debt loads also swelled, common to housing booms, with new mortgage debt accounting for 107% of total household credit debt during these five quarters (Statistics Canada 2021a). Striking evidence of the role of housing in wealth accumulation also comes from the United Kingdom. National wealth rose by £7 trillion between 1995 and 2016, and more than £5 trillion, three-quarters of the total growth, was attributable to the escalation in value of the housing stock (Macfarlane 2017; ONS 2017). Unsurprisingly, among a range of investment options, over half the respondents to a UK survey nominated residential property as providing the best return (Lowe 2011). Further finessing of national wealth data showed that while the increase in the value of dwellings was appreciable, more significant was the growth of land value beneath them.[2] Land is the greatest single contributor to UK national wealth, and its share has been steadily rising. Over the period from 1996 to 2018 the median contribution of land to the annual growth of non-financial assets in the UK's net worth was 67% (ONS 2019a). Land value has been growing at an even faster rate than dwellings and other improvements in the built environment. This has been a constant refrain in gateway cities, providing great incentives for builders and investors, while generating profound policy challenges to the creation of affordable housing.

The Volatile Housing Markets of Gateway Cities

At a Singapore conference in April 2015, Laurence Fink, Chair and CEO of BlackRock, offered his advice on successful investment. 'The two greatest stores of wealth internationally today is [sic] contemporary art… and two, the other store of wealth today is apartments in Manhattan, apartments in Vancouver, in London' (cited in Burgos and Ismail 2015). Housing as asset was given a geography by an interlocutor with compelling global credentials as the founder of the world's largest asset management empire. Fink's discerning eye focused on residential property in designated locations, gateway cities with a history of appreciating housing values (Martin 2011).

Gateway cities are hubs in international flows of capital, trade, and migrants.[3] Many are global cities, but whereas discussions of global cities are preoccupied with hierarchies and labour market classifications, the concept of gateway cities highlights interface and mobility, the movement of people, finance, goods, and information. Gateway cities are ports, typically nodes of ocean and air traffic. They are major landing points for international migrants, and immigration is usually the major source of population growth. They have white-collar, post-industrial economies, with a dual labour market of well-paid professionals and managers, and poorer paid service workers, disproportionately women, immigrants, and young singles. They are typically entertainment, fashion, arts, education, and media centres, disseminating both higher learning and the novelties of popular culture. As cultural and lifestyle centres they are noticed, even branded in the transnational imagination, and destinations of tourists and international students. They are places where national and international capital moves freely, entrepreneurial juices flow, opportunities and opportunism exist for striking a deal, and white-collar crime makes a profitable entry.

Gateway cities like London, New York, Hong Kong, and Sydney, tied into global flows of capital and labour, have become veritable honey-pots for national and global property investors (Fernandez et al. 2016; Ley 2017, 2021; Liu and Gurran 2017; Chung and Carpenter 2022). Global portfolio investment supplemented by wealth migration aided by golden visas have together brought a 'global wall of money' (Aalbers 2016, p. 134) to bear upon selected local housing markets. Within gateway cities, significant residential investment is initially concentrated in prime areas, the blue-chip neighbourhoods where returns are proven; but effects ripple out reaching even distant suburbs (Grigoryeva and Ley 2019). New York's new luxury high-rise condominiums of 'Billionaires' Row' around the southern edge of Central Park, including the Time-Warner Center, attracted many foreign purchasers (Story and Saul 2015). As properties inflated in value, ownership became more difficult to trace, with capital flows leading to tax havens with inscrutable security concerning the identity of beneficial owners. Over half the residential sales of over $5 million in Manhattan in 2014 were to shell companies, described by an international anti-money laundering agency as the getaway cars of financial crime (Transparency International 2016, p. 6). Some apartment units, bought purely for speculation, were never occupied, and after an early boom ebbed, vacancies were abundant.

Hot money that arrives quickly may depart quickly, creating housing market volatility that festoons instability and financial chaos in its wake.[4] The Asian Financial Crisis (AFC) in 1997 abruptly punctured housing bubbles in East and Southeast Asia. In Hong Kong, a rapidly inflating market ahead of the handover of the British colony to China had created euphoria, as flat prices rose 70%. But euphoria led to despair as a crash and then a slide removed all the gain by 2003. At that date over 100,000 mortgage holders were underwater, in a state of negative equity, their savings lost and prospects savaged (see Chapter 3). The AFC was a dress rehearsal for the GFC a decade later that brought economic chaos to each coast of the North Atlantic, especially Britain, Ireland, Spain, and the United States. The Case-Shiller home price index of 20 large US cities revealed the extent of the carnage that *The Economist* in 2005 had warned lay ahead (Wake 2020). Gateway cities (Los Angeles, Miami, New York, San Francisco, Washington) and retirement/leisure cities (Las Vegas, Phoenix), where prices had more than doubled since 2000 displayed the biggest price bubble and suffered the deepest price collapse. In contrast heartland cities like Dallas, Charlotte, and Atlanta had experienced little price inflation and saw limited price shedding. Old industrial cities had gained little and lost more. The volatility of price oscillations was most marked in gateway cities, the national centres of irrational exuberance (Shiller 2000).

The similarity of price behaviour among US gateway cities and their distinction from other large metropolitan areas deserves further comment. House price profiles among 27 large American cities showed that six coastal immigrant gateways formed a recognisable cluster in terms of price peaks and the amplitude of price oscillations (Dieleman et al. 2000). Such national – and international – synchronicity of housing markets in advanced societies has been recognised (IMF 2018b). A striking example are Sydney and Toronto, two gateway cities of similar size but 15,000 kilometres apart, whose parallel house price trajectories showed a correlation of 0.88 over the period from 1977 to 2002 (Ley 2007). Remarkably this robust relationship was much stronger than correlations between prices in Toronto and cities in other Canadian provinces (Ley and Tutchener 2001). A global signal had trumped a national one. Such 'synchronization of housing prices reflects the key role played by global factors, primarily through interest rates and global economic activity' (Terrones 2005, p. 2).

The Globalisation of Residential Markets

I recently received an e-mail from a Hong Kong broker working for an international real estate company. He has sent sales information regularly since our earlier conversation in Hong Kong, forwarding new international listings, especially those located in Britain, mainly Central London, a popular venue for Hong Kong investors. This recent alert concerned a new London, Thames-side, condominium with sales about to be launched in an exhibit at the Mandarin Oriental Hotel in Hong Kong's Central district. The development company for the London project is listed in Singapore, has a Scottish name, Frasers Property, from its colonial founding in 1883, has been owned since 2013 by a Thai billionaire, and the building was about to be marketed in Hong Kong. It is through international networks and institutions such as these that global residential markets function, exemplifying 'the unprecedented extensiveness of [global] real estate networks, the high level of intensity of real estate activity, and the speed at which real estate transactions occur' (Gotham 2006, p. 254).

The liberalisation of foreign investment regulations in the 1980s and 1990s permitted increasing capital penetration across national borders. Since then, and especially since the GFC, property companies have made repeated sorties from their national bases. Australia's Lendlease corporation has developed an English niche in the regeneration of London's council housing estates (see Chapter 6), while its 'Global presence… focuses on [15] major "gateway cities"' (Lendlease 2019). Large Asian developers have been particularly proactive, their size and connections giving them substantial economic power. Singapore's CapitaLand has become a significant player in China's urbanisation with extensive residential, retail, and office projects (Chapter 2). Nonetheless, 'Driven by a global vision', the company has a footprint in over 200 cities in more than 20 countries (CapitaLand 2019a). To avoid the cyclical instability of real estate, many Asian property developers have diversified into much broader holding companies. In Hong Kong, Li Ka-shing's Cheung Kong Holdings was restructured in 2015 to include the primary property business, CK Asset Holdings, while CK Hutchison Holdings became responsible for its global interests in telecommunications, utilities, retailing, and other sectors (Chapter 3).[5] Like other large Hong Kong and Singapore developers, Li used his political connections with the Chinese Communist Party to establish a robust presence early in China's urbanisation, where Cheung Kong undertook over 80 development projects.

Always a pioneer, Li Ka-shing was the first Hong Kong developer to diversify outside East Asia. In 1988 he led a consortium that bought the site of Vancouver's Expo '86 (Chapter 5), and within a few years Hong Kong's four largest developers had an active presence in major redevelopment projects in the city (Olds 2001). As part of his company's later pivot to Europe, Li began two large Thames-side projects in London, including Convoy's Wharf, redeveloping the original Royal Dockyard, where 3500 housing units will eventually be built. Just downstream a subsidiary of Hong Kong's New World Development is building 10,000 units on the Greenwich Peninsula (Chapter 6). After the lifting of state controls in 2012, large Chinese companies bought, sometimes exuberantly, in gateway cities, notably London, New York, and Sydney. Not all were successful, and the then largest in China, Dalian Wanda, and third largest, Evergrande, had to liquidate purchases to meet heavy debt obligations. Their missteps repeated the earlier failure of Canada's Olympia and York that overcommitted its capital in developing London's Canary Wharf.

These property corporations are typically marketing their units both locally and offshore. Their market is global, and eager buyers include Asia's rising new middle class as well as global high net worth investors (Hay 2013; Rogers and Koh 2018). Real estate comprises a key investment portfolio for the 'super-rich', particularly for investors based in Asia (Hay 2013; Forrest et al. 2017; Atkinson 2020). Their business plans vary (Ley 2010; Montezuma and McGarrigle 2019). The wealthiest may be seasonal residents, moving between holiday homes, or immigrants on a golden visa. Middle-class transnational investors are more likely to purchase a single or a small number of condominium units, in some cases a home for adult children studying abroad. When currency rates, interest rates, and local politics are propitious these overseas investors can exercise significant effects on gateway housing markets, especially in smaller gateway cities like Vancouver (Moos and Skaburskis 2010; Ley 2010; 2017; see Chapter 5). But even London's much larger market is impacted (Chapter 6); in 2013 over 1800 new-build dwellings in London were sold to buyers from Hong Kong and Singapore alone, 10% of all London completions that year (CBRE 2014). Developers routinely sell their prime London flats in Asian cities, including Hong Kong and Singapore. Weekend property exhibits are held at luxury hotels, where international sales are curated by global real estate companies.

In the past decade international sales have been greatly aided by new technologies which permit virtual viewing of a global housing stock (Rogers 2016). The real estate platform Juwai, based in Hong Kong and Shanghai, brings a global menu of real estate properties with separate portals for Asian buyers in China and, from 2020, for the rest of Asia. Juwai claims, under the mission statement 'Empowering Asian property investors to be global residents', to list six million properties a year to 5.5 million active subscribers (Juwai 2020).

The property capital of offshore companies and individual investors is typically welcomed, even invited, at least initially. Senior governments favour investment and facilitate it, while local government may participate in an accommodating growth coalition with the real estate industry. But the cumulative presence of investors can destabilise a local housing market, by ratcheting up prices with the displacement of wage-earner savings by investor capital in residential purchase. This decoupling of a local labour market from its housing market has precipitous social and economic consequences we shall consider in later chapters. It also causes a re-writing of the explanation of housing markets, making former fundamentals like local incomes less salient. Bob Rennie, the most successful condominium salesman in Vancouver, understands this all too well. 'I joked with the CMHC's board[6] a couple of years ago that the Vancouver market never went up on fundamentals, so why would we go down on fundamentals?' (cited in Gordon 2022). This book aims to extend Rennie's professional acumen into a broader scholarly discussion.

A Narrative of Key Relationships

Housing booms in gateway cities, their causes, consequences, and the role of the state as both instigator and sometimes mitigator of house price inflation, provide the basic architecture for the extended case studies of housing in Singapore, Hong Kong, Sydney, Vancouver, and London. Housing plays a central and distinctive role in the economy and society of each city, and that role is discussed in a detailed regional and historical contextualisation of their residential markets.

At the same time, empirical trends require conceptualisation into a broader set of arguments.

Booms are shaped by a range of economic, demographic, and political factors operating at regional, national, and international scales. In a complex cascading of effects, booms create their own outcomes, notably affordability crises, greater inequality, and grassroots political pressure. Affordability problems then lead to a new round of outcomes in civil society including migration, accommodation, and protest. In systems this complex, local contingencies abound, outcomes and causes are multiple, and the ranking of 'independent variables' is moot. Nonetheless, an idealisation of key characteristics and relationships may be identified in the following narrative that builds out from the three propositions that began this chapter, and highlights key factors to be identified in the case studies, including the role of 'surplus demand' from speculative investment, the participation of transnational housing market actors, and housing policy derived from specific state ideologies.

We start with the recognition that gateway cities are growth nodes, hubs between national and international economic flows, with population increase driven by immigration in contrast to the net out-migration of domestic-born households. There is commonly a crisis of housing affordability in gateway cities, as asset-seeking investment, 'surplus demand', often primed by local growth coalitions, decouples housing markets from local labour markets. That investment includes value-seeking global capital arriving from off-shore investors and wealthy immigrants, sometimes landing with golden visas, as well as regional and national asset-seekers. Off-shore household investors are part of a broader globalisation of real estate in gateway cities, which includes the play of mobile international property development and marketing companies, sovereign, pension, and private equity funds, plus opaque capital from tax havens, including money-laundered funds. Real estate globalisation has been facilitated by declining interest rates over the past 30 years and especially since the GFC, and the availability of new, transnational financial instruments and institutional arrangements. The excess of asset-seeking investment in a deregulated market leads to house price volatility, with exaggerated boom and bust cycles.

The neoliberal state's default policy is to encourage investment in home-ownership, regarding the home as an appreciating economic asset, where capital gains may offset shortfalls of wage income and declining welfare services. Household welfare is transformed as residential property ownership adds a major source to wealth accumulation. But such an arrangement may be politically unstable, in part from growing inequality with growing numbers unable to access affordable homeownership, while others confront serious risk from heavy mortgage debt loads. In some instances, the extent of inequality and marginalisation creates a state of residential alienation (Madden and Marcuse 2016) for those unable to access affordable, decent housing, including newcomers to the market excluded from homeownership. The neoliberal state is then obligated for its own electability to introduce demand management in a succession of cooling measures. State failure to mitigate the affordability crisis for local residents may lead to political mobilisation and possibly even regime change.

Most evident in gateway cities, the empirical prominence of residential real estate in both macro-economic relations and everyday life confers a new theoretical centrality to housing in a financialised, post-Fordist society.

Of course, this narrative is not as linear or chronological or complete in any one city as this idealisation might suggest. Not all relationships are equally evident in each of the five gateway cities. The grassroots residential alienation in Hong Kong and Vancouver is limited in Singapore and Sydney. The state's inflation-cooling measures so prevalent in Singapore are subdued in London. The narrative does, however, provide a framework that aids the introduction of comparative themes in the chapters that follow. Each chapter highlights some, but not all, of these relationships. The Hong Kong chapter features the actions of a property-based growth machine, leading to inequality, residential exclusion, residential alienation, and political mobilisation among young adults denied the wealth accumulation and middle-class status of homeownership. In Sydney the argument stresses the role of state-facilitated local and global investment introducing 'surplus demand' and declining affordability during the 2013–2017 boom. In London tenure inequality is emphasised, within a global housing market primed by vigorous neoliberal marketisation, asset-based social policy, and welfare austerity. The Vancouver story examines the state's daunting attempt to reregulate a deregulated and dysfunctional housing market distorted by transnational investment. Singapore represents the most successful case of homeownership as asset-based welfare, sustained by long-standing, fastidious state management of the housing market, while navigating significant economic and demographic challenges.

Over-theorised discussions of the property market risk presenting a system of relationships whose interlocking parts are too well-lubricated, even functional in their interdependencies. This study presents a more grounded conceptualisation, where institutions and their decision-making are taken seriously, including government departments, development companies, financial corporations, and civil society organisations. An impressive precedent is Rachel Weber's interpretation of real estate speculation in Chicago's downtown area, with her declaration, 'I give voice to agents in these different professions instead of giving agency to abstractions such as "capitalism" or "markets"' (Weber 2015, p. 31). At the same time, she acknowledges that those agents are always implicated in broader geographical and historical contexts which they do not fully understand and only partially steer.

This analysis emphasises the period since the GFC, but more broadly covers the last 30–40 years, an era coinciding with the crisis of the Fordist concordat, and the development of market-leaning neoliberal governance, though the shape of that governance inevitably has a variable expression in each city. The transition period of the 1970s–1980s has significance for housing in the approximate coincidence of three significant developments. First, it represented the crisis of Fordism, and with it the erosion of welfare state benefits, including the provision of subsidised social housing. Major financial reforms, notably in the US and the UK, deregulated banking and liberated the globalisation of finance and the proliferation of financial institutions and instruments (Lowe 2011). Competition for borrowers was accompanied by a lowering of mortgage rates and innovation in financial instruments, giving much more flexibility in credit provision, and encouraging consumers to carry heavier debt loads. The second transition was a phase change in real house prices in many western nations with a sustained upward trajectory beginning in the 1960s and 1970s after a long quiescence; it was only in the 1970s that real residential land values, on average, regained their pre-1913 level (Knoll et al. 2017). But from 1980 to 2012 real house prices doubled, a figure much exceeded in the five gateway cities. Clearly a long-term transition was occurring in the meaning of residential land as an asset. Third, a similar shift is found in Piketty's macro-analysis of the composition of capital in a sample of western nations, with a substantial rise in the share of housing capital in national capital totals after 1950, while private capital (roughly half of it in housing) doubled from 2–3.5 times the value of national income in 1970 to 4–7 times the value in 2010 in a group of advanced societies (Piketty 2014, p. 173). Piketty identifies two changes between 1970 and 2010 relevant here: privatisation, the decline of public capital and the rise of private capital, and also the continuing recovery of asset prices, including real estate. Together, these trends identify the growing centrality of housing in private capital formation in a post-Fordist society, and its status as an asset in wealth accumulation.

The principal objectives of this book are first, to examine the place of the homeownership market – its price trends, their causes and consequences, and its management by government – in the economy and society of five gateway cities, and, second, to interpret how these relationships fit within the more particular thesis of homeownership and an asset society.

Homeownership and Asset-based Welfare

A conceptual frame usefully binding this study's interwoven relationships is the evolving thesis of homeownership as asset-based welfare, and the broader theorisation of an asset economy (Adkins et al. 2020). The rise of neoliberalism, declining household pension benefits, stagnant real wages, the long-term growth of house prices, and the rising share of private capital (notably housing) as a multiple of national income converge to locate homeownership as the primary household asset in the formation of a system of asset-based welfare. Neoliberal government in its ideological drive to reduce social service costs and marketise social relations encourages residents to transition from state dependency to 'modern investor subjects' as homeowners (Watson 2010). Social housing policies are discontinued and replaced by homeownership incentives. At the same time stagnant or declining real wages and shrinking welfare state benefits require inflating house prices to secure state legitimacy in any partnership with homeowners. The home becomes a household's primary asset for wealth accumulation, while mortgage debt provides an induction to risk society. In some states asset-based welfare is an implicit, default position with limited formal state sponsorship. In others its relationships are guided, even extolled, by explicit state policy (Adkins et al. 2020).

The role of homeownership in a personal investment portfolio to provide welfare and retirement insurance exists in a number of East and Southeast Asian countries (Ronald 2008; Ronald and Doling 2010; Doling and Ronald 2014). This system was instituted in Singapore in the 1960s, and the interactive relations of residential asset and family insurance were underscored by the use of the compulsory retirement savings scheme, the Central Provident Fund, as a contribution to housing expenditures, with capital gain on housing investment intended to cover retirement and other welfare needs (Lee 2014). With the steering capacity of a powerful state, Singapore has continued to achieve, more or less, a medium-term balance between the use and exchange value of its government-leased flats. Hong Kong was another case where homeownership might have dispersed wealth and achieved political legitimacy in the presence of a weak welfare regime (Goodstadt 2013). The policy worked well enough with rising homeownership in the 1980s and most of the 1990s, but it was undercut by the Asian Financial Crisis and the bursting of the housing bubble in 1997. Unlike Singapore there was no effective government oversight to protect highly leveraged homeowners or provide an adequate continuing supply of quality subsidised housing. Since 2003 the ownership rate has stalled at around 50%.

The place of homeownership in asset-based welfare was also evident in social policy and welfare state studies, particularly in Britain, Australia, and other societies subscribing to a 'liberal-market' model of residential capitalism (Schwartz and Seabrooke 2008; Ronald et al. 2017; Adkins et al. 2020). The argument was set in motion by Kemeny (1980) in an important discussion of the relation between homeownership and welfare state regimes, where in principle, high taxation countries with comprehensive welfare states should have lower levels of homeownership, and vice versa. The private character of homeownership, he argued, created a conservative ethos unsympathetic to collective, public models of social security. In producing a form of 'private insurance' insulating a household from old-age poverty, Kemeny posited that homeownership would make welfare state services and the taxation that supports them less attractive. Not only does pension assistance become less necessary in old age, but also the front-loaded nature of ownership costs inclines first-time buyers to be wary of high taxation policy to support a substantial welfare state. With reduced homeownership costs in later life, homeowners continue to oppose high taxes, for the equity asset of their home compensates for smaller public pensions (Kemeny 1980, 2005; Doling and Ronald 2010a). Complicating this hypothesised relationship, while states with high levels of homeownership should tend toward weaker welfare states, not all European states have the same institutional arrangements in terms of housing and pension commodification (De Decker and Dewilde 2010; Doling and Ronald 2010b; Delfani et al. 2014).

Deregulation in the mortgage market from the 1980s provided many more financial instruments to attract homeowners and residential investors. In addition to more accessible credit, competition and innovation provided greater flexibility to creative uses of housing wealth. As the literature developed it became clear that the trade-off between homeownership and welfare was not limited to pension support, for home equity withdrawal was shown to be taking place at different life-cycle milestones including family and employment transition, medical emergencies, children's (or grandchildren's) education, and aid for children's entry onto the ownership ladder (Smith and Searle 2008). In the British case, a surprising finding was that only 10% of households 55 years and older were likely to make a withdrawal in a given year, challenging the argument of home equity's primary use as pension insurance (Searle and Smith 2010).

Using the home as equity that may be drawn down is one aspect of the financialisation of the housing market. Financialisation is the process 'by which something or someone is managed as a fund' (Aalbers 2016, p. 2). In a growing synergy, the expanded financial capacity of homeownership is matched by the increasing housing reach of finance, exemplified by the diversity and importance of mortgage loans in the lending portfolio of many banks, and the increased marketability of housing as a result of flexible means of borrowing. Deregulation of the financial sector in the 1980s unleashed a flood of global finance with new instruments and new institutions liberalising the acquisition and sale of property as asset in a growing number of nations (Ronald and Dewilde 2017). Financial instruments like mortgage-backed securities or REITs establish a second-order commodification of domestic property increasing its value and fungibility (Forrest and Hirayama 2015).[7]

Marketisation is a key word of neoliberalism. In Britain, Margaret Thatcher's transformational agenda identified housing as a seminal project where the use value of council housing could be converted to the exchange value of homeownership. Her right-to-buy policy, selling off council housing to sitting tenants at far below market value, was the front end of a larger ideological project to wrest British society away from welfare state services and toward household self-sufficiency, with housing ownership a market solution to create and sustain an entrepreneurial ethos (Watson 2010). Significantly, the spirit of right-to-buy was retained by the succeeding New Labour governments in the UK, and the Coalition that followed, with the positioning of citizens as individual asset managers adjusting to swingeing reductions to public welfare services. In this calculation, the family home was regarded as a leading component of a household's welfare assets, to be deployed as needed in the purchase of market services in lieu of 'free' or subsidised public services (Watson 2009; Lowe 2011). Access to homeownership and the advancement of residential property prices then became a common refrain in the growth coalitions of national and sub-national governments, where incentives to private investment have commonly led to inflating housing markets, especially in gateway cities. In response to good economic returns on house prices, government expects from homeowners the political return of re-election. This informal agreement might also include the advantage of low taxation (and/or tax privileges) to facilitate residential purchase. As long as homeownership rates were high and increasing, the case could be made that a democratisation of national wealth accumulation (though in unequal shares) was taking place (Hamnett 1999).

Since the 1980s, employee pensions have become less dependable and welfare state benefits invariably reduced. But another shortfall beyond state benefits has afflicted workers, a steady decline in the growth of real wages as the wage share of labour has fallen in comparison with the profit share since the 1980s (Bengtsson and Ryner 2015). A number of reasons for declining rates of real wage growth have been suggested, including competition from low international wages with globalisation, the erosion of unionisation, and the emerging dual labour market of a post-industrial economy, with the decline of middle-income households, and rising polarisation accompanying the expansion of higher- and lower-income groups (Grant et al. 2020). With its welfare state emphasis, the asset-based literature sometimes overlooked this additional wage-based impediment to household budgets. We will see that in the five gateway cities, with the notable exception of Singapore, real wage rates have fallen behind the rate of house price growth.

Observing these trends in Sydney, Adkins et al. (2021) made the connection with Piketty's finding that capital and wealth, notably asset-based wealth, were outpacing the growth of the economy and especially wages. Asset-based welfare became a centrepiece of Australian economic and social policy in the 1980s and 1990s, facilitated by unusually favourable tax structures (Nethercote 2019; Adkins et al. 2021). High house prices then are in good measure 'a product of the way in which public policies have constructed a particular "logic" of asset inflation' (Adkins et al. 2021, p. 553). In its bargain with the electorate, government has to maintain both access to homeownership for new households and high and rising house prices for existing homeowners, a balance that may become unsustainable. Events have been similar in Vancouver though the asset trade-off has not been laid out as explicitly as in Sydney. But Canada's neoliberal transition in the 1980s and 1990s led to a familiar suite of slow wage growth and welfare state cuts, culminating in the 1994 federal budget when most social housing programmes were terminated (Suttor 2016). With housing construction left to the private sector, developers have opted for more profitable homeownership, in detached houses and condominiums, over rental production. In Canada's gateway cities, immigration-driven population growth, speculative investment, and low-interest borrowing have propelled upward cost spirals. As real wages grew sluggishly far below inflationary house prices, homeownership became an aspirational (but often unattainable) objective.

In the post-GFC world, especially in those countries labouring beneath austerity policy, Ronald et al. (2017) observed that assets, notably homeownership, are all the more important in household budgets confronting diminishing welfare benefits, precarious employment, and, recently, the vulnerabilities of the COVID-19 pandemic. The extent to which asset-based welfare, with its primary asset of homeownership, is a sufficient policy to ensure household capacity before these multiple challenges will be an important question in the chapters that follow.

Corollaries of Homeownership in Asset Society

Typically, the literature on asset-based welfare assumes a national frame of reference. But with the globalisation of the real estate market, international actors are also seeking asset value, and a calculus of housing demand limited to domestic buyers will fabricate a substantial undercount (Gallent et al. 2017). Affordability is a primary affliction for home seekers in gateway cities and, in a corollary of the asset society, the dependability of value growth stoked by market stimulus will attract value-seeking investors from near and far alike in an open economy. The decoupling of housing markets from local labour markets provides substantial evidence of the power of speculative property investment to create severe unaffordability (Gordon 2022). While international investors play a significant part in speculative investment, the case of Sydney (Chapter 4) is a reminder that local investors should not be overlooked, especially when residential purchase is accompanied by advantageous tax concessions.[8] The piling on of individual and corporate investors, both national and global, with easy access to credit and the added liquidity from quantitative easing since the GFC, have led to extraordinary strains on the residential markets of the gateway cities we are examining – and on asset-based homeownership as a normative social policy.

Countering, or at least complementing, the supply-side emphasis popular with the growth machine of politicians and the real estate industry, a focus on investment that is not derived from the local wage economy leads to the specification of surplus demand as a key explanatory factor in creating unaffordable housing (Aalbers 2016; Gallent et al. 2017; Ley 2017; Ryan-Collins and Murray 2020). With its clear policy implications, this is an important argument and the case will be laid out for each city.

A second corollary follows the first. Housing booms may provide a problem for the state, which sees rising house prices but cannot guarantee continuing access to homeownership, leading to a growing minority barred from the property ladder and its promise of wealth accumulation. Having acquired a taste for sales to well-heeled investors, the private sector is often unable or unwilling to build sufficient affordable units, for which there is huge need. Aside from the special case of Singapore with its highly managed housing market, social housing programmes have been cut or abandoned in our gateway cities. Instead, the state has engaged in different forms of demand management to cool price booms, notably credit tightening and various forms of taxation, to be examined in the case studies. These cooling measures are crisis responses, because in general the state facilitates investment flows and rewards growth coalitions, for housing investment can act as a counter-cyclical stimulus to the economy. Consequently, the real estate sector is frequently privileged in its access to power and political decision-making. In addition to Hong Kong, Vancouver provides an illustration of the institutional construction of a real estate growth coalition (Ley 2021). But political mishandling, even denial, of Vancouver's housing crisis led to an electoral reaction at all three levels of government (Chapter 5). The city provides insight into the rare prospect of a political response that moves policy from deregulation toward a degree of reregulation, though to date it is unlikely whether substantial improvements in affordability have followed.

Concerning Method

There has been considerable fruitful discussion concerning comparative urban research of late (e.g. Robinson 2011, 2016; Stephens and Norris 2011; Lees 2012; Peck 2015). While not adding to that discussion directly, I can briefly present my position. Housing markets are embedded in distinctive geographical and historical contexts that shape them, and this study respects, but does not idealise, the richness of the single case. Local similarities and differences permit generalisation within cases as well as between them, and provide the basis for developing, importing, testing, and revising concepts. In past urban research I made extensive use of comparative method to draw out generalisation and permit concept formation. The easier study compared gentrification in six Canadian cities where similar urban forms and related economic, cultural, and political contexts limited potential variation among the cases, enabling generalisation and concept formation to emerge readily (Ley 1996). More challenging was a comparative study of relations between neighbourhood organisations and the welfare state in Vancouver and Jerusalem (Hasson and Ley 1994), where extensive contextual differences between the two nations presented an implausible basis for comparison. Yet by matching neighbourhood types between the two cities, for example elite or minority districts, informative comparative results were achievable as micro- and meso-scale similarities were evident despite major macro-scale differences.

The five cities in this study were selected to include representatives from two regions where homeownership as asset-based welfare has been identified, East and Southeast Asia (Ronald 2008; Doling and Ronald 2014) and western liberal-market nations (Schwartz and Seabrooke 2008; Adkins et al. 2020). The cities are all coastal, gateway hubs open to global flows of capital, migrants, trade, and ideas; indeed, the Singapore and Hong Kong currencies have pegs with the US dollar, facilitating the onset of global impacts. Located on waterfronts, there is a scarcity of developable land, with physical geography providing limits to urban development. Four cities are located around the economically vibrant Pacific Basin, and share a colonial past with the former imperial city of London, historic connections that have some continuing relevance for orderly legal and administrative systems, for widespread use of English, for student and immigration flows, and for family and corporate property investment. At the same time, London's greater size and more complete global connectivity introduce additional variations to any Pacific Basin homogeneity. The five are multicultural cities with immigration the major contributor to their population growth, and labour markets stratified in part along ethno-racial and gender lines. Though formerly manufacturing centres, they have moved increasingly into a post-industrial employment profile, containing an upper tier of white-collar professional, managerial, and technical jobs, and a large lower-paid tier of service jobs in sales, clerical positions, the hospitality sector, manual work, and a varied group of personal services. Particularly in the post-GFC period, relations between the cities have included flows from trade, immigration, education, tourism, and property investment. Hong Kong and Singapore have been origins, as we shall see, of property investment and post-secondary students directed to the other three cities. The Asian gateway cities have also been destinations for western corporations seeking product, service, and investment markets in the cities and their hinterlands.

In contrast to their similarities, the cities are located on four continents, at varied latitudes, and differ sharply in hinterland populations, resources, levels of development, and modes of government. Two are former colonies, two European settler societies, one a former imperial centre. Both differences and similarities appear in classifications of national housing markets. Australia, Canada, and Hong Kong were categorised by the IMF (2016) as having booming housing markets, with only a small downturn during the GFC. The UK was placed in a bust and boom group; a significant GFC correction was quickly followed by renewed growth in London. Singapore was cast by the IMF among states whose housing market was characterised by gloom, with a GFC price bust not followed by renewed boom conditions – though the IMF overlooked residential price control as a deliberate state policy. A second classification, based on types of residential capitalism, placed Australia, Britain, and Canada within a liberal-market group of nations on the basis of high homeownership levels and debt loads. The criteria imply Singapore could be added to the group, while Hong Kong would form a hybrid case (Schwartz and Seabrooke 2008; Lowe 2011).

An important distinction separates Singapore from the other cities. Its unique governance, blending an open economy with firm, essentially one-party government, and elements of quasi-municipal socialism, have not only sustained substantial resident ownership of state-subsidised flats on leased government land, but also developed an early model of household accumulation treating the home as a wealth-generating asset. The relative success of its housing regime, in contrast to the mixed experience (at best) of the other cities, makes the Singapore case particularly significant.

The comparative method here is incomplete. Each chapter examines a partial set from the narrative of key relationships outlined earlier, while other relationships remain as background context. So, for example, while all five gateways are immigration cities, a detailed treatment of immigration appears primarily in the Sydney chapter where it is significant in that chapter's emphasis on global effects in the 2013–2017 housing boom. While it is noted that a similar immigration profile characterised Vancouver's 2013–2016 boom, the chapter treats this as background to its main task, examining the rise of a politics to re-regulate the housing market, a development missing in Sydney. Again, while the state's reluctant prescription of cooling measures to address over-heated markets is noted in all cities (but least of all in London), it is highlighted in Singapore, because of the city-state's persistence and post-GFC success in contesting price inflation. Finally, though inequality is a feature of every city, it majors in the Hong Kong and London chapters as a result of the abject failure of asset-based welfare, which has precipitated social, economic, and political polarisation.

I had prior familiarity and existing contacts with the five cities, and the advantage of earlier research in Hong Kong, Vancouver, and (to a limited degree) in Sydney. The research began (for every city except Vancouver, my home base) with field orientation, a visit of 2–6 weeks that included observation, identification of data sources, and conversation with 15–25 local experts on housing and urban development with different professional roles and diverse theoretical perspectives. Interviews were conducted with scholars from different urban disciplines, with representatives of residential real estate companies, and public sector housing planners and managers. In some cities, interviews also included community activists and real estate journalists. The objective was to encounter multiple perspectives rather than lock onto a premature meta-narrative. On-line data bases were informative in providing detailed time series for key variables, notably house prices, while extensive use was made of secondary literature to establish contexts, precedents, and insights. Reports, newsletters, and other relevant materials were derived from organisations with significant research capacity, including the IMF, international property consultancies, planning agencies, government departments, NGOs, and think tanks. To provide relevant detail, the texture of events and places, and retrieve information missing from other sources, considerable use was made of local and regional media that were regularly reviewed over a 10-year period.

How generalisable are the processes and outcomes documented in these five cities? While each metropolitan area has its own institutional contexts within which housing markets are embedded and modified, asset-based accumulation, with homeownership the principal asset, has long been the explicit or implicit goal of developmental states in Asia Pacific (Ronald and Doling 2010; Izuhara 2016). China might be included in this group for residential ownership is also regarded as a principal economic development tool, a contributor to social stability, and a resource for family-based welfare, leading to extensive household investment in rental properties, with heavy debt loads among households and corporations alike. The principal features of the asset economy have also been located in liberal-market societies like the United States, Canada, Australia, and Britain (Adkins et al. 2020), and in parts of Europe, but not those countries with high rental and/or social housing populations (Lowe 2011; Delfani et al. 2014).

Theoretical expeditions are often tempted to draw *a priori* straight lines through complex empirical terrain, undercutting the power of their own conclusions. In developing generalisable concepts, necessary hard labour comes first, developing a composite empirical portrait of each city within which housing questions are embedded and shaped. The objectives in each chapter are first, to locate the significant place of housing in a local human geography, and second, to select themes from the asset-based housing literature prevalent or especially informative in that city. In this way, various facets of a homeownership-based asset society are examined in each chapter.

Notes

1. A grey rhino is a probable, slow moving, high impact, yet generally ignored threat.
2. Four-fifths of the increased value of the housing stock is attributed to the inflated price of the land upon which it is built.
3. A pioneer in this literature was Burghardt (1971) who stressed the business service function of gateway cities. For a recent review of the economic role of gateway cities, see Scholvin et al. (2019), though my emphasis is on transnational real estate capital and migration flows rather than the city-hinterland link of global production networks.
4. Housing crises do not fall equally on all housing groups. Residential price collapse following the GFC was borne disproportionately by households of colour (Pew 2011).

5. Li Ka-shing has been one of East Asia's wealthiest men, and in Hong Kong his business prowess earned him the popular nickname, 'Superman'.
6. The Canada Mortgage and Housing Corporation is the housing agency of the federal government of Canada.
7. While writing this section a local news story disclosed that REITS are newly active in buying older rental apartments in Vancouver and Toronto where they see potential for enhanced yield and long-term capital gains. Tenant advocates are concerned about rental affordability and security (Lee-Young 2020). See also Fields and Uffer (2016) and new examples of property financialisation in Aalbers (2019).
8. An analysis of 'non-primary' (investor) home buyers in the US showed they accounted for over 30% of US residential home sales from 2008 to 2012, and more in specific regions, more than enough to impact markets significantly (Alter and Dernaoui 2020).

CHAPTER 2

Singapore: Housing and Nation Building

This was the plan we had from the very beginning, to give everybody a home at cost or below cost and as development takes place, everybody gets a lift, all boats rise as the tide rises.

(Lee Kuan Yew in CNA 2012a)

Singapore is the outlier among the five cities, not because housing is not central to its economy, politics, and everyday life, but rather because of the fastidiousness with which a policy of homeownership as asset-based welfare has been pursued and protected by a vigilant government. Housing assumes a fundamental, multi-functional, nation-building role in Singapore, with ownership of good quality, state-built, subsidised housing available to citizens and permanent residents, giving them a stake in national prosperity, while instilling responsible citizenship. From the 1960s, pension savings could be used in housing costs, formalising an early model of asset-based welfare. The chapter examines how this asset-based policy has been sustained by an attentive state since the GFC, even as global capital and local wealth have introduced inflationary housing pressures to an open economy, while economic growth, declining fertility, and temporary immigration have brought sometimes destabilising political pressures. Government has introduced extensive cooling measures against renewed housing booms and built a protective firewall intended to sustain affordability for Singapore citizens, while restricting rights for temporary and permanent residents and external investors. Housing rights reproduce social identities of inclusion and exclusion.

When Singapore was driven out of the Federation of Malaysia and became an independent republic in 1965, none of the fears that had led to its eagerness to enter the Federation had been dispelled. It was a small tropical island of under two million people, with limited human or natural resources (not even abundant fresh water). With a fertility rate of 4.6 children per

Housing Booms in Gateway Cities, First Edition. David Ley.
© 2023 John Wiley & Sons Ltd. Published 2023 by John Wiley & Sons Ltd.

woman it faced the need for rapid economic development to employ its fast-growing population. Moreover, the island was vulnerable geopolitically: there were uneasy relations with Muslim neighbours, domestic race riots, and pro-Communist activism, with the added geopolitical anxieties of a Southeast Asian domino waiting to topple according to the Cold War paranoia of domino theory. A powerful political movement sought to tame this turbulence, the People's Action Party (PAP), which had won the 1959 election and has retained control of the national government ever since. The PAP's first Prime Minister, Lee Kuan Yew, a brilliant Cambridge-educated lawyer, remained in office until 1990, and in Cabinet as the honorary 'Senior Minister' to 2004, and finally 'Minister Mentor' in the government of his son, Lee Hsien Loong, until 2011. Lee Hsien Loong in turn was Deputy Prime Minister from 1990 to 2004, and became Prime Minister in 2004, while his wife, Ho Ching, became the Chief Executive Officer of Temasek the same year, a position she held until her retirement in 2021. One of Singapore's two sovereign wealth funds, Temasek was valued at SG$403 (US$286) billion in March 2022.[1]

This dynasty has governed Singapore paternalistically as a multiracial family where collective objectives transcend the freedoms of individuals. And as for any family, the question of suitable housing has been a central objective and aspiration; indeed, so central that housing policy is multi-tasked in the roles it plays in the reproduction of the national society. Both for government planning and in the everyday life of Singapore's civil society, housing is a major preoccupation and multifaceted resource. Homeownership existed as asset-based welfare, *avant la lettre*, and the task of government has been to grow the asset and share the increase, while ensuring continuing access for the next generation (Lee 2014). Having first established the place of housing at the heart of Singaporean nation-building, this chapter examines how housing-based asset accumulation has been sustained through a form of municipal socialism[2] that grants tight management control to the state. We examine how housing assets have been preserved and extended to new households in the post-GFC period by steadfast state policy confronting daunting economic, demographic, and political pressures.

The Busy Life of House and Home in Singapore

At various times during his leadership, Lee Kuan Yew evoked the legitimating hold of 'Asian values' upon Asia Pacific societies (Emmerson 1995; Ong 2006). These values included the traditional Confucian views of the family: the providing father, the obedient and nurturing spouse, the dutiful children, and emphasis upon family objectives as the highest calling upon personal loyalty. As paterfamilias in turn of the Singaporean national family, both Prime Ministers Lee have single-mindedly directed the affairs of the state, presuming that the effective monopoly of one-party government, the suspension of a jury system, an uncompromising law and order regime, compliant media, and meticulous state control met the needs of a developing nation. In return the benefits of rapid development as one of the four tiger economies have been broadly shared. Unemployment has remained very low, around 2% in the recent pre-COVID-19 period, and per capita incomes have risen dramatically, to the point when Singapore is ranked globally among the top three countries in purchasing power parity. Household net wealth rose by 75% from 2010 to 2019, and during this decade healthy life expectancy in Singapore became the highest in the world (IMF 2019a).

Housing policy has fitted closely into this encompassing governance strategy. In 2019 an astonishing 90.4% of 'resident households'[3] were classed as owners, the large majority living in government-built flats (SDS 2019). A virtual state monopoly on land ownership (over 90% of the land area) and housing provision (some 75% of residential units) has been legitimated by the creation of stakeholders, citizens who enjoy both homeownership and the predictable economic growth of that asset in public housing units purchased from Singapore's Housing and Development Board (HDB) on long leases and at subsidised prices (Chua 1997, 2003a; Goh 2005; Glass and Salvador 2018).[4] Flats may be financed by withdrawals from the Central Provident Fund (CPF), a compulsory employee pension plan, and mortgage loans are available from the HDB and, latterly, commercial banks (Phang 2015).[5] With some conditions, flats may be bought and sold on the resale market after a specified period of time at market prices, granting the expectation of significant capital gain for owners. HDB flats include a range of sizes and amenity levels so that residents can upgrade (and enhance value) within the public sector through their housing careers; 'every household tries to withdraw up to the maximum sum permitted out of its CPF account to pay for housing, not only to purchase the first flat but also to finance subsequent upgrading to a bigger flat' (Chua 2014, p. 523). This asset-based housing policy has contributed directly both to family wealth accumulation and to the growth of the national economy (Phang 2001).

The integration of pension and housing assets in 1968 means that in Singapore the role of housing in asset-based social security became a finely-crafted and evolving national imperative at an early date. The preservation and enhancement of home value has therefore been a key government policy as residents committed a large share of their personal wealth, including pension assets, to flat purchase. To maintain value, the HDB engages in comprehensive maintenance and upgrading of estates, such as the Remaking our Heartland programme (Glass and Salvador 2018). Upgrades are not only functional but, aided by community participation, include planning innovations to enhance place identity. Indicative of the orderly functional integration of Singaporean society, HDB's building and development division was spun off to the national sovereignty fund, Temasek, in 2004, and then to CapitaLand, the largest national development company, 51% owned by Temasek (Phang 2015).

The Housing and Development Board was established in 1960, before national sovereignty, and by 2019, 79% of resident Singaporean households lived in HDB housing units, almost all of them owned, typically on 99-year leases.[6] Large well-planned estates of high-rise towers, many substantial enough to be called new towns, with comprehensive services and efficient public transport, comprise the characteristic residential landscape of Singapore, its national 'heartland'. The amenity levels of these developments have been rising with the wealth and consumption expectations of citizens. As an elder statesman, Lee Kuan Yew reflected on this policy at a tree-planting ceremony at an HDB estate:

> Everybody owns their own homes and the value of their homes goes up as development takes place. Some are unwise enough to sell their homes, thinking they can buy another one, they then find they can't and have to rent a flat. But those who hold on to their homes, I've seen their property values going up, five times, 10 times, 15 times, 20 times. This was the plan we had from the very beginning, to give everybody a home at cost or below cost and as development takes place, everybody gets a lift, all boats rise as the tide rises.
>
> (CNA 2012a)

Moreover, the multi-tasking housing landscape has also contributed to the social and political ends of the state, as devised by the People's Action Party (PAP). The design of flats plays a didactic role, instructing Singaporeans how to live and how to organise family life. Various HDB advertising campaigns have taught residents how to decorate their homes (Jacobs and Cairns 2008), how to behave in a neighbourly way, how to feel a sense of belonging, how to welcome others, in short, the practice of 'harmonious high rise living' (HDB 2012a).[7] Neighbourliness promotes a durable national sentiment, a 'scalability from the local to the national' (Ho and Chua 2018, p. 295). The HDB's website has tutored community building, the nurturing of the national family:

> Our Heartland comes 'alive' when we come together to realise our common dream and aspirations. Our towns are brought to 'life' when the physical landscape and buildings are complemented by the everyday touches of caring and considerate neighbours, familiar sounds, sights

and people. Common interests and activities bring the community closer together and appreciative of each other. All these bring colours and vibrancy to the heartlands.

Beyond providing public housing, HDB is also a developer of community-centric towns and builder of active and cohesive communities. HDB has a slew of community programmes and initiatives that provides the finishing 'heartware' touch and brings HDB living 'to life' by encouraging residents to be positive change agents in their communities, to get involved and to take ownership of their community and living environment.

(HDB (2012a)

The evocative naming of 'Our Heartland', and the communal 'heartware' of HDB residents that celebrate 'life', is multi-layered. The capitalisation of 'Our Heartland' is significant, and so too is the possessive adjective, projecting a singular family name, a 'common dream', a quintessential social identity of shared belonging and ownership. Robbie Goh (2005, p. 147) has observed how the HDB heartlander, the beating heart of Singapore society, has been contrasted with the 'cosmopolitan', a foreign national or a Singaporean educated overseas. The heartlander is a true member of the national family, of secure ancestral status. Prime Minister C. T. Goh described the identity of 'heartlanders' as 'local rather than international', thereby playing a 'major role in maintaining our core values and our social stability' (Goh 2005, p. 148). The heartlander is traditional in sentiment and local in attachments – note the repetitive placement of 'community' as the appropriate spatial scale in the extract above. Goh notes that vernacular languages and historic religious faiths are both concentrated in the HDB estates rather than in the wealthy enclaves of private property around the commercial core.

But at the same time, the 'heartland' risks becoming off-centre in Singapore's urban geography. New large HDB towns like Woodlands, Jurong West, and Yishun, with a total population of over 700,000 in 2019, 95% in HDB units, occupy the distant north of Singapore Island. In contrast expensive ex-patriate districts of privately-owned housing units tend to be clustered closer to the strategic downtown core. The question of who is core and who is peripheral in this social geography provides an irritant to heartlanders and a caution to government, notably in the vigorous debate during the 2011 election campaign.

Robbie Goh, a perceptive writer on the lived experience of the HDB estate, has observed that it is 'the built environment of the heartland which both represents the experienced space of the average Singaporean, and symbolizes the general condition of Singapore society' (Goh 2005, p. 104). The well-defined lineaments of heartland identity preclude others from entry. Foreigners who are not permanent residents are not able to purchase property in the HDB estates. There is a further definition of insiders and outsiders that underscores the meticulous authoring of the built environment as a tool in the reproduction of the national family. Singaporeans married to foreigners are defined as single persons in the HDB housing queue and until recently were unable (like other singles) to buy HDB units. New, subsidised units have been off limits to singles beneath the age of 35 years. Here is a nudge from government to 'facilitate marriage and to nurture a culture where singles view marriage as a top life goal' (Strijbosch 2015, p. 1109). The restricted access of all single people to the housing market is rationalised in terms of their location outside traditional 'Asian family values' whose communitarian definition does not readily accommodate single people (Chua 1995; Wong et al. 2004b). The *kampong* (village) spirit is an ideal to be sustained and 'Our public housing policies have... played a crucial role' (Khaw Boon Wan, Minister of National Development, 2015). These social values, ideally comprising the three-generation family, are inscribed into the HDB landscape. There are incentives for multi-generational families to live close together, facilitating filial piety and limiting the need for state welfare expenditures on care for the elderly, while grandparents will look after children as parents work.

But in contrast penalties confront single people (Chang 2012). Discussion about relaxing this restriction in 2012 only underscored the firm priority listing of families, for comments by a senior PAP Minister made it clear that a principal concern against letting singles into the queue for new HDB housing was that they might pre-empt flats available for more highly valued nuclear families: 'the interests of married couples, especially those with children, may be adversely affected' (Ng 2012). Single people under the age of 35 would still not be permitted to buy HDB new or resale stock.[8] This restriction has led many young adults to continue living in their parents' home into their 30s, a circumstance that is unlikely to facilitate marriage at a youthful (and fertile) age. From the perspective of government, singleness is regarded as an incomplete state, a time of 'waiting' (Ramdas 2012); so too homosexual households fall outside the conventional requirements of 'Asian values' (Oswin 2010). Not surprisingly these populations find themselves alienated from policies that exclude them from the dominant social paradigm.[9]

State control of housing also permits management of inter-ethnic relations, another objective in constructing communitarian harmony. While Chinese ancestry is dominant in Singapore (accounting for 74% of the *resident* population of four million in 2020), there are also significant minorities of Malays (14%), and Indians (9%), with 3% others (SDS 2020). The complexity of the population, with residents including both citizens (3.5 million) and permanent residents (520,000), is further accentuated by the presence of 1.64 million 'non-residents' or 'foreigners' living in Singapore in 2020. The total population of 5.7 million in 2020 scarcely changed in the previous five years, and it was only during this period of demographic stability that the growth rate of the resident population slightly exceeded the rate of total population growth, reversing a long period when the non-resident share was gaining. As we will see, this adjustment is also the outcome of careful calibration.

Historically the colony of Singapore as constituted by Stamford Raffles in 1822 included planned districts of highly segregated minorities – Chinese, Europeans, Indians, and Malays with other Muslim groups – comprising a characteristic 'plural society' in the colonial tropics, a tapestry of social, spatial, and cultural difference (Furnivall 1956). Ethnicity is overlaid by religious and linguistic distinctions, leading to the possibility of entrenched separate identities. Remembering the vexing experience of the 1960s race riots, the PAP government regarded ethno-racial concentration as a threat to social harmony. In a 1989 pronouncement, for example, a party spokesman declared that 'living in separate enclaves, community leaders will develop narrow views of society's interests. The enclaves will become seedbeds for communal agitation. We will witness the unravelling of what we have knit so carefully since independence' (cited in Sin 2003, p. 535). In acts of precise social engineering, the Singaporean government deployed their widespread power in allocating new HDB flats so that ethnic minorities would be dispersed into ethnically integrated housing blocks (Lim et al. 2020). Tendencies to regroup in the HDB resale market were also checked, by the imposition of local ethnic quotas (Vangrunsven 1992; Sin 2003). The result is a low level of inter-group segregation, even in traditional Malay minority districts in the sector running east from the downtown core. In state policy, the necessity to avoid segregation has become the virtue of promoting multicultural integration:

> That is why we impose an ethnic quota in each residential block to ensure that all races are adequately represented in every town. This way, children grow up with neighbours and classmates of different ethnicities. This ensures racial integration and promotes mutual respect for one another's cultures, traditions and religious beliefs.
>
> (Khaw Boon Wan 2015)

However, the extent to which closer inter-ethnic ties – the formation of a multicultural family – has actually taken place is uncertain. Ironically the national emphasis on family values reinforces kinship networks, which are ethnically bounded. Singapore's multicultural integration is, it seems, an integration of weak ties rather than strong bonds (Chua 2009).

Residential dispersal policies also sought to de-fang opposition politicians who might develop electoral strength in concentrated ethnic districts. Here we see the power of single-party governance to cross over from cultural to electoral hegemony. To disperse the political strength of opposition supporters the PAP instituted not only the more conventional tactic of electoral redistricting, but also a novel system of electoral multiculturalism. Multiple-member constituencies were established, with each including a mandatory multi-ethnic slate of candidates. In a winner take all model, the slate with the most votes took all seats in a constituency, guaranteeing ethnic inclusion in Parliament. This ingenious model of both multicultural inclusion and also effective co-optation was reinforced by what might be called electoral persuasion. As the housing estates aged, necessary flat maintenance and also some upgrading became part of the HDB's mandate. Voters were advised that while a vote for the PAP would ensure local flat maintenance and upgrading, electoral success for the opposition would lessen a constituency's priority on the list for housing improvements (Chua 2000). In the 2006 election, for example, the campaign to win back the two opposition-held single member constituencies was accompanied by a promise of SG$180 million in local flat improvements if PAP candidates won, incentives declined at election time by the democratically-inclined voters.

A virtual monopoly power to author residential landscapes has given the governing party significant authority to steer the shape and trajectory of Singapore's civil society (Kong and Yeoh 2003). In the post-colonial state, single party government and a dominant family dynasty have secured this power, creating unusually direct links between political declarations and societal outcomes while establishing coordination across separate policy domains. Even the National Trades Union Congress is aligned to the PAP and its leadership may include a cabinet minister. Housing provision has become a nexus for nation-building, promoting loyalty to the national project, continuing success for the governing party, multicultural integration, a moral tutor for family and lifestyle formation, and a household financial asset with proven growth potential. The socially overdetermined HDB flat has multiple tasks to complete in the daily life of Singapore's heartland estates and new towns.

The Property State

Anne Haila (2000, 2016) has identified both Singapore and Hong Kong as property states, jurisdictions where land and its development play a particularly large role in national economic growth. The state is the dominant property owner in Singapore, and post-independence acquisition, expropriation, and land reclamation have taken the public share of land ownership above 90%. In principle, state ownership should moderate housing prices by precluding land hoarding by large private companies. In practice, the state's own fiscal dependence on land sales and price growth in HDB flats creates a more complicated scenario that in recent years has prompted political disaffection as price inflation has periodically limited access to the market, raising issues of affordability and housing debt.

But state intervention in the land market reaches far beyond the supply of public housing and the auctioning of state land. Government holds a share in some large property development companies, aiding the property sector to be a significant group in listings on the Singapore Exchange. Overseas property investment by individuals, companies, and the national sovereign funds is substantial. Singapore's Government Investment Corporation, one of two sovereign funds,[10] bought a 50% share of the large Broadgate office and retail centre in the City of London from the US-based fund manager, Blackstone, for £1.7 billion at the end of 2013, then the largest property deal in Europe since the Global Financial Crisis (GFC), beating out the Norwegian and other sovereign funds (Chassany 2013); the month before it had joined a partnership that included the Abu Dhabi sovereign wealth fund to purchase the Time Warner building in Manhattan.[11] In March 2014, the GIC was joined in London by Temasek, the state's other sovereign fund that was planning portfolio diversification in Europe from its new London base. With over half of its existing assets in China and Singapore, Temasek has been extending its reach in Europe and especially North America to become a more fully global player (Temasek 2020). GIC and Temasek are regarded as among the most active global sovereign funds, with a peak of over half of all sovereign fund deals in the first half of 2014 (Grant 2014). They are able to move flexibly with sizable expenditures into new investment niches; from January 2016 to April 2017, GIC moved into student housing, which was offering higher yields than residential and commercial property, and spent over US$3 billion in purchases in Europe, North America, and Australia (Roney 2017).

CapitaLand, 51% owned by Temasek, is one of Asia's largest property developers, and the most active foreign developer in China with more than 100 projects, including large mixed-use urban centres based on its prototype Raffles City brand in Singapore. By 2020, nine Raffles City projects, integrated retail malls with office space, had been completed in China (CapitaLand 2019a). Its most expensive project is Raffles City, Chongqing, a $3.6 billion, eight tower development designed by Moshe Safdie and opened in 2019 (Asia Times 2019). Aside from commercial projects, in the past 20 years CapitaLand has constructed 107,000 residential units, and developed and managed dozens of retail malls, the majority in China, while its serviced apartment company,

The Ascott Limited, passed the threshold of 110,000 global units in 2019, with China its largest single customer, but with dozens of properties in Europe.[12] China accounts for almost 40% of CapitaLand's total assets, just behind Singapore in total. As part of a diversification and expansion strategy, CapitaLand announced the purchase of real estate trusts for US$8 billion from Temasek in 2019, catapulting the company into the world's top ten real estate investment managers by size of asset. Part of the deal is a share exchange that made Temasek a majority shareholder in CapitaLand, thereby tightening the bonds between the private and public arms of the Singapore property family. Already active in 30 countries, CapitaLand announced its intention in 2019 to 'set ourselves on a journey to transform our company from an Asia-focused real estate player to a global one' (CapitaLand 2019a, p. 16).

For a city-state of 5.7 million, Singapore has a disproportionate number of medium- to large-scale developers with active overseas ambitions. City Developments has a varied portfolio in Singapore, China, and the UK, including a London-based hotel chain, and rental accommodation in England and Japan (City Developments 2020). The Keppel Corporation developed from a shipyard and marine company into one of Singapore's largest con-glomerates. Keppel Land, its property arm, derives three-quarters of its reve-nues in ten Asian countries, with Singapore, China, and Vietnam its core markets (Keppel 2019). In Asia, excluding Singapore, the company announced a pipeline of 45,000 residential units. Fraser and Neave is a long-established Singaporean conglomerate, with residences, serviced apartments, hotels, and business parks concentrated in China, Southeast Asia, Australia and Europe, and located in more than 70 cities globally (Frasers Property 2020). Like other developers, Frasers has recycled some assets (amounting to $7.7 billion) into real estate investment trusts (REITs), providing 'a virtuous cycle of growth and value creation' (Frasers Property 2020, p. 44). Far East Organization is listed as Singapore's largest private property developer. With overlapping ownership with the Sino Group in Hong Kong, its overseas investments are located in Malaysia, Hong Kong, China, and Australia. Finally, a newer company, Oxley Holdings, with projects in Singapore, Malaysia, and Cambodia has joined the thrall of the London market, pur-chasing the large Royal Wharf industrial site in East London in 2013, where it is building riverfront homes for up to 10,000 people (Allen 2013).

The London connection is also evident with individual Singaporean investors, prolific purchasers of overseas residential projects at weekend hotel exhibitions. London property experienced an upsurge in popularity after 2008 with depreciation in the value of the pound creating a massive exchange rate discount compared to a 20-year average (Chua 2012). During this period investors from Singapore were estimated to account for about 15% of overseas residential sales in Central London, a similar share to investors from Hong Kong and Malaysia (Chapter 6). In contrast, Singaporean investors were second only to British buyers, for a more specific product, new build homes in Central London (Pickford 2013).[13] Singaporean household investors are also active in Australia, Malaysia, China, and elsewhere in Asia Pacific; almost 100 Australian apartment properties were launched for sale in Singapore in 2015 (Savills Singapore 2015a), while Haila (2000) reports the sale of all 80 units in a (Hong Kong-financed) Vancouver condominium project during a 3-day open house launch in Singapore.

Overseas property investment by Singaporeans is evidently substantial. Nonetheless, indicative of the even greater scale of local residential investment, in an interview a real estate manager labelled this overseas purchasing activity as a 'sideshow'. Stimulated by the ownership returns from HDB flats, individuals and families have seen Singapore real estate as a primary asset for wealth accumulation. HDB flats offer a gradation of sizes and amenity packages, while 'upgrading', ascending the steps on the quality ladder, is a major national preoccupation, encouraged by the government. As family incomes rose, HDB's 'executive flats' provided an additional upper step and a bridge to the private condominium market (Tse 2015). Executive flats feature the accoutrements of aspiring middle-class living including in many cases space for a full-time domestic worker. By the late 1990s, the gap to private ownership was narrowed still further by the 'executive condominium' option, built and sold by private developers, but with HDB financing privileges, catering 'to Singaporeans, especially young graduates and professionals who can afford more than an HDB flat but find private property to be out of their reach' (HDB 2012b).

By 2012 the most expensive executive condominiums had broken the SG$2 million price threshold. The state has synchronised its housing policy with Singapore's growing per capita purchasing power, creating additional rungs at the top of the housing ladder and facilitating the leap to private ownership, for example by permitting HDB residents to purchase a private condominium, while retaining their (subsidised) flat that they can rent out on the private market (Goh 2005). In this manner, the state's desire to permit the accumulation of housing wealth has been constantly calibrated against the upward movement of family purchasing power.

The use of the Central Provident Fund as payment for a deposit and mortgage fees of an HDB home means that the home and pension funds are one and the same investment: 'the public housing flat is thus an "asset" that holds a lease-owner's accumulated retirement capital' (Chua 2015, p 30). This unusual financing of housing ownership is perhaps the most explicit example of asset-based welfare, with the home necessarily producing an investment that may be cashed in at retirement. Consequently, government is obligated to ensure rising flat prices, and absolutely guard against price reductions, as a political as well as an economic imperative. But such an imperative runs counter to affordability for new entrants, whose access to the HDB homeownership ladder is impeded. A balance must be discovered between acceptable returns to owners and price rises that would compromise first-timers' access to the ladder – unless government produces substantial subsidies. The price inflation in HDB flats following the GFC brought this delicate balance into question, and, as we shall see, contributed to a humbling chastisement for the government in the 2011 general election.

In many East and Southeast Asian countries, housing assets are regarded as a major vehicle for family upward mobility (Goldberg 1985; Ley 2010; Doling and Ronald 2014). In the low interest environment of the past two decades, property has become of even greater significance. In Singapore, with over 90% homeownership, property amounts to about 55% of household wealth (Deng et al. 2019). As a government manager in the housing sector told me, 'Everyone here wants to own two properties'. An urban economist matched his view: 'People only think of real estate as an asset, not just to live in. Here they think about property as an investment. It's all about the real estate ladder and upgrading'. This culture of property, related to what Anne Haila (2016) called 'the property mind',[14] was effusively reproduced in interviews with representatives of large real estate companies: 'We have a property is investment psychology. There's a psyche that you can't go wrong with real estate'; and again, 'Everybody here is an expert on property. It's a Chinese mentality that land and home are key. There's a deep-down happiness with increasing property values'. There is a life stage when ownership becomes pertinent: 'Home becomes the number one thing with marriage. A couple first buys an HDB flat and then steadily moves up toward the private market. Property is ingrained in the Asian mindset, it's close to the heart'.

The private ownership market is relatively small but growing, providing homes for about 20% of resident Singaporeans in 2019, three-quarters of the units in flats, and the remainder in 'landed properties' which include a modest stock of expensive detached and semi-detached dwellings, the peak of the housing pyramid. But the private sector is also the principal housing option for well-paid expatriates who are excluded from HDB flat ownership because of their status as foreign non-residents.[15] Together with elite Singapore residents and non-resident investors, these 'foreign talents' comprise the top end of the local private market. Despite their clear distinctions, HDB flats and private sector condominiums are nonetheless linked sub-markets moving in parallel price tracks (Ong 2000; Sing et al. 2006). The HDB has responded to market signals in its pricing formula, and though new flats are typically

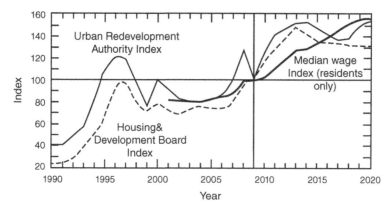

FIGURE 2.1   Home price and median wage indices, Singapore, 1990–2020. (Source: Author, from statistics in Data.gov.sg 2020a; b; Ministry of Manpower 2021)

priced at a discount below market rates, HDB resale price-lines follow similar trajectories, parallel with but below the private market (Lum 2012, p. 431).[16]

Both HDB units and the private ownership market (the URA index) experienced remarkable price growth and volatility from the early 1990s to 2013 (Figure 2.1). Pegged against a 2009 value of 100, the HDB resale market accelerated fourfold from 1990 to 1996, before plunging over 25% during the Asian Financial Crisis (AFC). Beginning from a higher base, the private residential index paralleled the HDB price line, tripling from 1990 to 1996, before it suffered a 40% correction. Since the bursting of this bubble, HDB units have shown less extreme year-to-year changes than private market units. A second bubble began to form in the private sector in 2006, with the price index swelling almost 50% before it was punctured by the Global Financial Crisis (GFC) in 2008–2009, falling back more than 20% over the next 12 months. But this relapse was short-lived and another burst of growth was in place by the beginning of 2010 and within a year the earlier peak index was far surpassed. Gains of 50% were recorded on the private housing index from 2009 to 2013, before decisive state intervention brought a series of cooling policies and some stability to the price line. It is no wonder with such excessive oscillations that particularly the private residential market in Singapore was regarded as 'one of the "frothiest" in the world' (Lum 2012, p. 422). Nonetheless for the long-term investor, the upward trajectory has provided satisfactory returns. Less satisfactory for investors has been the government-induced sluggishness in the market since 2013. Values for private dwellings and HDB resale flats showed slow but steady decline. Most likely, it was the volatility of the HDB flats on the heartlander estates that caused more uneasiness to government. The 1997 bust devalued HDB flats, and another bubble seemed to be forming from 2007 to the beginning of 2013 as HDB prices doubled. As we shall see, extensive cooling measures brought more Singaporean orderliness to the worrisome instability of the heartlander market.

The trajectory of HDB prices raises two interesting observations. First, though their oscillations are more muted overall than the private sector, the similarity of the price trends indicates seepage between the HDB market, restricted to Singapore residents, and the private market, wide open to wealthier residents, non-residents, and overseas investors. Yet, second, while there is seepage, there is also enough insularity to the HDB market that it successfully rode out the severe shock of the GFC, while the private market shed 25% of value, admittedly for a short term only.

Global Pressures...

Singapore is habitually listed at or near the top of market-friendly rankings like the World Bank's ease of doing business index. Economic reports emphasise the openness of Singapore's overseas trade in goods and services to external events, its global exposure to 'cycles in world demand and swings in global sentiment' (IMF 2012, p. 12). Singapore has also been a safe haven for footloose capital, including property investment, while welcoming foreign high net-worth individuals who may be admitted on a fast track to permanent residency (Pow 2011); the British manufacturer Sir James Dyson was the biggest catch in 2019, buying a large penthouse, and moving his firm's global headquarters to a Singapore heritage building (CNA 2019).

The volatility of the housing cycle over a short period (Figure 2.1) has been shaped by the openness of the Singaporean economy to global economic shocks and to the circulation of capital at virtual flood tide with rapid economic growth in Asia. Repeated applications of quantitative easing to counter impacts from the Global Financial Crisis (GFC) in the US and Europe have released surges of mobile capital seeking profitable sites in emerging economies (Yip 2019). In Singapore, the IMF noted a huge increase in the stock of cross-border assets (from outward capital flows) and liabilities (from inward capital flows) from 200% of GDP in the 1980s to around 1600% in 2010 (IMF 2017b, p. 51). Changes in capital inflows and the foreign share of private residential purchases match, but exaggerate, the oscillations of private residential prices (Figure 2.2). Notable is the substantial volatility in flows from the shock of the GFC between 2007 and 2009, and the precipitous withdrawal of foreign buyers after the 2011 increase of stamp duty on property transfers. Econometric analysis has attempted to isolate these pressures, notably from the US, as they transmit economic signals to Singapore's housing market both directly and through Singapore's macro-economy. Examining the post-GFC period, Chow and Xie (2016, p. 13) conclude 'that the surge in real capital inflows is strongly associated with real house price appreciation in Singapore' and larger in impact than 'real economic growth and real stock price inflation'. Domestic factors, though, certainly played their own part, with cheap mortgages, flagging new supply, and a strong economic performance in Singapore in 2010 and 2011 (real GDP growth of 14.8% and 4.9% and unemployment of only 2%).

A liberal approach in admitting foreign labour that grew by over 400,000 in the five years from 2006 – half of a remarkable total population gain of 850,000 – led to a rapid escalation of housing demand from 'human talents' and aided a fast recovery in prices from the GFC. In addition, home purchases in the private market from foreign investors climbed steadily following the market correction of 2009. They became an important driver of the private market, reaching a high point of 20% of new buyers in the final quarter of 2011. Together, permanent residents, foreigners, and company ownership raised the non-citizen share to a quarter of purchased properties (IMF 2012). Ethnic Chinese buyers from Indonesia and Malaysia have been leading overseas investors, followed by purchasers from China, the United Kingdom, and India, but in 2011 there was a surge of buying from China. Though only available to foreigners with the state's permission, the modest stock of 'landed' detached and semi-detached houses are the most expensive properties and most subject to foreign demand, and have displayed the sharpest oscillations with exaggerated peaks and deep troughs.

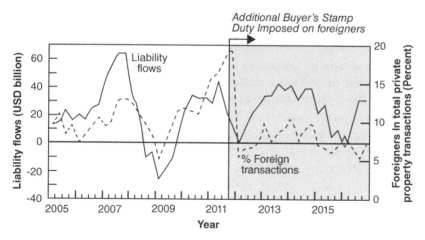

FIGURE 2.2 Capital flows and percent foreign residential purchases, Singapore, 2005–2016. (Source: IMF 2017b)

There is a matching geography to this sub-market, with properties in the 'core central region' of Singapore commanding the highest prices and also showing the most marked volatility. In contrast private units outside the central area, more likely to be owned by Singapore residents, have shown less variation. The central city, also the epicentre of the private condominium market, has been the entry point of new global price signals, which have subsequently diffused in a ripple effect to the suburban towns of heartlanders (Liao et al. 2015).[17] As foreign condominium ownership begins to reach into suburban districts, non-central price lines have risen, while remaining below the core central region. These externally-induced price shocks can then cross into the HDB market, although foreign buyers are unable to enter it.

Not surprisingly, it is the private housing market that is more sensitive than HDB flats to external shocks. The global financial crisis was accompanied by a marked downturn in private residential prices in 12 months to mid-2009, but this correction was quickly set aside, and by early 2011 in another speculative rush, prices were up by over 40% from their GFC base. Moreover, during this turbulent period the price line for the public HDB flats held by heartlanders continued to inflate as well, displaying remarkable resilience through the GFC and associated property crashes in the United States and Europe (Figure 2.1). The housing market has also remained a most attractive asset for Singapore citizens. Low unemployment, high levels of liquidity with historically-low interest loan rates (effectively negative with inflation factored in), lagging supply, and the rising real wealth of many citizens, together shaped effusive demand. During the post-GFC boom over 15% of Singaporean households held liquid assets in excess of US$1 million, an unusually high proportion (IMF 2012). While there is substantial inequality, real household income grew by almost 80% between 1995 and 2011; the top household income decile inflated by 126%, but even the lowest decile growth of 20% exceeded the overall income growth in the United States over this period (IMF 2012). In this context, as planned, HDB flats supply a significant source of investor income; at the end of 2012 as many as 43,000 HDB flats were being sub-let by owners who had upgraded to the private condominium sector while enjoying a premium rental yield and capital gains on their former unit (Chang and Chin 2013). The 'modern investor subject' (Watson 2010) has required little tutelage in Singapore.

The allure of residential investment introduces risk to different agents of the property state. With the post-GFC investment growth, risks of portfolio concentration have appeared for banks and households alike. Property loans accounted for 40% of total loans for Singapore's largest three banks, while property comprised over half of household wealth (IMF 2012). This concentration could be savagely exposed with serious economic shocks, notably significant increases in borrowing rates or an externally driven recession with higher unemployment and lower real wages. The price gyrations in Singapore's housing market in the recent past have proven its pronounced sensitivity to such externally induced shocks. The stabilising hand of government has, with some urgency, sought to bring order and predictability to such exuberance.

...and National Defences

In light of the exacting management exerted over Singapore society, and its substantial control of land supply, government intervention in the residential market is predictably pervasive and multi-faceted. Government has many tools at its disposal to manage housing supply and demand. It controls supply as a close to monopoly landowner, through Government Land Sales releasing developable leasehold property to the private sector. The scale of annual land releases is strategic; not only do auctions line government coffers, but they also permit market intervention through rationing or enhancing supply. Through the HDB the government is by far the largest supplier of new flats; it also exercises control on HDB flat eligibility (by citizenship, family status, age, and income), on flat re-sale, and on mortgage financing. Through the Monetary Authority of Singapore, its quasi-central bank, the state has additional capacity to steer the market through the lever of exchange-rate adjustment, macro-prudential measures, and taxing authority. Since the 1990s and especially since the GFC it has been fastidious in exercising these powers. Its bottom line has been simultaneously to permit asset growth for HDB owners while also maintaining access and affordability for Singaporean residents who are first-time buyers. Achieving this balance was sorely strained during the 2009–2013 boom, but the importance of success was revealed by the diligence of interventions.

Both the range and the scope of intervention tools are remarkable, and probably unequalled in range and deployment in any other open market society. Fine-tuning and re-calibration of these instruments are on-going, creating a complex and constantly evolving regulatory system. There is no space here to record each intervention but the principal actions in recent years are instructive.[18] In 2005 private home prices had not regained the 1995 level preceding the Asian Financial Crisis of 1997–1998 (Figure 2.1). That year government introduced a series of measures to prime the market, including policies to aid domestic purchasers, liberalising the use of their Central Provident Fund savings by raising the maximum loan to value ratio of housing loans from 80 to 90%, and by reducing the minimum cash down-payment (Lum 2012). At the same time foreign investors were encouraged by facilitating foreign ownership of apartment units, and permitting property to count as allowable investment for business immigrants seeking permanent residence (Lum 2012). External drivers of the housing market included regional growth in Asia Pacific and in-rushing capital flows, and to these were added substantial domestic job creation and immigration. Foreign capital was particularly active in the speculative condominium pre-sales submarket (Liao et al. 2015). Prices soared and government land sales were resumed in 2007, having been suspended in 2001 in an attempt to ration supply after the failure of housing market recovery from the crash of 1997–1998.

Meanwhile the HDB boosted its re-sale market in 2007 by easing flat subletting and enhancing access with more generous purchase grants; a renewed building programme was also announced. In the next two years, the private market fell back appreciably with the onset of the Global Financial Crisis, while prices for the HDB re-sale market continued to rise (Figure 2.1). However, the relatively small size of the private market and the liquidity of the banks precluded significant financial difficulties.

Anxious to protect local asset-seeking homeowners and financial institutions from another damaging boom/bust price cycle, the government introduced ten rounds of cooling measures between September 2009 and December 2013 (Lum 2012; Phang 2015; Deng et al. 2019; Yip 2019). The first measures included the abolition of interest-only loans, a reliable sign of the presence of speculative investors. Overall, the series of interventions were directed in particular against speculative purchases that involved short-term re-sale of property (or flipping); linked to it were financing restrictions on minimal down payments by owners of more than one property. Such activities faced steadily rising stamp duty charges. As the private market is the only niche for foreign owners, these cooling measures disproportionately affected overseas buyers. In March 2010 a quota was introduced limiting purchase of HDB flats by permanent residents, and reducing the housing grant for couples that included a permanent resident. The pecking order placing Singapore citizens first was made even more explicit in the Seller's Stamp Duty in 2011 that introduced differential exposure to foreigners, permanent residents and citizens. While foreigners were charged an additional duty of 10% on top of existing stamp tax for any residential purchase, Singapore citizens paid a lower supplementary value of 3%, and only on their third or subsequent dwelling purchase. Permanent residents fell between the two, with a charge of an extra 3% being levied on their second or subsequent residential purchase. The seventh round of cooling measures in January 2013 continued this process of graduated control, with permanent residents facing tighter HDB mortgage and subletting regulations plus an extra 5% stamp tax.[19] Additional penalties for foreign and company purchasers in the private market carried the stamp tax to 15%, while only Singapore citizens who were first-time buyers were exempted from the new rules. Differentiation penalising non-heartlanders carried over into 2014 with a quota limiting the number of HDB flats that could be sub-let to non-citizens in each apartment block, though by then the market had cooled appreciably.

Nonetheless in early 2013 there was no shortage of local buyers in the private market. The Head of Research at Savills' Singapore office estimated that 30–40% of buyers at new condominium launches were local investors purchasing their second, third, or additional flat. 'They are creating reasons to buy. It could be for rental income when the population grows to over six million, capital gains, or to hedge against the possibility of their children not being able to afford homes in the future' (Cheong 2013a). But after three more rounds of cooling measures in 2013 by the end of the year the market had softened, with prices and sales volumes down in both the HDB and the private market. Knight Frank's Singapore office reviewed the damage done to volume and prices from 'the onslaught of property cooling measures' (Knight Frank 2015). The Head of Research at Savills acknowledged that 'The debilitating effects of the additional buyer's stamp duty combined with the total debt servicing ratio framework continued to weigh on the residential segment' (Cheong 2014).

The clear intent of these rounds of intervention was to reduce investment and speculative activity that was forcing up flat prices in both public and private sectors – to reduce trading for exchange value so as not to jeopardise purchase for use value. The range of the instruments employed is remarkable, and their targeting of particular types of units and types of households is forensic. It is difficult to assess the efficacy of different tools; clearly the successive rounds of cooling after September 2009 point to the failure of earlier rounds – though supporters might claim that without them price inflation would have been even more pronounced. The first five rounds of market cooling were aimed primarily at external investors in Singapore real estate, motivated to enter Singapore's safe haven with liquidity from regional growth and quantitative easing in the United States. Overseas purchasers of residential property (excluding permanent residents) were active in the inflationary post-GFC recovery, peaking at 20% in the last quarter of 2011 (Figure 2.2). But foreign buyers fell off substantially in 2012, following imposition of an Additional Buyer's Stamp Duty of 10% directed at foreigners and corporate entities. The tax culminated several earlier cooling measures and seemingly was the decisive addition to earlier control measures. To secure its impact, stamp duty was increased in January 2013, so that non-residents faced stamp tax of 18%, plus an additional 16% if the property was re-sold within a year; off-shore investors backed off.

Demand control is challenging when many of the pressures are external; the convergence of so many positive demand signals in 2010 and 2011 gave price inflation the impetus of a locomotive. Even as the Singapore economy slowed down, the cash-fuelled residential market was buoyant. With the seventh round of cooling efforts in January 2013, there was a first day drop of 4–8% or more in the share price of Singapore development companies. But this response had occurred for earlier cooling efforts as well, and had lasted only a few days before share prices recovered. 'Cheap money', the *Financial Times*' columnist observed, 'has produced a market with the attention span of a small child' (Lex 2013). However, local experts were more sanguine, predicting that the most recent cooling measures in January 2013 would bring a flat line with no price growth for the year (CNA 2013a).[20] Some offshore reallocation of property investment by Singaporeans was also anticipated, 'to overseas residential properties, ie London and Iskander Region [Malaysia]' in wake of 'the recent cooling measures' (Knight Frank 2013a). Savills Singapore (2016) later reported that in 2015 Singaporean investors spent an astonishing figure of over US$26 billion on overseas properties, an increase of 50% over 2014.

Nonetheless, at the peak of the market in late 2013 average residential prices had gained more than 60% over mid-2009. Further refinements in determining limits to buyers' ability to pay were added in June 2013 by the Monetary Authority of Singapore's introduction of a Total Debt Servicing Ratio instrument (TDSR).[21] Households were highly leveraged, a fact that continued to draw attention from the IMF in their 2017 Report, though they also noted some improvement in debt ratios. The major restriction of this latest cooling measure was to limit total debt obligations to 60% of total income. Up to that point there was continued demand strength by local buyers in new suburban projects. But foreign buyers had become coy, and sales and rentals of high-end and prime central district flats were in retreat. As a local real estate expert saw it, 'As the authorities tighten the noose further on buyers, the question remains whether it will strangle the market or whether buyers are tenacious enough to break free' (Cheong 2013b). By the end of the year (and continuing into 2014) a subdued private home market suggested that the long series of cooling measures were biting, as both the HDB and private markets were losing ground and moving into a modest price correction (Figure 2.1). The measures had been targeted particularly against foreign buyers, and their preferred location in the core region saw prices fall first and fall furthest (Deng et al. 2019).

By December 2015, with eight consecutive quarters of gradual losses, no end was in sight to the housing market doldrums, attributed to global economic uncertainties, the cooling measures, and the accumulating stock of unsold new units. Sentosa Cove, the high-priced enclave for wealthy foreign investors, took a particularly hard hit. Characteristically, it had experienced rapid price growth of 80% between 2004 and the peak in 2013, but with cooling measures adding 18% in tax to the price for foreigners, and a flipping tax adding a 16% penalty to sales in less than a year, the bubble burst as demand collapsed (Stevenson 2015).

In contrast, private flats owned in the heartland outside the central region showed the smallest price loss. Having been compromised during the price take-off after 2008, housing affordability for moderate-priced units on HDB estates was restored by 2016 (Deng et al. 2019). Arguably, this was the primary objective of the exhaustive rounds of intervention, particularly in light of the heartlander rebuke to the PAP in the 2011 general election, with housing affordability a particular grievance.

By autumn of 2014, Savills September newsletter observed that the real estate sector was clamouring for loosening of controls, that the additional buyers' stamp duty was repelling foreign buyers while Singaporeans were deterred by the constraints of the total debt servicing ratio. In a 'transactional famine', sales volumes of new private units in 2014 were less than half the level of 2013 and less than a third of those of 2012. The net effects were that property investment capital was flowing out of Singapore. The next feature in the September newsletter summarised an article from the *Straits Times* that London regeneration projects (and notably the Malaysian-funded Battersea Power Station redevelopment) was looking for overseas buyers. Market softness carried into 2015. To the dismay of the real estate sector, 'the government's unyielding focus on keeping housing affordable and lowering household indebtedness levels' sustained continuing price decline (Savills Singapore 2015b). A slowing economy in 2015 coincided with a continuing marked decline in ex-pat demand; rents in the ex-pat favoured central core area had fallen by 26% between June 2013 and January 2016 (Savills Singapore 2016). Despite pressure from the real estate industry, government showed no inclination to suspend the cooling measures and announcements by the Monetary Authority into 2017 stated that they were unlikely to be lifted for some time with continuing low interest rates, weak economic growth, and global liquidity still searching out investment opportunities. By then prices had fallen nearly 11% over the previous 12 quarters.[22] The orderly decline suggested that a soft landing had been successfully achieved.

In addition, other potential risks identified by the IMF (2012) had become more visible. In unusual public declarations in the summer of 2013, Temasek, the sovereign wealth fund, warned of 'a lot of disruption and volatility' regionally with the slowing volume of American quantitative easing, and likely rises in the low interest rates that had produced such liquidity and cheap credit in Southeast Asian markets (quoted in Grant 2013a).[23] Ten days later Moody's lowered its outlook for Singapore's banking sector from 'stable' to 'negative', citing concern at the level of personal bank borrowing (primarily for property acquisition) in the face of potentially rising interest rates (Grant 2013b). Standard Chartered Bank warned of excessive leverage among Singaporean households, with housing loans as a share of GDP rising from 35% to 46% over the 2010–2013 period; almost 50,000 households held two mortgages or more (The Economist 2013a). In such 'perils of a gilded age', there was some concern that under adverse conditions the banks could be faced by a surfeit of bad property loans. The steady hand of government cooled these anxieties, reducing the price-to-income ratio and levelling off the price-to-rent ratio, two common indicators of a developing housing bubble (IMF 2017a).

In 2018 the government showed its continuing resolve to bear down on potential home price inflation. Prices were starting to rise, and wage gains had exceeded them for the top third of wage earners, raising the prospect of renewed excessive investment and price inflation. Greater developer activity was evident in Government Land Sales and purchase of private property parcels in collective *en bloc* sales; PRC developers with lower costs were increasingly prominent with inflationary land bids (Low 2017). Non-citizens, permanent residents, and foreigners, were again accounting for 20–25% of the private market, with Chinese, Malaysians, and Indonesians the leading purchasers, though overall sales volume declined steadily with the onset of cooling measures. Chinese buyers retained their post-GFC niche in the luxury Singaporean market, where they continued to be the leading foreign buyers, and equalled local buyers in number during most of 2019 (Reuters 2019). The Singapore builder, City Developments, announced foreign buyers had spent a billion dollars purchasing 70% of the units by value in two of its new condominium projects. In a limited response to such signs of exuberance the Buyer's Stamp Duty was raised in February 2018 for properties valued at over $1 million (the majority). In July, to the surprise and dismay of the residential property industry, the ABSD was raised by another 5% for individuals and 10% for entities – to be effective in 24 hours! Only residents (citizens and permanent residents) making their first home purchase would be exempted. Compounding the tightening effect, the loan-to-value limit on residential loans was lowered by another 5%. The market response was immediate with transactions of secondary (previously owned) private flats falling by over 40% in the following quarter, and by over 25% in the primary market. Prices for new units, which had risen in the previous four quarters, immediately flattened (Savills Singapore 2018).

In contrast to these demand challenges, when it comes to the supply of new residential units, government, as primary landowner, holds most of the cards. In pursuit of HDB affordability, it can seek to shield new public units from market pressures, and offer demand subsidies to enhance access for first-time buyers

(Lum and Zhou 2019). However, the state has competing objectives in housing provision, for while it will not want to encourage steep price rises, HDB owners have become used to asset growth, and public coffers also benefit from price inflation. Moreover, synchronisation of supply, which will come onstream a couple of years in the future, against demand, which can only be known in the present, is a far from perfect science for both public and private sector planners. Government clearly miscalculated in releasing very few new HDB units in 2006–2010, bringing only a little over 26,000 HDB units to the market in that five-year period.[24] In contrast with swelling demand and inflating prices, some 25,000 HDB units were built in each of 2011 and 2012, and a slightly higher rate of production was planned to 2016. Simultaneously, 21,000 private units were launched in 2012, and some 85,000 private sector flats were said to be in the pipeline, a massive increment that generated some anxiety of over-supply going forward (CNA 2013a). This elasticity of public and private supply is extraordinary, especially when compared to problems of lethargic supply growth in Sydney and London. To the sceptic, however, this largesse looked very similar to the massive release of HDB units at the end of the 1990s boom that contributed to a price correction of over 25%. Would the government response again be overshooting the market?[25]

Reproducing Labour: Housing Costs and Fertility

Singapore is the consummate entrepreneurial state, replicating policy initiatives tried in Western cities, which are modified and speedily implemented. Knowledge transfer and policy experiments have characterized its administrative practice (Lee et al. 2017). Re-valuation of urban heritage was learned from other cities and led to the saving of several ethnically themed precincts from the redevelopment bulldozer, with a keen eye for their tourist appeal (Chang 1997, 2000a; Kong 2011). From here it was a small move to a broader arts- and culture-based strategy, The Renaissance City Plan, and the presentation of Singapore as 'a Global City for the Arts' (Chang 2000b). A less refined version, and one that the government entered with caution, was the creation of two casinos as amenity leaders in integrated urban resorts for high-spending tourists (Zhang and Yeoh 2017).

Higher education has been identified as a means to move the island nation up the value chain to a knowledge economy, improving the job opportunities of heartlanders. Singapore is seen as providing a comparative regional advantage, producing an educated work force with R and D capacity for IT, biotechnology, and other advanced research and manufacturing sectors. The material expression of this vision was the campus of Biopolis (biomedicine) and Fusionopolis (IT, media, and engineering), 'a world class research hub' of over 3000 research scientists and engineers from 50 countries (Ong 2006). Higher education also presents business opportunities, through the export of educational services. So was born the idea of Singapore as a world education hub and its 'Global Schoolhouse' development strategy (Olds 2007; Sidhu et al. 2011). Currently, government is pursuing a plan for widespread digitalization to create a global technological innovation hub (IMF 2019a).[26] The intent here is to move toward a growth model that becomes labour-lean and less dependent on foreign migrants. In a fast-aging society, innovation and digitalization represent a substitution of capital for labour, with the heartlander population benefitting from continuous skill upgrading (IMF 2017a).

Singapore has also presented itself as a green city, a 'City in a Garden', with its impressive new urban park, Gardens by the Bay, on 250 acres of reclaimed land. Green initiatives have included the announcement of the city state as 'a global hydrohub', with urban water management 'soon (to) be one of the world's greatest business opportunities' (Singapore Economic Development Board 2009). Sustainability discourse suffuses the annual reports of the property development companies. By 2019 CapitaLand, the pace setter, was publishing its eleventh annual *Integrated Global Sustainability Report* where it proudly announced it remained listed 'in the Global 100 Most Sustainable Corporations in the World 2020 and The Sustainability Yearbook 2020. We also retained our listing on the Dow Jones Sustainability World Index for the 11th year and regained Global Sector Leader status in the Diversified sector for the Global Real Estate Sustainability Benchmark (GRESB) with the highest tier of a 5-star rating' (CapitaLand 2019b, p. 3).

These serial claims for a pivotal global role are symptomatic of a small island state that lives by its wits, discerning new trends and responding decisively and invariably ahead of the curve in Asia (Olds and Yeung 2004). Such innovation has contributed to the remarkable economic growth of recent years, adding to the successes of a global financial and trading entrepot located in one of the world's most vigorous growth regions. Up-skilling of the work force has occurred, with the professional, managerial, and technical share rising rapidly from around 25% in 1995 to over 50% in 2006 (Sun 2012a). GDP sped along at 5.8% per annum, 2001–2012, despite the ravages of the Global Financial Crisis, moderating to 3.5% from 2013 to 2019 (World Bank 2020). Over this same period the purchasing power parity in Singapore has more than doubled, and is second only to Luxembourg (World Bank 2020). The Gini coefficient based on net income (after taxes and transfers) has fallen slightly to a level beneath Hong Kong and the US (IMF 2017a). National unemployment has averaged 2.5% since 2001, though this obscures the still low rate of 3.6% for Singapore citizens, the heartlanders (Ministry of Manpower 2020).

An increase in wealth has stimulated the development of a consumer society in Singapore. Housing upgrading and investment are part of a larger consumer package pursued by an increasingly well-educated workforce. Among Singapore's large middle class, the 'five Cs' defined the consumer life-style package: cash, credit cards, club membership, a car, and a condominium. Each new shopping mall seeks to advance the extravagances of its rivals. Citing the National Day speech by Prime Minister Goh, Chua (2003b, p. 17) deconstructed the Prime Minister's declaration that 'Life for Singaporeans is not complete without shopping'. The major expenditure, however, remains a flat and for some years rising household debt loads have been primarily the result of leveraged flat purchases. The commitment to 'upgrading' facilitated by HDB innovations like the 'executive condominium' – with its promise of class distinction – may well lead to the 'overconsumption of housing at the expense of other aspects of daily life' (Chua 2003b, p. 10).

Rising wealth and the spreading of an urbane consumer culture have sharpened the contrast with a traditional lifestyle of familism. It is at this point that the population question enters the discussion. The island state shows in exaggerated form the inverse relationship between population fertility and a broadly based definition of modernisation that includes not only economic indicators but also such social indicators as female higher education and control of reproduction. Before 1960, colonial Singapore had a total fertility rate of over six births per woman of childbearing age, but this figure fell dramatically and by the late 1970s dropped below the replacement rate of 2.1. Thereafter, fertility decline among the resident population has become more gradual, with a rate typically between 1.1 and 1.2 in the past decade, identifying Singapore as one of the states of abnormally low fertility in the Asia Pacific region (Jones et al. 2009). The speed of change in fertility behaviour in the 1980s was so fast that the government did an about turn from vigorous population planning to pro-natalist policy in less than five years (Sun 2012a, b).

The reasons for Singapore's fertility decline comprise a complex of factors in which careerism, consumerism, and economic costs are all implicated. In field research I heard variations on a theme from young professionals and business managers.

> I would rather have my own flat than be married and have a child. I value my independence. It's very expensive to bring up children, not just money but also time and stress. I've heard of parents who take up to a year off work to help their kid get through a key exam.

Indeed, one of Singapore's large banks, in a gesture to support family life, proposed giving employees time off to aid their child prepare for the primary school-leaving examination, which determines their access to top secondary schools. A married professional woman, 30 years old, expressed her view about her own fertility behaviour and that of her friends: 'My friends, at my age, don't have children. They say maybe in three or four years. Likely they will only have one. It's the cost, really, education, housing, yes the costs.' Her perception of peer behaviour is correct, for government data confirm that the peak fertility years for women were delayed from 25–29 in 2000 to 30–34 by 2010, and a delay in conception will mean fewer children per family. Moreover, the proportion of single-person households is rising, especially among the majority Chinese population. Among Singaporean residents, 41% of men aged 30–34 and 29% of women were single, and this lifestyle group has been growing (SDS 2021). The trends were personalised by a business manager in his early 40s, working for a multinational firm:

> It's lifestyle changes. Women are more educated, marriages are later, there are more single people like myself. We are chained to different demands. The work stress is very high here and people have difficulty conceiving by their 30s. It's also very expensive, people keep jobs, you need two wage earners. Raising a child is not cheap and there's not much money left for kids after housing.

This final observation on the share of the household budget already committed to housing is worth further reflection, for 87% of resident households in 2010 were already homeowners. Shirley Sun's interviews with Singapore households revealed a similar set of responses, and added important nuances. Her data showed that higher-income households were the most likely to raise the cost-of-living argument against having children, although objectively they were the most sheltered from affordability constraints (Sun 2012a, p. 71). A plausible interpretation is that they had already committed substantial funds to the primary consumer item, their flat, and that this committed outlay limited the field of additional expenditures. Here is the 'overconsumption of housing' identified by Chua (2003b).

In a society where the major consumption item, housing, is also the preferred investment asset, the rising unaffordability of even HDB housing is bound to cut into other expenditure classes. Abeysinghe (2011) showed that the total fertility rate in Singapore is positively related to housing affordability, and as affordability has declined so have fertility levels. In an unpublished regression study, he found that only the level of female education accounted for more of the variance in fertility rates than relative housing costs. As Sun's

(2012a, b) data corroborate, it is not the absolute income of families that matters but rather income levels relative to housing aspirations. A key outcome is that low levels of affordability delay family formation.

The seriousness of declining fertility in the reproduction of Singapore's national family has encouraged a series of pro-natal policies, patriotic encouragement – including a rap song – and research. Joel Kotkin's wide-ranging comparative project, *The Rise of Post-Familialism* was undertaken primarily as a Singapore policy study. The common modern complex of highly-educated men and women, careerism requiring long work hours, delayed marriage, secularism and the lapsing of traditional values, together have a predictable outcome in household size. The fertility impediment of 'singlism' is a prominent feature of modern urban households in Singapore, as elsewhere. Two other factors relevant for our present argument emerge from Kotkin's multi-locational research. First, there is typically a negative correlation between the high population densities of high-rise living and household size; fewer children reside in a landscape of high towers, the quintessential HDB, and private residential landscape of Singapore. Second, there is abundant evidence that low levels of housing affordability are associated with low fertility. With expensive housing, households require two working partners for a longer period to establish an adequate financial underpinning for child rearing. 'The link between house price and the decision to have children came up repeatedly among people we interviewed in Singapore' (Kotkin et al. 2012, p. 16).

The Immigration Fix

While economic growth has accelerated, Singapore's fertility rate for more than a generation has fallen below population replacement levels, producing labour shortages and an aging population. Not surprisingly, unemployment has remained exceedingly low, averaging only 2.3% even across the 2007–2011 period that spanned the Global Financial Crisis. To address shortages the Singapore Government expedited an extensive programme of importing labour (Yeoh 2006; Yeoh and Lin 2012). Official estimates projected a total population of 6.5–6.9 million by 2030, driven primarily by the growth of temporary migrants from overseas who would by then have risen to 2.3–2.5 million, or 36% of the population (Government of Singapore 2013).[27] This proposal, envisaging substantial dilution of the heartlander share of the total population, created considerable resentment and unusual levels of critical commentary (Hodal 2013). Polling in 2015 prior to the general election showed that among 21 public issues, government scores were weak on population management (17th rank) and housing affordability (19th) (Blackbox Research 2015).

More than most states, Singapore has been an immigrant nation, created by waves of Chinese, Indian, and Malay arrivals, overseen for decades by a European colonial elite. Since the 1990s, substantial immigration has taken place in conjunction with the fertility collapse, labour shortages, and a booming economy. The population of Singapore citizens grew by only a quarter of a million from 2000 to 2010, while the total population rose by over a million (SDS 2010), so that 77% of growth was contributed by permanent residents (24.2%) and non-resident 'foreigners' (52.4%).[28] As a result, by 2010 Singapore citizens had slipped to a little below three-quarters of the total population. More ominously from a heartlander perspective, the foreign-born comprised almost 35% of the Singapore labour force in 2010 (Yeoh and Lin 2012).

Immigrant flows are contained in two well-defined tracks (Yeoh 2006; Ye 2016, 2017). The majority of newcomers are low-skilled workers from elsewhere in Asia employed in Singapore as domestic servants, in construction, manufacturing, and personal services. Domestic workers live with their employer family, while male low-skilled migrants dwell in employer-provided dormitories, bunkhouses, or cheap and overcrowded rental units. These cramped residences provided an ideal ecology for the incubation and spread of the worst COVID-19 outbreaks in Singapore; in July 2020 migrant workers accounted for a shocking 90% of COVID-19 infections (Li, A. 2020).[29] Workers have minimal rights, and commonly hold short-term work permits which are subject to abrupt termination on a number of grounds, including pregnancy.[30]

In contrast, the upper tier of the migrant pool comprises the 'human talents', some 240,000 in 2010, skilled professionals and managers from Europe, North America, and increasingly from Asia. This work force is regarded as crucial to Singapore's objective to be a global financial centre and a key hub in the global knowledge economy. As a result, this migrant group is treated generously with liberal opportunities and minimal restrictions. A related objective is the effort to recruit high net-worth individuals, and provide as incentives advantageous financial conditions, attractive leisure options, and high-quality residential environments in such elite enclaves as Sentosa Cove (Pow 2011, 2017). The Global Investor Programme and (until April 2012) the Financial Investor Scheme have been business immigration options with routes to permanent resident status and later citizenship for high net-worth individuals. The investor programmes have added to the considerable stock of wealthy households. The Swiss National Bank, pillar of personal wealth management, opened its *first* overseas office in Singapore in 2013, an acknowledgement that Singapore had become a major player in the wealth management trade. Right on cue, the day before the office opened, the Monetary Authority of Singapore announced the value of assets under management in Singapore had risen by 22% in the previous year to SG$1.63 trillion (Grant 2013c).

Tears in the Seamless Society: Housing Affordability

Strains have appeared in the balancing of economic, population, social, and political inputs and outputs in Singapore's national ecosystem in recent years. A growing economy needs increasing labour, but as we have seen Singapore's fertility collapse is unable to meet this need, and a liberal immigration policy has ensued. But that policy has led to heartlander resistance. With rising longevity as well as low fertility, the resident population is aging quickly, with the median age over 42 years in 2020, and expected to reach 50 years by 2040. Singapore is second only to Hong Kong in the speed with which it is transitioning toward old age dependency (IMF 2017a). In a wide-ranging interview Prime Minister Lee Hsien Loong lamented that the island was becoming a 'retirement home' (Bloomberg 2012). At the same time, he identified the policy conundrum:

> The immediate issue which we are focused on is the question of demographics, population growth, connected to that immigration, connected to that economic growth… It's a big issue. It's not something we are going to be able to solve one-off, but we'll be dealing with it over the next ten years, and longer. Because we're not producing enough babies, we need to top up with immigration. We must strike the right balance. We must maintain economic growth. So that's a complicated set of trade-offs.

The interconnected set of relations is well identified, but Prime Minister Lee stopped short of specifying an additional link – with housing. But the connections are clear as he addressed the housing question separately:

> We have had a property boom, almost a bubble. It's because liquidity is sloshing around worldwide and real interest rates are negative. People are looking for opportunities to invest their money and there aren't a lot of exciting opportunities where you see growth and possible breakthroughs right now. So that's a difficult problem for us on the overall property market. In the public housing market with new flats, we have control and we can build more and we can make them available and affordable. It takes a while but it can be done.
>
> (Bloomberg 2012)

Like the housing bubble of the 1990s, sluggish supply from the mid-2000s – a hangover from the demand bust following the Asian Financial Crisis – had been overwhelmed by a surfeit of demand with excess liquidity 'sloshing around' on global markets (Lum 2012). Residential affordability, the bedrock of asset-based welfare, was endangered in the private market, but not for new HDB flats, where the government 'have control'.

As stated by Prime Minister Lee, availability and affordability problems might be addressed by ramping up supply, and indeed some 25,000 HDB units were built in each of 2011 and 2012. However, new supply had slowed but not stopped price growth to the end of 2012, and affordability had developed as a serious issue. Price inflation placed the bottom half of the population under serious affordability pressures. Analysis of the *Straits Times* showed a growing crescendo of stories linking property prices with lack of affordability, debt, and foreign buyers. Over the period from 1990 to 2011, the highest incidence of such stories occurred in 2009–2011. These three years also coincided with half of all stories since 1990 that alluded to the existence or potential existence of a property bubble. In 2012, for the first time, the annual *Demographia* affordability survey included Singapore in its housing analysis. Using a 'median multiple' definition of affordability – the median home price divided by gross annual median household income – revealed a multiplier of 5.9 for Singapore's HDB flats (Cox and Pavletich 2013), a value defined as 'severely unaffordable', and just beneath the 90th percentile of unaffordability among several hundred cities in the analysis. Even within the closely managed HDB housing system, the cost of entry had become inordinately high.

A related aggravation to the heartlander was growing income inequality (Cheung 2013). Lifetime income trajectories for lower and upper quartile income groups have diverged substantially since the late 1990s (Abeysinghe and Gu 2011). In terms of income from work, the ratio of top to bottom decile incomes rose from 14.3 to 26.8 (IMF 2012). Growing income inequality was expressed in Singapore's high and then rising Gini index of 0.47 in 2011.[31] Even significant redistribution by the state had not been sufficient to address the scale of the problem.

Together these inequalities created considerable disaffection in the Singapore population and growing criticism of the governing People's Action Party. There were the abiding concerns of a democratic deficit among the increasingly well-educated population.[32] The offence of million-dollar ministerial salaries rankled poorer households as their own incomes fell below the rising cost of living. Those struggling to enter the HDB housing market found the increasing share of permanent residents a source of blame for inflating housing prices; rapid population growth (and ministerial allusions to a potential future size of 6.5 million) agitated commuters confronting ever more congested buses and trains. The concessions and privileges afforded overseas human talents were an affront to a heartlander population that feared for its own employment opportunities (Yeoh and Lam 2016). For young voters, the elderly family patriarchy of the Peoples Action Party had become out of touch in a sophisticated post-industrial city. The growing number of adult singles found themselves shut out from the HDB new flat market and its subsidies; I was told that the PAP's view of 'the Singapore family' that excluded singles could add $200,000 to housing costs for an alternative flat in the resale market, enough to generate a substantial level of frustration.

The Managing Editor of *The Straits Times*, an outlet usually in harmony with government policy, spoke for many when he wrote:

> This public sourness over property prices is a relatively recent phenom-
> enon given the history of rising prices here, which has been generally
> welcomed by the public. It shows there is a point beyond which re-
> sentment sets in, even if the majority see the value of their homes go-
> ing up. They worry about whether their children will be able to afford
> these prices in the future, and whether they themselves will be able to
> upgrade… (The) link between prices and incomes is, however, broken
> when the market is open to foreigners whose salaries have no connection
> to those of Singaporeans… How much should the government protect
> local buyers from the purchasing power of foreigners? … Making the
> HDB market – both for new and resale flats – exclusively for citizens is
> the best safeguard for the future.
>
> (Kwang 2012)

To achieve this desirable outcome, Mr. Kwang suggested that permanent resi-
dents, like foreigners, henceforth be excluded from the HDB market. The government's perennial struggle to balance affordability with homeownership asset growth was becoming unhinged. One outcome was the relentless series of cooling measures that eventually gained traction in 2013.

The 2011 General Election and Since

Critical views among heartlanders were widespread when I visited Singapore in late 2012. A real estate consultant whose company caters to high end foreign talents bewailed the government's misplaced focus: 'The 2011 General Election was a tipping point because the government was looking after for-
eigners better than locals. They need to treat their own people better than foreigners.'[33] A young government professional was even more outspoken: 'People of my age, we're really pissed off. Even as DINKS[34] the cost of housing is out of sight. Prices are pushed up by permanent resident buyers. There are more PRC Chinese among them. People don't like them, they're raw, unso-
phisticated.'[35] A taxi driver pointed out the cost of cars and HDB flats: 'It's too expensive, people are very stretched. They are angry. And the government wants to increase the population to six million. It's already too crowded'. The key election issues were summarised by Prime Minister Lee as immigration, affordable homeownership, and the escalating cost of living especially for

poorer Singaporeans (Tan 2011). In Singapore's interlocking ecosystem, these problems are interconnected and were regarded as such.

Internet sites and social media messaging played an important role in arousing sentiment prior to the May 2011 election, especially among the young, with sites like *The Online Citizen* offering critical news and commentary. These sites and social media platforms created a vigorous new public sphere (Tan 2012). The 2011 election was described by Prime Minister Lee himself as a 'watershed'. As we have seen there was significant disaffection, widely shared, but most clearly articulated by young households, those who described themselves as 'middle class but missing out'. Previous elections had poorly organised opposition parties; in the 2006 election, seven constituencies (six of them with multiple seats) were not even contested. In 2011 only one constituency gave PAP an electoral walkover, and the various opposition parties apportioned the districts to avoid competing against each other.

Housing affordability 'has long been a combustible election issue' (Tan 2011), with access to HDB housing considered a social right, and home asset appreciation regarded as the sanctioned means of upward mobility and economic security in old age. In the campaign preceding the 2011 election, Prime Minister Lee even warned that if a seat turned over to the opposition it would result in the devaluation of local residential property values, presumably because promised HDB improvements would not occur (Au 2011). As HDB prices rose so did expectations, with investment in additional flats seen as necessary to ensure children could get on board the ever-ascending price escalator. Residents, like government politicians, were expecting housing to achieve a large number of their objectives.

In National Day Rally speeches in 2009 and 2010, Prime Minister Lee combined the issues most vexing to heartlanders, housing, and immigration. As we have seen, a series of cooling measures in the housing market followed, together with plans for a substantial new supply of HDB units and land releases for private flats. These measures were executed selectively, with the most substantial tax barriers directed at immigrants and foreign buyers, with fewer barriers against permanent residents and least impediments to native Singaporeans. Promises were made to slow the growth of temporary migrants. But for some of the electorate these measures were too little and too late.

The election results in any other state would be regarded as a massive government endorsement, as the PAP won 81 of the 87 seats. But their popular vote of 60% was the lowest ever received, and an achievement the more impressive for opposition parties considering they were fielding candidates in six constituencies they had not even contested in 2006; in these seats, starting from nothing, they won on average 38% of the vote. PAP support rose in only three constituencies. 'Middle class but missing out' encompassed a broad swath of citizens: 'the ruling government's legitimacy to rule has become highly dependent on its ability to deliver affordable housing, as the 2011 general election demonstrated' (Chua 2014, p. 530).

Despite their decisive victory in terms of seats, PAP realised the election result was a slap on the wrist. Several ministers resigned from Cabinet, including Lee Kuan Yew, the Minister Mentor, who had been a dominant force in Cabinet for 52 years, and also the ministers for housing and transportation, two of the portfolios where government policy had come under severe criticism. Here indeed was a watershed. For his 2012 National Day Rally Speech, Prime Minister Lee returned to fundamentals, the basic building blocks of the government's construction of the nation.[36] His speech, 'Hope, Heart and Home' was delivered in Malay, Mandarin, and English. The governing party expressed a greater desire to listen to the voices of citizens, launching a consultation process, Our Singapore Conversation (2013), dedicated according to its website, to the same three co-ordinated themes:

> What makes Singapore our HOME?
> How can we have more HEART as a nation?
> What are your HOPES for our shared future?
> Join the Singapore Conversation.[37]

The allusion to shared aspirations around a communal home and a collective heart is a familiar refrain, calling forth the national family of heartlanders as an antidote to the frustration and anger expressed by individuals against the government. Boundaries for inclusion in that family have been tightened. The government announced a reduction in dependence on immigration, despite ensuing labour shortages, and this commitment was firm enough to be incorporated as a new parameter in economic forecasts (IMF 2012). Regulations were introduced to check numbers not only of low-income migrants but of 'human talents' as well through raising costs of work permits. The access of permanent residents to the HDB resale market was restrained (Chua 2015). At the same time substantial grants became available for first-time HDB flat purchasers.[38] A massive building programme of public units was announced. Public participation, what Prime Minister Lee called 'an inclusive dialogue', would play a greater role in policy experimentation (Lee et al. 2017).

At a local 'Our Singapore Conversation' community meeting in November 2012, housing availability and affordability were raised as a 'hot issue' (CNA 2012b). Khaw Boon Wan, Minister for National Development, told a heartlander audience of 300 that an imbalance of demand and supply for HDB resale flats was keeping prices high, but was confident that vigorous government action would restore affordability in the near future. Indeed, in the following year three rounds of cooling measures tamed the tiger of rising prices, temporarily at least. Simultaneously, a $2 billion package was

announced to boost the national fertility rate (CNA 2013b), a necessary cor-
relate of lesser dependence on foreign talents. Among the wide-ranging package of policies were housing incentives; a fixed proportion of new HDB flats
would be reserved for families with young children, and temporary HDB
rental units would be provided for them while they awaited their new home.
Two months on and there were more substantial announcements in a budget
debate from the energetic Minister Khaw to address the grievances that had
been bared in the 2011 election: single persons older than 35 years would be
permitted to buy HDB flats, while a 30% reduction in flat prices for first-
time buyers was under study so that 'their Singapore dream of owning their
own homes, like their parents, is safe' (Chang 2013). The plan would reduce
HDB flat prices from 5.5 times annual salary to 4 times, the level that existed
before the bull run in housing since 2008.[39] The proposal was one ingredient
of a review of the entire HDB philosophy, henceforth to address affordability
through de-linking prices of new HDB flats from what the Minister called
'the rapid rise of the bubble in recent years' (Chang and Chin 2013). It is clear
that house, home, and community would remain at the centre of achieving
Singapore's national project through mobilising its national heartland.

The month before the 2015 election, Minister Khaw Boon Wan (2015),
was at pains to keep the habitual Singapore conversation going:

> Hardware facilitates but it is the software – the *heartware* – which defines
> resilience. Do we care for one another in times of crisis? Do we put com-
> munity interests before individual interests? …Housing has played a crucial
> role… The HDB does not just build flats, it builds cohesive communities.

It is a tenet of faith with PAP that cohesive communities build a cohesive
nation.

Conclusion

The Opposition gains of 2011 were not sustained in the next election in 2015.
Selection of the fiftieth anniversary of independence as the election year, cou-
pled with the death of Lee Kuan Yew, father figure of the nation, a few months
earlier, led to a substantial rebound of PAP support, despite continuing resentment at growing inequality, higher housing prices, and immigration. But the
nostalgia had dissipated by the next general election in 2020. Just before the
election, polling showed general support for the government, though views concerning housing affordability had soured the most among the 21 issues in the
survey (Blackbox Research 2020). Anticipating vulnerability on this issue, the
Finance Minister announced that easing the property cooling measures 'is not

on our radar at this point', despite continuing pressure from the development industry (Makhtar and Amin 2020). The election results revealed PAP's support had fallen back to 61%, close to the disappointing level in 2011, while opposition representation rose slightly, though only to 10 out of 93 elected members.

The imprint of the 2018 cooling measure, and the continuous assurance by political and Monetary Authority leaders that there would be no short-term relaxation of the complex housing regulatory structure of the previous decade, together indicated that PAP had reached an accommodation with the intersecting and often opposing pressures of housing Singaporeans. It was a heartlander agenda that prevailed. Immigration would be limited; labour shortfalls would be made good by local skills upgrading, delayed retirement, and where possible, automation. Protection of heartlander assets and privilege in the housing market would be maintained with growing taxes and incremental barriers to the entry of foreigners and permanent residents from a decade of cooling measures. The de-linking of HDB prices for new flats from market-linked HDB resale prices would add to an affordability firewall assembled around public stock for first-time buyers.

Overall, prices would be managed with a regulatory chokehold on excessive inflationary gains, while allowing acceptable asset growth.[40] Nominal price gains of HDB resale flats had averaged 15% a year from 2007 to 2013, delighting many flat owners but antagonising a younger generation aspiring to join the housing ladder. That excess had to be corrected. Under the thumb of a battery of cooling measures, a slow reduction of the price index to 2020 restored an annual average increment of 5.3% between 2007 and 2020, just about an acceptable return to owners and a much more scalable gap to the HDB ownership ladder for aspirants, especially when aided by a first-time owner's grant. In its constant monitoring and regulation of the housing market, and re-calibration of supply and demand parameters, the Singapore government continues to juggle affordability against asset accumulation with forensic diligence and managerial authority missing in other gateway cities. With all of the regulatory instruments in its arsenal, this elusive balance must satisfy economic, demographic, and electoral imperatives.

Notes

1.   Currency values in this chapter are in Singapore dollars. 1 SGD = 0.76 USD on 1st January 2021.
2.   Haila (2016) notes the abiding influence of Fabian thought on Lee Kuan Yew, encountered during his studies in England.
3.   Resident households include citizens plus permanent residents, but exclude temporary foreign workers, some 30% of the total population of 5.7 million in 2018 (SDS 2019).

4. In a feature critical of housing bubble tendencies ('Avoid feast and famine in housing') the managing editor of *The Straits Times* noted that his own flat had appreciated at 9% p.a. over 27 years of ownership (Kwang 2012).

5. The use of the CPF, a form of pension fund, as a source of domestic property investment exemplifies the use of housing in a policy of asset-based welfare. In this instance pension savings are directed to personal housing investment to augment the pension fund. The CPF can also be used to invest in financial instruments, though with sometimes disastrous results (Lai 2013).

6. The HDB share is slowly declining (in 2009 it was 84%) as upwardly mobile resident Singaporeans enter the private condominium market.

7. For a similar mission to inculcate civility to migrant workers, see Ye (2017).

8. Liberalisation widened the access of singles to flats from July 2013. But the age threshold of 35 remained.

9. The private sector has been more forthcoming, creating a supply of 'small concept flats' of 500 square feet or less, colloquially known as shoeboxes, which are also a response by developers to expensive land costs (HSR 2012b).

10. According to the Sovereign Wealth Fund Institute, Singapore's two state-owned investment funds held assets of $870 billion in January 2021, third only behind the Norwegian and Chinese sovereign funds.

11. GIC's varied purchases also include an office building in San Francisco and several resorts in Hawaii. In the UK it underwrote a £1 billion mortgage fund for loans for troubled UK commercial real estate in 2013 (Hammond 2013). GIC also has several joint ventures in the UK with the largest British developer of student housing. In Shanghai it bought a development site for $930 million, the majority partner in a purchase with Hong Kong's Kerry Properties (Caillavet 2021). In Sydney it partners in funding the large Barangaroo redevelopment (see Chapter 4).

12. Chinese developers are also active in Singapore, both in the private and the HDB market (HSR 2012a). In 2014 Greenland Group announced a US$500 million waterfront project in Danga Bay just across the Malaysian border. It joins Guangzhou-based Country Garden Holdings who are also targeting the Singapore market in this region.

13. Singapore buyers purchased 23% of Central London's new-build units in 2012 (and 20% in 2013), while 27% went to UK owners. Hong Kong (16%) was the second overseas source of investors (Pickford 2013).

14. Haila's concept was developed from her work among Chinese societies in Asia Pacific. In its most explicit development, the authors trace the emergence of the property mind in an urban village in NE China (Sa and Haila 2021). My term, the culture of property, depicts an intersubjective setting where the property mind is already established and reproduced.

15.   The private sector also includes a diverse private rental market for short-term expatriates and also a considerable population of manual workers in poor quality apartments and dormitories.

16.   Data from the Urban Redevelopment Authority (URA) show that HDB resale annual price returns averaged over 7% in the ten years prior to the second quarter of 2013, slightly ahead of private sales at 6.5%.

17.   We will see the same spatial trend in Vancouver (Chapter 5) and London (Chapter 6) where price shocks enter the metropolitan area in prime central areas popular with foreign investors, and then diffuse outwards.

18.   A more detailed analysis found 17 separate policy interventions from government between September 2008 and January 2013 involving stamp duty and macroprudential restrictions alone (Knight Frank Singapore 2013a). A fuller inventory might begin in 1996 and also note three later rounds of measures from June 2013 to July 2018 (Yip 2019).

19.   The screws were turned further on Permanent Residents in August 2013, when their ability to buy HDB flats was suspended for a three-year period following accession to their PR status. The same government policy release broadened housing access to citizens.

20.   The 'mass market', i.e. the less than prime share of new ownership units, rose from under 50% of the private market before 2011 to over 70% in 2012; this trend favoured suburban sales, and was seen by local experts as a consequence of overseas buyers being discouraged by steadily rising stamp tax (Knight Frank Singapore 2013b).

21.   In addition to such macroprudential policies to moderate capital flows, the Monetary Authority has developed an exchange-centred monetary policy, supplemented by government-imposed fiscal policies (see IMF 2017b, pp. 57–59).

22.   There would be 15 quarters of consecutive small declines amounting to 11.6% from the 2013 peak before the tide turned for the private market in the third quarter of 2017.

23.   Within a week – such is the interconnection and nimbleness of institutions and subsequent decision-making in Singapore – the Monetary Authority had issued a new set of rules tightening household property loan eligibility to constrain credit exposure and over-leveraging 'in view of the current market uncertainties' (Knight Frank Singapore 2013b).

24.   In contrast over 150,000 HDB flats were built during 1996–2000, leaving a huge surplus when the housing bubble burst in 1997–1998 (Lum 2012).

25.   In December 2013 Minister Khaw announced a 'tapering' of HDB supply going forward as new units have 'begun to restore the balance' in the housing market. From 2011 to 2013 over 77,000 new build-to-order HDB flats had been launched (Heng 2013).

26. Singapore ranked second in Bloomberg's scoring of most innovative global economies in 2021.
27. In 2010, foreign temporary migrants accounted for 26% of the population of 5.08 million. The projected growth to 36% would contradict the government's promise following the 2011 General Election to limit the increase of overseas workers.
28. In the 1990s, Singapore citizens accounted for 37% of the total population gain of almost one million. In 2005–2010, citizens contributed only 18% of population growth while non-residents contributed 63%, with permanent residents gaining 19% (SDS 2012). This deep demographic deficit among heartlanders was a prominent issue in the 2011 General Election.
29. On 21st April 2020, Singapore registered 1426 new COVID-19 cases, 1369 of them among foreign workers.
30. These pressures contributed to the worst rioting in 40 years in December 2013, following the death of a migrant worker in Little India who was crushed by a bus. Following arrest, 52 Indian nationals were deported without trial under the terms of internal security legislation.
31. Later in the decade the index had fallen.
32. Singapore ranked 150th out of 180 nations in 2014 on the Press Freedom Index assembled by Reporters Without Borders, a disappointing score for a putative democracy.
33. Some blogs began to refer to the PAP as the Pro Alien Party. A number of blogs showed evidence of nativism and anti-foreigner sentiment.
34. Dual income, no kids.
35. Mainland migrants comprise a substantial foreign minority in Singapore's population. For the racialisation of this migrant group by Singapore citizens, see Ang (2018).
36. Signalling some personal culpability and remorse, Prime Minister Lee Hsien Loong accepted a pay cut of 36%, down to SG$2.2 million a year – still more than four times the salary of President Barack Obama (the Economist 2012a).
37. A number of concrete policy proposals emerged from these discussions. For an assessment of the most fully developed, see Phang et al. (2014).
38. In the constant struggle to balance the asset performance of HDB housing, and its affordability to new households, an enhanced housing grant (EHG) of up to S$80,000 for first-time buyers, and S$40,000 for singles aged over 35, was introduced in September 2019. The income eligibility band was broadened.
39. See Figure 9 in Deng et al. (2019).
40. With the price genie again threatening to escape regulatory confinement, another round of tightening occurred in December 2021, targeting (again) foreign investors.

CHAPTER 3

Housing Divides: Property and Society in Hong Kong

Land, housing, and property are at the centre of many of Hong Kong's deep contradictions – economic, social and political – in ways that are not often appreciated by other observers. Land and property can keep people permanently divided.

(Y.C. Richard Wong 2015, p. 207)

The market here always seems to be bullet proof.
(Simon Smith, in Riordan et al. 2021)[1]

Hong Kong and Singapore have been city-states competing as global hubs linking Asia Pacific with other world economic centres. They are peers, constantly seeking to emulate each other and mutually vigilant to new initiatives and achievements that might reconfigure the balance of success between them. They share a history as colonial entrepots, established to service trading routes between Asia and Europe, and more recently, as free-market gateways to the economic power of their hinterlands. They share the attributes of what Anne Haila (2016) has called a real estate dependent, property state, with land held by the government and leased to buyers in limited annual releases. But in Hong Kong, unlike Singapore, housing divides citizens. Weak government was co-opted by a powerful oligopoly of property tycoons, fuelling a formidable growth coalition, buttressed at first from London and since 1997 from Beijing. After the GFC, asset-seeking hot money from China and rounds of quantitative easing from the US overcame the city's cooling measures. Extraordinary price growth and crippling affordability problems marginalised the younger generation, and truncated access to residential ownership as an asset that could be leveraged into wealth accumulation and upward social mobility. A massive decoupling occurred of declining real

Housing Booms in Gateway Cities, First Edition. David Ley.
© 2023 John Wiley & Sons Ltd. Published 2023 by John Wiley & Sons Ltd.

wages from escalating flat (apartment) prices, while weak welfare protection added to generational social and economic exclusion. In a context of substantial generational and tenure inequality, residential alienation created a predisposition to political action among young adults.

In late September 2014, with students in Hong Kong on strike, and the Occupy Central/Umbrella Movement anticipated to begin within days, President Xi Jinping had summoned 70 members of Hong Kong's elite to meet him in the Great Hall of the People to promote Beijing's plan for the political future of the territory (Ng and Ng 2014). While the assembled elders were a roll call of Hong Kong's business aristocracy, the micro-geography of seating arrangements offered a more refined reputational guide. Seated at the President's right hand was the leader of the delegation, Tung Chee-hwa, Hong Kong's first Chief Executive, and vice-chair of the Chinese People's Political Consultative Conference. Sharing the honorific front row were wealthy property tycoons, beneficiaries of the Mainland's urbanisation, seated in a crescent ensuring unobstructed eye contact with President Xi. Next to Tung Chee-hwa was Li Ka-shing of Cheung Kong Holdings, then the wealthiest man in Hong Kong. To the right of Mr. Li followed a series of other Hong Kong property dignitaries: Henderson Land's Lee Shau-kee, the Kerry Group's Robert Kuok, Peter Woo, Chairman of The Wharf (Holdings) and Wheelock and Company, Lui Che-woo of the K Wah Group, Henry Cheng of New World Development, and so it continued. Leaders of Sun Hung Kai Properties, Swire, and Sino Land, other development titans, were also in attendance. It was a revealing moment confirming that influence resided not with political representatives, but with the wealthiest men in Hong Kong. Power was wealth, and wealth was, above all, property.

The most serious political crisis to that date in post-1997 Hong Kong exposed not only the concentration of power in the property sector; in this visible centralisation of authority, it also presented a reason for the existence of the fledgling democracy movement. Eight months later, after the protests of Occupy Central, when Beijing's political plan was debated in Hong Kong's Legislative Council, property elders from the front row of the September meeting hung together in a chorus of pro-Beijing endorsement. In a choreographed sequence, four of the property tycoons made public statements over a two-day period (Cheung 2015). Mr. Li warned of the economic costs if Beijing's political plan was rejected in the Hong Kong Legislative Council. Mr. Woo urged lawmakers to 'stand on the side of public wisdom', Mr. Lui lamented how the Occupy Movement had weakened Hong Kong's competitive position, while Mr. Lee made the princely offer of an annual HK$1 billion[2] gift to charity following the Hang Seng stock market's upsurge should

Beijing's political proposals be passed. But despite the advocacy of the property tycoons, China's messengers, Beijing's plan for minimal political change in Hong Kong was defeated. Amid procedural confusion, the political package failed to win the necessary two-thirds majority in the Legislative Council. Many Hongkongers wanted greater political reform, and subsequent events showed they would go to the barricades to pursue it.

In this chapter, we examine the place of the housing market in the development of a deep class divide in Hong Kong society, the existence of a growth coalition of government and business leaders sustaining the conditions that have led to this inequality, and the rise of a disenfranchised, youth-energised, opposition movement, frozen out from homeownership and the wealth accumulation, and middle-class status the property asset offers. The movement has multiple antecedents, including the democratic deficit inscribed in Hong Kong's Basic Law following its colonial precedent. However, because the property tycoons enjoyed oligopolistic power in Hong Kong, and were also intermediaries in the extension of Beijing's influence in the territory (Fong 2014), the nexus of property, power, and politics has been a central dynamic in the unfolding of the city's society, landscapes, and life chances. So is the residential alienation that accompanies exclusion from Hong Kong's property-based asset society.

The Tycoons and the Property Market

A number of property companies were long established in Hong Kong and some had evolved from the British *hongs*, the nineteenth century trading houses operating from colonial enclaves snatched from the Chinese coastline. Wheelock was founded as a tug company in Shanghai in 1857, The Wharf (Holdings) as a wharfage and warehouse operator in Hong Kong in 1886, while Swire expanded its Liverpool-based trading activities to Shanghai and Hong Kong by 1870. The Scottish traders, Jardine and Matheson, who began running opium and a more conventional tea and silk trade through Canton (Guangdong) in the 1830s, were early boosters of Hong Kong, and among the first land purchasers on Hong Kong Island. Jardine Matheson's subsidiary, Hongkong Land, remains a major owner and developer of commercial real estate in Central, the former colony's downtown.

In the late twentieth century, new property-based business empires were established by Hong Kong Chinese families. Cheung Kong Holdings was established by Li Ka-shing in the 1950s, Sun Hung Kai Properties by the Kwok family in 1963, New World Development in 1970, Henderson Land in 1976. These companies and others have flourished with the rapid expansion of the economy of the city and the industrialised Pearl River Basin in the past 50 years (Lin 1997). Each conglomerate had an early focus in property, but many have diversified into much broader holding companies. Always a pioneer, Cheung Kong led the way in geographical diversification, investing initially in China, and more recently, Australia, Canada, and heavily in Europe; by 2018, 59% of its gross earnings were derived from European assets (half of them in the UK), 12% from the Mainland and only 2% from Hong Kong (CK Hutchison 2019). Although the Li family deny a policy of disinvestment from Greater China, these data support the view that the family see more potential for value growth in other parts of the world.

The growing complexity of these conglomerates creates a large network of interconnecting companies, and not infrequent structural re-organisation. Cheung Kong was restructured in 2015 to include the primary property business, CK Asset Holdings, with CK Hutchison Holdings responsible for its interests in telecommunications, utilities, infrastructure, port services, retailing, media, and biotechnology. In contrast to such sectoral breadth, CK Asset's dependence on property invited cyclical volatility, and to ensure a steadier revenue flow it too has diversified its portfolio by acquiring energy firms in Australia, Canada, and Germany, a brewery and pub chain in the United Kingdom, and an aircraft-leasing business in Ireland. Its property activity has continued to expand beyond Hong Kong, with development projects in Singapore, London, and particularly on the Chinese Mainland. Cheung Kong/CK Asset has undertaken over 80 property development projects in China, and still held a land bank of 96 million square feet there (CK Asset Holdings 2019). However, its Hong Kong land bank had fallen to four million square feet, reinforcing the viewpoint that the Li family were disinvesting from Hong Kong.[3]

Property has historically been the largest sector by turnover on the Hong Kong Stock Exchange, accounting for between a quarter and a half of the market capitalisation by local listings (Olds 2001; Smart and Lee 2003). In 1997, on the eve of the handover, the property-dominated holdings of the top six business families accounted for almost 40% of the Hang Seng's market capitalisation: the Li family alone held 16% (Wong S. 2015). The property tycoons are major revenue generators and employers. At the apex, the entire Jardine Matheson conglomerate claims a global workforce of 470,000,[4] Cheung Kong Holdings some 300,000 in 50 countries in 2014 prior to restructuring. These are extraordinary heavyweights to be headquartered in a territory of 7.5 million people in 2020. The top four property holding companies based in Hong Kong, CK Asset Holdings, Sun Hung Kai Properties, Henderson Land, and New World Development declared combined profits of US$16.9 billion[5] in 2019 with a workforce of 110,000 (Forbes 2019). Indeed, the tiny territory of Hong Kong has been home to 25 of the world's 184 real estate billionaires, and 6 of the 20 wealthiest (Carlyle 2016); more recently the Hurun Institute's listing of the world's wealthiest real estate billionaires in 2022 placed Li Ka-shing first, with three other Hong Kong billionaires in the top ten. There is extraordinary market power behind such statistics, and the tycoons have wielded that power to reproduce their privileged status (Fong 2014; Wissink et al. 2017). Careful rationing of production from large land banks has ensured tight housing supply. For many years, the startling economic success of the tycoons, with accompanying rags to riches stories, identified them as figures of admiration and aspiration; hence Li Ka-shing's popular moniker of 'Superman'. However, as we shall see, in recent years such reputational pre-eminence has been undermined by a critical reassessment.

A handful of corporations has effectively controlled the territory's land market through a cosy *entente cordiale* secured by interlocking objectives with the ultimate landowner, the colonial and later the post-colonial government. While business-friendly, Hong Kong is far from a pure market economy. In a jurisdiction with limited land supply and where new development sites are rationed by the government in modest annual land releases, rapid population growth led to an entirely predictable, indeed planned, escalation of land prices. The considerable size of many government land parcels added to the cost premium, and disqualified all but the large companies from bidding in the land sales tender. The coherence of this elite growth coalition and the cost and complexity of property acquisition effectively shut out competition from foreign developers, permitting the flourishing of an oligopoly of fabulously wealthy local commercial empires. In some years Cheung Kong and Sun Hung Kai between them supplied half of all new residential units in the territory, while the top five companies often built 70% of new supply.[6]

Entry to this hermetic circle started to be broken open only in the past decade when equally large Mainland developers, some of them possessing the borrowing advantage of state-owned enterprises, began to undertake geographical diversification in response to the unpredictability and limits of the Chinese property market and the currency volatility of the yuan. Despite the globalisation of Chinese Foreign Direct Investment between 2004 and 2018, 64% of Chinese corporate direct investment in real estate went no further than Hong Kong (Li X. et al. 2020). Anticipating profit margins of up to 30–40%, but unfamiliar with the Hong Kong market, some developers sought joint partnerships with local corporations; others, with deep pockets or willing to tolerate high debt loads, more bravely (sometimes recklessly) bought sites independently, typically by buying at a premium above local purchasers.[7] From 2011 to 2019 about a fifth on average of government land sales in Hong Kong were won by Mainland developers, an unprecedented outcome. The tight oligopoly of the top five Hong Kong property firms that had secured 90% of land acquisitions in 2011 was severely dented as Chinese firms won 70% in 2017 (Li X. et al. 2020). A striking Mainland entry was the HNA Group, one of four Chinese companies that went on a brazen global spending spree during the 2014–2017 window of extensive capital out-flows from the Mainland. Though originally a regional airline in South China, HNA developed an audacious property-buying appetite until crippling debt (and the Mainland government) caught up with it. In 2016–2017 it bought four plots on the large redevelopment site of Hong Kong's former Kai Tak airport at a cost of US$3.5 billion (Bloomberg 2018). Its purchase prices far exceeded local expectations, and with land cost the principal item in property development this incursion of Mainland capital would certainly stoke higher residential prices. HNA, however, overreached its fiscal capacity, and was obligated to unload its Kai Tak purchase in 2018 to address unsecured debt.

Capital controls introduced by the Chinese state in 2017 slowed this corporate outflow. Mainland developers were also chastened by the different economic culture in Hong Kong. A softening of the market penalised companies who had overspent in land acquisition, especially as more seasoned developers were able to offer price discounts to move their product. In these challenging circumstances some Mainland developers scarcely covered their costs, and for the short term at least, withdrew their development interest.

Hong Kong's Land Supply

There have always been sceptics concerning the population carrying capacity of Hong Kong's land base. Dr. Sun Yat-sen, who graduated as a medical doctor in Hong Kong, alluded fondly to the 'barren rock' which he noted had been a negligible asset to imperial China but not to imperial Britain (Kwan with Kwan 2009, p. 23). But the problem of developable land in rugged topography can be exaggerated. Scarcity is also socially constructed. As a colonial legacy, over 60% of Hong Kong's land area is protected as a country park, green belt, or conservation area, while only a quarter of the territorial land is developed (Wong et al. 2018), and a mere 7% is allocated to residential use. The top four property companies together have land banks of over 100 million square feet (approximately 1000 hectares) in the New Territories, currently zoned for agricultural use. In addition, they hold significant development property in Hong Kong and Kowloon.

Government, however, is the ultimate land owner, freeing developable sites for lease in annual land sales. It also has the power to 'resume' ownership through compulsory acquisition of leased land for public purposes. Resumption powers have been used sparingly despite calls to liberate large land banks and other non-urban uses in light of severe shortages of affordable housing. But from colonial times to the present the government's inclination has been to restrain land supply. The 1984 Joint Declaration on the future of Hong Kong included an annex on land policies that restricted land sales by the colonial government to 50 hectares a year, a figure less than half the releases of previous years (Li 1990). Though the limit was exceeded following 1984, it did provide a brake on the scale of land releases. This restriction on land sales was subsequently carried forward after 1997.[8] In a fast-growing society a modest annual land release guarantees a high land price policy, with revenue from leasehold sales intended to contribute significantly to government budgets (La Grange and Pretorius 2005). Between a quarter and a third of government revenues are commonly derived from land sales and associated stamp duty taxes. In the deep recession following the bursting of the property bubble after 1997 this proportion was substantially reduced. However, in the renewed boom, it rose, reaching a peak of 42% in 2017–2018.

Dependence on high land prices for government revenue is rationalised by the desire to remain a business-friendly, low-tax environment. Hong Kong has low personal taxes, with 17% the highest marginal rate (and based on local not global income), no capital gains or dividend tax, no inheritance tax, and low corporate taxes. This is an exceedingly favourable regime for business success and wealth accumulation. But it redistributes costs onto citizens who wish to gain their own property asset; they pay the premium of high land prices for flats as a form of hidden tax, and that tax has been biting ever deeper. Moreover, government land revenues are applied not to a housing fund but to the Capital Works Reserve Fund for the expansion of infrastructure that typically adds to the positive externalities, and thus the value, of land. In short, the land value lift achieved by public infrastructure expenditure disproportionately benefits wealth accumulation by existing lease holders, leading to growing economic inequality between owners and tenants, with the biggest increment gained by the largest landowners. Big property holders have thus been gaining unearned and untaxed rent from their land banks directly from state investment, enhancing their market power, and exacerbating the economic division of society.

Such a land regime led Anne Haila (2000, 2016) to identify both Hong Kong and Singapore as consummate property states, 'where real estate plays an important role in the economy, public revenue and the wealth of people' (Haila 2016, p. 16). But despite comparable colonial histories, common land shortages, and shared public ownership, their land policies have led in different directions (Hui et al. 2004), for in Hong Kong the state has less frequently deflected its land power to beneficial public policy, has favoured rather than managed the property industry, and in producing public housing has done so inadequately and to minimal standards. Land rent that in Singapore has been redistributed to the 80% of residents living in good-quality Housing and Development Board flats, has in Hong Kong usually accumulated in public coffers and the assets of a land-holding oligopoly. Recognising, like Anne Haila (2016), the relevance of Henry George's populist analysis of land value to account for the biased holding of land rent in Hong Kong, Alice Poon, a former employee of the property tycoons, launched a vigorous exposé of their power, and introduced the politically critical term, 'real estate hegemony' to the public discussion of land and society in the territory (Poon 2006, (2010)).

Collusion: A Cohesive Growth Coalition

The overlapping objectives of government and business leaders in land policy identified a network of political and economic elites. In principle this growth coalition obeyed the economically-driven Basic Law, the effective constitution of post-1997 Hong Kong, and in practice it reproduced the everyday reality of economic and social inequality and polarisation.[9] The Basic Law was written to sustain the interlocking government-business elite nexus built during the colonial period, a nexus that privileged economic development and marginalised social development (Goodstadt 2013). The ethos of 'big market, small government' prevailed. Despite Hong Kong's substantial capital reserves, it was a tenet of faith that growing commitment to social redistribution would undercut the low tax, free-market ideology defining the city's economic culture and growth trajectory. Consequently, despite the acute housing need that grew cumulatively as affordability steadily deteriorated, there was no equivalent response in public expenditures. While absolute funds for housing did increase, the housing file was stuck at around 5% as a share of total public spending (HKHA 2019). In contrast, the privileged status of the tycoons as owners of capital was endorsed by the Mainland government and as a matter of course by Hong Kong's political leadership (Fong 2014). During the Umbrella Movement, Chief Executive Leung was caught off-guard by an international reporter's question, as he expressed caution that democracy would mean that the balance of power in Hong Kong would be shifted to low-income earners, meaning a different 'kind of politics and policies' (CY Leung, in Noble and Zhu 2014). While Leung was clearly wary of such a political re-alignment, his preference for a non-democratic oligopoly was distasteful to many Hong Kong people.

The compatible objectives of economic and political leaders propelled a turbo-charged property growth machine (Molotch 1976, 1993), operating with unusually few checks and balances. While it is possible to have compatibility without necessary collusion in a growth coalition (Ley 2021), some evidence in Hong Kong suggested that both of these conditions were present, while public perceptions enlarged visible evidence of developer interests influencing public decisions. A case in point was the suspension of the popular subsidised homeownership scheme in 2001, removing an indispensable rung in the housing ladder for poorer households. Its termination occurred on the advice of Donald Tsang, then Chief Secretary in the Tung administration, because public homeownership was regarded by the development lobby as competing with private flat development. The land bank assembled for Tung's ambitious public housing programme was then broken up for purchase by private developers (La Grange 2007; Goodstadt 2013).

Significant public opposition arose in 2001 to plans to convert the newly-completed and unoccupied Hunghom Estate in Kowloon from public homeownership schemes to private title. Nonetheless, the public asset of Hunghom was sold to a partnership between Sun Hung Kai Properties and New World Development that eventually turned a considerable profit after renovating and selling the flats (Chu 2010). At the same time an apparent case of cronyism was apparent in the Cyberport project. A state-proposed IT hub, to be built on public land with a valuable waterfront, morphed into a large, high end residential estate of 2800 units. In addition to a digital technology business park, construction included tower blocks of luxury flats with a Bel Air branding, described by selling agents as 'a luxurious ocean-front resort'. With the difficult market conditions of the dot-com crash, it was the profitable residential component that guaranteed the continuing viability of the entire project (Baark and So 2006). Cyberport had been talked up as a public–private initiative with Li Ka-shing's son, Richard, and in the eyes of critics the government role seemed to make public land available to a single developer in a secretive deal. To the dismay of other developers, the land transfer occurred without competitive tendering and without transparency. Meanwhile, with calamitous deflation in the residential market, angry Hong Kongers saw their own real estate equity vanishing by over 60% while the bottom lines of the large developers continued to swell with apparent sweetheart deals from the SAR government. The language of collusion between business and political elites began to appear with increasing frequency in Hong Kong civil society (Smart and Lam 2009).[10] In a 2006 survey, 82% of Hong Kong people believed that there was government-business collusion, while 44% regarded the problem as 'serious' or 'very serious' (Ma 2011, p. 704).

Land use conflicts became more salient in the daily consciousness of Hong Kong residents. According to the issue, a cross-section of civil society was mobilised; besides impacted local residents, a growing assortment of environmental, heritage, anti-poverty, planning, and architectural NGOs joined the dispute, with protests that might include street demonstrations, effective messaging via social media, and sophisticated use of international precedents to undermine government proposals. A common model would be an action by a state agency that transferred a public resource, usually land, for the benefit of large private developers, with incomplete transparency in the decision process. Giving the impression of negligence in sustaining a broader public interest, government action drew a critical media and community response. Such public–private transfers were perceived to be the typical *modus operandi* of the Urban Redevelopment Authority (URA), with the added indignity that, in a classic example of state-led gentrification (La Grange and Pretorius 2014), the action of a public authority led to the eviction of working-class residents and small businesses, and the subsequent sale of the cleared land for construction of luxury towers of flats, many sold to local and overseas investors.

A celebrated example was the demolition of Lee Tung Street (or 'Wedding Card Street') in gentrifying Wan Chai (Ip 2018), the location of many small printers who had developed the niche market of wedding invitations and other printed items (Smart and Lam 2009; Ley and Teo 2014). The URA announced redevelopment of Lee Tung Street's tenements for residential towers in 2003 and compulsory purchase with compensation began. Some residents and shopkeepers and a broader preservation lobby opposed the project and offered an alternative plan. Resistance continued over a two-year period but the URA engaged in a policy of attrition, completing compensation agreements with a majority of owners and tenants. Having assembled the land and paid off existing owners the URA sold the site to a joint venture of Sino Land and Hopewell Holdings to construct luxury flats and a themed retail street. A gentrified simulacrum of the old street has been reconstructed as a pedestrian mall, fronting The Avenue, high rise apartments built in 2015, where in 2020 a studio of 339 square feet was on sale for HK$9.5 million. According to promotional literature, The Avenue, 'is popular with expats and business professionals' (OKAY.com 2018). Many of the units are owned by investors, and in early 2020, a single real estate firm was offering 25 units for sale with another 153 available for rent. The hand in glove alliance of a public agency and prominent developers was repeated elsewhere, not infrequently overruling community voices who wanted to stay put in favour of a broader market of buyers and investors.[11]

With growing public resentment, the property tycoons who had once been regarded with admiration as rags to riches role models were seen more critically.[12] A priest's naming of Li Ka-shing as a property market 'devil' at a small Hallowe'en celebration was widely reported. Housing specialists I consulted noted Li's changing status (Ley and Teo 2014): 'Formerly Mr. Li had been a model; now people resent his heartless monopoly. The tycoons are too greedy; they are only leaving other people a bowl of rice' (social worker). 'Now people hate the monopoly of developers. They used to be our heroes, but no longer. They are now seen as greedy and in collusion with government' (urban planner). There was a nascent critical awareness that 'Hong Kong is ruled by developers... Li Ka-shing is our official ruler' (community organiser).

The dots between property and power were joined in Alice Poon's seminal book, *Land and the Ruling Class in Hong Kong*, a critical exposé of the workings of Hong Kong's property empires (Poon 2006). Poon had been a former personal assistant to Kwok Tak-seng, the patriarch who co-founded Sun Hung Kai Properties, and also a senior manager at Kerry Properties. The first edition of her book was published privately in 2006 in Richmond, British Columbia, where Ms. Poon had emigrated. The first Chinese-language version appeared in Hong Kong in July 2010. It was a bestseller and reprinted several times that year. The book gave voice to the unease of Hong Kong people with the growing political and economic asymmetry in the city, and provided a language for understanding it; as an interviewee told me, the book 'touches the heart of many people here living under their rule'. Poon's authority as an author came from her eye-witness position within the property empires; the political force of the book came from the fact that what she saw and heard radicalised her understanding. The term she publicised, 'real estate hegemony', provided a framework for understanding the growing marginality of Hong Kong's aspiring middle-class from the asset of homeownership.[13] Striking a raw nerve, the term diffused widely. A survey in 2011 by the Hong Kong Institute of Asia-Pacific Studies revealed that 85% of respondents were familiar with the term and 78% believed in its existence (cited in Ip 2019). Truly, 'hegemony has recently become the buzzword in Hong Kong society' (Lee and Tang 2016, p. 3404).

The culpability of property tycoons is one dimension of hegemony but perhaps not the most pernicious. Another is the naturalisation of development/ redevelopment in everyday life, including market manipulation (Ley and Teo 2014; Lee and Tang 2016). Just before publication of Poon's book, *The South China Morning Post* reported on two 'unusual sales transactions' in the luxury flat market, one involving New World Development's *The Masterpiece* in Kowloon, and a second, Henderson Land's project at 39 Conduit Road in Mid-Levels, whose large units and spectacular views made it perhaps the most expensive residential tower in Hong Kong. In both cases lack of transparency by the developer gave the impression of substantial early sales, which might entice additional buyers. In the Mid-Levels case, Henderson claimed 25 luxury units had sold, when in fact 24 of them were assigned through the same law firm to shell companies in the British Virgin Islands (Fun 2015). A few months earlier, soon after the building's launch, the developer announced the sale of a five-bedroom luxury duplex at an extraordinary price on the 68th floor of the *46-storey* building. The seller contemplated even higher prices for its 88th floor penthouses! Inquiry showed that the developer had exaggerated the vertical scale (and hence the views) by removing all floor numbers ending with the unlucky number 4, and also excluding floor numbering from 40 to 59. While Henderson Land claimed they were following an established marketing strategy, no other developer had re-arranged the numbering system with such abandon. Moreover, it later transpired that 20 of the 25 sales had been cancelled, including the 68th floor duplex. Community uproar led to a police investigation revealing that only four buyers were responsible for the cancelled sales, and most were offshore registered companies. Unusually, deposits were returned to buyers in the aborted sales, adding to the suspicion of a scheme to boost prices and sales through fake transactions. In the under-regulated real estate sector, voluntary codes of ethics offer no consumer protection. Lack of transparency grants knowledge to the seller permitting manipulation of under-informed buyers (Fun 2015).

The pinnacle of collusion-turned corruption came with two sensational criminal cases that drew international attention. In May 2014, the trial began of Thomas and Raymond Kwok, co-chairmen of Sun Hung Kai Properties (SHKP), charged with bribing Rafael Hui, Chief Secretary and top civil servant under Chief Executive Donald Tsang. Mr. Hui in turn was charged with receiving HK$34 million in inducements to be Sun Hung Kai's 'eyes and ears' in government, releasing information relevant to the company's business plans. In a remarkable show of resolve, Hong Kong's Independent Commission Against Corruption (ICAC) indicted two members of a premier business family and the top government official beneath the Chief Executive. Thomas Kwok, Rafael Hui, the Executive Director of SHKP, and an official at the Hong Kong Stock Exchange were found guilty and given prison terms, while Raymond Kwok was acquitted. Meanwhile, a long simmering case was being investigated by the ICAC against Hui's boss, Chief Executive Donald Tsang, for misconduct in accepting favours from businessmen concerning use of a penthouse while in office. Charged on three counts, his case went to trial in 2015, though enquiries had begun in 2012. It was a very public criminal proceeding. With appeals, Mr. Tsang was in Court five times from 2015 to 2019, and spent 12 months in prison, before he was finally acquitted by the Court of Final Appeal in 2019. Besides the discomfort the protracted legal process exacted on Mr. Tsang and his family, the repeated court appearances and their wide coverage internationally kept the question of the credibility of the Hong Kong government constantly before Hong Kongers.

The Kwok/Hui and Tsang trials sustained evidence of collusion in high places between the political and business elites. In the second half of 2015, polls showed only 38% of Hong Kongers trusted the SAR government (HKUPOP 2019).

Housing Prices and Their Causes

Hong Kong's housing roller coaster is apparent from the price index released by the territory's Rating and Valuation Department. After 1970, prices moved sharply upward but with significant corrections in the mid-1970s and 1982–1984 (Li 1990). Thereafter an extraordinary price ride began with a doubling of prices from 1985 to 1989, and a further three-fold increase from 1989 to 1994 (Figure 3.1). These surges and abundant supply helped create a property bourgeoisie, with a doubling of homeownership to 50% of households in the 20 years to 2001 (Forrest and Lee 2004; Yip et al. 2007). Price appreciation underscored the role of housing as an economic asset and the housing ladder as the most widespread vehicle for social mobility, while the dispersal of wealth accumulation also provided some ideological coherence to the colony's political legitimacy. Serial upgrading on the residential ladder followed a route through the levels of public and private tenancy and on to the dream of entering the private ownership market. 'Getting aboard' the homeownership express meant riding the rails to asset-based accumulation and social respect. On the other hand, failure to reach the first rung of the ownership ladder left public and private tenants with little hope of advancement. Already, pre-1997, the wealth accumulation accompanying property ownership was establishing deep divides in Hong Kong society.

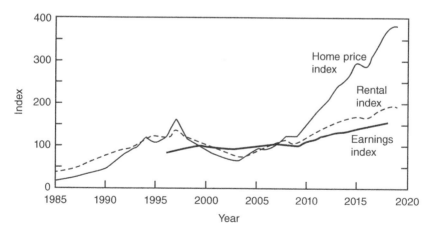

FIGURE 3.1   Residential price index (re-sales), 1985–2019, rental index, 1985–2019, and nominal earnings index, 1996–2018, indices = 100 in 1999. (Source: Census and Statistics Department 2019b; Rating and Valuation Department 2020)

The spectacular price inflation after 1985 created substantial wealth accumulation. I was told by a transnational business immigrant from Hong Kong how capital gains by households from the sale of housing assets in the 1990s permitted comfortable re-location to Vancouver in the anxious years before 1997 (Ley 2010, p. 129):

> The source of wealth of many Hong Kong immigrants is the huge real estate boom of the mid 1980s to mid 1990s. In some cases, real estate prices went up ten times in less than a decade. Pre-buying of an apartment could lead to forgiveness of a 10% down payment. With a 90% bank mortgage, by the time the apartment was built a year later you'd already made money. So, no personal money went into the purchase, and with low interest it was a very cheap investment and very lucrative. A small apartment of 500 square feet cost less than $HK100,000 in the 1980s and sold for $HK500,000-$1 million in 1993. With two of these it was very easy to bring money to Canada, and have savings of $HK500,000-$1 million after house, car, and business immigration costs. You aim to pay off a big chunk of the housing cost, maybe a half in the down payment. Often, you'd buy two [houses] to give rental income [in Vancouver]. Invest in property and the stock market.

This is an informative testimony to the effects of housing wealth in creating a privileged class of residents. Up to the Asian Financial Crisis (AFC), Hong Kong's asset accumulation performance was not much different from Singapore's. Returns on property could exceed annual incomes, so the preference in both Hong Kong and Vancouver was to buy two properties, one for residence and one for investment. But timing in the market is everything, and middle-class aspirations were brutally undercut by the trauma and post-colonial embarrassment of the real estate bust, a painful six-year rout precipitated by the AFC, immediately after the 1997 handover. As the housing bubble burst, prices fell continually, with an eventual collapse of 60–70% of value from the 1997 peak, a price point that was not regained until 2011. In 2003 the SARS epidemic coincided with the bottom of the crash, which by then had consigned over 105,000 mortgage holders to a state of negative equity (Poon 2006, p. 52).

Indicative of the cruel impacts of the property bust on family life, Hong Kong's long-declining fertility rate, among the lowest in the world, fell below 1.0 between 2001 and 2005, reaching 0.95 in 2003. Hong Kong people were in a sour mood, and the middle-class rebelled on 1 July 2003 in a massive march of 500,000 against a Beijing-imposed security bill that highlighted how far the government was out of touch with public priorities. Property grievances were also in the air, as some of the home-owning protestors described themselves as the 'League of Negative Assets' (Lo 2005). Remarkably, while middle-class assets were crushed – and golden visa emigration from Hong Kong was abruptly terminated – the bottom lines of the tycoons were resilient. Despite the depressed land market, Cheung Kong Holdings declared annual profits of HK$8.8 billion in 2002, Sun Hung Kai Properties, HK$8.52 billion; Henderson Land, HK$2.15 billion; and New World Development, HK$1.3 billion (Poon 2006). Resentment began to grow at the asymmetry of economic fortunes during a painful house price correction; it would soon become more activist.

The first Chief Executive of Hong Kong, shipping magnate Tung Chee-hwa, resigned before the end of his second term. The 2003 march of disapproval against the government's security proposal, together with the bursting of the property bubble and the SARS outbreak, added up to a pitiful beginning to the post-1997 one country, two systems epoch. Tung was replaced as Chief Executive in 2005 by Donald Tsang, a Harvard-educated civil servant. By then, the economy was growing again, credit was cheap, Mainland money was entering the territory, and inflation of residential real estate resumed (Figure 3.1). As a new bubble inflated, prices rose by 275% from 2004 to spring 2015. Tsang's period of leadership was marked by the restoration of a colonial ethos of 'big market, small government', and the slashing of government housing supply. The severe reduction of new public housing units aided the recovery of the private market, and with short-term pauses prices continued to rise rapidly.

Concerns about a lack of affordability had been voiced in the colonial period, but by the arrival of the third Chief Executive, Leung Chun-ying in 2012, Hong Kong was appearing every year as by far the least affordable among the more than 300 cities examined in its annual survey by the *Demographia* consultancy.[14] In addition, the territory consistently appeared at or near the top of a list of gateway cities with unsustainable housing bubble tendencies and most at risk of (another) serious price bust (UBS 2018). With rapid price inflation and no real wage increase, in 2018 a Hong Kong resident would have to work for 22 years before being able to afford a 650 square foot flat. As a housing economist remarked to me in 2014, '$4 million for 500 square feet in the New Territories! It's a broken system'.

The economist was castigating both the cost and also the shrinking size of new flats as a supply response to a product that had long strained the affordability of the working Hong Kong population. Micro-flats or 'nano-flats' (Singapore's 'shoe boxes') became increasingly popular after 2010 among buyers desperate to cling to the ownership ladder and its promise of asset accumulation. Requiring a smaller initial down-payment, they were also bought as investment properties, and in recent years price growth per square foot of smaller units has exceeded those of larger flats. The unit size of micro-flats continued to decline as overall residential prices rose. In early 2018, a project on Hong Kong Island included a micro-unit of 209 square feet that sold for HK$7.86 million (US$1 million). A consultant's survey taken at the same time showed that while over 40% of Hongkongers felt excluded from the ownership market, half of the remainder were considering micro-flats as a home or investment purchase (Sito and Li 2018). Convergence was occurring with the miserly size of public housing units. While two-thirds of public rental units were less than 430 square feet, the share of private ownership flats of this size rose from 5% of new stock in 2010 to 45% in 2019. In a telling indicator of overall affordability problems, production of the smallest units of under 215 square feet increased from 64 units in 2014 to 3200 under construction in 2019. The presenters of this data wryly note that these tiny dwellings are 'just enough space to park 1.6 regular-size 4-door cars' (Wong et al. 2018, p. 04). One of the smallest units, at 128 square feet, is more minute than the parking stalls provided in the same project. The developer describes this tiny batch as 'the best choice' for young couples with 'a desperate need for small flats' (Bland 2017).[15]

The constrained government land sales and the high land price policy have naturally led to a widespread view that deficient supply lies behind the price boom. This hypothesis is readily supported by residential completions (Figure 3.2). Despite population growth that added 350,00 residents in the 2000s and over 400,000 in the 2010s, new residential supply has fallen significantly. The last decade of colonial rule saw average annual production of 28,300 market units; following the handover, production fell to 24,000 units annually in the next decade, while from 2008 to 2017 completions collapsed to a mean of 11,700 units a year (Wong et al. 2018, p. 08). This diminishing trend in private completions has been matched by shrinking public sector production. From 1988 to 1997, production of public rental and subsidised ownership units exceeded 30,000, seven years out of ten. This threshold was exceeded four times in the next decade, 1998–2007, but not at all from 2008 to 2017 (Wong et al. 2018, p. 16). As affordability needs and prices have grown, public and private supply have faltered.

This precipitous decline in new units indicates marked inelasticity in supply, a feature common to housing markets in other gateway cities (but not Singapore). A conservative interpretation would point, as critics have in London, Vancouver, and elsewhere, to residential supply impeded by bureaucratic delays and restrictive zoning (remember that 60% of Hong Kong's land area is in some form of protected status). While this argument bears some

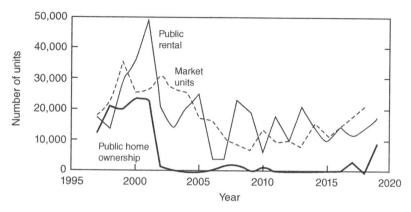

FIGURE 3.2   Housing completions in the public and private sectors, 1997–2019. (Source: Li 2016; Census and Statistics Department 2019b)

weight, it overlooks (as in London) the large land banks of developers that are drip-fed into housing production. As the state rations the supply of land, so the development industry ekes out new projects; through the wilful construction of scarcity, both are inevitably forcing up prices for end users to their own benefit. Moreover, another anomaly to a supply-side argument is evidence that housing prices have been insensitive to changing levels of land releases through the government sales programme. This unexpected outcome is attributed to the small scale of new supply from land sales relative to the entirety of the housing stock (Li et al. 2016). Yet widespread economic commentary continues to liberate supply as the primary means to address the severe affordability crisis.[16]

At first sight the demand component would seem less efficacious than supply in shaping prices. While household income grew slowly after 2003, the take-off of apartment prices substantially uncoupled housing costs from income growth. The gap continued to widen through the 2010s, while the volume of property transactions fell steadily much to the vexation of sales agents. The government's residential price index rose spectacularly (Figure 3.1), by 24% in 2009/10, by 21% in 2010/11, by 12% in 2011/12, and by 18% in 2012/13. Double digit inflation continued in 2014/15 (16%), 2016/17 (17%), and 2017/18 (13%). In June 2018, a car parking stall at a Sun Hung Kai apartment building in Kowloon – appropriately named *The Ultima* – changed hands for HK$6 million (US$760,000), a profit for the seller of HK$2.6 million over less than nine months. Property owners were exuberant at such returns, while those outside the ownership tent were falling despairingly ever further behind. Investors would inevitably pile on their capital to an asset offering such consistently high returns. But how has declining relative market power from incomes been associated with such escalating prices?

Some Hong Kong buyers are fully implicated in this price escalation. Local investors have been an entrenched (if variable) feature of opening day apartment sales.[17] Beneath the tycoons is an affluent class, some of them employed in senior positions in Hong Kong's post-industrial economy, others property-rich from earlier purchases, and all of them seeking good investment returns. In 2018 an estimated 69,000 residents had liquid assets (deposits, mutual funds, stocks, and bonds) worth more than HK$10 million (US$1.27 million). But three-quarters of their total wealth was in property, holding on average 3.2 properties each, 1.3 of them located overseas (Bray 2019). Nothing could equal the perceived returns/risk ratio of property. In a regression study of Hong Kong's price index, Hui and Yu (2012, p. 224) concluded that 'most market fundamentals are not significant in guiding property price movements… (they) are driven more by investment demand than by user demand'. The study also reinforced the role of the assisted homeownership schemes in lubricating upward movement on the housing ladder. In summary, Tang (2008, p. 359) has accurately described Hong Kong as 'a society organized around real estate development', a property state where 'the exchange value of property has an absolute supremacy over the value of use' (2008, p. 357).

The primacy of property as an asset for accumulating wealth is repeated (and doubtless reinforced) by its salience in public discourse. A key word search in the *South China Morning Post* (SCMP), regarded locally as the most credible local newspaper (Centre for Communication and Public Opinion Survey 2011), revealed more than 6000 Hong Kong-based stories that included the key words 'property prices' published between 1980 and 2012. Other prominent key words included 'foreign investors' (4216 stories) and 'property investment' (1558). Interviews with a dozen housing professionals confirmed that the property market provides a meta-narrative in everyday life similar to that expressed in Singapore (Ley and Teo 2014). 'The major business of all Hong Kong people is their property' observed a housing economist, while a second noted that, 'Real estate is everyone's passion; it's a hobby, a cultural value.' A housing journalist concurred: 'Everyone in Hong Kong loves property, left wing, right wing, no difference. It's onward and upward.' A pervasive culture of property as asset in Hong Kong has been carried overseas by Chinese emigrants, leading to high homeownership levels in destinations like Sydney and Vancouver (Ley 2010). Among investor immigrants in Canada, primarily ethnic Chinese, income derived from real estate and rental property leasing was the largest Canadian revenue source – and a primary reason for the Canadian government's termination of the programme (CIC 2014).[18]

But the abundant media stories on 'foreign investors' raise another demand dimension. The globalisation of housing markets means that especially for open economies like Hong Kong and Singapore, demand pressures do not stop at national borders. Besides local investors, two large bodies of capital converged on Hong Kong from the Chinese Mainland and the United States after the 2008–2009 Global Financial Crisis. Chinese investors were keen to diversify their portfolios and gain higher returns outside the regulatory environment of the Communist government. A large Chinese stimulus package in November 2008 enhanced liquidity and liberated capital toward quality purchases. Data amassed by the Centaline Property Agency reveal that PRC investors accounted for about 10% of sales by value in Hong Kong's luxury market in 2007, rising rapidly to 18% in 2009 following the stimulus package, reaching a high point of 39% by 2012, and remaining between 15 and 24% through 2017. Mainland buyers have strong preferences for new over second-hand apartments, and their share of luxury purchases by value in the primary (new) market reached almost 50% in 2012 and maintained an average of over 20% by value every quarter but one during the 2010–2017 period. An abrupt drop in 2013 coincided with economic liberalisation in China and demand management taxes in Hong Kong leading to widespread capital flight (FT 2016; IIF 2016). A switching of Mainland investment to gateway cities including Sydney and Vancouver, contributed to booms in their housing markets (Chapters 4 and 5). It is surely no coincidence that the marked decoupling of residential prices from Hong Kong incomes after 2009 coincided with the arrival of footloose Mainland capital (Figure 3.1). At this date house price lines also diverged further from rental price trends. The parting of ownership and rental trajectories is an indicator of bubble tendencies with rents aligned more closely with local fundamentals than external speculative funds.

One advantage (among many) of Hong Kong investment for the Mainland property buyer is Hong Kong's exchange rate peg to the American dollar. Investment inside the dollar club provides an advantageous hedge against fluctuations of the yuan, as well as freedom from irksome and changeable property regulation in China, and access to the lucrative Hong Kong market. The linkage with US monetary policy is a final feature leading to demand overload on Hong Kong assets, including property. Regression analysis of economic fluctuations in Hong Kong between 1995 and 2010 suggests that US macro-economic factors were of equal rank to local factors in long-run trends, though local Hong Kong factors prevailed in short-term trends of less than a year (He 2012). Mainland effects played a lesser role in this earlier period before 2010. But after the Chinese stimulus in 2008, Hong Kong property was 'inflated from both ends: rock-bottom US interest rates keep

mortgages cheap, thanks to the dollar peg; and [fleeing] Chinese money…
has bid prices upward' (Minas 2010).

The first of three rounds of US quantitative easing, following the Global
Financial Crisis, together with the same policy in other parts of the developed
world, released high levels of liquidity, with capital seeking assets with good
returns in open economies. The growth region of Asia Pacific countries experienced upward pressure on their currencies, requiring intervention by central
banks. The head of the Hong Kong Monetary Authority (HKMA) noted the
effects on the property and stock markets: 'The launch of QE3 and the short-
term improvement of the European debt crisis will increase the risk of overheating in Hong Kong's asset market' (Norman Chan, in Tsui 2012). The
prediction was quickly borne out and the following month the HKMA intervened five times to weaken the Hong Kong dollar which was being bloated by
incoming capital flows from QE3 (Davies 2012).

Bank deposits rose by almost a half during the three rounds of US
quantitative easing, resulting in a credit boom in Hong Kong that inflated
property and stock markets. With QE3 capital piling on top of earlier flows,
in 2012 Hong Kong had by far the highest ratio of bank credit to GDP in
Asia. The territory's Aggregate Balance, an indicator of net external capital
inflows, rose precipitously from less than HK$5 billion in mid-2008 just
before the first round of quantitative easing to over HK$150 billion by the
end of the year, peaking at HK$420 billion in the fourth quarter of 2015
(Savills Hong Kong 2018a). But such capital is volatile and sensitive to
repatriation at the onset of any shocks, or even small interest rate increases
in the advanced economies. Aware of the instability and fragility of financial
flows, Norman Chan, head of the HKMA, was under no illusion of the
extent of the risk: 'The ongoing quantitative easing by advanced economies
is unprecedented in both scale and duration. The risk of overheating in the
property sector to financial stability in Hong Kong is no smaller than that
seen in 1997' (cited in Noble and Jacob 2013). Four years later, with prices
again on a tear, the Financial Secretary, Paul Chan, showed equal concern:
'The risk in the property market is very high; sentiment in the property
market is very exuberant' (Cheng 2017). Investors were out-numbering end
users as buyers in new flat launches, and in light of the buying euphoria
developers were boosting prices in successive flat releases. But six incremental gains of US interest rates over the next 28 months reversed capital flows
and by the end of March 2019 with significant outflows the Aggregate
Balance was reduced to HK$75 billion, threatening to end the golden
period of negative real interest rates, and place upward pressure on Hong
Kong mortgage rates.

The globalisation of property markets meant that local, regional (the Mainland), and global actors were all at play as investors in Hong Kong residential property. Here was the effective, over-determined nature of demand, with pressures much greater than local incomes, population growth, or other conventional real estate fundamentals. We will see to varying degree the same relations in other gateway cities.

Low borrowing rates and abundant capital provided the exuberance for the market's 'animal spirits' (Akerlof and Shiller 2009); hot money drove Hong Kong price lines ever higher. The peg with the US dollar provided an additional advantage to Hong Kong property buyers as imported interest rates fell below local inflation rates, creating a condition of negative real interest on mortgage loans. From the last quarter of 2009 onwards to the end of the 2010s decade negative real interest rates added to the attraction of housing as asset; the parallel hot market in the 1990s before the bubble burst in 1997 was similarly a period of negative real interest when the inflation rate exceeded interest rates (Yiu 2010). But the current boom was always vulnerable to increases in American interest rates, which could quickly re-define the local investment equation.

Into 2018, the band played on. In August, Sun Hung Kai Properties sold out a project in a weekend, with 7300 buyers submitting bids for 328 flats; the developer's weekend haul was HK$2.8 billion (Lam 2018). Hong Kong returned to first place in the basket of gateway cities on the UBS housing bubble risk index. However, the long-dreaded strengthening of the US dollar laid bare the vulnerability of the territory's property market to trans-Pacific rate hikes. The initial signs of residential price cooling were apparent by the autumn of 2018 with the first mortgage rate increase since 2006, and the weakening of the Hang Seng stock market index, typically an accurate antecedent of property losses.[19] The effects of the US-China trade war were also a drag on the economy, while new supply of 21,000 private housing units in 2018 exceeded official targets. A confluence of conditions that had led to a sustained 15-year boom, now conspired to lead to a modest deflation of prices. But like previous pauses in price acceleration, the correction was short-lived and by early 2019 the judgement was that 'Hong Kong's housing bubble looks like it will live on to burst another day' (Dunkley 2019). In May 2019, UBS even predicted another ten-year bull market, and Wheelock Properties sold out a 500-unit project in a single day, banking a record one-day total of HK$4 billion in revenue (Li and Arcibal 2019). But May 2019 recorded the boom's high water-mark. Despite favourable market predictions, the end of the long cycle of price inflation was accomplished by a combination of local, regional, and global shocks. On 10th May, the US-China trade war escalated dramatically, and in June, massive protest marches and subsequent violent street conflict dragged down Hong Kong's economy. With tourism and retailing the first to show significant decline, residential prices fell in the second half of 2019. Then the coronavirus outbreak brought an added crisis to East Asian markets, followed by the repressive security legislation imposed upon Hong Kong from Beijing. Capital flows that had long boosted the market reversed, with significant portfolio investment leaving Hong Kong for more stable settings including Singapore, the United States, and the United Kingdom (Savills Hong Kong 2020b).[20] For now, the boom had run its course.

High-priced residential property provides an outlet for the circulation of both licit and illicit capital, and is widely recognised as a major front for money laundering. It is well-known that capital controls in the PRC are often evaded, and that Hong Kong is a major hub for washing undocumented capital and transmitting funds onwards to global markets, often via anonymised accounts in offshore tax havens. High-priced property sales may be completed by companies incorporated overseas with concealed ownership. The 'ML [money laundering] threat is assessed as medium-high' (Government of Hong Kong SAR 2018, p. 40). Some indication of this activity is provided by the Suspicious Transaction Reports passed on by staff to Hong Kong's anti-money laundering agency, the Joint Financial Intelligence Unit, most often by bank officials, who have suspicions about the provenance of a fund transaction. These reports of suspicious financial transmissions with regard to money laundering run into the tens of thousands annually, peaking at over 90,000 in 2017 (JFIU 2019). Bank (and other) officials may be exaggerating the threat by practising excessive diligence in compliance, but threats are real. In any case, with such an overpowering workload, relatively few suspicious transactions are ever investigated. Shadow banks are responsible for laundering huge sums of money out of China, principally from Guangdong province through Hong Kong and Macau. According to a report based on Chinese government data, underground banks handling over US$30 billion (HK$235 billion) in illegal money transfers were terminated in the first half of 2016 (China Daily Canada 2016). One underground bank that was foiled, with over 200 arrests, was alleged to have illegally exported HK$245 billion out of Guangdong in 2014 alone (Lau 2016).

A further indicator of the magnitude of undocumented capital movement through Hong Kong was the presence of the busiest global office of the Mossack Fonseca law firm, source of the Panama Papers (Mai 2016). A number of Mossack Fonseca accounts were traced to the families of prominent members of the Chinese Communist Party. Funds flowed through Hong Kong to anonymised accounts in off-shore destinations, facilitating tax avoidance. The Panama Papers also revealed that both Sun Hung Kai Properties and Cheung Kong Holdings, Hong Kong's leading developers, held subsidiaries in the British Virgin Islands (Robertson and Farrell 2016); one Sun Hung Kai subsidiary with business dealings in Australia, held at least 33 BVI companies.

The Response of Government Policy

Despite its commitment to the open market, with admiration of 'the world's freest economy' coming regularly from America's Heritage Foundation, the Hong Kong government has responded repeatedly if often unsuccessfully to its own housing question. Despite charges of collusion with the property tycoons, its policies have not always favoured the development sector, at least in the short term. Critics also charge that ultimately the policies have failed. But while the housing affordability crisis has certainly deepened, there have been substantial attempts at mitigation with undoubted benefits, notably the continuing replacement of squatter and dilapidated housing. There is an ample policy toolkit to address high-priced boom markets with bubble tendencies (Igan 2012), and Hong Kong policies have included both supply and demand side interventions. In its most recent country report, the IMF (2019b) endorsed a 'three-pronged approach' by Hong Kong authorities to address housing market problems. They comprise supply responses through a public housing programme, increased levels of stamp duty to discourage 'speculative activity and external demand' through targeted tax policy (IMF 2019b, p. 17), and macroprudential measures to mitigate banking risk from under-resourced local borrowers.

Supply initiatives are long-established. Extensive World War II destruction and refugees escaping the Chinese Civil War led to a large squatter population in Hong Kong entering the 1950s. The colonial government began a significant housing programme, building 880,000 public rental units from 1954 to 1997, both to house an industrial workforce as well as an expression of necessary, if miserly,[21] social welfare (Smart 1989; Castells et al. 1990; Yung 2008; Yip 2014). With ongoing population growth and riots in 1966 and 1967 overflowing from the Mainland's Cultural Revolution, a continuing public housing policy became a requisite feature of social stability as well as labour policy. Public housing was targeted at below median-wage working households, and included a housing ladder comprising, besides public rentals, smaller aspirational homeownership schemes that permitted purchase of public housing units at a discounted price as well as loans for private flat purchase. By the 1980s these programmes were well-entrenched in colonial policy. Acknowledging ongoing, and often dire, housing need, the colonial government built an impressive 31,000 public housing units a year in the decade leading up to the handover. Almost a third fell under the popular Home Ownership Scheme, priced 30% or more below market units, bringing households into the asset economy. At handover, almost half the population lived in public rentals or subsidised ownership flats (Chiu 2007).

This supply-side intervention was to be expanded after 1997 by Hong Kong's first Chief Executive. However, Tung Chee-hwa's ambitious plans for 85,000 new units a year – 50,000 of them public-sector to address continuing housing need in dilapidated and sometimes informal private rentals – were ultimately derailed by the Asian Financial Crisis. The public sector did ratchet up production to 40,000 units in 1999 and an astonishing 70,000 in 2000; with accelerated output by the private sector, almost 100,000 units were completed in 2000. This extraordinary flood of dwellings was intended to shorten the wait time for public housing entry and to lubricate opportunity on the housing ladder, through the expansion of the Home Ownership Scheme and a plan for tenant purchase of public units (Yip 2014; Li SM. 2016). Indeed, Tung aimed to make 70% of Hong Kong households homeowners and asset sharers by 2007. The fulfilment of this ambitious policy portfolio would have moved Hong Kong much closer to Singapore's model of a broad-based asset society where ownership of leased flats would disperse wealth accumulation to a large majority of citizens. In hindsight, this was a critical moment not only for housing, but also for inequality and social harmony in the territory.

But it was an opportunity lost. Instead of the usual state response of too little, too late, Tung's ambitious programme was too much, too soon. His supply cornucopia coincided with the fallout from the Asian Financial Crisis, a deep recession, and the collapse of housing demand, precipitated by high interest rates, significant debt loads, and unprecedented levels of negative equity among homeowners as prices tumbled by over 60%. Tung was persuaded by property interests to drastically cut back public supply targets and sell off amassed property sites to the private sector. The Hong Kong government abandoned the shaping of housing policy as accessible asset-based welfare and relapsed to the development paradigm controlled by the property tycoons.

Like Singapore at the same time, government overreached as market conditions changed rapidly, and the property industry urged a reduction of public supply, especially of public home ownership, now seen as challenging sales in the private market. Tung Chee-hwa's administration yielded, terminating its subsidised homeownership drive, and declaring a moratorium on land sales that continued for some years. Its visionary supply-side policy was in tatters, as publicly-assisted housing fell from a 2000 peak of 70,000 units to 14,000 in 2003 at the bottom of the wrenching price collapse (Figure 3.2). Tung's successor, Donald Tsang, reacted against public intervention and resumed the paradigm of 'big market, small government' (Tsang 2006). Aside from a brief and unambitious flurry in 2007 and 2008, the homeownership scheme was virtually abandoned by Tsang and his successor CY Leung until its restoration at the end of Leung's administration in 2017, and its advancement by the fourth Chief Executive, Carrie Lam, in 2019. The public rental programme, too, was downsized, producing on average 14,500 units annually from 2003 to 2019. Despite re-invigorated demand and a steadily rising price line, private sector production was surprisingly tepid with an average of only 11,700 annual completions from 2008 to 2017, less than half the output of the previous two decades (Wong et al. 2018).

CY Leung's administration restored a more liberal land sales policy, actively seeking new developable land. Housing was his primary policy goal, and rounding out a very busy first 15 months, the government released a consultative document in 2013 announcing a target of 47,000 new housing units a year, 60% of them to be public sector completions. This scaled-down version of Tung's plans is apparent, but like the earlier version, announcements are an imperfect predictor of achievements; from 2014 to 2018 public plus private housing completions averaged 29,300, well below the target. Since the Umbrella Movement there has been a frenzy of public planning and think tank proposals around housing supply, including Carrie Lam's interest in a vast land reclamation scheme around Lantau Island.[22] In her first year in office as Chief Executive, Lam, too, identified housing as her top priority, including expanded homeownership, with deeper subsidies, closer to the Singapore HDB model.[23] Indeed, projections to 2021 forecast an increased annual production of 40,000 units, with the private sector contributing just over half the dwellings (Wong et al. 2018). This increase is consistent with a conclusion of the IMF's recent report on Hong Kong's economy: 'increasing housing supply is critical to resolving the structural supply-demand imbalance' (IMF 2019b, p. 25). However, the IMF report under-emphasises capital and investment flows from China and the West, and their disruptive impact on the housing market.

There is also a political problem confronting proposals for an energetic building programme, experienced both by CY Leung and Carrie Lam. In a small territory, civil society groups emerged to challenge development in many locations, whether country parks, village lands in the New Territories, near-shore land reclamation, or urban redevelopment that impinges on heritage sites or provokes charges of gentrification. Contestation and locational conflict became a frequent by-product of government development schemes, postponing and sometimes precluding housing construction. A more fraught political environment has included the mobilisation of oppositional and often generational interest groups. The administration has been sometimes willing, however, to pick its fights, surprisingly on occasion challenging the development industry in the broader public interest. In 2018 the Lam administration introduced a vacancy tax that required developers to release all new units in a project in a timely manner. As well as phasing launches of new projects to avoid flooding the market and threatening price levels, developers had also been accentuating shortages by hoarding some completed units from sale until a later date when prices would have risen. The vacancy tax penalised such practices. A second blow for the property tycoons came in the 2019 policy address where Ms. Lam challenged land bank hoarding, suggesting she would invoke the Lands Resumption Ordinance to extract new sites for housing from extensive corporate land holdings.

Cooling Measures

Nor has the development sector appreciated the cooling measures introduced by government to contain exuberant demand. We saw earlier that since the GFC there has been a formidable incursion of investment capital into Hong Kong assets, notably property, emanating from desires for portfolio diversification in China and from quantitative easing rounds in the United States. With the decisive failure of ambitious supply-side policies in the Tung administration, Donald Tsang, his successor as Chief Executive, was eventually forced to turn to demand management, with the first of an array of stamp duties and macro-prudential policies, expanded substantially during the Leung administration, aiming to control access to flat purchase. If the supply-side initiatives had been targeted primarily to aid the poorly-housed, demand management through taxation was directed against investors and non-local purchasers, in order to retain market access for Hong Kong residents, notably first-home buyers. Like Singapore, a series of cooling measures of growing intensity represented a model of state intervention that introduced some fresh points of conflict with the development lobby. Donald Tsang could no longer maintain his hands-off policy as prices rushed toward the 1997 peak of the price bubble. Increasingly, Hong Kong residents, especially first-time buyers, were being left behind. In the 2009–2010 fiscal year, home prices had risen 24% on the official price index, and were on a tear to exceed 20% again in 2010–2011. This volatile context invited rampant speculation, and to counter the speculative flipping of properties in an environment of easy credit, the Special Stamp Duty (SSD) of November 2010 introduced a sliding tax scale on re-selling. A duty of 15% would be billed on re-sales for dwellings held less than six months, with reduced duties for longer periods of ownership.

CY Leung's administration aspired to Tung Chee-Hwa's earlier interventionist ideology sympathetic to restoring an accessible housing ladder with secure public housing at its base. Housing was Leung's primary policy concern. The existing level of taxation was clearly inadequate to provide direction to the private market. The basic or *ad valorem* stamp duty, a long-established tax on real estate transactions, had been raised to 4.25% for the most expensive properties in April 2010. Leung's government doubled the tax in 2013, and raised it again in November 2016 to 15% for all buyers of new properties, except for first-time buyers who were also Hong Kong residents. Controlling residential price inflation was fundamental and urgent and in October 2012 the anti-flipping SSD was increased by 5% to a maximum of 20% for a re-sale of less than six months, and its duration extended to three years after purchase. Simultaneously, an additional and notable innovation was a Buyer's Stamp Duty (BSD) of 15% to be exacted against residential properties purchased by non-Hong Kong residents.

The short-run effect of the 2012 cooling measures was significant notably in the luxury market where Mainland investment was focused, though overall prices faltered only in the minor correction in 2016 (Figure 3.1); otherwise, the price index rose by over 80% between 2012 and 2018. More significant was the role of stamp duties and macro-prudential measures on the volume of residential transactions which fell by almost 40% in 2013, following the introduction of the BSD and the increase to the SSD in the preceding October. However, this effect was short-lived for primary transactions rose in the 2014–2018 period, despite the increase in the *ad valorem* stamp duty in November 2016. More troubling was the sluggishness of the larger secondary (re-sale) market (Figure 3.3), where sales volumes slumped after the 2012 interventions and did not revive. 'No one buys. No one rents. The market is dead' complained an agent (Sito 2013).[24] A similar 40% slump in secondary transactions had occurred in 2011, following the first stamp duty increases in 2010. These two substantial reductions in sales volume indicated an extensive erosion of Hong Kong buyers as well as outside investors. The stamp duties bit deeply into the profit margins that allowed local buyers to indulge in the ritual of 'trading up' (Liaw 2011).

The Buyer's Stamp Duty established a striking demarcation between Hong Kong and the Chinese Mainland. It was widely known from the media and real estate agencies that Mainlanders were the principal extra-territorial purchasers, especially of new luxury flats, and the BSD made a remarkable, perhaps invidious, distinction *within one country*, identifying Mainland buyers as interlopers whose purchases were penalising Hong Kong people and were therefore in need of management.[25] It was a matter, as economist Richard Wong more broadly saw it, of *Hong Kong Land for Hong Kong People* (Wong

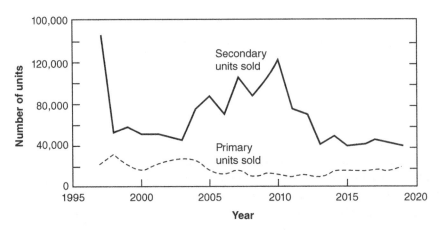

FIGURE 3.3 Primary (new) and secondary (re-sale) residential transactions, 1997–2019. (Source: Land Registry and Midland Realty Property Data and Research Centre)

Y.C.R. 2015). Some might see the BSD as a sanctioned, institutional form of a localist ideology that within a few years would be rejected by Beijing in the sternest terms. For a purchaser who was not a Hong Kong permanent resident, the cumulative stamp duties would now add 30% to the cost of purchasing a property valued at HK$30 million or more.[26] The extensive barrage of stamp duties targeting re-sale flipping, high end purchases, and foreign ownership was clearly a protective measure defending local buyers against speculative, external capital. The severity of these barriers curtailed Mainland purchases, but not, as it turned out, permanently.

Demand management also made extensive use of macro-prudential policy to buttress mortgage security for Hong Kong borrowers and lenders. The HKMA added eight rounds of macro-prudential measures between 2009 and 2017 to try to alleviate the risk of consumer vulnerability through excessive leverage.[27] They included attempts to limit the extent of credit accessible to more marginal borrowers through several rounds of tightening loan-to-value (LTV) and debt-to-income ratios, steadily removing more risk-laden buyers from the market.[28] These measures, notably LTV limits, had been of some use in mitigating banking risks from non-performing loans during the 1997 real estate bust (HKMA 2017). But macro-prudential measures in the Hong Kong context, 'while effective in containing leverage played a limited role in containing house price appreciation' (IMF 2019b). A much larger analysis in 57 countries found that while limiting the size of debt servicing to income ratios did successfully limit credit growth, stamp duty-type taxation more effectively limited house price booms and the development of housing bubbles (Kuttner and Shim 2013).

Overall, the continuing inflation of the property bubble indicated that the battery of demand-management measures at best arrested prices in the short term, though they also limited the number of transactions, in both the primary and the secondary markets. The Buyer's Stamp Duty was immediately followed by a large decline in Mainland purchasing in 2013, though some buyers were enticed back by price discounts by developers for luxury homes to offset the tax.[29] Macro-prudential measures could likewise be circumvented by borrowers using the riskier funds of non-bank financial institutions. Developers joined this market, offering mortgages of up to 80 or 90% of apartment cost, way above the loan-to-value cap imposed on the banks.[30] Stamp duties were certainly regarded as impediments to house sales by the development lobby. In January 2014, at a meeting of the Hong Kong Development Forum, Hong Kong and Mainland executives railed against the demand-management policies of the previous 18 months; the Chairman of a private equity company criticised them as 'targeted at mainland talents, as they are the major buyers of Hong Kong's luxury houses' (Yu and Yu 2014). The answer to high prices, according to an executive with the Mainland's sovereign wealth fund, was not to block Mainland property investment but instead to add to Hong Kong's developable land supply. However, without any lifting of the offensive stamp duty, Mainland buyers were back in the luxury residential market later in 2014, with a number of expensive homes bought by companies, thereby concealing the property's beneficial owner. Compounding stamp duties had become just a cost of doing business for very wealthy investors. With Mainland buyers exceeding 20% of the primary luxury market, the double *ad valorem* stamp duty was raised to 15% in November 2016. After a brief adjustment, investment continued and by early 2018 Mainland investors were scooping up over a quarter of luxury new-build properties, despite a tax charge of up to 30%. While the IMF staff analysis concluded that 'these stamp duties have been effective in curbing house price increases' (IMF 2019b, p. 19), it is hard to disagree with the UBS assessment that 'Regulatory measures proved ineffective to restrain insatiable investor demand and speculative price expectations' (UBS 2019, p. 9).

Inequality in the Housing Market and Beyond

Discussion of price lines and housing production numbers gives only an indirect and partial view of the experience of housing market inequality in everyday life. While public interventions were frequent and substantial, more persuasive is the UBS assessment that they failed to unhinge the injurious effects of hot money combined with a land policy constructed to produce scarcity. For Hong Kong residents with property assets, there has been extraordinary wealth creation; for the rest, there is a meta-narrative of housing as unaffordable, unavailable, under-sized, and frequently of low quality.

Housing consumption both reflects and reproduces a stark inequality of wealth accumulation. A high Gini coefficient of 0.54 defined a significantly unequal income distribution, rising before and after the handover, and by 2008 Hong Kong was named the most unequal city in Asia (Goodstadt 2013, p. 73; Chen et al. 2018). The assets of the 40 or so billionaires – more than half of them real estate magnates – in the territory in 2014 corresponded to almost three-quarters of Hong Kong's annual economic output, a steadily rising level of wealth concentration said to be exceeded globally only by Swaziland (Chu 2014)! By 2019, Hong Kong was home to 71 US dollar billionaires, more than twice as many as lived in Japan (UBS 2019). Wealth concentration tripled between 1988 and 2020, when it was higher by far than any national economy (Piketty and Yang 2021).

Taxation policy has systematically favoured the business elite. There is no dividend tax, and the richest five tycoons made close to $24 billion in dividends alone in 2016 and 2017 (Wong, M. 2018).[31] The statistics pile up, and all indicate a state where rising inequality has become institutionalised. Hong Kong's wealth gap has steadily broadened. By 2018, a fifth of the population lived below the poverty line, with higher rates for children and much higher rates for the elderly, for single parents, and recently arrived households with at least one Mainland member (Census and Statistics Department 2019c).[32] Even the IMF's Executive Board urged diplomatically that the Hong Kong government dedicate more of its large revenue surplus to social policy, recommending 'a comprehensive medium-term fiscal package', to address 'longer term structural challenges associated with housing market imbalances, population aging and income inequality' (IMF 2019b, n.p.). The SAR government, however, absolved itself of responsibility, blaming the growing immiseration on an aging population, an improving economy, and changing demographics (Chiu 2018). This response was also an admission that the state did not adequately care for the elderly, that a growing economy does not aid the poor, and that open borders do not prosper many Asian immigrant minorities.

The relentless deterioration of housing affordability was documented by the annual *Demographia* report. Against a median affordability index of 4.3 for the entire set of cities in the survey, a score falling in the 'seriously unaffordable' category, Hong Kong's index value was 20.3 in 2019, at the very top of the 'severely unaffordable' scale, and far above the value of 11.9 for Vancouver in second place (Cox and Pavletich 2020). When Hong Kong was first added to the *Demographia* ranking in 2010 its index was already 11.4; it has always been the most unaffordable city listed and with a steadily increasing extreme value.

The index is restricted to private ownership, and the poor are normally in public or private rentals. Among Hong Kong households, 31% live in public rental housing; another 15% live in larger and more desirable subsidised homeownership flats (HKHA 2019). The quality of public rental accommodation is variable, and has not thrown off its earlier status of representing a minimal entitlement. Buildings are aging, with a quarter of all units in 2019 more than 35 years old (HKHA 2019), in a climate where building materials speedily deteriorate, and where I was told that 'an old property is 20 years old'. In contrast only a fifth of units were ten years old or less. Despite improvements, units remain very small, with 83% less than 40 square metres (430 square feet), and almost a quarter below 20 square metres. With an average household of 2.7 people, flats are cramped and barely functional. Most are located in the New Territories, distant from the focus of job opportunities. Nonetheless, some households remain in public rentals even as their income rises, because of the very low rents, typically only 15–25% of the per square metre cost of a private apartment (HKHA 2019; Wong Y.C.R. 2015).[33]

An ethnography of poor families of Mainland wives and Hong Kong husbands has documented the marked deterioration in dwelling size and disappointment about dwelling quality among Guangdong women joining their partners in Hong Kong. Whether in public or private rentals, 'hyperdensity, crowding and clutter are the norm' (Newendorp 2008, p. 107). With a 300 square foot unit sometimes home to three generations, family tensions were common, and the 'extreme lack of space may have been largely responsible for wives' difficulties in adjusting' (Newendorp 2008, p. 122), Despite these forlorn conditions, the wait time for public housing for a lengthy waiting list has more than doubled since 2014, reaching 6.1 years for general applicants, and over four years for single elderly residents in early 2022 (HKHA 2022).

Conditions are varied in private rentals. While investor-owned flats might offer good though expensive accommodation, poorer households make do in low quality, older tenements, where shoddy construction and inattentive management accentuate deterioration, squalor, and sometimes danger. The Urban Renewal Authority (URA) – which had a vested interest to reveal inadequate conditions in private buildings it sought to demolish – declared in 2011 that 110,000 families were living in 'homes that are neither healthy nor safe' (cited in Goodstadt 2013, p. 89). Filth, risk of flooding, and electrical faults in overcrowded buildings were a recipe for disaster. Moreover, tenure was insecure due in part to the URA itself, especially in more central areas where the Authority was mandated to assemble older properties for redevelopment, compensating both owners and tenants (Ng 2002). Its actions often led to charges of gentrification, for once clearance of poor-quality rental apartments was achieved, the URA sold on its sites to property developers who replaced them with high-priced flats (La Grange and Pretorius 2014).[34] A senior manager of the URA acknowledged as much in an interview: 'We are accused of gentrification all the time, but this macro-economic impact of redevelopment is unavoidable'. In the case of *The Masterpiece*, an upscale mixed-use project in the old neighbourhood of Tsim Sha Tsui, a member of a development review committee critically singled out the URA's role: 'Instead of serving the public by regenerating their living environment, the URA becomes a developer and creates gentrification' (cited in Lai and Liu 2010). The accusation seemed on target for an older, low-income block had been transformed by the developer, New World Development, with the smallest one-bedroom unit in *The Masterpiece* marketed for HK$24.5 million in 2009. But such land use transition was usually tolerated as a law of nature. I was told by an urban planner that, 'Redevelopment is the taken-for-granted here… even the poorest accept the inevitability of demolition and redevelopment. Their dream is a new public housing unit. People welcome redevelopment'.

Below the bottom rung of the housing ladder, homelessness counts identify 1200–2000 people who live on the streets. There has always been a much larger population in various types of informal housing. The public housing policy initiated by the colonial government settled occupants of squatter camps, and various forms of informality remain: rooftop shelters, and especially the growing numbers of subdivided flats. One rung above homelessness, an estimated 210,000 Hong Kong residents live precariously in illegally partitioned flats in old tenements and former industrial buildings. These elongated units may be as narrow as 6 feet, 100–150 square feet in size, cramped, congested, and unsafe. The housing code is infringed but there is little enforcement when alternate accommodation is unavailable. Subdivided flats typically house the elderly and the working poor. A survey in 2018 in several older Kowloon neighbourhoods found 1700 small flats subdivided into 5500 tiny units with minimal fire safety, conditions propitious for disease, and modifications threatening the structural integrity of the building (Zhao 2018). Most subdivided units were windowless, with minimal ventilation; electrical hazards were common, while insect infestation was often a problem. Nonetheless rent per unit area might be comparable with prices in far more prosperous areas. NGOs like the Society for Community Organisation have drawn attention to this precarious and unsafe housing through various forms of advocacy. In Hong Kong's fraught housing environment, the micro-flat has become the end result in both the public and the private sectors, and marks the failure of both market housing and public policy. With a weak welfare state, personal assets matter for household flourishing in Hong Kong, but for many, the fundamental asset, a home of their own, is totally inaccessible.

Growing disparities and polarised experiences in the housing market pointed to the shallowness of Hong Kong's welfare safety net to offset the institutional advantages granted to class privilege. Like its colonial precedent, 'The Basic Law made business pre-eminent in the political system, and the government's subsequent deference to business interests seemed almost limitless' (Goodstadt 2013, p. 59). This seems to be the only possible conclusion to the present state of housing conditions. Reflecting public sentiment, three of the first four Chief Executives in Hong Kong since 1997 came to office declaring that housing was their top priority. Yet progress has been agonisingly slow, policy failures not infrequent, and with uncontrolled price inflation each Chief Executive lost their credibility and legitimacy with the Hong Kong public well before their term ended.[35] From 2009 to 2019 house prices surged 250%, while incomes rose 25% (IMF 2019b), making homeownership an alluring but disappearing mirage (Figure 3.1). The decreasing number of housing transactions showed that far fewer residents could access that market without investment capital or substantial family aid. Reversing the rapid ascent to ownership status in the years before the handover, households who were owner-occupiers declined from 53.6% of domestic households in 2008 to 49.6% in 2018 (Census and Statistics Department 2019b).

Growing income polarisation has accompanied a largely service-oriented, post-industrial employment profile (Chiu and Lui 2004). The wages of low-skilled service workers barely kept up with inflation in the period from 1997 to 2014 while housing costs rose faster despite the bursting of the housing bubble (Gu 2014).[36] Surprisingly this is the cohort with whom some university graduates are grouped. While Li Ka-shing's wealth rose from $13 billion in 1997 to $32 billion in 2014, starting salaries for university graduates rose by a nominal 1% annually, with significant losses in real terms (Gu 2014). According to a think tank, the New Century Forum, there was a real income loss of almost 10% in first jobs for graduates between 1992 and 2017. Compared with the inflation of home prices, the real median income of graduates more than halved during this time period. With fewer high-paying positions than there were qualified applicants, some graduates were settling for unskilled and low-paying jobs (Ng and Choi 2019).

The growing inequality and polarisation of society was experienced as such. The proportion of Hong Kong people who defined themselves as lower class rose from 18.4% in 1997 to 26.5% in 2006, while numbers fell for those who self-identified as middle class (Ma 2011). Unexpected downward mobility was inevitably shrinking housing options for young adults. The lack of new subsidised homeownership completions from 2003 to 2016 removed an important route to the privately-owned housing ladder, middle-class status, and wealth accumulation. As a result, the waiting list for existing subsidised homeownership units among single applicants aged under 30 years quadrupled from 2007 to over 60,000 in 2014 (Yao 2014). More desperate still were applications by young singles for public rental housing, where eligibility criteria would block them from selection for many years (Ng 2018b). Young graduates hoped that a public rental unit might qualify them for the subsidised homeownership scheme, and thereby one day give them a toehold on the ownership housing ladder, the path to wealth accumulation.

Another adjustment has been to extend the period of residence with parents. In general, it has been a traditional pattern in Chinese households that children remain at home until marriage. Census data for 2016 indicate that a high proportion of young adults remain in the parental home: 48% live with parents among those aged 25–34 and 16% are still at home among the 35–44 age cohort (Census and Statistics Department 2019d). The census table does not identify separately three-generational households; the category of 'persons living with spouse and/or child(ren)' is tabulated 'regardless of whether they were living with parents or not'. It was the three-generational family living together in a small flat that was so distressing and conflictual in the sample studied by Newendorp (2008) . A survey of a thousand young adults, aged 18–35, revealed that more than 80% were living with their parents, but showed nuanced responses to extended residence in the parental home (Forrest and Yip 2015; Forrest and Xian 2018). The reality of barriers to setting foot on the housing ladder was apparent. A majority (70%) lived at home because they could not afford other options, and recognising their limited market power, a similar share (74%) would be happy to rent in the public sector (Forrest and Xian 2018, Table 1). Not surprisingly, insurmountable obstacles to entering the private market – half the sample never expect to own – correlated with the distant hope of qualifying for a publicly-subsidised homeownership unit among a large majority of the young adults. Yet at the same time, living with parents had some rewards, including closer family bonding and the ability to save money (Forrest and Yip 2015).

The biennial report of the Hong Kong Council of Social Service, an umbrella organisation of the city's NGOs, published in May 2014, provided its continuing series of statistical indicators on Hong Kong's social development (HKCSS 2014). While all but two fields in the social development index were advancing, the HKCSS singled out the housing index for critical attention as its score showed a significant negative trend, and by an increasing amount, in every report since 2006. The Council offered some ominous overall observations on its findings:

The drastic drop of the Housing sub-index illustrates not only the housing problems faced by the Hong Kong people, but also the potential risk factor for the stable development of a society… "Housing" is the prerequisite for stable development of society; the government should seriously tackle the housing problems. The situation will worsen if government intervention is absent, and the discontent of the people will increase, which may cast challenges to the rule of the Government.

A few months later the Umbrella Movement shut down the streets of Central for 79 days. Four years on, the Council's 2018 report revealed that the housing index had deteriorated still further (HKCSS 2018).

Residential Alienation and Its Discontents

Government had lost its legitimacy as an enabler of upward social mobility through ownership of a housing asset for educated young adults among the unequal and polarised population of Hong Kong (Cheng 2017). Homeownership provided the asset that was the economically proven and culturally affirmed path to wealth accumulation. But the path was blocked. The real wages of college graduates had fallen below those of their peers a generation earlier, while fuelled by speculative investment, apartment prices had skyrocketed. At their age, even access to public housing was a long shot. Remaining at home in a cramped family flat denied their independence but for many was their best option. The widely reported collusion in the growth coalition of government and the property tycoons gave them no hope that the chokehold of a tightly controlled housing regime would be broken. This was a Hong Kong version of residential alienation (Madden and Marcuse 2016), exclusion from an asset that would provide social status and economic security.

A think tank, the Hong Kong Ideas Centre, issued a report in 2015 on youth aspirations and conditions in Hong Kong based on a survey of 1500 young adults, aged 15–39 (HKIC 2015).[37] A third of respondents expressed dissatisfaction with Hong Kong, while 40% supported civil disobedience in pursuit of justice objectives. Respondents were asked to identify grievances from a pre-determined list. While this list included items of social policy including housing, poverty, youth opportunities, and interaction with the mainland, it did not include items on democracy or governance other than a vague reference to social harmony. When asked to rank their grievances, housing featured prominently: high rents and home prices, insufficient public housing, and the poor quality of dwellings were the greatest source of frustration. Concern was expressed at the perceived trespass of Mainlanders and Mainland values challenging Hong Kong identity and sovereignty. Consistently, youth aged 20–24 were the most aggrieved, with 43% dissatisfied with the state of Hong Kong society.

These results reinforced the prominence of housing among Hong Kong's dissatisfied young adults. Amidst the plethora of studies of Hong Kong life during this introspective period after the Umbrella Movement, a 2016 survey by the Civic Exchange think tank raised considerable concern with its finding that Hong Kong people were so alienated that 42% wanted to leave the city (DeGolyer 2016); of these potential departees, only 1% would choose to move to the Mainland. Some 70% felt the city had deteriorated as a place to live. The quality of government and the quality and cost of housing raised the most dissatisfaction from a suite of 10 public and private services, and of the ten, housing was the issue respondents cared about most deeply and regarded as the clear top priority for government action.[38] Partitioning the sample by age confirmed the usual pattern with the most dissatisfaction expressed by young adults. Some 60% of those aged 18–29 would choose to leave Hong Kong and 52% of those aged 30–39, with growing unwillingness to leave through older groups. The same gradation appeared when specifying the most important issue, with 43% of the 18–29 cohort placing housing as the top priority issue for public intervention. Within the housing domain, 99% identified prices as an important problem and 92% the need to build more public housing.

In this window, post-Umbrella Movement and pre-2019 protests, polls show a high level of localism especially among young adults, matching the mobilisation of localist political parties, an identification of housing as the principal grievance (in surveys that did not usually include democratic reforms as subjects for assessment), growing antipathy toward the Hong Kong (and Beijing) governments, and a level of urban alienation that included both emigration and civil disobedience as potential outcomes. While these views were shared widely, they were expressed most strongly by the 18–29-year-old-age cohort.

The burden of age in stratifying life chances in labour and housing markets has been noted elsewhere, with lobbying around such rallying cries as Generation Rent in London or Generation Squeeze in Vancouver. But in Hong Kong the burden thrust on a generation is multiply determined. Alienation from political elites, a democratic deficit, together with banishment from wealth accumulation through blocked mobility on the housing ladder, overdetermine the marginalisation of young adults in Hong Kong. This alienation was revealed in multiple attitudinal surveys and found its release in the new-found solidarities of street protest in the Umbrella Movement and the persistent rallies and guerrilla actions of 2019–2020.

Housing and labour market marginalisation were contextual structural factors that predisposed young adults in particular to mobilise around a democratic deficit, the expanding Mainland presence in Hong Kong, and the growing militarisation of police suppression of protests.

Conclusion

An assessment of motives behind participation in the Umbrella Movement found a broad tent of grievances that included both a democratic deficit and economic injustice (Cai 2017). In this chapter I have suggested that a critical source of the growing marginalisation and alienation of young adults, measured in multiple surveys, was growing exclusion from the homeownership ladder, with ownership the marker of household independence, the badge of social status, and the principal asset for wealth accumulation. Because of the power of the Hong Kong growth machine and the overseeing control from Beijing, economic change required political change. Residential alienation predisposed generational civil disobedience.

In October 2016 a Senior Editor at the *South China Morning Post* published an unusually strident column which excoriated a proposal to build flats of 61.4 square feet, smaller, he noted, than a prison cell. Prophetically he thundered, 'When – not if – we have the next iteration of the [February 2016] Mong Kok riot, let's not ask "why" or "how" any more' (Lhatoo 2016). The link between housing inequality and political unrest has been recognised by speakers from near and far. Hong Kong economist Richard Wong has written that 'Upward mobility is a distant option for those without property; they have become unhitched from Hong Kong's economic future. These economic and social divisions in society have spilled over into political divisiveness' (Wong Y.C.R. 2015, p. 212). An experienced observer from afar could see that such an unequal allocation of housing opportunities lacked political sustainability. Lee Hsien Loong, Prime Minister of Singapore, cast doubt on the survival of the one country, two systems agreement unless there was resolution of the housing question (Marlow 2020).

Thomas Piketty has drawn attention to the growth of capital relative to income as a source of wealth in advanced societies. A rentier model has become prevalent in the low interest rate, asset-heavy investment environment of recent decades. Housing has become a major asset, and its inflated value has contributed to a significant expansion of housing capital compared to income (Piketty 2014; Piketty and Yang 2021). In Hong Kong the ratio of net private housing wealth to national income rose from 122% in 1980 to 209% in 2013 (Wong Y.C.R. 2015, p. 216). In advanced nations generally, growth in the value of housing has dominated private wealth expansion. This is the full cost of exclusion from the ownership ladder in Hong Kong and elsewhere, an inability to accumulate wealth in the primary household capital-generating sector and to enjoy social mobility to middle-class status. The gain lies with property owners and especially development tycoons, whose wealth accrues minimally from their incomes and primarily from largely untaxed rentier sources. The loss has been borne disproportionately by young adults, alienated from property ownership. This unstable relationship became toxic as the inequality vice tightened, government was not responsive, and local democratic rights to effect change were rejected by Mainland overlords.

Notes

1. Simon Smith is the Asia-Pacific Head of Research and Consultancy at Savills Hong Kong.
2. 1 HKD = 0.129 USD on 1st January 2021.
3. This view was fortified by CK Asset's sale of a majority share in its flagship Hong Kong office tower, The Centre, to a consortium led by Mainland state-controlled groups in 2017. The sale price of US$5.15 billion was said to be the world's highest for a single-building transaction. A year earlier the Li family had sold the Century Link complex in Shanghai to a Singaporean group for US$2.95 billion, the world's second most expensive commercial sale (Wineland 2017). Divestment of high-value assets in China and Hong Kong aided an investment pivot to Europe.
4. Jardines maintains its Hong Kong head office, while it is incorporated in Bermuda, and its primary stock market listing is in London. Though a highly diverse conglomerate, almost all of its revenue is generated in Greater China and SE Asia, while property, featuring its subsidiary, Hongkong Land, was its leading profit sector in 2018 (Jardines 2019).
5. The Hong Kong dollar is pegged to the US dollar, trading in a narrow band of HKD7.75–7.85 to USD1. This peg plays an important role in Hong Kong's political economy, including its property market.
6. Cheung Kong and Sun Hung Kai built 68% of new flats launched in 2014 (Savills Hong Kong fact sheet 2014).
7. Two Mainland developers bought a remote coastal site in a government land sale in 2017, adjacent to a sewage treatment plant and an industrial area, for a price that exceeded market expectations by 50%. Their expensive purchase would inflate the local price base, and inevitably force up the final cost of flats (Zhao 2017).
8. From 1998 to 2018 government land sales for residential purposes only exceeded 20 hectares a year on four occasions (Savills Hong Kong 2020a).

9. The distinction between inequality and polarisation is usefully defined and operationalised by Hamnett (2003a, especially pp. 75–78).

10. Smart and Lam (2009) show the increasing prevalence of the term, 'government-business collusion', in Hong Kong Chinese media after 1997, reaching 2611 references in 2005.

11. The issue of compensation is key here, and the URA was able to offer enough incentives on Lee Tung Street, and elsewhere, for existing owners and tenants to relocate (Ley and Teo 2014).

12. Henry Tang, unsuccessful candidate for Chief Executive in 2012, famously challenged young people not to complain about property prices but ask themselves, 'Why can't I become the next Li Ka-shing?' But for this audience his exhortation seriously missed the mark.

13. For a critical view of the real estate hegemony thesis, see Wong S. (2015, 2018). His key argument points to occasions of internal division among the tycoons and between the tycoons and the administration. But hegemony is never perfect, and can occur through ongoing ideological convergence without direct collusion – for example consensus on the foundational ethos of 'big market, small government'.

14. *Demographia* publishes an annual affordability index and interpretive text (from a pro-development perspective), for cities in eight countries in the anglosphere.

15. With declining and delayed marriage rates, one of the world's lowest fertility rates, and among the longest life expectancies (Census and Statistics Department 2019a), the demand for small units is substantial.

16. See for example, The Economist's (2012b) attribution of 'constricted supply' as 'the biggest factor' driving price escalation in Hong Kong.

17. See, for example, Li's (2017) portrayal of Hong Kong residents who are buyers of multiple units in new building launches.

18. Canada's Business Immigration Program, formerly the world's biggest golden visa option, was intended to prime economic development in the resource and manufacturing sectors. Golden visas have become increasingly popular with cash-strapped governments, but Canada's experience of over 30 years concluded that policy objectives were not being met (Ley 2010; CIC (2014). See also Chapter 5.

19. Savills Hong Kong (2018b) computed a correlation of 0.87 between movements of the Hang Seng and the luxury residential market since 1997, with the stock market typically leading by 3–6 months.

20. 'The challenging market has resulted in low levels of Hong Kong inbound investment of HK$1.54 billion in 2H/2019, a sharp fall of 71.1% YoY compared to 2H/2018. In contrast, outbound investment increased significantly by 41.9% YoY, from HK$30.6 billion to HK$43.4 billion between 2H/2018 and 2H/2019. Capital outflows from Hong Kong to Singapore, the US and UK rose by 4,909.2%, 113.4% and 67.4% respectively' (Savills Hong Kong 2020b).

21. Leo Goodstadt, a long-time observer of the precarious status of social policy in Hong Kong, detailed the minimal shelter standards of both public and private sector buildings. In the 1960s, compared to a statutory minimum of 35 square feet of living space per person, the colonial government tolerated an average of first 24 and then 16 square feet for an adult, and 8 square feet for a child, in their Resettlement Blocks (Goodstadt 2013, p. 93).

22. Lam's bold proposal called for the reclamation of up to 1700 hectares off Lantau Island to house over a million people, the majority in public housing. Its impact on housing needs would be great, but the project suffered from a long lead time, vast cost, and political opposition. Brownfield sites and under-utilised agricultural land in the New Territories have also been suggested as new sources of developable land for housing. Perhaps most controversial in elite quarters have been calls to develop part or all of the Fanling golf course. Lam's later plan (October 2021) envisages massive construction in the northern New Territories.

23. The homeownership scheme has always been popular, and in a new 2018 launch, 258,000 applications were made for the 4431 deeply discounted flats (Ng 2018a). These odds barely improved upon the 1 in 60 chance of success in an earlier HOS launch in 2015.

24. At the end of 2013 the Centaline Property Agency predicted that dramatic declines in transactions from the series of cooling and macro-prudential credit tightening would lead to 1000 redundancies among real estate agents. New deals fell even further in the commercial market.

25. A survey in 2017 showed that 72% of respondents thought that purchases by Mainland investors were responsible for 'Hong Kong's housing problems' (HKUPOP 2017). This was the leading selection from half a dozen on offer (with multiple answers permitted).

26. For example, a Mid-Levels penthouse sale in 2018, priced at HK$175 million, to an anonymous foreign company, 'Booming Success Limited', required payment of a 15% Buyer's Stamp Duty plus a 15% *ad valorem* Stamp Duty, for an additional total of $52.5 million (Savills Hong Kong 2018c). These taxes were a significant revenue windfall for government, amounting to $5.96 billion in the month of June 2018 alone.

27. For the eight rounds of macroprudential tightening of the housing market between October 2009 and May 2017, see IMF (2019b, Annex V). Each round might include several measures. The IMF report also lists six stamp duty revisions between November 2010 and April 2017. Clearly there was considerable diligence exercised in attempting to manage escalating housing prices and their fiscal consequences.

28. Reduction of the LTV rate from 90 to 80% in 2015 added four years to saving for a down-payment for a small HK$4 million flat for a young professional couple (Siu and Li 2015).

29. Discounts were typically 10–15%. For example, Swire cut flat prices on a luxury project in Mid-Levels by 12% (and more for multiple purchases) during a depressed market in 2016.

30. In September 2016, non-bank financial and real estate entities combined to offer 90% funding for apartments valued at HK$8–$12 million. The equivalent bank LTV ratio, mandated by the HKMA, was 60%. On a property of $8 million, with the non-bank option the buyer would lower their down-payment by $2.4 million over standard bank financing (Li 2016). Large developers were offering mortgages of 80, 95, or even in one case, 120% of cost in a softening market (Shanghai Daily 2016).

31. In 2011, Raymond Kwok, Chairman of Sun Hung Kai Properties, received HK$1.36 billion in untaxed dividends, and a personal salary of HK$2.52 million. His taxable income was less than 0.2% of the total package (Tsui and Sender 2012).

32. There is some debate concerning these statistics. They measure income, but the government argued they were misleading as they did not represent assets (e.g., social benefits and imputed housing subsidies), and therefore presented an incomplete view of a household's well-being. According to which assets are included, the poverty rate would fall from 20 to 10–15% in 2018.

33. In households with expenditures below the median, average public housing expenses amounted to only 13% of monthly household expenditures in 2014/15, but the equivalent figure for the bottom 50% in private rental was a scarcely sustainable 44%. In households with incomes below the poverty line, 65% of expenditure was spent on housing and food (HKCSS 2018).

34. The issue of adequate compensation was an incentive that encouraged many owners and tenants to vacate their homes willingly. In this respect gentrification in Hong Kong includes a dimension usually missing in western cities (Ley and Teo 2014).

35. For an account of housing and other social policy failures that highlight incompetence among the Chief Executives and their senior staff, see Goodstadt (2018).

36. The wage outcome reflects the labour market of the post-industrial city that Hong Kong has become, with a bi-modal employment structure of advanced and personal services. Studies have shown surprising levels of closure between labour sub-markets, impeding social mobility (Forrest et al. 2004).

37. Data were collected in January–March 2015, the immediate aftermath of Occupy Central, and included 1505 telephone interviews, 8 focus groups, and 47 in-depth interviews with youth experts. I am grateful to Justin Tse for translating key parts of the report and press release.

38. As with the 2015 HKIC survey, democratic reforms were not admitted as an item for consideration.

CHAPTER 4

Sydney: Investors, Offshore Relations, and the 2013–2017 Residential Boom

Rental housing is an investment pursued by all strata of Australian society.
(Badcock and Beer 2000, p. 106)

Real estate, it seems, is the true national sport.
(Sisson et al. 2019)

Despite the aspiration of its first chief executive, post-1997, Hong Kong failed to develop as an inclusive homeowning asset state. But a more sustained connection between house prices and asset-based welfare has occurred in Australian state policy since the 1980s (Nethercote 2019; Adkins et al. 2020, 2021). An informal contract balanced low wages and declining welfare against homeownership and price inflation. Sydney, like Vancouver, is part of a democratic colonial settler society, with immigrants, like residents, sharing an elevated desire for homeownership. But like Vancouver, Sydney now suffers from unaffordable housing for a growing population. Exploring the role of investors as 'surplus demand' in priming housing booms and declining affordability, this chapter works with Maurice Daly's (1982) thesis that property bubbles in Sydney's history were globally induced, by foreign capital inflows, high mineral prices on the world market, and immigration pulses meeting labour needs. The argument is extended to Sydney's 2013–2017 house price boom, now in a Chinese, no longer a British, hegemon of trade, immigration, and property investment. Price inflation far exceeded wage growth during the boom, further blocking entry to new buyers behind a barrier of rising unaffordability. But complicating Daly's thesis, local as well as foreign investors were implicated, with wealthy citizens benefitting from favourable tax policy and cheap credit.

Housing Booms in Gateway Cities, First Edition. David Ley.
© 2023 John Wiley & Sons Ltd. Published 2023 by John Wiley & Sons Ltd.

The role of housing as investment was evident from my first day of fieldwork in Sydney in 2013. I attended *Home* a conference intended to showcase the newly established state agency, UrbanGrowth NSW. The event was organised primarily for the building industry and local government, and the attentive audience of several hundred heard Brad Hazzard, the New South Wales Minister for Planning and Infrastructure, open the floodgates to residential development. On its website the new agency declared itself to be a 'development champion', and the Minister locked into a familiar narrative in stating that UrbanGrowth NSW had been formed to ease a serious backlog of housing supply, to remove barriers and red tape. 'We need a can-do culture not a series of hurdles'. Greater Sydney required 550,000 new homes over the next 20 years, but recent production had only attained 15,000 new units a year. More supply was essential because growth was firmly on the agenda: 'Sydney is not full. It's a world city. World cities don't stagnate, don't die, they grow'. In helping Sydney to grow, the task of UrbanGrowth was to facilitate, not produce, new dwellings. Mr. Hazzard announced to his audience that the private sector 'is the way forward. Without you there is no property development in New South Wales'. The objective was affordable housing, 'making sure those who want a home can have a home at affordable prices'. The Chairman of UrbanGrowth underscored the profile of the population at risk of missing out in a high-priced market: 'A home for our children and their children to occupy. This is the bottom line'.

The conference was held in Penrith, a distant western suburb of Sydney, part of an outer region often stigmatised as poor, poorly serviced, and too far from the central city to be an attractive commuter destination. Following a morning of speeches, conferees were taken to Thornton, an 1100-dwelling demonstration project under construction near the Penrith railway station. Thornton was planned as a compact and affordable development by UrbanGrowth's predecessor, Landcom, a New South Wales crown corporation and property developer whose mission was now superseded by UrbanGrowth (which ceded Landcom's development function to the private sector).[1] Thornton comprised denser design, innovative social mixing, units of different sizes, and some laneway homes (or granny flats) above garages. Here was a new paradigm, an innovative prototype for the government's '21st Century Living Programme'.

Thornton's major public space was then a cricket oval encircled by a white picket fence, and interested conferees met at the cricket clubhouse. The marketing director offered a profile of on-site enquiries for the just released first phase of construction: 'all types, first home buyers, some retirees, about *one-third investors* ...' In a distant suburban, master-planned community, tasked to showcase a new sustainable and affordable homeownership paradigm, I expressed surprise at the inclusion of so many investors as a significant buyer group. My uninformed question, however, gained no traction. 'No worries, this is normal, it just means more rental units'. That same first quarter of 2013 in New South Wales as a whole – a market dominated by Sydney – Australian investors were estimated to have bought almost 25% of new residential properties, while overseas buyers accounted for another 16% (NAB 2013). I learned at the start of field research the scale and reach of rental property investment, extending the exchange value of housing unproblematically into the most distant corners of the Sydney metropolitan area, and into a carefully stewarded project proclaiming environmental, economic, and social sustainability. Minister Hazzard's speech, with its supply-side emphasis and abhorrence of barriers to efficient markets was a faithful recital from an established government and development industry play-book, identifying 'housing supply as Australia's defining housing problem, and regulatory reforms to alleviate "barriers" to supply as a paradigmatic solution' (Phibbs and Gurran 2015, p. 718). Whatever and wherever barriers existed in the Australian housing system, the door was wide open for the investor community.

While house prices were not problematised at the *Home* conference, Sydney was entering another cyclical housing boom. This chapter will discuss the usually unexamined effects of the surplus demand of investors upon housing affordability during the 2013–2017 boom, and how they challenge the place of housing in Australian public culture as the centrepiece of a consensus on asset-based welfare (Adkins et al. 2021). Asset accumulation flourishes in the unregulated, low-interest environment represented by Mr. Hazzard, and is characterised by investor-driven volatility during periodic booms. The 2013–2017 boom will be interpreted following Maurice Daly's (1982) emphasis on international flows of investment capital, labour, and trade as property drivers in his study of over a century of real estate booms and busts in Sydney. Does that emphasis hold good in the twenty-first century when Australia's external linkages are now closer to Asia than to Europe? How does the international scale of Daly's argument interlock with the national project of housing as asset-based welfare? While committed to affordable homeownership, we will see that the state's explicit policy towards property investors, international and national, for both political and macro-economic objectives, has uncoupled incomes from prices, denying access to homeownership for many first-time buyers. The chapter examines surplus demand from residential investors that undercuts housing affordability, and the particular role of global investors during housing booms. To jeopardise affordability is also to jeopardise the premise of homeownership as asset-based welfare.

Sydney's House Price Profile

Greater Sydney has a population of over five million, with a sprawling footprint suggesting an even larger city. Its low densities, derived from the settler's dream of owning a quarter-acre block in a continent of seemingly endless horizons, makes infrastructure provision expensive. It is an abiding planning lament that necessary provision of infrastructure services constantly lags behind demand for property development and inhibits its outward march. The metropolitan area is conventionally divided into three rings, disrupted by linear development along radial rail lines: first, a mostly higher status and post-industrial inner ring, parts once industrial and working-class, and including older elite, gentrified, and partly redeveloped neighbourhoods around Sydney's Central Business District (CBD); second, a middle ring of aging homes with an immigrant concentration and recent apartment densification; and third, an outer ring of mixed status suburbs (like Penrith), with young families and some concentrations of poverty, far from the city, short on infrastructure, and suffering from traffic congestion in the journey to work. The metropolitan region's social geography could also be partitioned by sectors that distinguish between more prosperous eastern waterfront and northern suburbs, and less prosperous and more distant suburbs stretching to the south and west.

At different times, investment and price gains have favoured one of these three rings over another. Stapledon (2012, 2016) observed that the 1968–1974 real estate boom was associated primarily with a sharp land value gain in the outer ring, a development consistent with automobile-based suburbanisation in western societies at that time. But consumer interest and development energies then switched to the inner ring, coinciding with what Blair Badcock (1992) identified in Adelaide as the city's 'heart transplant' in the 1970s and 1980s. This continuing reinvestment in the inner city has involved gentrification in many Sydney neighbourhoods (Engels 1994; Rofe 2003); indeed, I was told that inner city Sydney 'is gentrified out'. Against a 1971 index of 100, land values in Sydney rose to 469 by 1986 in the inner ring, within six kilometres of downtown, to 409 in the middle ring, up to 25 kilometres from downtown, and to only 309 in the outer suburbs (Valuer-General 1986). These differentials were sustained into the present century with a growing emphasis on compact city development, as inner-city gentrification was reinforced by offshore investment in condominium apartments. Land values for a residential property in Ultimo, a regeneration apartment district in the inner ring, rose from $100,000 in 1996 to $390,000 in 2011; in the stylish Victorian terraces of Paddington, gentrification led to even greater inflation, from $213,000 in 1996 to $961,000 15 years later.[2] Land value gains in the outer ring were more modest, despite larger lots: from $86,200 to $210,000 in Penrith in the far west, and from $66,600 to $174,000 in Campbelltown in the far south (LPI 2012).

In terms of historical price trends, Stapledon (2012) has assembled an estimate of Sydney house prices dating back to 1880. While price cycles are evident from his analysis, with oscillations indicative of booms and busts, in real long-term variation not much happened in Sydney's overall price structure until the 1960s. Inflation-adjusted prices fell below an 1880 index value of 100 for the next eight decades, and only crossed this threshold in the 1960s.[3] But in the following five decades *real* prices quadrupled. Median *nominal* prices of established (pre-owned) detached houses in Sydney doubled from 1986–1990 and doubled again from 1998 to 2004 when they nudged half a million dollars.[4] After a short pause inflation continued, with a final doubling from 2009 leading to a median price of $1,050,000 in June 2017. Prices fell back in 2018 and the first half of 2019, though they were recovering when the COVID-19 pandemic introduced a major shock to the entire real estate system in 2020. But, resilient, the market surprised analysts by showing significant recovery in late 2020 and 2021.

The price trajectory shows an asymmetry of larger upslope gains and smaller downslope losses in each real estate cycle, leading cumulatively to an extended boom period. Unlike Sydney's real estate history up to the 1960s, booms are no longer followed by busts, or at least busts of equal magnitude. Any downslope decline represents a case of *reculer pour mieux sauter*, indicating a long-term inflationary market running for 50 years, intensifying in its upward motion.

The details of the 2013–2017 boom are shown in Figure 4.1. Quarterly median nominal prices collected by the state of New South Wales differentiate between strata sales (multiply owned dwellings on a single land title) and non-strata sales (a single dwelling on a single title). Rents are recorded from new landlord–tenant contracts. Non-strata homes in Greater Sydney led the price surge, rising by over 70% between June 2013 and June 2017, reaching a peak median price of $1,075,000. There was substantial new supply of strata apartments (condominiums) during this period in Sydney's inner and middle zones, but nonetheless strata prices rose over 40% in the same four-year period. Like earlier recent booms, downslope losses did not cancel upslope gains. Price declines bottomed out in summer 2019, but with losses of only 16% for non-strata dwellings and 9% for strata units, before a new upswing began, temporarily arrested in mid-2020 by the shock of the COVID-19 pandemic.

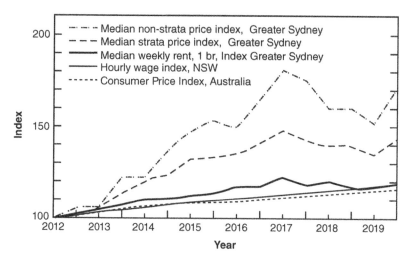

FIGURE 4.1 Economic indices through the 2013–2017 boom, Sydney. (Sources: DCJ 2020; ABS 2020d, Table 2b; RBA 2020c, Table G1)

The remaining variables in Figure 4.1 describe a very different profile from the ownership price gains. Median rents for a one-bedroom unit shadowed the sales price curves, but with a much flatter trajectory, rising only 16% between June 2013 and 2017; the downslope in the next two years was an almost imperceptible 4% loss. The price to rent ratio is often taken as an indicator of bubble tendencies, and the dramatic divergence of rent and price levels indicates significant frothiness in the sales market. Rental levels do, however, closely match the trajectories of both median wage levels in New South Wales and the national Consumer Price Index – indeed, wage and CPI changes are almost identical and can scarcely be separated on Figure 4.1. Wage levels rose only 9% from 2013–2017 (CPI rose 8%), falling behind rental growth, and far behind inflating home prices. However, on the downslope of the boom, wages caught up with slowly declining rents, though when prices bottomed out in the summer of 2019, wage workers were much further behind the strata and non-strata ownership prices than they had been in 2012.

Two general points emerge. During the boom, the housing price lines became uncoupled from local fundamentals, represented by wages, rents and CPI. Prices were marching to a different, investment-driven drummer. Second, when the boom ended the asymmetry was not corrected. Prices remained an order of magnitude above 'fundamentals', more de-coupled than they had been when the boom began. The divergence between indicators of the local economy and the price lines of residential property broadened another band, further disconnecting many local wage-dependent residents from access to the ownership market. Increasingly, these indicators reveal two worlds, an everyday existence including rents, wages, and consumer prices, and a world of asset prices, investments, and debts eroding the path to home-ownership, and with it a foundational layer of the Australian dream of asset-based accumulation.

The housing price boom of 2013–2017 generates three sets of questions that will guide much of our discussion in this chapter. First, what are the consequences of such an explosion of house price inflation for the residents of Sydney in terms of housing affordability, and more broadly economic inequality? Has the creation of such housing wealth redefined life chances sufficiently that it is shaping a new arrangement of housing-based classes? How has the property-centred creation of wealth affected residents themselves and their assessment of their own home as asset?

Second, how does such a boom market sustain its gravity-defying motion? What goes up we are told, has to come down, and this is exactly what the Sydney housing market did in its property cycles from the 1880s into the 1960s. How has property sucked up so much potentially productive capital into its own investment vortex since then? What about relevant property-based institutions, the real estate sector and financial institutions? How have their priorities been configured by the alluring opportunities of housing capital? The unsustainability of such price inflation since 1970 has frequently led to imputations of a property bubble.[5] *The Economist*, with its diagnostics of ratios between prices and rents or prices and incomes, habitually sees Sydney (and Australia more generally) as displaying an alarmingly unstable market. If incomes or rents are indicative of local economic fundamentals, why have such fundamentals had so little effect in dragging back runaway prices?

Third, such an emergent and potentially unstable real estate-capital nexus should not be ignored by government. How has the state intersected with this property-based exuberance? Is there a coherent housing policy that may be traced through this period? How have housing plans evolved? Indeed, is there a plan, or does superficial rhetoric match the frothiness of real estate and its aspirations? Is 'policy', more a matter of facilitators and barriers, variously drawn and withdrawn, where unintended consequences replace clearer objectives? Have ideas about welfare been largely replaced by the uncertain payoff of property assets?

Consequences of House Price Inflation

Like many territories of European, particularly British, settlement overseas, Australian colonists were pursuing a dream that had frequently been inaccessible in their home countries, the dream of homeownership. Possession of a home on a quarter-acre block became a founding myth of the young nation, 'a culture of home-centred individualism that has long existed as one of the most defining traits of the nation' (Allon 2008, p. 26). Allon traces the culture of homeownership through the popular press, television, and conservative political values. She makes the important point that by the 2000s it was not simply the use value of the home that was embraced, but also the exchange value of the house as a property deal, revealing a calculating asset-seeking rationality. This orientation was advanced by the financial deregulation of the 1980s that liberalised mortgage credit, accompanied by financial policy that lowered interest rates. But the credit boom was to an important degree an investor boom. Ryan-Collins and Murray (2020) note that the investor share of bank home loans grew from 14% of home lending in the decade to 1995, to 38% from 2000 onwards, and reached 50% during 2014–2015, filling out the narrative of housing as investment commodity.

With institutional support and a buoyant economy, the Australian dream of homeownership became normative, endorsed by government, and widely achievable in the early post-1945 period, reaching a pinnacle of 73% ownership in 1966, flat-lining until the 2000s, but falling to 67% by 2016 (Burke et al. 2020). Lisa Adkins et al. (2020, 2021) have identified an understanding between government and the electorate to compensate weakening social welfare and faltering wage gains against the inflating asset of homeownership reinforced by significant tax concessions. These benefits were scarcely objectionable when ownership was widely accessible, but become problematic, indeed discriminatory, when new entrants face insurmountable barriers due to inflated prices uncoupled from inadequate wages. In the early years, homeownership could be secured in a conventional nuclear family with a single wage-earner, but house prices have risen since 1961 at twice the rate of average full-time earnings (McLennan and Long 2020). With price inflation, a full- or part-time second wage was necessary until that too was insufficient to cover a deposit and monthly payments.

The uncoupling of wages and house prices was again starkly evident during the 2013–2017 boom (Figure 4.1), a period when nominal annual wage growth in Australia continued to falter, falling to one percent in 2016 (IMF 2018a). There had already been great concern about deteriorating affordability in the housing literature in the 1990s and 2000s, with an assessment in 2002 that 'the affordable housing crisis is now a real threat to the continued economic well-being of Sydney'; but there was also 'a conspicuous lack of political will or desire to engage with the problem' (Randolph and Holloway 2002, pp. 332, 353). The burdens became even less sustainable after 2013, and the HIA/Commonwealth Bank affordability index fell by almost a quarter from December 2013 to June 2017 (HIA 2018).[6] Even with low mortgage interest rates, the average household would commit 49% of their gross income in 2018 to servicing their 80% loan to value ratio on a median value dwelling in Sydney; their 20% deposit would consume 185% of their annual household income (AHL Investments 2018).

The rate of house price growth in Australia after 1995 was among the highest in the western world, while some state capitals were among the most unaffordable cities. According to *Demographia*, for some years Australia recorded 'seriously unaffordable' housing indices in each of the five largest state capitals, the worst ranking possible.[7] Of the more than 300 cities reviewed by *Demographia*, Sydney and Vancouver vie for second spot for unaffordability most years behind Hong Kong (Cox and Pavletich 2020). Inevitably those penalised are potential new entrants to the market, the young, immigrants, first-time buyers, and lower-income groups. First home buyers had fallen to only 14% of mortgage holders among all owner-occupiers in New South Wales with a housing loan by 2018 (AHL Investments 2018). Older owners who entered a more favourable earlier market have benefitted with substantial gains in their home equity, but younger groups are heavily penalised, with ownership dropping for those under 35 from 60% in the mid-1980s to below 40% in 2015. Among the 35–44 year-old group substantial ownership erosion also occurred, from nearly 75% to just over 60% (Yates 2016).

With current trends, homeownership is projected to fall to 62% by 2030 and to just over 50% for the 25–55 cohort; the average buyer is now in their mid-40s and will be paying off a mortgage until age 67 (Burke et al. 2020). A young Sydney professional with a PhD confided that

> Prices are outrageous. I've been here seven years and not been able to crack the [ownership] market. I rent in an up-and-coming neighbourhood. If I bought, I'd be looking at $900,000. My best friend's father arrived here in 1978. Now he lives in an architect-designed bungalow.

Such generational asymmetry in life chances challenges social cohesion; it can also dislocate labour markets, especially when essential staff do not have viable housing opportunities (Berry 2003).[8] Parents might help with a deposit, with inter-generational transfers usually reproducing existing inequalities. Whereas in the immediate post-1945 period, a single wage-earner had been the typical home purchaser among 25–44 year-old family heads, by 1981 that figure had fallen to 46%, and to only 13% in 2016 (Burke et al. 2020). While several motivations created the dual-income family, saving for home purchase was often uppermost, contributing to delayed child birth and smaller families. Family size is just one of the adjustments families have had to make to navigate a housing market littered with unsurmountable costs.[9] Accepting very high debt levels is another burden to realise the aspiration of homeownership. Australia has one of the highest household debt rates among OECD peers, with liabilities reaching 220% of net disposable income by 2017 (OECD 2018, p. 20); in 1995 the figure had been 68% (Badcock and Beer 2000, p. 121). This imbalance drew some critical observations from the IMF's (2018a) consultation report, which warned that aside from household impacts, a housing bubble would jeopardise banks with high mortgage exposure.

Many households, however, reluctantly realise that the Australian dream has become unattainable and that renting is likely to be a permanent rather than a temporary stage of the housing career (Pawson et al. 2017). As rents follow local labour market fundamentals more closely, they have fallen behind the rate of house price inflation. But rental housing is not necessarily affordable. The thousands of rental units created by investment in condominium apartments are typically high-priced to cover the owner's mortgage payments (Easthope 2019). At the other end of the rental spectrum are the undesirable equivalents of Singapore's migrant bunkhouses, Hong Kong's tiny subdivided flats, and Vancouver's dank basement suites. Sydney too has its largely unregulated informal housing offering basic accommodation to low-income groups (Gurran et al. 2022). Other home-seekers work between a range of housing adjustments: multigenerational family households, home-sharing, crowding, couch surfing, and for some, homelessness.

A systemic problem is a growing shortage of secure and affordable rental units for the bottom 40% of income cohorts. Direct and indirect displacement of this population by inner city gentrification has been continuing for decades. Disadvantage has moved outwards as privilege has centralised (Randolph and Tice 2014). Earlier housing booms were associated with lower-income departure; net domestic out-migration from Sydney exceeded 60,000 with the price boom of the early 1980s, while during the price hikes in 1989–1990 net losses reached over 100,000 (Ley 2007). Out-migration was led by lower-income groups including the unemployed (Hugo and Bell 1998).

An additional limitation of the rental solution is that in an asset-based economy, a failure to own means an inability for tenants to benefit from wealth accumulation through capital gains on a principal residence (Badcock 1989). Of course, real estate is not a guaranteed investment, but in the growth-oriented gateway cities price inflation has been the norm, in Sydney now for almost two generations, and as we shall see financial policy has fanned the flames of a market hotspot. The rental solution, usually born of inequality, breeds further inequality. Survey data show the mean household net wealth of Australian tenants in 2018 was around $200,000, compared to

$1.3 million for owners (Adams et al. 2020).[10] Three-quarters of the wealth of owners was derived from housing assets (as well as 80% of their debt). The top income quintile of the population included 30% of all owner-occupiers but 45% of housing investors (Adams et al. 2020).

Maurice Daly and the International Drivers of Sydney's Property Market

Some research has isolated single factors to explain Sydney's house price inflation and its consequences – declining interest rates over the past 30 years seem a compelling candidate – but surely this is insufficient to account for such upward turbulence? In a discussion of 1980s prices, Maher (1994, p. 7) wisely observed that 'housing markets are dynamic and complex, responding to a wide variety of forces which interact unpredictably at a variety of scales'. In an Australian capital city context, he saw the changing relations of supply and demand to be sensitive to economic and income restructuring, demographic processes, the availability and cost of credit, interest rates, inflation, and land supply, with some of these categories further subdivided. Ten years later, another wide-ranging discussion reviewed Australian house prices in the 1990s. The authors identified nine broad sets of house price drivers, showing overlap with Maher's list a decade earlier, and like him separated them for ease of discussion, while recognising that 'their impacts interact in complex ways not fully understood' (Berry and Dalton 2004, p.74).

It would be useful to establish a coherent narrative or theoretical sketch to bind together a number of the factors that are analytically separated, clarifying how at least some of them interact together. A compelling narrative integrating a range of factors and interest groups was presented by the Sydney geographer, Maurice Daly, who examined the early 1970s boom-bust property cycle, 'an extraordinary event for Sydney, and for Australia' (Daly 1982, p. 1), and from this base reviewed other property bubbles in the city since the mid-nineteenth century. External investors and open borders were two guiding themes in his examination of Sydney's property market. In the 1970s bubble, the massive participation of government, private corporations, and civil society had encouraged an analysis that emphasised made-in-Australia causes. But this view was too myopic, too scale-bound for 'the critical international influence was understated or overlooked' (Daly 1982 p. 4). That influence included exports from a mining boom, a peak in immigration from 1968 to 1972, and a great deal of liquidity, with mobile capital and cash-rich property developers following migrants from Europe, notably from Britain. Lagging supply helped inflate prices further. The cost of land rose 2.5 times in six years before the bubble burst in 1973. Daly summarised his argument:

> At each decisive step in the nation's development, Australia has had to rely on foreign capital and foreign manpower to support her growth. The reliance on these external sources has imbued every facet of Australia's development, including the growth of her cities and even the fluctuations of their property markets … Most significantly, the external forces have been vital in shaping the boom-bust sequence which has been illustrated for Sydney in the 1970s.
>
> (Daly 1982, p. 138)

Notable in Daly's exposition were the varied external influences integrated in his interpretation: a mining boom, international trade, investment capital, and immigrants who served both as labour and also as housing consumers, together bringing a massive overseas intervention to the property market. In a settler society, globalisation has always been a real estate fundamental.

Book reviewers were mixed in their response. Johnston (1983) found the book to be an 'excellent start' to a political economy of Sydney's property boom, but too detailed and yet too brief as an exposition of 'general processes'. In contrast, Goldberg (1984) regarded Daly's analysis as 'of enormous relevance to regional scientists'. Goldberg, a Vancouver-based urban land economist, found the parallels with Canadian property markets so close that he tended 'to forget from time to time that Sydney, Australia was the subject of the study and not the Canadian real estate boom of the early 1970s' (Goldberg 1984, p. 103). For Goldberg, the generalities were strikingly present as one moved to other comparable cities. In the era of accelerated globalisation, largely since Daly's analysis, it is not surprising that his thesis might continue to ring true. The boom-and-bust oscillations of housing bubbles are repetitive phenomena and neither exceptional nor ephemeral (Sisson et al. 2019). With globalisation all states display more permeable national borders to global flows and forces. Examining Vancouver (Chapter 5), we will see the international component again understated in explanation, for reasons that had much to do with political ideology concealing the material interests of a growth coalition.

Sydney's 1968–1974 bubble was initially in commercial property coinciding with the arrival of a post-industrial urban economy, with head office, financial, and business services creating demand for office expansion in downtown cores. The last fling of the boom saw the arrival of new overseas capital from the Middle East and in particular from Asia Pacific championing speculative condominium apartments in selected inner-city neighbourhoods. The commodification of this new housing sub-market was marked by off the plan (or pre-build) sales in advance of construction, a practice we examine in more detail in Vancouver (Chapter 5) and London (Chapter 6). In Sydney, a remarkable 80–100% of units were pre-sold; local and international investors rather than end-users were the typical purchasers (Daly 1982, p. 69).

Reading back from the 1970s property bubble in Sydney, a similar pattern was repeated in earlier cycles of Australia's economic history. 'Ultimately the causes [of property bubbles] are to be found in the extreme openness of Australia to the world capitalist economy and the demands for capital, labour and trade associated with this, and the inherent jerkiness of the capitalist mode of growth' (Daly 1982, p. 150). With some prescience, and supporting a fundamental role for these variables, Daly (1982, p. 195) concludes his argument with a prediction: 'The pressures of the resources boom on materials, labour and money are likely to keep the prices high, and many potential home-buyers will be simply unable to enter the market'. There is evidence that the importance of this immigration-export-led growth–real estate nexus has been sustained. Moving on from the boom of the 1970s to the boom at the end of the 1980s, national GDP rose by 5.75% in 1988, the highest level since 1970. International migration alone added an average of 50,000 people a year to Sydney between 1987 and 1990, coinciding with a house price boom that peaked in 1990, despite a *rising* bank rate that reached over 16% that year, making mortgages prohibitively expensive.[11]

Daly's emphasis on international drivers of the property market has been reinforced with the acceleration of globalisation following neoliberal reforms in the 1980s and 1990s. Sydney was identified as a southern hemisphere global hub. This status presupposed membership in an interlocking network of cities open to international flows of capital, labour, trade, and ideas, animated by transnational corporations, and seeking market efficiencies with an entrepreneurial ethos. Downtowns were increasingly dominated by corporate head offices, a dense network of financial and business services, and media, communication, and entertainment centres. 'Sydney, especially inner Sydney, has become Australia's leading switching point into a globalised financial capitalism … Sydney is Australia's gateway city for finance, people, trade and information' (O'Neill and McGuirk 2002, p. 246). The service economy steadily replaced manufacturing in the labour market, with jobs divided into an upper tier of well-paid professional and managerial jobs, and a lower tier of sales and personal service positions, often precarious, and disproportionately filled by women and recent immigrants. As such, employment-based inequality was built into the DNA of the global city.

The international linkages and land use characteristics of the gateway city sustain Daly's emphasis on the significance of external relations in the property market. The 2000 Olympics represented a characteristic world-embracing project of the entrepreneurial global city – a project to be repeated in short order by Vancouver (2010) and London (2012). Around the downtown area, the expanding district of Chinatown-Haymarket contains a population of diverse Asian nationalities, where Thais now out-number residents born in Mainland China, many living in new high-rise residences (Anderson 2018; Anderson et al. 2019). Nearby, just to the south of downtown and alive in global city imaginaries, Central Park on Broadway is a vast, $2 billion, mixed use, condominium project on a former brewery site near the University of Sydney and the University of Technology. Its starchitects (Olds 1997) include Foster and Partners and Jean Nouvel, whose green tower with a hanging garden has won numerous awards. Its marketing and co-living options ('dual entry keys') make it clear that this building is aimed at well-to-do international students at one of the nearby universities.

Such projects are also eloquent markers of the globalisation of real estate. Central Park has been a joint project of the Singapore-based (and Thai-owned) Frasers Property and the Japanese developer Sekisui House. In 2017 the Singapore Government Investment Corporation (GIC), a national sovereign fund, purchased two of Central Park's student housing blocks (Roney 2017). Meanwhile on the western edge of the CBD, the Barangaroo project has attracted a medley of global investors to a vast, 22-hectare former port site. Barangaroo is a $6 billion waterfront project being redeveloped into an office-residential-tourist complex.[12] Its initial sponsors were Lendlease, an Australian developer with a global reach, and the Canadian Public Pension Investment Board (CPPIB), who each invested $1 billion in 2010. The investment was rolled into a trust in 2012 and the original investors were joined by the Hong Kong Monetary Authority, the Qatar Investment Authority, an Australian pension fund, and an Australian corporate fund. In 2017 CPPIB cashed out, and its share was taken by Singapore's GIC, making three national sovereign funds supporting the trust, appropriately named International Towers Sydney (Barangaroo Delivery Authority, various years). Starchitects adding a global imprimatur to the buildings in Barangaroo include Renzo Piano, Richard Rogers, and Tzannes Associates. Almost a third of buyers in its first condominium release were foreign investors (Smyth 2015). The scale and investment power of Barangaroo has transformed adjacent land values; the long-established public housing in Miller's Point became expendable, and over 500 tenants were displaced (Morris 2017). To rationalise neighbourhood gentrification, the state government promised a larger stock of new units would be built elsewhere with proceeds from the sale.

Central Park and Barangaroo illustrate the role of global players financing, developing, and buying large property projects in gateway cities like Sydney. They intimate also that globalisation has sustained the role of external institutions identified by Daly in his analysis of the Sydney property market. In the next part of the discussion, we shall examine what differences have occurred in a twenty-first century housing boom when the imperial regime of Daly's period has given way to an Asian, and more particularly, a Chinese mode of economic incorporation.

From the British Empire to an Asian Hegemon: Australia Pivots

Australia is a client state of the PRC. There's a very big market in promoting Australian residential property there. I've spoken on these road shows in China. We tick so many of their boxes. Sydney luxury high rises are of great interest

(a property journalist, 2013)

The more distant in time Sydney's property booms, the more fully they enter the imperial regime of Britain overseas, the 'context of all contexts' (Sisson et al. 2019) in considering Sydney's housing market. This is not the place to narrate the huge economic, cultural, and political impact of Australia's colonial past and surviving colonial present,[13] which Leonie Sandercock (2003, p. 23) has identified more generally as 'the enduring historical connection between empire, immigration, labour markets, and racism'. To this complex must be added the organisation of space and real estate practices (Troy 2000; Shaw 2007), emphasising the aboriginal dispossession and displacement that Porter (2018, p. 240) has called 'the foundational story of Australian cities'. A centrepiece of Australia's immigration regime for the nation's first seven decades was the White Australia Policy, formally established in 1901 under pressure from labour groups the same year as the birth of the nation. In addition to competition in the job market, anti-Asian sentiment was also powered by social Darwinism, including late nineteenth century ideas of racial hierarchy and the widespread eugenics movement that morphed into virulent race superiority in fascist propaganda between the two World Wars. In this charged ideological environment the White Australia Policy was a more explicit form of the anti-Asian legislation, including head taxes and immigration exclusion, that was variously rolled out in Europe overseas – the legislated racism of European settler societies that also included South Africa, Canada, New Zealand, and the United States.[14]

In the British dominions the racialisation of immigration policy naturally benefitted immigrants from the British Isles. The numerical peak of British immigration to Australia was from 1947 to 1976. Four out of five migrants travelled to Australia by assisted passage after recruitment from a network of UK offices. In 1957 emigration was boosted by a 'Bring out a Briton' programme, and two or three ocean liners left England each week, filled with 'ten-pound tourists' on assisted passage, until they were replaced by air travel in the mid-1960s (Jupp 2004, p. 138). These were overwhelmingly the immigrants whose impact on the housing market Daly identified. Between 1965 and 1975, straddling Sydney's boom-bust cycle, over 620,000 immigrants landed in Australia from the British Isles, over 45% of the entire immigrant body (Jupp 2004, p. 191).

Like Canada and the United States, Australian immigration policy slowly liberalised in the post-1945 period. By the late 1960s, policies of European preference were being dissolved. In part this was a response to universal human rights movements, in part it resulted from a decline in immigration demand from European sources. The White Australia Policy was steadily dismantled and terminated in 1973, the same year that Britain entered the European Community. From 1975 British immigrants required visas to enter Australia; 150 years of assisted passage ended in 1982 (Jupp 2004). Also similar to Canada and the United States, legislative liberalisation from the 1960s onwards led to increasing diversity in immigrant origins. Asian-born Australians increased rapidly from a quarter of a million in 1981 to 665,000 in 1991 (Jupp 1995). Ethnic Chinese were the largest single group, though they arrived from multiple Asian origins. In Sydney only 13,000 residents in 1981 were born in Mainland China, but by 2006 numbers had risen to almost 110,000 (Hugo and Harris 2011),[15] and to 224,000 in the 2016 Census. Many additional Sydney residents originate from the broader diaspora outside Mainland China, so that almost half a million Sydneysiders identified as wholly or in part ethnic Chinese in 2016.

Real estate booms began to include a new set of actors. Early intimations of the transition had occurred during the 1978–1981 round of property investment. A significant shift in the geographic origins of investment capital occurred with the tiger economies of East and Southeast Asia becoming notable sources (Daly 1982, p. 31). By 1984, Japan, Hong Kong, Malaysia, and Singapore were accounting for more than half of the foreign direct investment in real estate (Adrian and Stimson 1986). The primary strategy of capital preservation by Asian investors led to a tolerance of low returns but assurance of long-term security. These Asia Pacific influences became pronounced in the 1986–1990 boom, solidifying a fundamental reorientation of Australia's global economic relations (Hajdu 1994). The UK's share of foreign property holdings fell from 62% in 1973 to 16% in 1988; scarred by the 1973 collapse, many enterprises had withdrawn from the Australian market. In contrast, Asian corporations had responded strongly, rising from 12% of foreign holdings in 1973 to 75% in 1988, led by Hong Kong and Japan. And although the British Isles had contributed over 45% of immigrants to Australia during Sydney's property boom in the 1965–1975 period, by 1985–1990 the share had fallen to 19% and to less than a tenth by the end of the century (Jupp 2004, p. 191). While a majority of Australians still described themselves as of British or Irish ethnicity in 2001, far fewer had been born there. Perhaps the most striking contrast is in Sydney, home to almost 60% of Australia's China-born population, and where that population now exceeds the English-born (Anderson et al. 2019).

Coinciding with a changing immigration profile was the evolution of Australian trade relations. By 2017–2018 two-thirds of Australian trade was with countries in Asia (DFAT 2019). A renewed mining and energy boom in the 1990s, with Japan its principal customer, led to the resource sector dominating Australian exports into the twenty-first century. A more prolonged boom began in 2004, leading to the doubling, from 9% to 18%, of the share of the resource economy relative to GDP by 2012 (Egan and Soos 2014, p. 531). In 1992 Japan had taken a quarter of Australian goods, primarily from the resource sector, but economic stagnation and the appetite of rapid Chinese industrialisation for raw materials saw China become the leading customer, with a 28% share of exports in 2012, led by iron ore. That year the resource economy accounted for almost 60% of Australia's exports of goods and services. Once again, a mining boom accompanied by offshore capital investment became part of the context of the renewed take-off of the housing market.

Australia's economic and demographic pivot to Asia has been easier than a cultural and geopolitical recalibration for a population that retains a majority European origin and sentiment (Ang 2016; Anderson et al. 2019). In this regard the milestone White Paper, *Australia in the Asian Century*, launched by Prime Minister Gillard in 2012, represented a catch-up for cultural and policy domains, with its emphasis on collaboration, cultural understanding, and more liberal entry visas for Asian visitors (Henry et al. 2012). The White Paper was aspirational, for international trade interdependencies continue to contrast with national cultural independence, marked most recently by the repeated quarrels between China and the Scott Morrison government in 2020–2021, initially over the use of Chinese soft power to influence Australian hearts and minds.[16] The coincidence of these altercations with the US–China trade disputes and the AUKUS security pact, underlies Australia's fundamental geopolitical relationships. So too its membership in the Five

Eyes intelligence partnership continues to locate Australia firmly within the security agreements among Commonwealth countries and the United States.

The Economic Contexts of the 2013–2017 Housing Boom

If its cultural relations with Asia remain ambiguous, Australia's recent economic geography has been unequivocally bound to north-south flows of trade and travel. China has become Australia's largest trading partner, with relationships lubricated in trade missions, notably Prime Minister Turnbull's visit with an entourage of 1000 business delegates in 2016, the largest trade mission overseas by an Australian government (China Daily 2016).[17] China's ascendancy has been spectacular, receiving only 2–3% of Australian goods and service exports in 1990, a mere tenth of Japan's share at the time. A mineral export boom sustained continuing growth and prosperity from the bust of the early 1990s until the COVID-19 induced downturn in 2020. Indicative of the importance of the sector, since the global financial crisis of 2008–2009, 'swings in Australian resource and energy export earnings have correlated very closely with swings in nominal GDP' (Department of Industry 2020a). Like the earlier real estate booms Daly reported, the ownership and capital sources of the mining sector have been located overseas. Some 60–80% of mineral and energy ownership is foreign (Black et al. 2017), and until 2010–2011 this sector led the flows of inward direct foreign investment. Sydney, as principal global city, has collected its economic tithe in head office and business service growth from the mining sector in its national hinterland. Its property market has flourished.

Despite repeated warnings of the imminent end of the mineral boom, a slowdown in 2014–2016 was temporary, and activity remained robust into 2020, with mineral and fuel export receipts doubling in the past decade (DFAT 2019; ABS 2020b).[18] Even allowing for COVID-19 effects, exports of mineral resources and energy were expected to reach close to $300 billion in 2019–2020, the highest figure ever recorded, and accounting for 58% of goods and services exported (Department of Industry 2020b). The Chinese share of resource exports, notably iron ore, had risen to 53%, while Japan continued to lead the export totals for energy, principally LNG and coal, though closely followed by China. Significantly, in terms of Australia's dependency on a single customer, the PRC's share of all exports rose to 36% in 2018–2019 (Department of Industry 2020b). Such dependence on a single customer and a single export sector must bring some risks of international exposure and with them, vulnerability.[19] China received 80% of Australia's iron ore exports in 2019–2020, a commodity which itself comprised more than a fifth of total exports. Yet China is exploring additional iron ore sources in Brazil and Africa, which is certain to discipline Australian producers.

Besides the resource sector, tourism and education have been among the top five Australian exports by value, and China has again been a major client. Just as Japanese tourism followed mining investment in Australia in the 1980s and 1990s, so Chinese tourism rose dramatically from a low base after 2009, more than tripling between 2010 and 2019 to 120,000 arrivals a month (ABS 2019). That year China edged ahead of New Zealand to become the leading source of short-term visitor arrivals (RBA 2020a). There were over 750,000 visitors from China to New South Wales in the 2018–2019 reporting year, half as many again as the United States in second place. Chinese visitors are the biggest spenders per capita, and have led visitor expenditures since 2010, spending three times the amount of the United States in second place (DFAT 2019). This cash largesse can be significant for the housing market, for Chinese tourism has been associated not only with purchases of luxury goods but also with the inspection and purchase of real estate. Indeed, tourist expenditure provided a loophole for exporting capital overseas that could be used to contribute to home purchases, particularly during the Chinese New Year holiday.

Educational travel and services have also increased in value rapidly. Australia's international education business has grown substantially from small beginnings 30 years ago, coinciding with a rising shortfall of public funding to tertiary education. Education exports exploded in value from $500 million in 1992 to $12 billion in 2019 (Atkin and Connolly 2013; RBA 2020a). From less than 100,000 in 1994, international student numbers had quadrupled in Australia by 2006 (Fincher and Shaw 2009). International education contributes substantially to the rapid growth of temporary migrants in Australian cities, with significant implications for the downtown and inner-city housing market, especially in Sydney and Melbourne, the locations of leading universities. Around half the resident population of the administrative City of Melbourne comprised students by the mid-2000s, while at least half of them were foreign students living primarily in newly constructed apartment towers (Fincher and Shaw 2009).

Students are overwhelmingly Asian in origin, led by China and India, with Chinese purchase of educational services rising rapidly from 2014 (RBA 2020a). Close to 100,000 PRC students were enrolled in educational institutions in New South Wales in 2018, most in Sydney (ABS 2019).[20] International education has become a significant component of temporary migration and also of foreign apartment purchases by parents for student children, particularly close to top universities (Brooks and Waters 2013; Robertson 2013).

The Central Park apartment complex provides one such pairing of living and studying, adjacent to the University of Technology Sydney, and a short walk from the University of Sydney and the University of Notre Dame (Sydney). Central Park is on the edge of the larger Chinatown-Haymarket district where one in three residents is a tertiary-level student, primarily Asian, at a nearby university or other post-secondary institution (Anderson et al. 2019). Sydney's Chinatown has re-invented itself as a youth destination for young Asian residents and visitors, a 'hybridized, modern and youth-oriented register' (Anderson et al. 2019, p. 153). The large tourist market in Chinatown is dominated by PRC visitors and by young adults aged under 30. High-rise apartments to accommodate the burgeoning international student market have been a significant addition to a formerly low-rise landscape.

The trends in these economic indicators tell a common story of the emergence of a deepening transnational economic field linking Australia and its principal global city with China (Robertson and Rogers 2017). The PRC's share of Australian economic activity has risen quickly to a primary position in the major export sectors of minerals, tourism, and educational services. This economic presence has gathered momentum during the past 10–20 years in each sector, in phase with China's burgeoning growth as a source of temporary and permanent migrants. As we shall now see, these flows of economic activity and migrants have been joined by capital flows, including investment in real estate, rounding out the key overseas variables identified by Maurice Daly as drivers in earlier Sydney property booms.

Off-shore Residential Investors: Evidence from the Foreign Investment Review Board

From afar, the Foreign Investment Review Board (FIRB) provides an international gold standard in screening and monitoring offshore investment proposals. But closer scrutiny suggests FIRB is a somewhat tarnished standard-bearer. It is a minimally resourced advisory board to Government (the Treasury), while audit work on specific investment applications is referred to the Treasury and the Australian Taxation Office, which also handle enquiries and other day-to-day work. FIRB has had only one full-time executive member who is also the Head of Treasury's Foreign Investment Division. The remainder of the Board have comprised a small group of government and business specialists who meet face-to-face monthly, and more regularly electronically. The Board's meagre budget in 2018–2019 of $500,000 was largely remuneration for members' costs (FIRB 2020). Nonetheless, the Board approved 8724 applications for proposed investments that year with a value of $231 billion. The scale and significance of the work belies the frail resources of the Board.[21] As we shall see again in Vancouver (Chapter 5), the tasks of screening and monitoring the investment-immigration-real estate nexus are typically heavily under-resourced.[22] Moreover, rejection of applications to FIRB has been minimal.[23] Between 2015 and 2019, of 80,000 applications that were considered by the Board, only *14* were rejected or declined (FIRB 2020, p.19). However, almost half the files were approved with conditions, commonly related to tax exposure. FIRB's tone to foreign investors repeats Australia's preference to facilitate FDI rather than obstruct it (Li and Hendrischke 2020).

If FIRB's screening function identified very few bad apples in the application barrel, its monitoring function is also less robust than anticipated. The Board is transparent about this limitation, beginning its tabulations in each annual report with caveats about the use of its data. First, users are reminded that data reveal investment proposals not actual investments; as we shall see there is often a large gap between intentions and actions. Second, as there are screening exemptions, not all potential investments are captured. Third, government may change the threshold for exemptions, making time series analysis problematic. For example, in 1999 the threshold for exempting commercial real estate applications from review was raised from $5 million to $50 million, removing many proposals from subsequent assessment, and compromising longitudinal comparison. Fourth, administrative decisions by the Board may have the same effect. In December 2015, recognising that investor households searching for a single residence were covering their bases by submitting multiple proposals for alternate residential options, the Board introduced a fee for each application. The value of residential real estate applications more than halved in the next fiscal year. Similarly, the China–Australia Free Trade Agreement lifted the threshold for screening Mainland private investment applications from 2016, also limiting application numbers (Li and Hendrischke 2020). In annual reporting, categories are merged, and new categories appear in successive years, providing a roadblock for comparative study. The Board's cautions on time-series analysis are well-placed. But these cautions are commonly disregarded by media commentators (and some scholars) who use the statistics as if they were infallible, overlooking their social fabrication.[24]

Consequently, the annual FIRB data are used here cautiously. Beginning in 2002–2003, we highlight only major trends that can be triangulated against other information sources. A first point to note from the annual totals is the sheer scale of overseas investment applications. Approvals for mineral exploration and development in Australia led the economic categories and amounted to almost $300 billion in their most active period from 2007–2008 to 2010–2011 (FIRB various years). But in 2011–2012, minerals were nudged aside in value by commercial plus residential real estate investment proposals. The residential component alone had not received approvals exceeding $21 billion in any year in the previous decade, but during the property boom from 2013–2014 to 2016–2017 overseas residential investments amounting to almost $200 billion were approved; commercial real estate added another $170 billion – though it is important to repeat the earlier caveats that these numbers are indicative of proposed capital flows, not flows themselves.

It is possible to extract the contribution of different countries to this pattern of real estate proposals. Up to 2012, the leading investment nations were the United States, the United Kingdom, and Singapore. But from 2012–2013 until 2017–2018, as real estate proposals grew rapidly, Chinese investors were by far the leading recipients of real estate approvals, accounting on average for 27% of all approvals, by value. Even in 2016–2017, following the introduction of application fees to winnow out dubious multiple applications, PRC-based real estate approvals exceeded $15 billion in value; the year before, when the fees had applied for just over half the financial year, Mainland approvals had totalled $32 billion. However, in a faltering market at the end of the boom, Chinese approvals accounted for only 7% of the overseas real estate total in 2018–2019. The years of the Sydney residential boom coincided with maximum foreign investment approvals, and within this group, with the highest level of Mainland China participation.

We learn much less in the FIRB reports about the geography of real estate investment approvals in Australia. Fortunately, a detailed in-house analysis of 2010–2015 data by Treasury staff found that foreign investment approvals for residential real estate were highly concentrated spatially in a small number of postcodes in Sydney and Melbourne, with two-thirds of all national approvals falling within these gateway cities (Wokker and Swieringa 2020). Applicants are normally required to invest in new dwellings, stimulating the residential inventory, aside from temporary residents (like students) who can purchase an established (or new) dwelling for their own use while in Australia. Indeed, the largest single housing category by value in the FIRB record is new buildings, where 'developers [could] sell up to 100 percent of new residences to foreign interests' (FIRB 2012, p. 26). Such sales were not obligatory as the developer had to present the real estate product to a local market as well as overseas buyers. The FIRB found it worth pointing out that while the developer was permitted to sell all off-plan dwellings in the project to offshore buyers, 'the dwellings cannot be marketed exclusively overseas' (FIRB 2012,

p. 26).[25] The 2017 IMF review of the Australian economy noted 'a marked increase in the interest of foreign buyers to acquire residential real estate in the eastern capitals from 2012', while the Reserve Bank estimated that 'one fourth of new apartments in the eastern capitals over the past few years were purchased by foreign buyers' (IMF 2018a, p. 17).

What can we conclude from FIRB's accounts concerning applications from foreign investors? First, approved proposals for all sectors amounted to very large investment totals which grew to reach $231 billion in 2018–2019. In considerable part these flows were aspirational as they exceeded actual FDI flows by some order of magnitude. But if inflated, the FIRB approvals were indicative of investment desires, many of which would be realised. Second, the residential plus commercial real estate category surged from 2013–2014 to 2016–2017, with investment approvals for $363 billion, or 45% by value of all FIRB approvals those years. It was residential projects which bulged during this period and fell back thereafter, while commercial real estate approvals held a steadier course. Third, a detailed assessment covering 2010–2015 showed that a high proportion of these residential approvals were concentrated in a minority of Sydney and Melbourne postcodes (Wokker and Swieringa 2020). An earlier Treasury analysis had located FIRB approvals for apartment buildings in the inner-city rings of Sydney and Melbourne (Gauder et al. 2014).

Fourth, many overseas countries were sources for real estate investment proposals. In 2015–2016, the peak year of real estate approvals by value, eight countries originated approved proposals for over $2.5 billion each, five of them in East or Southeast Asia. But, fifth, leading them was China with 38% of approvals by value that year. China had been a small contributor to real estate proposals before the Global Financial Crisis, with 3% of approvals by value from 2002 to 2007. But from 2013 to 2017 real estate applications from China rose rapidly and accounted on average for 29% of successful proposals. Sixth, and finally, during this same period, median house prices in Sydney soared from $650,000 in 2013 to $1.05 million in 2017, an increment of 62% in just four years (ABS 2020a). Sydney's 2013–2017 housing boom coincided exactly with the peak of real estate investment approvals originating in China.

China and the 2013–2017 Real Estate Boom

A Chinese-Australian manager at an international real estate consultancy spoke to me in 2013 about Asian buyers in Sydney.

It began with Hong Kong after 1984[26] and has been going now for 30 years. The floodgates opened and the water has been flowing ever since. China, Hong Kong, Malaysia, Singapore, Korea. This is a safe haven, for both migrants and investors. Right now, the money is from China, and it goes to London, Sydney, Vancouver, a few other places. We sell London properties into Shanghai, and the contract is signed through a bank in Hong Kong. They want to disperse their funds, establish a family satellite in Sydney through education, and other family visas follow later.

A manager at a second real estate company reflected on his experience selling Sydney property to Chinese buyers.

For the last 10 years most new apartments here have been sold off the plan to Chinese. The locals couldn't buy the concept. Chinese and Hong Kong money is everywhere. The past five years they've purchased all the $10 million plus transactions in the northern and eastern suburbs. A lot of people want to get money out of China. You have to get money to Hong Kong first. For moving money in and out you can't beat Hong Kong. Australia is easy to get to, and has no income tax on global assets. The GDP is rising quickly. Australia is like a paradise. It's a prudent choice.

In contrast, other observers, notably some academics and government spokespersons, saw a limited role for Chinese investment in real estate. In a sense, both judgements were correct, for the sceptics were typically considering national transaction levels, while the real estate professionals were looking at eastern capital city purchases. Writing at the beginning of the boom, economists at the Reserve Bank of Australia identified the principal features of foreign property investment in the previous decade: 'Foreign purchases appear to be most concentrated in new rather than established dwellings, in higher- rather than lower-priced dwellings, in medium- and high-density dwellings rather than detached dwellings, and in inner-city areas of Sydney and Melbourne rather than other locations' (Gauder et al. 2014, p. 11). That the surge in real estate investment proposals originating overseas coincided so precisely with the boom in Sydney house prices between 2013 and 2017 suggests a causal relationship. And the prominence of applications from China, among the ranks of foreign investors, during the same period does not appear to be a coincidence. Additional sources and other relevant contexts support this conclusion.

First, we should note synchronous foreign investment underway in Vancouver (Chapter 5), where there was also a price surge during this same period, attributed in part to purchases from East Asia. Like Sydney, Vancouver prices rose substantially, by over 60% between July 2014 and July 2017. This was a period of sustained capital flight from China, with the depletion of the PRC's foreign exchange reserves by a trillion US dollars over 30 months from 2014–2016 (IIF 2016). The Juwai real estate platform estimated that US$180 billion in real estate investment left China in 2015 plus 2016 (Juwai 2017). An apartment price surge in Hong Kong and the marked decoupling of residential prices from local incomes after 2009 had coincided with the arrival of footloose Mainland capital (Chapter 3). However, in 2013 there were reports from Hong Kong that cooling measures following this investment surge were sending 'Cash-rich mainland Chinese… scouring overseas for better options' (Reuters 2013). Sydney, Los Angeles, Vancouver and London were among the residential markets that these investors selected.

Second, a series of property cooling measures in China to contain an inflating domestic market added to the volume of companies and private households encouraged to look overseas during this same window (Liu and Gurran 2017; Ma 2021). The 2011 'purchase restriction policy' and other moves to control prices by limiting speculation led investors to less regulated economies in the West.[27] Price gains from apartment sales in China were in relative and then absolute decline as developers as well as household investors in an overbuilt market looked offshore. Surveys by wealth management companies active in the PRC during this period showed an outwards compulsion among the country's high net-worth individuals, with 40–60% of respondents in different surveys seriously considering emigration. A survey of Chinese HNWIs in 2016 revealed that over 70% of respondents had already made overseas property investments (FT 2016), principally in the United States (28%, notably Los Angeles and San Francisco), Canada (23%, Vancouver and Toronto), and Australia (21%, Sydney and Melbourne). Australia's comparative position became more attractive with the suspension of Canada's popular Business Immigration Program in 2012, and a substantial rise in stamp duties charged against Mainland apartment buyers in Hong Kong the same year. Exchange rate fluctuations, and the volatility of the PRC housing and stock markets stimulated geographical diversification as a portfolio goal and as a potential prelude to emigration. In a global low interest rate environment, new apartments in Sydney and Melbourne represented a secure asset in a politically risk-free setting. A major advantage was a steadily improving exchange rate, as the Australian dollar depreciated by a third against the Renminbi from 2011 to 2015. Other important motivations for household investment abroad included educational opportunities for children, and environmental and sometimes political quality of life factors.

Not infrequently, purchase of an apartment for adult children pursuing higher education in Sydney or Melbourne provided a toehold for subsequent family migration to a setting of high environmental quality. Education, short-term tourism, and migration provided an integrated and sequential realignment of a family from China to Australia (Wong et al. 2017). Education and tourism were way-stations that could lead to migration and home purchase. This sequence was well-recognised by Chinese developers active in Sydney. In a media statement, the Chairman of the Greenland Group lauded the role of students and tourists as locational pioneers in this integration of consumer desire for Australia. 'We are extending the China market abroad and we prioritise our investments to countries where Chinese immigrants, students and tourists like the most' (Cranston and Thistleton 2013). Transnational family ties were often maintained, with the source of household business wealth located in China, prompting head of household location in the PRC with short-term family visits to Australia. This 'astronaut' family model repeated the earlier pattern of Hong Kong migrants in the 1990s, and like them often involved purchase of a home plus an investment property.

Third, especially after China's purchase restriction policy in 2011, many Mainland property development companies made their landfall in Australian cities. They had deep pockets; Greenland was looking at overseas investments of US$10 billion a year, with Sydney and Melbourne as favoured cities (Cole 2013). In Sydney, there was a concentration of activity in and around Chinatown-Haymarket, in part providing accommodation for Asian-origin students. The district also became a hub for real estate services, proffering advice, marketing, and mortgages (Anderson et al. 2019), in 'one of the most popular locations for property investment in Sydney for local and offshore Chinese buyers' (Wong 2017, p. 98). Following Hong Kong-based property development in and around Chinatown, Mainland developers followed with commercial and residential projects, the largest being the half billion-dollar Greenland Centre with 490 residential units. At the off the plan launch of its first stage in 2013, over 80% of units were sold in the first few hours, almost all to ethnic Chinese buyers, half of them off-shore (Wong 2017), although construction had not begun and completion was not anticipated for another four years (Cole 2013). At a nearby condominium, The Quay, funded by the state-owned Industrial and Commercial Bank of China. pre-build sales were described as frenzied (Wong 2017). Australian developers were in on the action too, with Lendlease's nearby Darling Square project selling out almost 600 off the plan units in a single day; a third of the buyers were foreign (Ruehl 2015).[28] Meriton was a successful pioneer in selling Australian residential property directly into China. Henry Triguboff, property tycoon and owner of Meriton, joined the dots: 'Our (real estate) market is the Chinese market, just like coal and iron ore' (Cranston and Thistleton 2013).

Built by well-known Mainland development companies, downtown and inner-city projects have been popular with PRC corporate investors; by the end of 2014 Greenland had acquired four downtown sites (Cole 2015). Commonly office acquisitions were converted to condominium apartments. Other PRC developers embraced the 'going out' strategy with gusto, and proliferated in and around the CBD including large players like Dalian Wanda, Poly Real Estate, Shimao Properties, and Aqualand;[29] seven of the ten largest Chinese developers were active in Australia by 2014 (Knight Frank Sydney 2015). The real estate arm of the Ping An insurance company completed two inner city condominiums as joint ventures with Australian developer Mirvac, and then boldly moved into a $1 billion commercial and office redevelopment on Circular Quay with Lendlease and Japan's Mitsubishi Estate Asia (Cole 2016). Nearby, in an exchange between international real estate titans, Dalian Wanda bought an office tower on Circular Quay from Blackstone for $425 million, intending to transform it to luxury apartments.[30] Smaller companies imitated the lead of majors. Ten small Shanghai developers combined to form Shanghai United in 2015, with a mission to look for overseas investments for survival. Within two years they had sunk $600 million in commercial and residential projects in Sydney and other Australian locations, with plans to invest another $1 billion (Smyth 2017). Together, Sydney and Melbourne attracted more Chinese real estate investment in 2014 than either London or New York (Knight Frank Sydney 2015).

High-rise condominiums downtown and in the inner city have been preferred by local and off-shore Chinese investors; they require a smaller outlay than detached homes, and rental yield is dependable. New apartment construction surged between 2009 and 2015, as planning approvals in Australia *tripled*, while new detached houses plateaued in number (Rosewall and Shoory 2017). Spectacular growth occurred in higher density dwellings – in Sydney's inner and middle rings, apartment approvals escalated by 78,000 units, 2012–2015 (Shoory 2016). Analysis of specifically high-density development sites purchased in Sydney showed that 48% by value were acquired by foreign investors in 2015–2016, and 55% the year before (Knight Frank Sydney 2017). The cheap Australian dollar, and favourable funding available to state-owned enterprises like Greenland, permitted Chinese buyers to out-bid local competitors for development sites. The evidence suggests success for the Australian government's policy of having foreign real estate investors augment housing supply, as condominium apartments owned by foreign investors would commonly be rented out to local tenants.

The condominium market has attracted both local and foreign investors as well as owner-occupiers; over 60% of apartment units in Sydney are owned by investors (Troy et al. 2020). Local real estate agencies have adjusted to this diverse market, adding Mandarin-speaking realtors, or whole teams. The day I interviewed an international real estate consultancy in Sydney they were assembling a new China-based unit dedicated to recruiting candidates for Australia's new Significant Investor Visa. Mainland buyers are officially only allowed to export US$50,000 a year. The manager at the consultancy did not know how funds exited China to make purchase in Sydney possible. He observed, however, that contracts were normally signed through lawyers in Hong Kong, and that 'any PRC buyer must have a Hong Kong bank account'. It was not unusual, he said, for 35–50% of condominium units to be sold to foreigners. In the case of Central Park, there had been launches in Hong Kong and Shanghai, and some 35% of units had sold offshore; another 40–50% had sold to local Asian-origin buyers. The manager was 'very grateful' that this market had sustained condominium sales in preferred districts during the post-GFC period. This market segment was important enough that when FIRB applications from China began to wane, concern was raised by the real estate industry. While the role of Chinese investment had been disputed by some sources at the peak of the boom, as prices eased after 2017 there was general agreement that shrinkage of Mainland investment was a leading cause. Observers pointed to tighter capital controls in China, to a credit squeeze by Australian banks, and to the role of additional state taxes on foreign buyers.[31]

Gifted Migrants from China

Immigration was an integral feature among the external drivers Daly cited in shaping Sydney's housing bubbles, and the city's population growth has become ever more dependent on immigrant arrivals. The 300,000 China-born permanent and temporary migrants in Sydney are often highly qualified and committed to the acquisition of further economic and cultural capital: 'Chinese emigration has been led, in particular by the highly educated and the wealthy, who are increasingly pursuing educational, work and investment opportunities overseas' (Anderson et al. 2019, p. 35).[32] These Mainlanders have followed the earlier path of Hong Kong migrants in the 1990s in pursuing elite entry visas. During this earlier period over 60% of immigrants who arrived in Australia through expedited business tracks came from ethnic Chinese populations in East and Southeast Asia (Wong 2003). Like the larger Canadian Business Immigration Program, the leading places of origin were

Hong Kong and Taiwan, with fewer Mainlanders.[33] However, in recent years Mainland-born arrivals have been prominent in the non-points tested skilled migration visa stream; from 2015 to 2019 over 20,000 Mainlanders plus family members qualified for the Business Innovation and Investment Visa, by far the largest national group holding this visa (DHA 2019).[34] In addition, Mainlanders have been prominent applicants for the Significant Investor Visa, established in 2012 and requiring an investment of $5 million in the Australian economy; in its first seven years, 85% of 2338 SIVs were granted to citizens of China, sponsored overwhelmingly by the states of Victoria and New South Wales (DHA 2020). Both Melbourne and Sydney commonly score near the top on international quality of life rankings, like the much-cited listing by the *Economist Intelligence Unit*.[35] Melbourne is usually ahead, which may explain its ascendancy over Sydney in attracting holders of the SIV, high net-worth individuals able to practise a kind of residential tourism that optimises seasonal settlement in Australia's high-amenity environments, shared with the opportunities of other global destinations.

But these remain relatively small numbers compared with the business immigrants who landed in Vancouver, enough to substantially affect the local housing market.[36] They are also a minority compared with the much larger overall migration to Australia from China of 330,000 between 2011 and 2018 who contributed a significant market share to new house and apartment sales. They have been a 'highly skilled, education-related and investment-focused' migration (Wang et al. 2018). Among Mainlanders arriving in Australia between 2006 and 2016, 56% were homeowners by 2016, some 20 points higher than other immigrants (Moallemi and Melser 2020). Members of Asia's vast emerging middle- and upper middle-class, they had successfully navigated their way through the Chinese housing market, where substantial fortunes had been made. They were also alert consumers during Australia's housing boom, buying for their own use and as local investors. The pervasive importance of property for upward mobility was a lesson well-learned in China and this culture of property was carried to Australia.[37]

Even allowing for hyperbole, the role of ethnic Chinese buyers was deeply ingrained in the minds of the real estate industry in Sydney and Melbourne. A much-cited Credit Suisse report noted that not only were Mainland buyers purchasing 18% of new dwellings in Sydney, but also observed that they had become the marginal buyer prepared to raise the price threshold in a competitive market (Janda 2014). These perceptions were amplified in the media and popular culture (Rogers et al. 2015; Wong 2017). An on-line survey of Sydneysiders, skewed towards Australian-born residents of above average social status, and undertaken near the peak of the real estate boom, revealed that foreign investors were regarded as the largest single cause of current unaffordable housing, prompting a majority to agree with termination of foreign investment in Australian real estate (Rogers et al. 2017).

From External to Internal Relations: Investor Profiles

The argument to date has tried to follow the spirit of Maurice Daly's emphasis on the external drivers of residential price cycles, extending his narrative to the 2013–2017 Sydney boom. A coherent story can be told incorporating, as Daly did, a mineral boom fuelled by extensive investment by offshore companies in exploration and extraction, which overlapped with a subsequent foreign investment surge in the property market during a period of expanded liquidity that saw the arrival of foreign investors, buyers, development companies, and financial institutions. The immigrants Daly emphasised now have a more nuanced profile; besides permanent residents arriving as skilled workers from China and other Asian destinations, there were thousands of temporary migrants, principally Asian students, who sustained a new central city housing sub-market, and even shorter-term arrivals, large cohorts of Asian tourists, some of whom (like the students) were scouting out residential investment and possible permanent migration. A major departure, then, from the 1968–1974 boom is that the migrants during the earlier period were sustaining permanent settlement through long-established links with Britain and northwest Europe, while in 2013–2017 migrants emerged in a more mobile transnational field, from Asia in general and China in particular, Australia's major trading partner and the leading source of FIRB's foreign real estate proposals.

Property is a most attractive investment asset in Australia. Over the past 25 years, CoreLogic data show that the annual price gain on a median-valued house averaged 7.6% in Sydney; the annual price appreciation for apartment units was 6.3% (AHL Investments 2018). The Australian Bureau of Statistics (ABS) distinguishes between housing loans granted by financial institutions to owner-occupiers compared with investors (Figure 4.2). The loans profile for New South Wales is largely shaped by the variations of borrowers in the Sydney housing market (ABS 2020c). While the profile for owner-occupier loans contains oscillations there is a clear upward trajectory, with lower lending totals in the early years and higher total loans near the present as we might expect in a growing and inflationary market. The loan profile for investors shows greater volatility. The crater around the GFC is broader, extending from 2007 to the end of 2009; the GFC had a more adverse effect on risk-taking by those pursuing

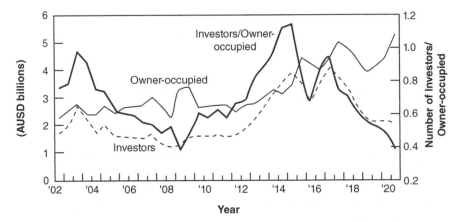

FIGURE 4.2   Housing loans granted to investors and owner-occupiers, New South Wales, 2002–2020. Commonwealth of Australia / https://www.abs.gov.au/ausstats/abs@.nsf/exnote/5601.0 / last accessed December 30, 2022 / CC BY 4.0

primarily exchange value. Similarly, there is a more effusive surge early into the 2013 boom where (to use a rugby metaphor) investors continued to pile on until early 2018, even exceeding the loans value for owner-occupiers for a period in 2014. But when prices fell, the players left the ruck abruptly; by 2019 investment loans were almost halved. Compared to the modulated loan behaviour of owner-occupiers there is a good deal more volatility in the acquisition of investor loans, with aversion revealed in 2007–2009 and 2018–2020 contrasted with the swarming behaviour during the 2013 to 2017 boom.

Australian and foreign borrowers are not differentiated in the ABS data base. An indicator gauging the share by each buyer group is provided by estimates maintained by the National Australia Bank (NAB) since 2010. The Bank's *Residential Property Survey* attempts to provide this more nuanced interpretation from a national expert panel of around 300 real estate specialists. In addition to predicting market price trajectories by state, the panel assigns buyers to one of five categories: owner-occupier, first-time buyer-owner, first-time buyer-investor, Australian investor, and foreign buyer/investor. Responses are further differentiated by building age, distinguishing new from established, pre-owned properties. The data are of course best guesses but they are compiled by industry specialists and provide useful general guidelines. In a depressed market in the fourth quarter of 2019, first-time buyers were the most active of the five buyer categories in New South Wales, expected to account for close to 40% of all purchases of new properties. Foreign buyers had largely lost interest in the market with less than five percent of all sales, while Australian investors had declined to about 25% of the market (NAB 2020). At this stage of the housing cycle, made-in-Australia investment was trumping investment from overseas, while first-time buyers (and upgraders) were making hay in a depressed market, repeating their behaviour in 2008–2009, during the GFC, when they also benefitted from an enriched First Home Owners Grant (Randolph et al. 2013). Contrast these relations with the pattern during the peak of the 2013–2017 boom (Figure 4.2). At that time, the NAB survey placed foreign residential purchases in New South Wales at their high point, with 20% of the market for new properties (NAB 2015); the Reserve Bank estimated that a quarter of new apartments in Sydney and Melbourne during the boom were purchased by foreign buyers. But even at this point, foreign buyers were outnumbered by the 30% market share of Australian investors. Australian plus foreign investors as a whole were equalling or just exceeding the market share of owner-occupiers in this frothy new home market.

Reading across these two varied data bases some general conclusions may be suggested. The ABS loans data indicate that owner-occupier loans for all dwellings in New South Wales grew steadily though irregularly through the 2002–2020 period with the highest totals in the last five years of the period (Figure 4.2). The loans secured by investors in contrast had a far more irregular profile, with exaggerated oscillations. A dramatic peak of borrowing in 2013–2017, coinciding exactly with Sydney's price boom, separated investment troughs in 2007–2010 and since late 2018. At the peak of the boom, in 2014–2015, investor financing exceeded the total of owner-occupier financing, suggesting the disproportionate role of investors. It is worth noting the withdrawal of first-time buyers from the market during the peak investment period. The lowest 20% of annual first-time buyer purchases between 2002 and 2020 all fell during the boom between 2013 and 2017, while the highest 20% are concentrated between 2007 and 2009, coinciding with the GFC when investors fled from the market, and again in the COVID-19 recession in 2020. The third curve on Figure 4.2 shows the ratio between investor loans and ownership loans; for a period during the boom investor loans were dominant.

The NAB data on market share distinguish between new and pre-owned ('established') dwellings. Our emphasis has been on the smaller new build sector, because this is the portion of the market that foreign investors are guided to by legislation; their proportionate share in the pre-owned sector is predictably lower. The data also reveal that the share of foreign buyers in the new-build sector was substantial and highest during the 2013–2017 boom – but even so, a still higher market share was filled by domestic investors. This is an important conclusion, and leads us to investigate the so-far understated role of the domestic investor, and to pivot from external to internal drivers of the housing market. Of course, some of the domestic investors would be immigrants and some of these would be Chinese Australians. Nonetheless, the prominence of the domestic residential investor in Australia complicates Daly's narrative on external drivers alone of Sydney's housing booms.

The Domestic Property Investor and Tax-Subsidised Rental Assets

After a circuitous journey through Sydney's 2013–2017 residential price boom, we can return to the vignette with which this chapter began, and to the discovery that 30% of purchase enquiries for a new affordable subdivision in Sydney's far western suburbs came from investors. In this region, far from the typical territory of foreign investors in new high-density apartments in the CBD and the first two residential rings, we might assume that enquiries came primarily from Australian residents. A thorough recent examination of landlords in the middle and outer suburbs of western Sydney sheds light on this behaviour (Pawson and Martin 2021).

Australians have an unusual proclivity for rental investment. A large online survey of Sydney residents noted that almost a fifth of respondents held rental property (Rogers et al. 2018). Pawson and Martin (2021) cite somewhat lower figures of 14–16%. But even this lower estimate identifies Australia as exceptional among its Anglophone peer nations. Despite the ubiquitous image of the 'buy to let' small landlord in the UK, the British incidence of landlord status is only half the lowest of the Australian estimates. The possession of property as asset reaches deep into the national psyche (Adkins et al. 2020, 2021): 'Once upon a time the most important pursuit was becoming a homeowner; now it's becoming a landlord' (Allon 2008, p. 6). The following narrative from a Sydney property professional is symptomatic:

> My father grew up in a small town in rural Victoria. He moved to Sydney when he was a young teen, dropped out of school, and began working as a carpenter's mate. He had the idea of getting ahead with property. He saved for a house on the outskirts of Sydney, and had a competition with his mates as to who could pay their's off first. Then he bought a small rental property, and in time a few others. He did it for security, as an asset for old age. It's the ideology of the Great Australian Dream, a house on a quarter-acre block, the individualist in a property-owning democracy.

It is an ideology too of the resolute, self-sufficient individual who has little interest or tolerance with government tampering with such freedoms. Here is the epitome of choosing a housing asset for retirement over taxation for state services in Kemeny's (2005) welfare trade-off. Commonly, government endorses this ideology of the self-reliant citizen practising asset-based welfare. As we saw in the last section, the can-do culture included expanding loan portfolios for the rental investment segment of the housing market during the 2013–2017 boom.

In Sydney reinvestment at the core together with gentrification of the inner city has driven poverty to selected suburbs, and with it, conversion of properties to rental units (Randolph and Holloway 2005). The unexpected return of private renting has coincided with the polarisation of labour and housing markets and the retreat of the welfare state (Pawson et al. 2017). These trends converged in gateway cities, a convergence which we will see most dramatically in London (Chapter 6). The small private landlord with home-based equity can readily secure a low-interest loan from financial institutions. This asset-based welfare, with an eye to old-age security (exemplified in the case of the apprentice carpenter, above), complements government orientation to marketisation and encouragement of capitalist subjectivities.

But western Sydney research showed that the apocryphal apprentice carpenter may no longer be a typical small landlord. A mail and online survey disclosed that on average landlords held 3.2 rental properties, and were well-educated with high incomes (Pawson and Martin 2021). The business strategy of landlords was to employ debt financing, 'using capital growth to lever into further property acquisitions, and rental income to enhance investor ability to service loans' (Pawson and Martin 2021). These results were amplified by a broader analysis of taxation data, contrasting the populist representation of the rental home investor as 'Everyman' with the statistical profile of a higher income minority (Hulse et al. 2020). Moreover, like the Western Sydney results, most rental units were part of a multiple unit portfolio, indicating access by owners to substantial investment funds. The view of the investor as Everyman normalises and conceals relations that benefit primarily those with a pre-existing economic advantage; the portrayal of equal access of every mum and dad to rental investment camouflages the socio-economic construction of privilege.

Tax law expands the contribution of rental investment to multiplying wealth inequality. There are material advantages to the status of investor in the tax code (diminishing perhaps the perception of investment risks). Accentuating asset-based welfare, since 1999 tax has been applied on only half the capital gain made on selling investment properties. Since the tax is applied at the marginal rate, savings are much greater for higher-income investors. The other celebrated incentive to property investment has been negative gearing, a tax concession permitting losses on rental property to be applied against taxable income from other sources including earnings. Since wealthier citizens own rental property, and will pay a higher marginal rate, so tax relief accrued by negative gearing will favour them disproportionately, especially when interest rates are higher and more interest can be offset. Data from the Australian Taxation Office showed that in the 2014–2015 tax year some 13% of taxpayers were negative gearing, but among wealthy occupations like surgeons and anaesthetists the number approached 30% (Jericho 2017). Far more owners (62%) were able to arrange their finances so that they claimed a rental loss than those who claimed a rental profit; of course, in a booming market the real objective was eventual capital gain when the property sold, with the bonus of reducing until then the annual tax load from personal income. With these tax concessions, governments have an additional incentive to maintain high house prices. Not only is there a home owning majority, but a growing number of those homeowners are also property investors. A market correction would bare the vulnerabilities of over-leveraging property assets among both groups. This anxiety was especially pertinent during the 2013–2017 boom when investors were extending themselves with risky interest-only mortgages.[38]

These distinctive Australian incentives to invest in rental assets, thereby raising property prices, have received sustained criticism, in part because their regressive impact is unambiguously recorded by annual Taxation Office statistics (Blunden 2016; Pawson 2018). Even the IMF's pro-market endorsement of supply-side housing measures also recommended 'reducing structural incentives for leveraged investment by households, including limiting negative gearing in residential real estate' (IMF 2020, p. 17). Limiting the tax breaks from capital gains and negative gearing had been a policy of the Labor Party in the 2019 federal election. The opportunity cost of these concessions was evident in Labor's housing policy that advocated construction of 250,000 rent-subsidised dwellings over ten years, for 60% of the current annual loss to the Treasury from the rental tax concessions. Labor had promoted a similar policy in the 2016 election, and the Coalition had countered by fear-mongering. With explicit reference to the ideology of home as asset-based welfare, Government ministers had urged that 'Labor's housing tax plan will deliver a reckless trifecta of lower home values, higher rents and less investment ... [homeowners would be harmed] if you take $1 off [the value of] their house, the asset they have worked hard for, that's going to see them to retirement' (Karp 2016). Labor's housing policy was rejected in both the 2016 and the 2019 elections, testimony to the electorate's continuing preference for an asset-based welfare ideology. Rather than provide social housing and reduce tax concessions to landlords,

Coalition politicians preferred to reward a rentier model of passive investing – and the electorate agreed. Burke et al. (2020, p. 19) have drawn the appropriate conclusion in terms of growing inequality: 'This becomes an entrenching cycle, resulting in considerable accentuation of the property wealth divide … as more and more households become investors supportive of the existing policy environment, e.g. negative gearing that underpins their investment.'

From Financial Policy to Cooling Measures

Economic policy makers were concerned by the winding down of foreign investment in the mineral sector after 2012 (IMF 2018a). Reducing interest rates from 4.25% in early 2012 to 1.5% in August 2016 was a calculated response, very satisfactory to investors, both local and foreign. Even more welcome to foreign investors was the additional rapid depreciation of the Australian dollar, which fell by more than a third against both Chinese and American currencies between 2011 and 2015. In considerable measure, declining interest rates and a weakening dollar exchange rate were linked and engineered to partially offset and counterbalance anticipated investment losses in the mineral sector with investment in consumption, and especially in property. A cheap dollar, low interest rates, and lending competition between financial institutions encouraged borrowing and residential investment. The subsequent piling on of property investors contributed to the dramatic price gain of 62% in established Sydney houses between 2013 and 2017. More than two out of five mortgages in much of 2014 and 2015 were interest-only, usually a sign of speculators betting on continuing price inflation. It seemed that stability in the housing market had been trumped by the desire for FDI to replace the decline of the mineral boom – though as we have seen, while foreign (primarily Chinese) property demand has been significant, there is evidence that more residential investors were Australians benefitting from low mortgage rates and tax subsidies. The boom shut out Australian first-time homebuyers from the market, and their numbers fell dramatically. As popular anxieties were given voice by the media, Australian legislators and regulators reluctantly introduced price cooling measures, comprising a familiar suite of macroprudential and tax measures.

Australian banks are heavily involved in the property sector with loans to house buyers commonly accounting for over half of all bank lending, more than loans to business or government (RBA 2020b). But the frothiness of the market – incited by financial and tax policies – introduced unpalatable risk and uncertainty for the nation's regulators. Supervisory direction was given to tighten or terminate mortgage lending to foreign applicants. Problems were exacerbated as it became evident that the apartment boom was fuelled in part by capital from fictitious offshore companies. At the end of 2014, the banks, chastened by the Australian Prudential Regulation Authority (APRA), toughened underwriting and in some cases froze loan applications. Interest rates were raised on investor and interest-only loans (Debelle 2018). Higher deposits were required in districts with apartment oversupply. But there was no signal from the RBA that overall interest rates would be raised. Moreover, the regulators were not stingy; investor lending could still grow, but growth was limited to 10%, while interest-only loans were still permitted up to a fairly generous cap of 30% of new lending. This set of prudential measures did not satisfy international rating services and in 2017 Moody's, Standard and Poor's, and Fitch all lowered or downgraded the Australian banking sector, finding elevated risks in their level of household loans (primarily mortgages) in the face of a possible significant property market correction. Through the boom the level of household debt had risen appreciably, from 171% of disposable income in 2013 to 196% in 2018. A key issue was raised by the IMF Consultation: 'Housing market imbalances and high household debt have become important vulnerabilities' (IMF 2018a, np).

The state of New South Wales eventually announced taxation as a familiar instrument to cool the fever in the housing market. But not too much, as state governments benefit from high house prices in their revenue columns through property transfer and other taxes (Vogel et al. 2020, pp. 20–21). In New South Wales, foreign investors were obliged to pay 4% stamp duty on property transactions from June 2016 on top of the standard rate, rising to 8% in July 2017, with an additional 0.75% of total land value chargeable for a land tax, rising to 2% in July 2017. While they gave the impression of fiscal discipline, the taxes were considerably lighter than equivalent cooling measures in such peer cities as Hong Kong, Singapore, and Vancouver, and paled against the devaluation of the Australian dollar. The ensemble of fees, taxes, credit tightening, and rule enforcement had only a temporary effect on price growth for the first nine months of 2016 (Knight Frank Sydney 2017), and prices for established houses in Sydney rose another 17% in 2017. But the intervention had a chilling short-term effect on foreign investors, including those from China (Gottliebsen 2016), leading to an abrupt drop in investor loans in late 2015 and the first half of 2016 (Figure 4.2). Considerable anxiety was expressed in real estate circles that after 'a stellar run with Chinese purchases', the market for new apartment units in Sydney and Melbourne might collapse as access to new credit from the four major banks was impeded (Cole 2016; Chancellor 2017). However, shadow banks and other lending sources were found, the market rebounded, and a Credit Suisse report, based on stamp duty collected by state government, announced that from September

2016 to June 2017 a quarter of new housing supply in New South Wales was being bought by foreign purchasers, primarily from China, who were able to evade financial barriers erected both at home and in Australia (Janda 2017). But this was the last year of the boom. High prices had little room for further growth, and the barrage of measures by government and regulators in Australia and China finally began to bite.

Housing Policy: What Policy?

We have seen the instrumental use of the housing market during the 2013–2017 boom to provide a partial offset for dwindling foreign investment in the resource sector. Lower exchange rates and a low interest policy added fuel to the combustible mix of domestic asset-seeking, Chinese property capital, scarcely regulated investment flows through the FIRB, inflationary tax breaks on rental property, banks committed to growth through mortgage lending, and population increase (largely through immigration) in the high quality of life settings of Sydney and Melbourne. Existing severe problems of housing affordability and the plight of first-time home owners were held hostage before the entirely predictable conflagration of residential prices from 2013 to 2017.

Pawson et al. (2017) have rightly identified this institutional ensemble as a 'lightly regulated housing market'. A broad review of homeownership in Australia concluded that, like other 'market liberal' societies, 'Australia has very little formal housing policy' (Burke et al. 2020, p. 28). Housing outcomes are frequently tangential to financial policy or tax policy. Other recent scholarship concurs: 'We have not, in this research or earlier papers in the series, encountered a well-developed, explicit, planned and modelled housing market strategy for any metropolitan area or state in Australia' (McLennan and Long 2020, p. 10). Sydney itself is 'a city continually devoid of a dedicated housing policy' (Troy et al. 2020, p. 18). A historical explanation of *laissez-faire* in the property market may perhaps be found in the legacy of a colonial culture of individualism, invoking 'a strong, culturally embedded resistance to regulation, combined with an equally strong belief in the significance of homeownership and private property rights' (Gurran et al. 2016, p. 33).

Aside from a small residual supply of new units, support for social housing was largely suspended in government policy. At its peak in the 1980s state production of public housing had amounted to 12% of annual new stock, but with right to buy and other measures the public sector component has fallen to less than four percent of total dwelling units, low by the standards of advanced societies. Subsidised production has been short-term and exceptional, and there seems to be little appetite to do more. The 2007 federal Labor government did initiate several affordable rental programmes and committed over $5 billion to the construction of 20,000 social housing units as part of a stimulus plan (Yates 2013). But this output contrasts with a very much higher level of need, a national estimate of more than 500,000 affordable rental units. As we will see again in Vancouver, the years of neglect have taken their toll, and new initiatives have a hopeless backlog of affordable housing shortfalls to address (Yates 2011).[39]

Moreover, popular support for redirecting the *status quo* is uncertain. Labor's plan in 2016 for a substantial affordable rental program paid for by reducing existing tax concessions on rental investment was nixed by the electorate. Small grants to first-time home buyers, while welcome, have been scattered too wide and too thin to address the serious public policy failure, the affordability impasse confronting many younger Australians in attaining homeownership.[40] The primary achievement of the grant was as an economic stimulus encouraging buyers to bring forward their date of purchase and help fill the void of lost economic activity (Randolph et al. 2013). So though marketed as an aid to first time buyers, it has been an expensive economic lever, enabling 'government to enrol the housing market as stimulus' (Randolph et al. 2013, p. 71). The substitution of economic policy for social policy with no remainder is one of the repetitive characteristics of neoliberal governments, and the toolkit constructed from this ideology has rarely included social housing policies. Moreover, the popular planning policy of containment or densification may well sacrifice affordability in the pursuit of sustainability (Beer et al. 2007).

There has been a good deal of state hand-wringing over the affordability crisis in Sydney (and beyond), which has steadily worsened (Yates 2011; Phibbs and Gurran 2015). Media and populist anxiety precipitated a flurry of government activity, consuming much paper, committee work, and research time. But the crisis has deepened. Some authors emphasise the repressive regime of neoliberal ideology and practice in blocking appropriate policy directions (Beer et al. 2007). Others emphasise the advantageous placement of property industry lobbyists able to capture the policy agenda (Phibbs and Gurran 2015). The outcome in practice has been to highlight the role of market housing supply, and to contest apparent planning barriers that impede private sector construction. This was exactly the focus of Minister Hazzard's remarks at the 2013 *Home* conference. But housing supply has been strangely price-inelastic, with totals scarcely responsive to rising populations and prices. It is not as if supply cannot respond quickly and substantially to demand, as the remarkable multiplication of high-rise apartments in inner Sydney showed during the 2013–2017 boom. But these dwellings were built substantially for a local and foreign investor market, and not as affordable housing, the outcome promised by Mr. Hazzard and the short-lived UrbanGrowth NSW once 'hurdles' were removed.[41]

The private developer operating under market conditions was the mast to which Mr. Hazzard nailed his affordable housing colours. The results in terms of affordable production have been meagre. In a large urban renewal project in Sydney, where Landcom, as government land developer, was a leading player, and disruptive planning hurdles were absent, the affordable housing yield amounted to less than one percent of the first 11,000 units completed (Gurran et al. 2016). This miserly share was not expected to rise when the project was complete. The failure of supply is widely recognised and has been pointed out as a systemic weakness in the housing market (IMF 2018a). Its implications are severe, for if supply cannot respond effectively to demand pressures, those pressures are capitalised in higher prices (Burke et al. 2020). This price outcome (rather than a supply outcome) will add to the attractiveness of housing as an investment asset. And as investors swarm, anticipating capital gains, partly tax-forgivable, wealth polarisation is amplified, and low- and moderate-income groups face displacement from the housing market.

This scenario identifies a fundamental weakness in the asset-based welfare deal established by Australian politicians in the 1980s and 1990s (Adkins et al. 2020, 2021). It has continued as *de facto* policy to the present with wages in Australia growing by only 3.1% a year in a recession-free economy from 1999 to 2019 while property prices rose by an annual average of 7.6%. The trade-off sees a decline in real wage-based income and welfare benefits compensated for by homeowner privileges, including appreciating house prices and tax concessions to aid the acquisition of rental property. Using housing as an economic stimulus ensures prices are moving for the 65% who are homeowners and keeps the investors coming. Housing as asset-based welfare is perhaps the closest one can find to a consistent housing policy. But with acute affordability problems and declining homeownership, it is a policy that is building structural inequality into Sydney society.

Conclusion

'Housing has been turned into a financialized and debt-fuelled speculative asset class in which prices have decoupled from household incomes. In effect, the market became the policy.' (Randolph 2020, p. vi). The cheerful assumption in theory and policy of a binding relationship between wage levels and house prices for new entrants to the market has been undone. Their decoupling means that many purchasers are deploying wealth that has not emerged from the current labour market, while most of those depending on their job-related income for home payments are (without family assistance) increasingly out of luck or seriously overcommitted. Like other gateway cities, the penalised groups include the young (unless they receive intergenerational transfers) the newly arrived (unless they bring equity derived elsewhere) and lower-income groups generally. The winners are the already advantaged, those owners who chanced into early property ownership through the accident of date of birth, and local and foreign investors who have successfully leveraged existing wealth into continuing accumulation through property assets.

The 2013–2017 residential boom in Sydney bared these relationships. As Maurice Daly had shown for earlier booms, foreign players were very much in evidence. Australia's economic pivot to Asia drew the nation into a force field that has established significant economic contexts for national development, especially in the gateway cities of Melbourne and Sydney. First Japanese and then Chinese hunger for Australian raw materials proved the prelude for capital and tourist flows, and in the case of the Chinese both permanent settlement and the temporary migration of students seeking a western education and perhaps a western *pied-à-terre* for themselves and later their families. Their presence created a more hybrid Sydney, and one of the Asian values that intensified in the city was the culture of property, affecting in particular the downtown and inner-city apartment market, a market whose opportunities migrants and investors had learned in China, Hong Kong, Singapore, and elsewhere to be the primary source of wealth accumulation. The overseas rush of capital from China after 2010 brought not only property-seekers but also property-builders. In short order, large and small Chinese development companies arrived with considerable economic strength, buying downtown and inner-city sites for apartment construction. They serviced an existing market of residents and recent immigrants, and expanded it in a feedback loop to investors on the Mainland.

Australian financial policy openly facilitated these processes. Seeking new foreign capital sources, with investment in mineral exploration and development seemingly winding down, both interest rates and the exchange value of the dollar were allowed to fall. The FIRB, viewed from afar as a sensible filter to unregulated foreign investment, was in fact heavily underresourced, approved almost all applications, and had insufficient capacity to enforce conditions imposed on approvals. With the continuing growth of the housing markets of state capitals, banks had committed heavily to household mortgages. Their enthusiasm in the early years of the 2013–2017 boom to support investors with high loan-to-value and interest-only mortgages had to be reined in by prudential regulators. But investors were not only, indeed not primarily, foreign. Tax benefits from rental investment and the proven returns from residential assets drew many Australians into residential purchases. Though they included some weaker punters, the main beneficiaries of tax concessions were higher income groups with resources from available capital and home equity loans playing the Aussie rules of wealth accumulation.

It was exchange-value, the house as asset, not use value, the house as dwelling, that drove the boom. As investors joined the rapidly inflating market, first-time buyers withdrew in droves. In some months during 2014 and 2015, banks in New South Wales were granting a larger share of total loan value to investors than to owner-occupiers. Nor was housing a primary policy field. Economic policy drove interest rates down while currency value also fell; though the asset-seeking and inflationary vulnerabilities in the housing market were recognized, they were regarded as an acceptable risk. Even when affordable housing policies were legislated, like the first homeowners grant, they served also as a counter-cyclical economic stimulus. But first-time home buyers are an endangered group. As levels of homeownership fall, authors are seeing the Australian dream as a fading promise: 'ownership as a tenure has burnt itself out and private rental is the growth housing sector' (Burke et al. 2020, p. 71). But the largest group of households with housing stress problems are private renters, and affordable rental units are primarily located in the outer suburbs – like affordable ownership stock (Randolph and Holloway 2002).

While there is clearly a deficiency in supply of affordable housing, which the private sector seems unable to address, the participation of investors in the 2013–2017 boom highlights the role of asset-seeking demand, displacing first home buyers in Sydney like Hong Kong, Vancouver, and London. This development is consistent with the marketisation imperative of neoliberalism, and with the attendant commodification (and financialisation) of house as asset. There is a further trend in Australia, a nation that lies at the free market end of market liberalism (Burke et al. 2020, p. 60), and notably in Sydney. Ryan-Collins and Murray (2020) have observed that in half of the three-month intervals through the decade of the 2010s, the value of the median Sydney home inflated faster than the median wages of a full-time worker. As I was told by a property journalist: 'The small investor in bricks and mortar consolidates a very strong culture here'. Asset growth with derived rents define a rentier society, with a version of what Piketty (2014) called *les petits rentiers* as major beneficiaries.

In November 2020, during the COVID-induced recession, the Reserve Bank reduced its interest rate from 0.25% to 0.1% as a continuing incentive to consumption (Clayton and Pupazzoni 2020). The Bank hoped the change would also rein in the Australian dollar, which had risen some six percent from its pre-pandemic level, though remaining beneath its exchange level during most of the 2013–2017 boom. To raise inflation and encourage investment the Bank also announced a substantial quantitative easing programme. The stimulus was expected to enhance housing consumption and push up housing prices – and it did. Once again instead of housing policy, the housing market is being used as a vehicle of financial policy to inflate and float the economy, as it did ahead of the 2013–2017 boom. In fact, this relationship goes back further, for hadn't Maurice Daly written that 'in the 1970s, however, the most persuasive influence on variations of property values had been the changes in the supply of money' (Daly 1982, p. 134)? Maintaining high – and unaffordable – house prices seems to have become a policy necessity.

Events in Vancouver were strikingly similar during this same residential boom. But rather than repeating this chapter's analysis, with contextual variations, the next chapter focusses upon a significant difference between the two cities. In Vancouver political resistance to excessive unaffordability led to regime change, and a multi-pronged attempt to *re*regulate a socially dysfunctional housing market.

Notes

1. Landcom was formed in 1975 to provide affordable serviced land in Sydney's outer suburbs for home purchase. Over the years, Landcom moved closer to a private sector company, and extended its geographical reach, while holding to sustainability criteria. According to its website, its 'challenge is to balance community good with commercial gain'.
2. 1 AUD = 0.77 USD on 1 January 2021.
3. The largest spike during this period came in 1949 with the lifting of wartime price controls, animating a market whose real prices had fallen considerably below the 1880 index of 100. This pattern of unchanged real house prices between the late nineteenth century and the 1960s exists for many industrial economies (Knoll et al. 2017).
4. This chapter uses second quarter, nominal median prices for established (existing) houses in Greater Sydney from the Australian Bureau of Statistics (ABS 2020a). This series dates to 2002, and has been extended back to 1970 by Abelson and Chung (2004).
5. Sydney is invariably among global gateway cities that are assessed as overvalued and at risk of bubble formation in the *UBS Global Real Estate Bubble Index*. See also the discussion of a real estate bubble in Berry and Dalton (2004) and Egan and Soos (2014). With continuing price inflation, bubble talk rarely goes away (Khadem 2020).

6. The index is set at 100 when 30% of earnings are taken by mortgage payments for a median-priced house by a first-time buyer. A figure below 100 indicates a mortgage load greater than 30%. The Sydney index fell from 65 in December 2012 to near 50 in June 2017, corresponding to a mortgage load of about 45%.

7. Though widely used, the *Demographia* index has weaknesses, notably the omission of mortgage and tax rates, which significantly impact housing affordability. Nevertheless, the index offers a useful general national and international comparative metric over time.

8. Even before the 2013–2017 boom, key workers – teachers, nurses, police, firefighters, and paramedics – faced house prices more than five times their earnings in 84% of Sydney's local government areas (Bankwest 2011). Affordable LGAs were overwhelmingly in Sydney's outer ring. Of the five groups, only firefighters and police officers could afford a median-priced house in peripheral Penrith.

9. See Flynn (2017) for an international analysis of the depressing effect of expensive housing on family size.

10. Burke et al. (2020, p. 25) cite somewhat different results from different data bases, but maintain a substantial owner: tenant premium of 9:1 (for 2015–2016).

11. During the immigration peak from 1987 to 1990, the Australian population growth rate of 1.8% a year was the highest in the industrialised world (Burnley et al. 1997, p. 18). In recent census periods, Sydney has typically accounted for some 30% of Australia's foreign-born population growth (Hugo and Harris 2011).

12. See Rogers and Gibson (2021) for a critical assessment. The headline on Barangaroo's Fact Sheet reads, 'Barangaroo is reaffirming Sydney's position as Australia's global city'.

13. In an urban context, see amongst others, Hage (1998), Shaw (2007), and Porter (2018).

14. The extent to which race was a dominant category of human differentiation was illustrated by the influential Sydney geographer Griffith Taylor, who received some public notoriety by opposing the White Australia Policy in the 1920s (Strange 2010). He argued that 'Mongoloid' people should be admitted to Australia because they were better fitted than Europeans to thrive in the austere climatic conditions of the arid interior. Race classification continued to be a central element in Taylor's human geography, using such criteria as hair texture and a head breadth index. In his landmark edited volume, *Geography in the 20th Century* (Taylor 1953), he contributed a chapter on "Race and Geography" summarising his work naturalising racial classification.

15. An additional 37,000 Sydney residents in 2006 were born in Hong Kong. Over half of the Mainland and Hong Kong populations in Australia were living in Sydney in 2006 (Hugo and Harris 2011).

16. Clive Hamilton's *Silent Invasion* precipitated considerable anxiety in Australia about the alleged infiltration of Chinese influence into Australian society and politics, with the work of China's United Front agency guiding public opinion (Hamilton 2018). A similar sentiment was experienced in Canada in 2022–23.

17. The mission followed the signing of the China–Australia Free Trade Agreement in late 2015.

18. There was, however, a significant slowdown in investment in minerals and energy sources, reflecting potentially weaker market conditions. New investment approved by the Foreign Investment Review Board (FIRB) averaged almost $70 billion a year from 2007 to 2012, but fell to an average of only $20 billion a year from 2014 to 2019 (FIRB various years).

19. China's economic rebound from COVID-19 and its successful stimulus policy led to a dramatic rise in its share of Australian goods exports to 49% by mid-2020 (Cranston 2020; Smyth 2020), accentuating the question of Australia's trade vulnerability, and questioning the economic wisdom of the Morrison government's anti-Chinese posture.

20. The ABS data tabulate students by nationality not ethnicity. Including numbers from Hong Kong, Malaysia, Singapore, and elsewhere would make the ethnic Chinese population considerably larger.

21. A Parliamentary review of foreign investment in the housing market in 2014 criticised the assessment processes at the Treasury and FIRB as 'a systems failure'. Weakness in rule enforcement was opening the door to rule evasion. In response FIRB stated that a 10-fold increase in review time would be needed to achieve the proposed assessment level (Reuters 2014).

22. Compare also the tens of thousands of Suspicious Transaction Reports that swamp Hong Kong's hapless Joint Financial Intelligence Unit (Chapter 3).

23. The NSW government undertook an investigation of almost 200 allegedly illegal residential transactions involving FIRB files in 2015. One case involved the head of Evergrande, a top PRC developer, who had transgressed FIRB regulations by buying an existing home in an elite district through a shell company for $39 million. With the transaction deemed illegal, the property was compulsorily re-sold, to a Chinese–Australian businesswoman (Chancellor 2015).

24. The immigration-investment-real estate nexus provides rich pickings for examining the social construction of official statistics. The official score card of economic activity generated by business immigration in Canada, dutifully reproduced in government and media accounts, was an aspirational fabrication (Ley 2010). So too income data in the Canadian Census are heavily skewed in Vancouver by the failure among wealthy immigrants to report global incomes as required (Gordon 2022).

25. Until challenged by Vancouver City Council, off-shore sales in Asia of entire Vancouver condominium buildings had occurred around 1990. In some cases, these buildings were never marketed in Vancouver (Ley 2017).

26. The year of the Sino-British Declaration on the future of Hong Kong which guaranteed the colony's return to China in 1997, prompting a large exodus of wealthy and middle-income households for over a decade. See Chapters 3 and 5.

27. Li and Hendrischke (2020) identify 2012 as the key year the Chinese state liberalised overseas direct investment by companies. In 2013 the approval threshold for outward investment was raised from US$100 million to US$1 billion.

28. With a head office in Barangaroo, Lendlease has a major global presence: "We identified 17 target gateway cities. Today, we operate in 15 of these, of which ten feature major urbanisation projects" (Lendlease 2019). Lendlease has become associated with controversial inner-city regeneration projects in London (Chapter 6).

29. By July 2016 Aqualand, the Australian arm of a Shanghai property developer, had bought nine development sites in and around Sydney's CBD; its typical business plan was to add value by converting commercial space to luxury condominiums (Chen 2016). In addition, Aqualand entered a joint mixed-use development of Central Barangaroo, where it would build the commercial and luxury residential component; it increased its share in 2019 by buying out partner Oxford Properties, the real estate arm of Canadian pension fund OMERS (Tan 2019).

30. Wanda was then the most successful Chinese commercial developer and its flamboyant founder, Wang Jianlin, was China's wealthiest businessman. His purchase on Circular Quay, Gold Fields House, probably evoked earlier travels by Chinese seeking fortunes in the Australian goldfields. Wanda, however, was too ambitious by far in the scale of its overseas conquests in the US and Europe, and was placed on a regulator's watch list in 2017. It has been earnestly deleveraging to reduce its debt load; the Circular Quay property was divested to Chinese buyers in 2018.

31. See statements by David Irvine, Chair of FIRB and Carrie Law, chief executive of Juwai, in Smyth (2018).

32. At the same time, while recent migrants tend to follow the skilled visa options, it is important to remember Burnley's (2002) earlier documentation of the diversity of Chinese communities in Sydney.

33. But like their peers in Vancouver, these professionals and managers were often unable to replicate their success in Sydney, with serious family implications including the astronaut strategy, as families were fragmented between the place of family income in East Asia and the place of family residence in Sydney (Mak 2001).

34. About 7000 business and investment visas were awarded annually, so PRC applicants secured almost three-quarters of the total during these years.
35. In 2016 the EIU listed Melbourne in top place among the 140 global cities it ranked. Remarkably, Australia included 5 of the top 16 spots on the list (and Canada 3 of the top 6), granting both countries leverage in attracting footloose capitalists (Knight Frank Sydney 2017).
36. See Chapter 5 and Ley (2010, 2017).
37. See Zhang and Wang's (2019) examination of "property talk" among Chinese Australians through the WeChat app.
38. When an interest-only loan rolled over to a principal and interest loan, payments could increase by as much as 30–40% (Debelle 2018).
39. This has not daunted some incisive scholarship and public engagement, including Pawson et al. (2019) and Pawson et al. (2020). The latter concludes with short- and long-term proposals for addressing the affordable housing dilemma.
40. The First Home Owner Grant brought funds totalling $2.5b to Sydney in its first ten years (Randolph et al. 2013). Another grant programme, HomeBuilder, was launched in 2020 as part economic stimulus for construction and part homeowner assistance.
41. UrbanGrowth NSW was disbanded in 2019 after a short six-year life, and Landcom was resuscitated. Brad Hazzard left the Ministry of Planning and Infrastructure after three years. Lack of institutional and ministerial continuity compromise coherent short- and medium-term policy.

CHAPTER 5

Vancouver: From Housing Deregulation to Reregulation?

In landing upon this part of my diocese I am filled with a deep interest in its future. A vast city may one day pursue a world-wide commerce here. What shall it be? A spot devoted to restless competition & thirst for gain, or shall it exhibit to the world a people not slothful in business, fervent in spirit, serving the Lord?

(George Hills 1860, in Bagshaw 1996, p. 72)

That is the nature of the housing market … currently land and development is one of Canada's biggest exports.

(Egloff 2017, in Planner 2017)[1]

Like Sydney a coastal metropolis in a European settler society, Vancouver has an even shallower urban history. George Hills, first Anglican Bishop in the newly declared Colony of British Columbia, made his mainland landfall at New Westminster in February 1860, after the short sea crossing from the small community of Victoria on Vancouver Island. When Hills had landed in Victoria by steamer from England via San Francisco the month before, he encountered a raw frontier society disrupted by gold rush frenzy. Victoria itself had exploded from a village of several hundred around the Hudson's Bay fort to a noisy tent city with several thousand temporary migrants, with men constantly on the move to the gold deposits of the Fraser Canyon and beyond. Many were Americans arriving from the California goldfields, creating a geo-political chill in the vast territories, nominally claimed by Britain but unin-corporated, administered by the Hudson's Bay Company, and scarcely occupied by Europeans prior to the gold rush aside from a few small coastal settlements and scattered trading posts.

New Westminster, the trans-shipment point for Fraser River traffic inland, was one such settlement: impenetrable virgin forest only a year earlier,

Housing Booms in Gateway Cities, First Edition. David Ley.
© 2023 John Wiley & Sons Ltd. Published 2023 by John Wiley & Sons Ltd.

but in early 1860 a village of 300, Hills reported, plus a recently arrived garrison of Royal Engineers from Britain, commissioned to show the flag, provide policing, establish basic infrastructure, and conduct land surveying to allow regulated settlement (Harris 1997). Amid the arrival of republican Americans, among a motley crew of gold prospectors from Europe, China, and the eastern colonies of British North America, the disquiet of the Hudson's Bay Governor at their presence, and waxing support for annexation to the US both locally and in London, the Colony of British Columbia was hastily declared in the summer of 1858, and the Royal Engineers despatched. In New Westminster, the enterprising Hills met the local population, examined church sites, conducted religious services, and explored forest trails leading northward from the Fraser to the deep-water Burrard Inlet. He was told that the Inlet, to be the town site of Vancouver and its early suburbs, was the location of villages and camps of several First Nations but had no European settlement. The 'Native Question' troubled Hills. His diary entries recognised the European source of the disruption of aboriginal society, and recorded his outreach work with the indigenous population, including plans for village schools.

Although New Westminster was then the principal mainland settlement of the Province of British Columbia, which would enter Canadian Confederation in 1871, the site of the 'vast city … with world-wide commerce' that Hills correctly prophesied, would be some kilometres to the north on Burrard Inlet. Vancouver, founded in 1886 as terminus of the nation-binding, trans-continental Canadian Pacific Railway, had grown to a metropolis of over 2.5 million by 2021, absorbing New Westminster as a suburban satellite. Land and its sale have always been a preoccupation, sometimes an obsession. At the end of the 1880s when Vancouver had a population of 3,000, commercial services included 16 real estate firms and 12 grocers (Wynn 1992). With a frantic boom in the late 1900s, the city had over 1000 real estate agents by 1912, one for every 100 members of the population (Donaldson 2019). Property ownership was a priority for the culturally and demographically British settler society, with fortunes won and lost amid land speculation and real estate hucksters (Holdsworth 1977). Investment syndicates from London, New York, and Chicago fuelled the excesses of the 1908–1913 real estate boom and bust, with the overseas capital piling onto BC real estate skyrocketing by almost 1200% through the boom (Donaldson 2019). Besides supporting resource sector and infrastructure development, overseas capital flows from Britain and the United States supported the ventures of landowners and property developers, including British Pacific Properties, owned by the Guinness family, and London-based Grosvenor Estate, companies that remain active to the present.

In this chapter, the continuing dalliance with land among Vancouverites is examined for the period since the 1980s, while this historical prelude is a reminder that the present is the current act of a long-running play (Gutstein 1975; Donaldson 2019). Like other gateway cities, immigration remains the dominant source of metropolitan growth, and following liberalisation of Canada's immigration laws in the 1960s, a speedy transition occurred in the 1970s and 1980s from a European to an Asian plurality among new arrivals to Canada and especially to Vancouver (Ley 1995, 2010). By the 1980s a new frontier was opening for commerce, immigration, and capital, no longer in Europe, but now (like Australia) in Asia Pacific. British Columbians grasped this opportunity, leading to a renewed immigrant rush for land. In its 'restless competition and thirst for gain' the post-colonial society has clear continuities with the youthful colonial society revealed in Hills' diary. He would have been interested, too, by the improbable role played by the descendants of the First Nations he thoughtfully observed in 1860, suddenly active agents in Vancouver's housing market in the 2020s.

While the story of Vancouver's housing market growth since the milestone of the 1986 world's fair is reviewed, the principal objective of this chapter is to examine attempts to *re*regulate a housing market made dysfunctional by the incessant flow of unregulated investment capital and the marketisation of state policy within a neoliberal regime. Substantial golden visa immigration, in addition to offshore buyers, established a strong transnational residential sales network between Vancouver and East Asia after 1986, adding significant speculative investment to local demand. By 2016, the aspiration of homeownership as asset-based welfare had reached a dead end for many residents. With modest incomes and exorbitant prices, Vancouver had been the least affordable city in North America for a decade. The decoupling of housing and labour markets under the auspices of an uncritical growth coalition had decimated affordability, precariously inflated mortgage debt loads, shut out first-time buyers, and aggravated spiralling inequality. Pressures had diffused into the rental market, where older, affordable rental buildings were demolished and replaced by unaffordable condominiums, attractive to local and off-shore investors. With widespread gentrification, displaced tenants adjusted their housing goals downwards, and those on the bottom rung of the housing ladder fell off, leading to abiding homelessness.

After a renewed investment surge (like Sydney's) from 2013–2016, affordability became a serious local irritant and led (unlike Sydney) to political reversals in regional and federal elections. Politicians were defeated who had welcomed the asset-based model of capital gains from investment-fuelled house price inflation. In the space of three years, 2015–2018, elections brought new municipal, provincial, and federal governments with manifestos to redirect deregulated and unaffordable residential real estate away from an exclusive emphasis on unhindered markets, the assumption of homeownership with wealth accumulation through price increases, and towards a paradigm of government intervention, demand management, and a supply emphasis on rental tenure. This chapter examines the continuing efforts to address a housing crisis by reregulating aspects of the housing market through taxation-driven demand cooling and the revival, after 25 years of neglect, of construction and renovation of social housing. Simultaneously, weak institutions overseeing the investment–real estate nexus have been strengthened, and the excesses of market opportunism have been curtailed. A federal National Housing Strategy has been launched. But the deregulated past leaves a heavy legacy that cannot easily be corrected.

A broader remit of this chapter is to contribute to the small literature that examines attempts to reregulate housing markets towards use value and social justice objectives in the post-GFC period (Wijburg 2021), even if it underscores the difficulty of this challenge and the stubborn tendency for deregulated, financialised markets to be self-sustaining (Stellinga 2022). Consequently, this chapter presents a fuller engagement than others with political change and policy innovations. The wider significance of recent trends in Vancouver is that they address the question, what is possible beyond asset-based welfare?

Vancouver Housing: The Back Story

A staple-based export economy, derived from abundant forests, mineral resources, and salmon fisheries, propelled British Columbia through its first century as a province, with Vancouver its primary entrepot.[2] But interest rates of 20% brought the 1970s to a calamitous close, precipitating a bust in a speculative housing bubble, where prices had virtually doubled from 1979–1981, and leading to a three percent decline in homeownership in Vancouver from 1980–1982 (Harris 1986; Skaburskis 1988). A deep recession followed, with the resources-led provincial economy contracting by 8% in 1982, and unemployment reaching double digits for most of the decade (Barnes et al. 1992). A right-wing provincial government introduced a familiar neoliberal suite of service cutbacks, privatisation, deregulation, and entrepreneurial forays, notably the World's Fair, Expo 86, held in Vancouver.

Simultaneously, the economic success story of the 1980s was the growth of Asia Pacific, notably Japan and the four tiger economies. For an exhausted economy in British Columbia, opportunities beckoned (Goldberg 1985; Ley 2010). Vancouver secured sister city relations with Guangzhou, and all three levels of Canadian government led frequent trade missions to Asia Pacific to prime sales and investment. In 1989, Canada became a founding member of the Asia Pacific Economic Co-operation network, providing a forum for Pacific Basin initiatives. Expo 86 was held as a marketing venture, with an eye to attracting further interest from East Asian investors, and in an act of supreme symbolic and material significance, at the close of the Fair the entire Expo site was sold to a Hong Kong consortium, led by Li Ka-shing, Hong Kong (and China's) most successful property developer (Olds 2001). Within a few years, Hong Kong's four largest development companies were engaged in major projects in and around downtown Vancouver. This initial landfall of housing development capital launched a transnational field of real estate investment that has continued ever since, for as I was told by a Hong Kong-Canadian realtor a few years later, 'Where the big fish swim, the smaller fish follow' (Ley 2010, p. 55).

The initial attraction of Vancouver for Hong Kong property investors was that it permitted portfolio diversification in a city with very positive growth potential, on the shortest air route from Hong Kong to a North American urban centre, and it contained an established ethnic Chinese population providing economic and cultural resources. But there was also a geopolitical event, the impending return of the British colony of Hong Kong to Mainland China in 1997, that encouraged the dispersion not only of capital but also of capitalists. And here Canada held a trump card: its Business Immigration Program (BIP) that provided liberal entry to immigrants who qualified to enter Canada either as *entrepreneurs*, committed to start or take over a business employing at least one Canadian, or as *investors*, initially venture capitalists but in later years investors in funds secured by the provincial government (Ley 2003, 2010). The BIP proved very popular to wealthy Hong Kong families and to a substantial number of Taiwanese – equally concerned by Chinese geopolitical ambitions – who landed in British Columbia in the 1990s. Mainland Chinese dominated the BIP after 2000. Including all entry streams, the small territory of Hong Kong was the leading source of immigrants to Canada for the decade following Expo 86, with the BIP the primary vehicle for bringing High Net Worth Individuals (HNWIs) from Greater China to the Vancouver housing market.

Though the BIP was always a smaller element in Canada's suite of immigration options, its clients have been strongly concentrated in Toronto and especially Vancouver. Among the investor stream, the wealthiest immigrants, it has been estimated that half landed in British Columbia, essentially Vancouver (Ware et al. 2010). Over the period 1980–2012, and including secondary migration primarily from Quebec, some 200,000 people arrived in Vancouver through the BIP, a large enough population to have impact in the housing market of a metropolitan area of two million in 2001 (Ley and Tutchener 2001; Moos and Skaburskis 2010). Capital flows accompanied the capitalists. Even in the early 1990s, banks were estimating annual fund transfers of $2-$4 billion from Hong Kong to Canada (Mitchell 2004; Ley 2010, pp. 67–73).[3] By visa definition, business immigrants were millionaires; even in the mid-1990s individual investor immigrants had on average available liquid capital of around $2.25 million. Including the entrepreneur stream of the BIP, between them the 1988–1997 cohorts of the two BIP groups had available funds of around $35–$40 billion for deployment in Vancouver. Wealthy migrants moved rapidly into homeownership at a rate substantially higher than the rest of the population and purchased additional investment properties (Ley 2010; Hiebert 2017).[4] Indeed, income derived from real estate and rental leasing was by far the largest revenue source in Canada for Investor-class immigrants (CIC 2014, Table 5.6).

With a Greater Vancouver population of half a million by 2021, the Chinese-Canadian residential market can support its own enclave economy of builders and real estate agencies. Among the largest, Royal Pacific Realty was founded by a Hong Kong immigrant in 1995 and 20 years later numbered 1200 staff, working primarily within a transnational field of ethnic Chinese immigrants and Asia Pacific investors in Vancouver's high-priced neighbourhoods (Royal Pacific Realty 2015). Its most successful agent sold more than 100 properties each year from 1990 to 2014 (Ley 2017). Advertising in Vancouver's *Sing Tao, Ming Pao, World Journal* (Taiwan) and *China Journal*, provided her listings seamless coverage to buyers from Hong Kong, Taiwan, and the People's Republic of China (PRC). A long-established Vancouver agency, and to become the largest independent real estate company in Western Canada, Macdonald Realty, pivoted to East Asia under its Taiwanese-born CEO, and opened marketing offices in Hong Kong and Shanghai. The company announced that 21% of its City of Vancouver residential sales in 2014 priced from $1 to $3 million were bought by purchasers from Mainland China, and 70% of properties priced in excess of $3 million (Lee 2015). Macdonald's experience has been confirmed by a release from the new Canadian Housing Statistics Program showing that recent immigrants (landing 2009–2016) owned detached houses with assessed values more than 50% higher than Canadian-born residents, while Investor-class immigrants from China owned houses with an average assessment at $3.3 million, over twice the value of the Canadian-born (Gellatly and Morissette 2019).

Large Vancouver property developers are attentive to the Chinese market locally and in East Asia. Concord Pacific was created by Li Ka-shing's 1988 consortium to redevelop the Expo 86 lands. It has maintained a Hong Kong sales office, as it has expanded from its Vancouver base through Western

Canada, Toronto, Seattle, and to London (UK). No less attuned to the Asian market is Westbank, with residential projects primarily in Canada, the western United States and Japan, and six marketing offices in East Asia. Its Director of Marketing and Sales acknowledged on the company's web site that 'China is now a big part of this business. … right now I have a rule when we talk about projects, if the Chinese market doesn't want it, I have no interest in it' (Westbank nd). Westbank's business model demonstrates the importance of speculative residential purchase of Vancouver residential property among East Asian investors, in part through the weekend property fairs at luxury hotels which have also been so important for Sydney and London condominium sales (see Chapter 6). These global investors have contributed to the disruption of a national narrative of asset-based welfare in Vancouver.

Ownership, Assets, Gains

Explicit in the formation of a transnational residential market stretching across the Pacific is a discourse and practice of market relations stewarding homeownership as the 'natural' model of urban development (Lauster 2016). This understanding expanded to fill the vacuum left by the state's abdication of its social housing role (Suttor 2016). Renewed recession in Canada in the early 1990s raised the demand for welfare services beyond the capacity of government revenues, as the national debt ballooned from $250 billion in 1981 to over $800 billion in 1994 (in 2019$). In its radical 1994 budget the federal government slashed services, including its commitment to new subsidised housing production; five of six social housing programmes that had produced over 500,000 units were abruptly terminated (Carter 1997). Aside from modest initiatives addressing homelessness and deeply disadvantaged groups, for the next 25 years the market monopolised housing production.

A free-market solution to housing fitted snuggly with British Columbia's right-wing Liberal government, in power from 2001 to 2017. The government was a dedicated partner with the property industry in propelling a real estate growth machine (Ley 2021).[5] Property companies were the single largest group of donors to the BC Liberal party, and from 2013 to 2017 its chief fund raiser was Bob Rennie, the 'Condo King', who led a very successful Vancouver real estate marketing company. Both government and the property sector saw huge benefits to the investment that flowed freely into Vancouver's real estate. For the Province it significantly enhanced tax revenues, while the growing equity among homeowners was intended to produce a satisfied and pliant electorate who had shown the good sense to invest in BC land and property. High residential prices were a commendation for good government. At the peak of a boom in 2016 that had decimated housing affordability, the Finance Minister could see only good news: 'It's a challenge that virtually every other jurisdiction would like to have, because it is a challenge that is associated with a growing economy' (Hager 2016).

By their own lights, the Liberals had scored highly during their period in power (Figure 5.1). From 2001 to 2010, real benchmark prices[6] for detached houses in Greater Vancouver rose from $494,000 to $929,000; in the next six years growth accelerated to $1.69 million. While median real family incomes rose a meagre 26% during the Liberal administrations from 2001 to 2017, real prices accelerated by 242%. The gap had been stark enough earlier, for real incomes *declined* by 5% from 1986 to 2001, while detached houses added $209,000 (42%) in value. Decoupling of this magnitude makes a nonsense of attributing prices to local incomes. The ratio between real prices and real incomes rose from 4.5 in 1986, the Expo year, to 8.1 in 2001, when provincial Liberals came to power, and to 22.3 in 2017, the year they were voted out of office. The annual rate of return to an investor or homeowner over that 15-year period would provide an impressive and sustained bonanza. Ian Young, the *South China Morning Post's* savvy Vancouver correspondent, laconically wrote that 'In Vancouver, house owners made more sitting on their assets than [the] entire population did by actually working last year' (Young 2016a). Rentier capitalism rode on the back of asset-based homeownership.

Vancouver, like Sydney (Chapter 4) and other gateway cities, had received a further flood of investment with major capital flight from China between mid-2014 and the end of 2016, when the PRC's foreign exchange reserves were depleted by close to a trillion US dollars.[7] The volume of home sales hit an all-time record in Greater Vancouver in 2015, as real detached house prices

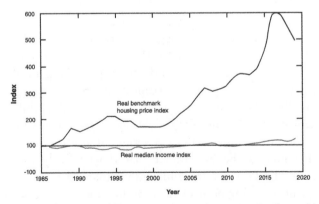

FIGURE 5.1   Real house price and income indices, Vancouver CMA, 1986–2019. (Sources: adapted from REBGV (various dates); Statistics Canada 2021b)

rose 18% during 2015, and a further 29% in 2016. Vancouver's Mayor Robertson, formerly in denial of the role of offshore investment capital, reversed his position after speaking to the mayors of Sydney and New York: 'We're among a group of big cities that have attracted billions of dollars each in investment … it's hit us like a ton of bricks' (Fumano 2017a).

Price inflation well above the Greater Vancouver mean had occurred in Vancouver's Westside, with the strongest absolute gains, and also the suburbs of Richmond and West Vancouver (Figure 5.2). Richmond, adjacent to Vancouver International Airport, with an ethnic Chinese plurality, has the highest immigrant share of any Canadian municipality. West Vancouver, stretching from Burrard Inlet up the North Shore mountains, offering city and ocean views, is the wealthiest suburb, while the city's Westside, closer to downtown, contains some of the most expensive neighbourhoods in the region. Business immigrants are highly concentrated in these three districts, which include 21 out of the 22 census tracts in the metropolitan area in 2011 with very high location quotients for recent wealthy arrivals: Vancouver Westside had ten such tracts, Richmond, eight and West Vancouver, three.[8] Prices fell consecutively moving eastwards from these three districts through the metropolitan area. A ripple effect was present with price changes tending

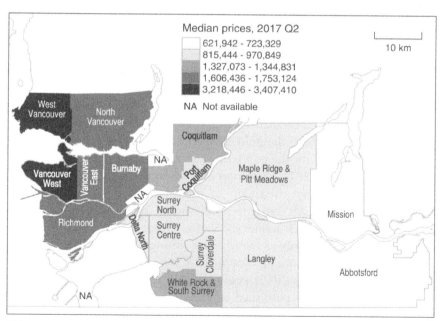

FIGURE 5.2   Median house prices, Vancouver municipalities, June 2017. (Sources: Adapted from Grigoryeva and Ley 2019)

to spread outwards over time from the most expensive districts, notably from the primary epicentre of Vancouver's Westside (Grigoryeva and Ley 2019).[9]

Substantial asset gains for existing owners represent asset penalties for new buyers and the next generation who must pay the steep entry price to this sequestered real estate. The lobby group Generation Squeeze (2020) has presented this inter-generational zero-sum game effectively, computing that average home prices in Metro Vancouver would have to fall by *three-quarters* to be affordable to a typical 25–34 year-old worker; at present this young adult must work full-time for 26 years to save a 20% deposit on that average home. Exclusion from ownership and the wealth accumulation accompanying might well provide grounds for residential alienation.

Spring 2015: An Emerging Counter-Narrative

We learned earlier that Larry Fink, Chairman and CEO of BlackRock, had recommended that 'The two greatest stores of wealth internationally today is [sic] contemporary art ... and two, the other store of wealth today is apartments in Manhattan, apartments in Vancouver, in London' (Burgos and Ismail 2015). Sales and affordability trends in Vancouver indicated that Fink's remarks had located a money trail. Nominal price gains in 2015 for the previous decade for all residential types in Greater Vancouver had averaged almost 8% a year, and close to 11% for detached houses (REBGV 2015). Districts favoured by wealthy Asia Pacific immigrants had done even better over the decade: 17% a year average gains in Vancouver's elite Westside neighbourhoods, 13% in Richmond, and 12% in the expensive suburb of West Vancouver.

Other institutional metrics concurred. The Royal Bank's Housing Affordability index[10] continued its irrepressible upward march in the first quarter of 2015, reaching the unlikely level of 86% of gross average household income required for the purchase of an average Vancouver-area bungalow (RBC Economics 2015). A second metric was provided the same year by the annual affordability assessment of metropolitan housing markets by *Demographia*, comparing median house prices with median household incomes: a ratio above 5.1 defines the worst category, severe unaffordability. Vancouver was second only to Hong Kong among a suite of cities in lack of affordability, and its disturbing ratio of 10.6 was its highest since the survey began (Cox and Pavletich 2015). Adding fuel to the fire that spring, the largest regional credit union published an alarming forecast on labour market-housing market relations. The report anticipated significant out-migration by qualified workers driven from Vancouver by their desire for affordable ownership of a detached home (Vancity 2015). With current trends, in only five years and even assuming dual income households, the median incomes of 82 out of 88 in-demand positions, including police officers, general practitioners, and civil engineers, would fall below the necessary housing cost threshold.[11] The housing crisis would precipitate a labour crisis. This extraordinary mismatch between wage returns and housing costs overturned any conventional model of a tight relation between local wage incomes and local house prices.

In this dire housing context, Larry Fink's investment recommendation was cited by David Eby, an opposition New Democratic Member in the BC Legislature, during question period on 14 May 2015 to Rich Coleman, Liberal Deputy Premier and Minister Responsible for Housing.[12] Eby asked whether the minister intended to measure the level of international (and domestic) speculative investment in Vancouver's market. Minister Coleman replied: 'I will tell the member that it has virtually nothing to do with the ministry for housing at all … Government doesn't have any policy around this … we do not discriminate against foreign ownership … the reason it [housing] is attractive internationally is because it's pretty reasonable compared to other cities like London, Singapore, Tokyo … There's no initiative at this time in government to go and interfere in the marketplace with regards to housing' (Hansard 2015).

Three features of this declaration to do nothing draw attention. First, was the remarkable claim by the Housing Minister that Vancouver house prices were 'pretty reasonable' compared to others when the RBC index identified a housing crisis, while the *Demographia* standing rated Vancouver's affordability as considerably more dire than London's or Singapore's. The fallibility of the Minister's response was self-evident. Second, was the claim that the question of foreign ownership had nothing to do with government. This was equally contestable, for Canadian governments had led trade and investment missions to Asia since the 1980s, and had used the instrument of business immigration to attract entrepreneurs and their property capital to Vancouver. Third, was the Minister's reluctance to gather property ownership data to gauge the level of foreign investment in the housing market, action requested by growing public agitation, but regarded by the Minister as unwarranted 'interference' in the marketplace. The Minister had made a similar reply to a question on foreign ownership in a media interview: 'It's not come up as an issue for us' (CTV 2015). The provincial Liberal Party's unwavering support for growth machine outcomes, with homeownership shaping asset-based welfare, allowed no place on a Cabinet agenda for transparency or corrective measures.

The lack of statistical data about who owned Vancouver's housing could then become a convenient excuse for fobbing off critics. Complaints by residents that international investors were uncoupling labour-housing relationships, lead-ing to a lack of affordability and related hardships, were met by the BC and City of Vancouver governments with the response that any evidence of such activity was merely anecdotal and thus not credible. But as Minister Coleman made clear, there was no intention by government to collect such data and provide unambiguous answers. Larry Fink's statement, it seems, was just another anec-dote. A second string to the bow of investment deniers was a blanket charge of racism against anyone – including Chinese-Canadians – who suggested that capital from Asia-Pacific was inflating the Vancouver market (Fung 2016).

However, public events intervened, even if the Minister would not. In frustration at the cost of housing, and the departure of even well-paid friends from Vancouver, Eveline Xia, previously a non-political young professional, started a Twitter account in spring 2015, with the #Don'tHave1Million (MacQueen 2015). She publicised the grave issue of affordable housing for professionals and other labour force members, with the benchmark price for a detached home in Greater Vancouver having exceeded $1 million. Other housing events coincided with her campaign, including a downtown confer-ence, *HOUSE: Rethinking the Housing Affordability Crisis*, in early May, and the releases of the *Demographia* and Vancity reports, attracting a media scrum and creating some political traction. Xia's message generated significant local support and a downtown rally was held, and then a second, with participa-tion from some opposition politicians, beneath the slogan 'Give us data'. Her campaign was raised in Question Time in Parliament, and caught the atten-tion of Vancouver's Mayor, who called for a property speculation tax. Mayor Robertson (an earlier denier of investor culpability) wrote publicly to the Premier of BC, Christy Clark, on 22 May requesting the tax and other hous-ing reforms. With surprising speed Premier Clark responded (publicly) with the party line that any housing interventions might compromise the equity asset of existing homeowners and suggested that the city reduce its own prop-erty fees and taxes to aid affordability. Housing assets were a sacred trust for this government; if they were protected, there was no housing problem.

Though Minister Coleman had told the Legislative Assembly that no studies and no data were available on foreign residential investment, with growing public dissent (Young 2015), the Premier in her letter to Mayor Robertson referred to a short report prepared by the Ministry of Finance, with data from the BC Real Estate Association (BCREA). The flimsy analysis by a growth machine partner – quickly debunked by local specialists – denied the significance of foreign investment in the housing market, a practice repeated since the first round of sharp house price increases after 1988 (Mitchell 2004; Ley 2010). The Premier's source of authority was the vested interest of the BCREA. The province's coffers, as well as property industry bottom lines, have benefitted greatly from East Asian capital flows. Each investor household that arrived in the Business Immigration Program (BIP) selecting BC as a destination brought the province their mandated loan of $400,000 (later $800,000), available without interest for five years. Not surprisingly, managers at Citizenship and Immigration Canada in Ottawa had earlier informed me that the provincial governments were the principal lobbyists for the BIP. Indeed, when the federal government had turned the screws on the BIP, threatening new financial disclosure legislation in the late 1990s over allegations of immigrant tax avoidance, the left-of-centre New Democratic Premier of BC had been one of the BIP's strongest advocates (Ley 2013). In a letter to the federal government, Finance Minister Petter resisted the threatened disclosure law, which 'has led to fears of increased taxation and appears to have weakened Canada's international reputation as an attractive place for individuals to reside and invest. This is of particular concern to British Columbia because the recent influx of new residents has been a major source of economic growth in the province ... We have fears that people will not come or will leave' (cited in Chow 1997). The convergence of interests between the BC provincial governments and the property sector encourages the same perception of collusion that many Hong Kong people saw between the property tycoons and their own government (Chapter 3).

By summer 2015 the housing issue had gained media traction as house prices continued their upward momentum. I was informed by a local journalist that newsroom editors were encouraging staff to find housing stories for an insatiable public interest, and newspapers were funding costly investigative journalism on real estate topics. With gravity-defying price increases, plunging affordability, and implacable provincial government denials of offshore investment, or indeed that a housing problem existed, stories were not hard for journalists to find: 'Something is grotesquely wrong with Vancouver's housing market, and the time for denialism is over' (Young 2015); 'Why don't we have real estate data?' (McMartin 2015); 'First step: Accept there's a problem' (Gold 2015). Civil society was rousing.

The Angus Reid Survey and the Shaking of an Ideology

The Angus Reid Foundation is a non-profit, non-partisan research institute dedicated to a fuller understanding of a wide range of national and international trends and issues of public interest. In light of widespread public concern, the Institute undertook a survey of housing issues in June 2015 with an on-line representative sample of over 800 Vancouver residents, both owners and renters

(Angus Reid 2015). Its statistically valid findings, reflected and contributed to the swirl of public fascination and frustration around housing. The report, *Lotusland Blues*, added to the spectre of a deeply troubled housing market in need of urgent correction. By denying a problem existed, elected officials showed the extent of the growing gap between their housing ideology of asset-based welfare and the experience of those they governed.

The Angus Reid survey found that its sample could be divided into four ideal types based on housing experience: the happy, the comfortable, the uncomfortable, and the miserable. Together happy and comfortable groups amounted to 55% of respondents. Theirs was a predictable profile. They were largely homeowners, outright owners or with manageable mortgages. They were likely to be aged over 55, were retired, or lived fairly close to work. They were more likely to be Liberal (politically conservative) in provincial elections, and were fortunate beneficiaries of an asset ideology with enviable rewards for long-time homeowners. In contrast, uncomfortable or miserable respondents (45%) were split between owners and tenants. They had larger families at home and were younger. As newer buyers they had larger debt loads, while a number of tenants were priced out of ownership, though it was their preferred tenure. These groups lived further from job opportunities and had lengthier commutes. They were more likely to have supported New Democrats (left of centre) in past elections. All four groups affirmed that housing was the most important issue facing metropolitan Vancouver.

A striking finding was that the miserable had the highest share of university graduates, but also a high level of residential alienation (Madden and Marcuse 2016). Their solution was to exit, with a remarkable 85% seriously considering departing metro Vancouver. Here was validation for Eveline Xia's #Don'tHave1Million campaign, plus the recently completed Vancity (2015) survey that showed an unaffordable ownership market confronting young professionals in strategic occupations. A small majority of the uncomfortable category shared the same sentiment, so that overall, 43% of all respondents were anticipating exit, 'seriously thinking of leaving Metro Vancouver because of the cost of owning a home here.' To an asset ideology, such an outcome was regrettable but politically manageable as long as it remained a minority view. A housing as asset ideology assumes market rationality, that homeowners will vote in their best economic interests and support policy that advances their wealth accumulation. Most respondents seemed to fit that profile, and the provincial Liberals played to their bias. In response to a journalist's question about cooling a hot housing market, following precedents in other cities, the Minister of Finance replied: 'If by cool you mean actually reduce the value of people's major asset, their home, clearly we're not interested in taking that step' (Jang 2016).

A survey (and my participant observation) showed, however, that residents, even homeowners, are more complex in their value commitments than market rationality allows for. During this period, at a number of community and media presentations on Vancouver's housing crisis, I encountered one deeply held anxiety from audiences more frequently than any other: 'I'm worried about my children. What will they do for housing? Where will they live?' This response appeared decisively in the Angus Reid survey, with 87% expressing worry that the next generation would find ownership unaffordable in their community. To the extent that the ideology of the asset economy reduces the identity of citizens to commodity consumers advancing their personal economic interests, it projects a one-dimensional marionette that misrepresents the complexity of human decision-making. For residents held plural, indeed competing, values. Even the desire for capital gains had limits if they corrupted the life chances of children and grandchildren, an eventuality that Liberal Party asset ideology did not accommodate.

Survey results indicated that the happy and comfortable groups recognised that while they were benefitting from inflationary house price trends, these trends were hurting their communities and the overall metropolitan region (Angus Reid 2015). A large majority of both owners and tenants described home prices in Metro Vancouver as 'unreasonably high', with a consensus that the problem was caused primarily by investment by 'foreigners' and 'wealthy people'. There was also a consensus that different levels of government had responded poorly on the housing file. Dissatisfaction ran high, expressed by 68% against municipal government and 72% against the provincial government (Angus Reid 2015). Most ominously for the provincial government, 58% who had previously voted Liberal were dissatisfied with a housing policy that had accomplished little other than inflate their property assets. By almost a two-to-one margin, and reflecting concerns expressed for their children's housing prospects, respondents (well over half of them owners) advocated for the affordability of first-time buyers and *against* protecting the investments of existing owners. A clear plurality of all four housing types rejected an emphasis on asset protection. Even more explicit was response to a question on government intervention *vs.* free market policy: 70% agreed that, 'Government should be more involved in the housing market in order to improve affordability', with only 30% affirming that, 'Government should stay out of the housing market. The free market should determine prices.' (Angus Reid 2015, p. 11). A similarly high plurality of respondents endorsed an array of state interventions: taxation policy to cool the market, limits on foreign property purchase, and collection and publication of data on the names of property owners, including home addresses.

Just as the precise relationship between attitudes and behaviour is contentious, it is always an empirical question to what extent political opinion will lead to political action. If many of Angus Reid's respondents were considering an exit strategy from Greater Vancouver's toxic housing market, in an act of political agency more chose an active voice in electoral politics (Hirschman 1970). The result of the 2017 provincial election proved that the dysfunction of the housing market undermined loyalty to the provincial Liberals' ideology of asset-based accumulation.

Governments and Elections: All Change

The media maintained a continuing flow of investigative stories from 2015 to 2017 that opened up new fronts in revealing the dysfunction of the unregulated, market-knows-best housing strategy. They included disclosures on the frequent use of tax havens as sources of Vancouver property investment, with disproportionate Vancouver entries among the Panama Papers (Young 2016b), while a related series of stories on money-laundering revealed the chronic vulnerability of Vancouver real estate as a result of compliance loopholes in legal, real estate, and banking practices (Cooper 2016; Tomlinson 2016a); the existence of tax evasion, likely extensive, was mooted in real estate deals financed by offshore capital (Young 2016c), while pre-sale residential flipping was identified as a source of price inflation and probable further tax evasion (Tomlinson 2016b; Gold 2017); rebuttals were made of charges of racism against critics who discussed real estate investment from offshore capital (Fung 2016; Todd 2021); and potential collusion between growth machine partners, local and provincial governments and the property sector, was raised (Hoekstra 2017).

Opinion polls confirmed the continuing unpopularity of the provincial Liberal government revealed in the 2015 Angus Reid survey. The residential market was out of control, with the composite Greater Vancouver price[13] up 32% between June 2015 and June 2016. Eventually, responding to mounting public frustration, in July 2016 the provincial government broke with its real estate allies and hastily introduced a 15% tax on offshore purchases of Greater Vancouver residential property, belatedly mimicking precedents in Singapore and Hong Kong. Not only was the government making an abrupt policy shift, but it was also admitting what it had previously denied, that offshore capital was a significant factor in house price inflation, just as a majority of citizens had asserted.[14] The real estate boom was temporarily checked, and the composite residential benchmark price fell by two percent in the second half of 2016, and by five percent for detached houses alone. But this still left an average detached house price of almost $1.5 million across metropolitan Vancouver. For the survival of the provincial Liberal government, the action was too little and too late.

In contrast, the Official Opposition, the left-of-centre New Democratic Party (NDP), presented a set of strong interventionist housing policies that included construction of over 100,000 affordable rental and co-op housing units over the next decade, a significant number against a provincial population of 4.6 million in 2016, a number of rental safeguards, and a vacant homes tax on absentee speculators. A task force (later the Cullen Commission) to combat real estate money laundering and tax fraud was also promised. By 2018 these policies had developed into a comprehensive 30-point housing plan (Province of British Columbia 2018), incorporating a number of the demand management policies advocated by the electorate in the 2015 Angus Reid survey.

With housing regarded as the primary regional issue in both 2015 and a later 2018 Angus Reid survey, the NDP's proposals landed in rich electoral soil. In the May 2017 provincial election, the Liberals had to run on the results of their market friendly, housing as asset ideology, while the NDP presented a critical revision endorsing regulation and social provision. The election results gave the NDP a just viable one-seat majority with the support of Green Party members. The NDP gained the 10 seats it needed for victory in Vancouver and its suburbs. The swing to the party was highest in the new suburbs, the homes of the larger, younger families whose housing experience had been either 'Uncomfortable' or 'Miserable' in the 2015 Angus Reid Survey[15]. The new NDP government adopted many of the cooling measures endorsed by respondents in the Reid survey.

The first clue to the critical mood of the electorate to political incumbents had come in the October 2015 Federal Election with the displacement of the Conservative government. The federal Liberal Party,[16] led by the energetic Justin Trudeau, declared an election slogan of 'Real Change (Now)' and took up an unfamiliar campaign position as the most left-leaning of the major parties. In visits to Toronto and Vancouver, Trudeau promised a more interventionist position on housing, with tax incentives for building and renovating rental units, and with funds to repair and construct social housing. In a then vaguely formulated national housing strategy Liberals promised to resume leadership of the housing file which they had largely abandoned in 1994. The electorate turned nationally against Conservatives with an extraordinary renewal of federal Liberal fortunes.[17] In metropolitan Vancouver, federal Liberals made substantial gains.

The final electoral reversal and dismissal of incumbents occurred at the municipal level. Vision Vancouver had been formed as a left of centre municipal party but in the public eye had failed to check the relentless pace of neighbourhood change or address desperate affordability problems (Hutton 2019). Indeed, there were public perceptions that Vision had grown too close to the development industry. Endless condominium development was forcing up land prices, but providing units affordable only to investors and retirees downsizing from a detached dwelling. In 2014, Vision had elected the mayor and seven of the ten councillors. Consistent with the Angus Reid polls of 2015 and 2018 local government was also held responsible for the dysfunctional housing market, and Vision lost all of its council seats in the 2018 election. Seeing the writing on the wall, the three-term Vision Mayor, Gregor Robertson, decided to retire and not contest the election.

Between two housing surveys in 2015 and 2018 the mood of survey respondents soured further (Angus Reid 2018). Responses were very similar in 2018, but a more pessimistic sentiment of residential alienation had set in. The share of respondents happy with their circumstances had shrunk, while the group classed as miserable had risen. Significantly, 20% of owners (and 67% of renters) hoped to see a market crash of 30% or more! Whether born of desperation or altruism, this is a remarkable expression of ownership values, showing again the contingency of the housing as asset ideology.

Towards Reregulation? Clipping the Libertarian Wings of the Real Estate Council

Regulation and reregulation began under the force of public and media pressure before the May 2017 provincial election. Under duress the Liberal provincial government had inaugurated demand management in the housing market with a 15% tax directed against foreign purchasers in July 2016, a strategy that would be greatly expanded by the new NDP administration. In the same way, the court of public opinion, informed by everyday life and investigative journalism, became a *force majeure* that could disrupt institutional practices that had been tolerated by a growth coalition.

The provincial government had deregulated the Real Estate Council of British Columbia (RECBC) in 2005, freeing it to self-manage the professional conduct of provincial realtors and to ensure appropriate consumer protection.[18] The removal of an arms-length regulator, however, opened the door to opportunistic activities in the hot market that prevailed in Greater Vancouver for most of the period since deregulation. A serious failing of the Real Estate Council became excessive negligence in guarding against money-laundering exposure, an endemic risk in high-priced markets. The anti-money laundering Financial Transactions and Reports Analysis Centre (FINTRAC), a federal agency, had been critical of realtors' non-reporting on residential sales, observing 'deficiencies in most aspects of the real estate sector's compliance programs that render it more vulnerable of being used by criminals to launder illicit funds' (FINTRAC 2016, p. 2). Although real estate offices are legally required to report suspicious or large cash transactions, FINTRAC received only *seven* such reports from Vancouver realtors over a four-year period. A compliance review showed significant or very significant deficiencies in 55 out of 80 BC real estate companies audited, precipitating serious risk levels. Among fundamental deficiencies, 'Attempts to verify sources of money were found to be inadequate or non-existent' (Tomlinson 2016a). So was a failure to secure proper identification from clients. Such negligence blocked attempts to locate the sources of cash funds or the identity of buyers, fundamental to anti-corruption practices.

The Canadian Real Estate Association responded pugnaciously to FINTRAC's charges, accusing the agency of producing confusing guidelines and creating extra work for their members. The impasse remained evident a year later when I attended a consultation on real estate practice. Agents were disparaging of FINTRAC documents – 'incomprehensible legalese' – and its assessment of deficient reporting. The agency was concerned with 'minutiae' and 'trivialisation', a 'black hole' that never replied to realtors' queries. Whether these complaints were legitimate or not, the communication failures they revealed provided a disturbing vulnerability to irregular real estate activities.

A second failing of deregulation was tolerance of unprofessional behaviour, including the practice of shadow flipping, or selling assignments as they are innocuously called in the industry (Tomlinson 2016b). Shadow flipping inflates home prices through repeated short-term selling among investors before an existing transaction has legally closed, conducted usually without the knowledge of the initial seller. Complaints by sellers and anxious ethical realtors to RECBC were fruitless. With growing media exposure and public displeasure, the BC government established an investigatory panel and declared a crackdown on shadow flipping. The panel found much more than shadow flipping was at fault. There were weak governance standards in the Real Estate Council, with inadequate monitoring of conduct and insufficient response to complaints. Penalties were minimal and could easily be rationalised as a business outlay. Compliance with reporting standards for money-laundering risks was weak. Castigating the Council, the Province's top financial regulator declared, 'The issues … in your sector of late are affecting many areas of the financial sector that we regulate and creating many other risks' (Cooper 2016). A past president of the Real Estate Institute of Canada wrote that deregulation had brought 'a systemic failure of ethics and standards and a culture too focused on fees – not service' (McCarthy 2016).

Following a scathing review, the Real Estate Council's powers of self-regulation were removed and it was reconstituted as a public entity with a majority membership from outside the real estate industry, and an overseeing Superintendent of Real Estate. Despite firm opposition from the BC Real Estate Association, one of the Superintendent's first priorities was to remove the practice of dual agency, where a single realtor represents *both* buyer and seller, inviting opacity and mis-representation in the course of real estate transactions (Fumano 2017b). Its mandate, emphasised in the first Annual Report of the new entity (RECBC 2017) was to strengthen consumer protection and enhance regulation of real estate professionals. After the publicised failures of the recent past, an important task identified by the Council Chair was 'rebuilding public confidence' in the real estate profession (RECBC 2017, p. 4). Continuing education for realtors was introduced, and disciplinary fines raised from a maximum of only $10,000 per infringement under deregulated governance to $250,000 going forward.

But the dragon of shadow flipping was too profitable to be slain in one attack. The government's crackdown on assignment selling was directed at existing properties. But there has also been a very profitable business in flipping pre-sales of condominium units before construction was complete (or had even begun) and formal ownership registration has occurred, a common practice in speculative markets that significantly raises prices. Lending institutions require a proportion of pre-sales before construction begins in order for the developer to secure a loan.[19] Guaranteed pre-sales to dependable clients have become a normal means of financing building projects, and large Vancouver condominium developers like Westbank and Concord Pacific are tightly integrated into Asia Pacific investment circles where pre-sale purchases provide a popular asset. Pre-build assignment contracts, potentially allowing (illegally) untaxed short-term price gains through repeated sales 'off the books' (re-sales), are popular among 'friends and relatives' of the developer, including real estate agents with a successful record of multiple sales (Gold 2017). Some re-sales occurred through public channels. In May 2018 a single agent, under the web title 'Vancouver Presale Condo Assignments for Sale' was listing for re-sale 16 units, priced above $3 million each, above the 40th floor in Westbank's still far from completed iconic downtown tower, Vancouver House. These large upper floor apartment units were advertised at a median cost of $5,388,000; the listings included 25 'lucky' 8s in their prices, the most favoured number in Chinese numerology. Some buyers may be senior employees. Gold (2017) provided details of two pre-sales to senior employees in one of their company's downtown towers. These view properties at or near the top of the building were priced well below market value, and not then available to the public. In one instance a price lift of $3.7 million occurred over two years, in the other, the price gain at sale was $4.5 million in three years.

An investigation of six suburban condominium towers showed the presence of several dozen realtors in an often-opaque process (Tomlinson 2018). Other pre-sale purchasers had no Canadian address or a foreign address; some units were bought by numbered companies. The average gross profit between initial pre-sale and eventual purchase and occupancy by an end user was $145,000. One realtor stated that through privileged access to a project he and his clients had bought 120 units pre-sale; most of the units were flipped with profits, he claimed, as high as $300–400,000. The inflationary price lift was passed on to end users. The unregulated and opaque nature of shadow flipping provides the potential for illegal concealment of taxable income, including liability to income tax, the foreign buyers' tax, the goods and services tax, and capital gains tax on an investment property. Pre-sales with shadow flipping of condominium units was not addressed until the comprehensive regulation programme of the NDP government sought to establish a register of the pre-sale market. Such a register is of interest to the Canada Revenue Agency (CRA), which has been stymied from probing into tax evasion in the dark corners of shadow flipping in the past.

Serious Reregulation?

Aware of the priorities of its electorate, the NDP provincial government introduced a 30-point Housing Plan, *Homes for BC*, in its 2018 Budget (Province of British Columbia 2018). The Provincial document was matched by almost simultaneous and closely related policy shifts by the Federal Government and the City of Vancouver. This inter-governmental consensus in re-directing housing policy by all three levels of government, revealed some intent to reregulate and intervene in a dysfunctional housing market that included an investment ethos, asset-based wealth accumulation, and dependence on the private sector.

The provincial Housing Plan was a significant and ambitious document, likely the most comprehensive set of housing policies in BC history. It comprised five sections: (1) Stabilising the market; (2) Cracking down on tax fraud; (3) Building the homes people need; (4) Improving security for renters; and (5) Building partnerships for affordability (Province of British Columbia 2018). Significantly, it begins with actions for demand management, including the unprecedented recognition of the inflationary effects of market manipulation, including speculation, money laundering, and tax fraud, revealing acute recognition of significant opaque processes in the housing market. The Housing Plan's first six policies identify areas of new or increased taxation, including 'taxing speculators who are driving up housing costs', increasing the foreign buyers' tax to 20%, increasing its geographical coverage, increasing the property transfer tax (stamp duty) for homes selling at above $3 million, introducing additional 'school' taxation, again for homes priced above $3 million, and taxing short-term rentals (Airbnbs). The intent here is first, to cool the market by checking speculative, inflationary, and off-shore property investment and second, to tax the accumulation of property wealth. The speculation tax is directed at residential owners (with exemptions) who pay minimal taxes in the province, and includes dwellings that are seasonally vacant. Explicit in extending the foreign buyers' tax was a penalty for tax evasion, suspected to be common among some members of this investment group (SITE Economics 2017; Gordon 2022).[20] Equally explicit was the progressive increase in transfer and school taxes that was intended to tax wealth accumulation through a housing asset advantage: 'Those who have benefited the most from the rising real estate market should contribute their fair share' (Province of BC 2018, p. 11).

The tax fraud section of the Plan began with the creation of a register of contract assignments, to address 'shadow flipping' in the condominium pre-sale market, recognising that this practice is rife with tax fraud possibilities. Disclosure of assignments would reduce their profitability and thereby reduce pre-sale price inflation. An equal lack of transparency was to be corrected in the land registry, where 'beneficial ownership' was concealed through the use of numbered companies and proxy owners. A new registry would require beneficial owners to be identified, and this information made available to taxation and law enforcement authorities. Only after addressing demand management – some of these policies imported from public recommendations in the 2015 Angus Reid survey – did the Plan turn to the question of affordable supply. Partnership with public and private housing providers and other levels of government was to be fronted by a $6.6 billion fund from the Province as a platform for the construction of 114,000 affordable rental units over ten years. Recognising the problems of labour availability in high-priced markets, another $1.8 billion over ten years was dedicated to middle-income rental housing. Specific programs were identified to build women's shelters, student housing, indigenous housing, and modular units for the homeless.

A section of the Plan was specific to the large and growing rental population in BC. Initiatives promised to tenants included a rental grant to place alongside the long-established homeowners' grant. Current rental supplements would be increased and rental protections against unjust evictions would be enhanced. Existing social housing, much of it built in the 1970s and 1980s would be repaired and retrofitted to meet earthquake and environmental code upgrading. Tax exemptions would be available for purpose-built rental housing. A final section of the Housing Plan emphasised, correctly, that the scale of the affordable housing crisis – 'the problems our province faces are immense' – could not be addressed by one level of government alone, or without significant partnerships with housing providers. A Housing Hub was introduced as a one-stop centre to facilitate these partnerships, and where needed to act as a project co-ordinator. Notable by its absence was policy to ease access to homeownership.

The *Homes for BC* Plan evinced some optimism for partnerships because all levels of government were motivated to act on the housing file, as indeed they had been during the 1970s in a golden era of social housing provision in Canada (Suttor 2016; Ley 2020). Certainly, the Federal Government gave every indication of being a willing partner in housing provision, restoring a major federal role in housing that had disappeared in the crisis budget of 1994 and had not been reinstated. If the *Homes for BC* Plan was ambitious, the Federal Plan was seemingly audacious. Canada's National Housing Strategy (NHS) was released three months before the BC Plan in November 2017, with the Canada Mortgage and Housing Corporation (CMHC) named as the lead federal agency (CMHC 2017). In recent years, CMHC's principal role has been to provide mortgage insurance to conventional loans from financial institutions (Walks and Clifford 2015). It was now mandated to deliver housing outputs from a substantial ten-year fund of over $70 billion.[21] The opportunity created some institutional euphoria, with CMHC's President announcing the NHS bottom line goal: 'By 2030, everyone in Canada has a home that they can afford and that meets their needs … The hope of affordable, adequate homes for all is what guides us. It is our north star, our *raison d'être*' (Siddall 2019).

Despite such unattainable hyperbole, this was indeed 'Canada's First Ever National Housing Strategy' and its expressed targets remained impressive: to build 160,000 new units, and repair and update 300,000 older social housing units (CMHC 2021). Target populations were primarily the most marginalised, the deepest in need, but middle-income rental affordability was also significant. Like the BC Plan, it was a project looking for partners. The breadth of the NHS reached beyond housing delivery to housing research, which received an unprecedented budget of $24 million a year for 10 years. Recognising the significant gaps in data collection – publicised by Vancouver's 'Give us data' rallies in 2015 – Statistics Canada was contracted to address key gaps, including the relative contribution of national and foreign housing ownership. Important data resources were created through the new Canadian Housing Statistics Program, leading to research opportunities that can finally address the ownership question quantitatively (Gellatly and Morissette 2017, 2019; Gordon 2020, 2022). The research mandate also included the formation of housing research networks with an annual housing conference in Ottawa.

For the third leg of government, municipalities, we will consider the City of Vancouver, the largest municipality in the metropolitan area with a growing population of 700,000 in 2020. Since 2008 the City had been governed by a mayor and council dominated by the Vision Vancouver party. Initially established as a reform group, the party had offended neighbourhoods by intrusive spot rezoning to raise densities. But the new structures were invariably high-priced condominiums, which replaced older, more affordable units, and pushed up land prices without solving affordability needs. For some years the municipal party had been in denial about the effects of offshore investment, further widening the gap between itself and popular perceptions, until the mayor's contacts with other global cities, including Sydney and New York, persuaded the Council majority of the globalisation of Vancouver's housing market.[22] Finally recognising that its policies were not addressing residents' needs, in November 2017 the City introduced a 10-year Housing Vancouver Strategy that made major adjustments to its policy emphases (City of Vancouver 2017). Mayor Robertson's 2017 preface was something of a *mea culpa*. The plan he wrote, 'was directly informed by what we heard from local residents: we need urgent action now to ramp up not just the supply of housing, but the right kind of supply' (City of Vancouver 2017, p. 3). Implicit was a prior failure to learn from residents, and an unqualified policy pursuit of supply without questioning its fit with resident needs. While the change of direction came too late to save Vision Vancouver – it was obliterated in the 2018 Civic Election – the new Council, with a left of centre majority, maintained the Housing Strategy.

The Housing Vancouver Strategy outlined key objectives: 'a significant shift toward rental, social and supportive housing'; action to address speculation and support equity; protection of diversity of incomes and households among residents; protection of existing affordable housing; renewal of partnerships for affordable housing, 'particularly non-profit, co-op, and indigenous housing partners'; and increasing support and protection of renters and the homeless (City of Vancouver 2017, pp. 9–10). Like the BC Housing Plan, the Vancouver strategy led off by recognising the global nature of investment demand, even adding a twist of sophistication to the analysis:

> Vancouver and other major cities around the world are experiencing significant speculative housing demand from investors, who view housing as an asset that can generate significant financial returns. This phenomenon is often referred to as the "financialization" of global housing markets and characterizes the purchase of housing as investments rather than homes … investor demand has contributed to housing market distortions, creating an environment where, in many respects, housing serves investors before people seeking a place to live.
>
> (City of Vancouver 2017, p. 11)

This statement represented a remarkable admission of the presence of the housing as asset ideology, and (though not explicit here) an about turn for a mayor who had earlier denied the role of offshore investment, decried as racist contrary arguments, and supported seemingly unlimited condominium (*i.e.* ownership) development.[23]

Ownership is the dominant tenure model in Greater Vancouver, and the common aspiration, and during the freewheeling period of market domination since the 1990s, ownership had been the implicit national housing policy (Hulchanski 2004; Gurstein and Yan 2019). But there is a significant realisation by all three levels of government that, at least in the gateway cities of Vancouver and Toronto, the future lies with rental tenure not ownership. The primary emphasis on rental support and new construction in all three policy documents is striking. The NDP government had even given BC municipalities the option of a new rental-only zoning category that would preclude the displacement of tenants by future condominium development, a trend that has carried gentrification to the suburbs (Jones and Ley 2016). But the existing market is highly stressed, with high rents and vacancy rates commonly at or below one percent. The Vancouver Housing Strategy targeted the construction of 72,000 housing units over 10 years, half of them rental, including 17% social and special needs housing. In the ownership share, 49% would be condominiums or townhouses, leaving only 1% of infill units for small detached dwellings (City of Vancouver 2017). In addition, the City's innovative empty homes tax to discourage speculative purchase without occupancy, the first vacancy tax in North America, would incentivise owners to rent out vacant units, thereby adding to the overall rental stock.

Current policy is encouraging densification through the demolition of detached houses and older apartment buildings on main arteries and around rapid transit stations. Replacement units have typically been 3–6 story condominiums, but the Vancouver Housing Strategy envisages taller rental construction on arterials with various developer incentives including additional densities to permit modest inclusion of affordable units. More controversially, the city is mooting 6–12 storey market rental and social housing within detached housing neighbourhoods. With a cooling condominium market, and with sufficient density incentives, developers are presently motivated to explore rental, including affordable rental, opportunities. But with existing high land values, it is hard to see how rents can be affordable,[24] certainly as affordable as the older units they replace.

Assessment: Reregulation Achieved?

The convergence of objectives in virtually simultaneous major housing policy documents by municipal, provincial, and federal viewpoints is striking and could be propitious. If not a collective, then at least a common, realisation is revealed by these documents of a necessary departure from the existing neo-liberal economics of asset-based welfare. First, 'surplus' demand has been problematised, recognising the market power of investors who are not primarily part of the local wage economy and who bring external capital resources to bear that overwhelm those of local wage-earners. Second, this capital inflow means a growing decoupling of local housing markets and labour markets with chronic affordability problems. Third, in major cities real estate investment has become global as housing markets have become transnational. Fourth, a freewheeling housing market has many imperfections, including distortions in Vancouver introduced by speculation, tax fraud, and money laundering that require public intervention. Fifth, taxation is one appropriate vehicle to manage speculative demand. Sixth, an unqualified endorsement of supply-side measures is mistaken and does not meet public needs; what is required is 'the right kind of supply', affordable supply, to meet the housing needs of current workers and other residents. Seventh, the unanimous view of all three levels of government is that the right kind of supply means a shift to rental apartments in high-priced markets. Notable is the absence of an ownership initiative such as the UK's expensive help-to-buy scheme. The federal government's modest shared equity scheme for first-time buyers set out in the NHS had cost caps that made it unworkable in the expensive Vancouver and Toronto markets. Eighth, an ideology of housing as asset was challenged in a policy set that cooled price inflation, did not promote ownership but supported rental tenure, and recognised the necessary role of government to direct housing toward the meeting of resident needs rather than investor spreadsheets.

This is a substantial and coherent set of conclusions that together indicate a reconfigured understanding of the housing market, implying an equally innovative set of public policies. However, the economic environment included other factors that were less propitious to this new interventionist policy. National financial policy by the Bank of Canada kept interest rates at rock bottom fuelling the ownership market and speculative activity until it was undermined by rising inflation in 2022; it was still possible to secure a five-year, fixed-term rate of under two percent from a major bank in early 2021 for a mortgage at the unprecedented gross housing debt service ratio of 6–7 times household income.[25] Prudential measures applying mortgage stress tests were not demanding. There was every indication that the Bank of Canada was employing its conventional strategy, with the housing market serving to stimulate the economy coming out of the pandemic recession. And the market responded with a very specific and unanticipated COVID-19 boom that inflated average national residential prices by a third between May 2020 and May 2021, according to the Canadian Real Estate Association. A work-at-home boom penalised urban cores and small apartments and favoured purchase in distant suburbs and small towns. The pandemic itself transformed policy priorities as the federal and provincial governments added enormous debt loads to counter the economic freefall that occurred as the pandemic struck. Inevitably other funding commitments would be re-examined.

Nor did the turn to rental tenure in current policy erase existing tax advantages for owners. In June 2021 an expert panel examining the improvement of housing supply in British Columbia presented its final report, advocating 'bold, fundamental changes' as a necessity to address affordability (Expert Panel 2021). Reflecting the pro-business majority among panellists,[26] recommendations paid no attention to demand management and moved directly into supply recommendations, including the familiar industry calls for more timely planning decisions, more predictable development fees, and coordinated inter-government relations, including 'flexibility' in local zoning. Alone, these three calls to action would have been consistent with the *ancien régime* of growth machine ideology. But the two remaining calls to action went beyond the emerging inter-governmental consensus. In advocating for affordable, social housing it recognised correctly that the private ownership market *and* the private rental market were not meeting the needs of an increasing number of households. A significant role for the non-profit sector with funding to support 10% of housing starts was advocated. Fifth, and unexpectedly, the Panel recognised the wealth premium generated by ownership, that 'Policies favouring homeownership exacerbate wealth inequality' (Expert Panel 2021, p. 36). To correct a tax-based inequity they recommended, removal of the annual BC homeowners grant,[27] and a review of the federal capital-gains tax exemption on principal residences, or failing this, comparable tax compensation to renters. This recommendation prioritised rental tenure to an even higher degree than the inter-governmental consensus.

The response from political parties that had authored the reform-oriented provincial *Homes for BC* and the federal National Housing Strategy to this fifth call to action was immediate and decisive. The same day that the Expert Panel's report was published, BC's housing minister rejected termination of the homeowner grant, while the federal finance minister dismissed any change to the capital gains tax exemption on a principal residence (MacLeod 2021). Neither recommendation was politically viable before an electorate comprising a clear majority of homeowners.

What has been accomplished so far by the three housing manifestos? The City of Vancouver offers an annual assessment of progress on its 10-year Housing Vancouver Strategy. Its 2021 report noted some modest successes (City of Vancouver 2021a). For the first time in many years, purpose-built rentals and social housing comprised over half of new housing approvals, amounting to 3800 units, accomplishing a turn to rental tenure, or 'the right kind of supply' that is a major goal of the Strategy. This sustains a three-year trend where purpose-built rentals plus estimated secondary rentals from condominiums amounted to two-thirds of new supply, though purpose-built rental approvals alone have only met 80% of the benchmark.[28] In addition the city's new vacancy tax raised levies of over $110 million for City affordable housing projects in its first three years, and also, with Airbnb restrictions, incentivised hundreds of owners to rent out empty properties (City of Vancouver 2020). Social and supportive housing production has run 15% above target over the same period. At the same time the goal of affordability has *not* been attained with approval of only a third of the low target of 400 annual new units affordable to incomes of below $80,000. These rentals are typically a minority share in market rental buildings, constructed under rezoning that allows a higher density bonus to accommodate an affordability contribution. This minimal achievement of lower cost units is an indication of the weak fiscal base of cities in Canada in addressing affordability in high-priced land settings.

Moreover, there is a significant problem in the city's budget stream that may challenge affordability policy. In attempting to contain tax raises, council became dependent in its capital fund on development cost levies and community amenity contributions from developers accompanying land use rezoning. While such charges are a form of land value tax that enable some of the land value lift from rezoning to be recouped for public purposes, there is a danger in projecting anticipated future levies and contributions directly into the city's budgetary planning (Cheung 2018; Todd 2022).[29] The 2012–2014 capital plan included a budgeted 12% contribution from levies and contributions, rising to over 20% in the 2019–2022 capital plan (City of Vancouver 2021b, p. B-71). Critics pointed out that with this budgetary dependence, councillors and planning staff would be predisposed to approve rezoning proposals, notably larger projects with density bonuses generating greater levies and contributions. Such projects will inflate land prices and hasten redevelopment pressures from copycat proposals. This conflict of interest could readily lead to a convergence of public and private goals and the re-creation of a property growth coalition.

With the variety of housing programmes and partners it is difficult to give a full assessment of the progress of the more recent provincial and federal housing initiatives. Housing projects take several years to reach completion, especially those that involve partnerships, so a slow start with subsequent acceleration in housing production would be expected. In the first two budget years of the provincial Housing Plan, 7,500 affordable and supportive housing units were completed across BC (BC Housing 2020). Another 2600 units were underway through a range of different non-profit and private partnerships through the HousingHub for middle-income, working households.[30] Plans to rehabilitate more than 60,000 existing social housing units in the province were in place; they date primarily from the golden years of social housing in the 1970s and 1980s, but now require capital renewal, repairs, and rehabilitation.

The provincial government's tax initiatives to cool the housing market produced measurable results. An independent review of the Speculation and Vacancy Tax showed it generated $231 million in public revenues in its first three years, primarily from foreign owners, which were applied to affordable housing funds (Ministry of Finance 2022). The tax also incentivised perhaps 20,000 vacant units in Metro Vancouver to be rented out, adding to the overall rental stock. As price moderating measures, the cooling tax regime had significant, but short-term, consequences. Following the initial 15% foreign buyer tax in summer 2016, annual price growth of 32% in July 2016 fell dramatically to a year-over-year decline of 2% by December (Figure 5.1). But the loss was short-lived, and by July 2017, a year after the foreign buyer tax announcement, 12-month prices were once again on a tear. The budget by the new NDP provincial government in February 2018, with a range of tax measures and a clear intent to manage speculative purchase, was followed by a 12-month price decline of 6% for all residential types in Greater Vancouver and 10% for detached houses (Gordon 2020). However, a year later the price line had bottomed out at the start of the COVID-19 boom, and by February 2021, three years after the aggressive cooling budget with its announcement of the 30-point housing plan, overall residential prices had regained the level of February 2018, and were racing ahead for detached houses in distant suburbs and ex-urbs.[31] The clear conclusion is that in high demand markets like Vancouver tax interventions have a short shelf life unless they coincide with some larger shock (like the Brexit vote that reinforced the deflationary pressure of tax increases in prime London) or successive tax increases (as in Singapore).

By far the best-resourced level of government in Canada is the federal administration in Ottawa. It reported fully on the first three years of the National Housing Strategy (NHS) in May 2021 (CMHC 2021; Government of Canada 2021). The proliferation of programme streams and the lack of spatial granularity make it impossible to assess the effects of the NHS on the Vancouver housing market. But some general assessments are possible. There is solid support to repair and re-capitalise legacy social housing units built over 30 years ago, typically with non-profit providers. Commitments for $14.5 billion have been made so far to repair 75,000 existing units across Canada and provide another 70,000 new social rental units (Government of Canada 2021).[32] The largest expenditure stream is for new rental construction, mainly affordable, with 14,500 units under construction or completed over the past three years.[33] This is a decent start, but numbers are quickly diluted when spread across Canada, and over several years. Consistent with the overall tenor of the inter-governmental consensus, ownership programmes are small, only two percent of planned NHS expenditures, with few applications from BC for shared equity mortgages. In contrast, other NHS supply initiatives had committed financing for almost 20,500 new units in British Columbia.

A potentially significant action adding some legislative leverage to the NHS is the National Housing Strategy Act (2019), which affirms the right to adequate housing as a fundamental human right recognised in international law, and requires the federal government to maintain a National Housing Strategy and report to Parliament every three years on progress towards achieving NHS goals. In addition, a National Housing Council was appointed and a Federal Housing Advocate, supported by the Canadian Human Rights Commission.

Meanwhile, the reprieve from price inflation earned by the 2018 Budget and its extensive cooling measures has ended. As in London, the unexpected COVID boom favoured detached homes in distant small towns, some a ferry ride away from the city. In Greater Vancouver, despite the work of the governmental housing partners, residential prices were up 14% year over year in May 2021 and by 23% for detached houses. There was minor improvement for tenants with the metropolitan vacancy rate rising from 1.1% in 2019 to 2.6% in 2020, but affordability had not improved. The misery had returned. When Angus Reid repeated its housing poll in April 2021, this time with a Canada-wide sample, Vancouver-region respondents showed continuing growth of those whose housing experiences were 'miserable', now extending to over a quarter of the sample (Angus Reid 2021). Only a third of respondents wanted prices to keep rising; many homeowners wanted them to fall. Three-quarters of Vancouver tenants could not afford to buy or never expected to be able to buy a home. By June 2021, polling showed that housing affordability had displaced the pandemic and returned to top rank among perceived public issues (Insights West 2021). There was massive disapproval of all three levels of government on housing issues.[34] Residential alienation was back. The reforms of the intergovernmental consensus had not yet brought the affordability solution the public required.

Conclusion

Vancouver offers a salutary lesson to a search for alternatives to the ideology of housing as asset-based accumulation, alternatives that have scarcely been sought in Hong Kong, Sydney, or London. Until 2016, the state welcomed the globalisation of its housing market with wealth accumulation accompanying homeownership, even though affordability was shredded. British Columbia's neoliberal government actively solicited investment capital, including real estate capital, especially from Asia Pacific. If it was not in collusion with an enterprising real estate sector, their interests were mutually intertwined, creating a formidable property growth coalition that benefitted from a robust transnational housing market. The federal government meanwhile had almost entirely abandoned the social housing file in 1994, while its Business Immigration Program liberally dispensed golden visas, seeking wealthy migrants to jumpstart economic development. They failed to do so, but their imported capital had helped inflate Vancouver's housing boom for a generation. The metropolitan area was repeatedly identified as the least affordable housing market in North America.

But by late 2018 some revision had occurred to this governing ideology. Alienated by the cavalier negligence of the housing market despite resident duress, voters in BC rebelled at the ballot box and governments fell, provincially, federally, and municipally. Ambitious interventionist housing manifestos were adopted by all three newly elected administrations implying a significant change of emphasis, and a surprising convergence of goals in an inter-governmental consensus. Resources to undergird the manifestos appeared substantial, with a can-do zeal evident at the federal housing agency, CMHC. Fresh support for the ownership model, fundamental to asset-based accumulation, was minimal in scope and affordable rental construction became a principal objective. Unqualified supply was no answer; it had to be 'the right kind of supply', affordable supply. The social housing sector was renewed with the promised renovation of older buildings and construction of new housing in conjunction with non-profit partners. Surplus demand from speculative off-shore investment was problematized, and multiple taxes introduced to restrict it.[35] An emphasis on housing needs (indeed housing rights) seemingly trumped the embellishment of investor portfolios. But the COVID-19 boom burst through these defences. By May 2021, year-over-year average residential price growth in Vancouver was back in double digits and highest for detached houses. Efforts towards reregulation face seemingly insurmountable barriers (Stellinga 2022). Politically, an inter-governmental consensus is no more secure than the outcome of the next election. The tyranny of high land costs from post-1986 property inflation overturns market-based affordability solutions, including rental solutions, even when high density up-zoning is permitted. Moreover, in a built-up metropolis, construction of new rental (or condominium) units is invariably achieved by demolishing older, more affordable apartment buildings (Gold 2022).

Breaking through these generalities, an unexpected regional specificity has recently added a new salience to Vancouver's housing landscape. When Bishop Hills imagined in 1860 what manner of great city would occupy the thick rain forest between Burrard Inlet and the Fraser River, his compassionate mind would have included a respectful place for the long-established aboriginal population. But in fact, the First Nations were later dispossessed of ancestral lands, villages were demolished, and populations were displaced to small suburban reserves and to urban poverty in and near Vancouver's Downtown Eastside (Blomley 2004). However, their treaty land rights were never legally extinguished, and the state is now negotiating land disposition with three Coast Salish bands with overlapping claims to metropolitan Vancouver as ancestral territory. The three First Nations have established a company, MST Development Corporation, which claims, following recent land negotiations, the largest land holdings among regional property developers. MST owns, sometimes in partnership with the federal government, 65 hectares of newly acquired prime real estate across their historic lands. In the City of Vancouver alone, the First Nations are planning 20,000 housing units (Fumano and Culbert 2022). The largest project is the 36-hectare Jericho Lands, a former National Defence site in the heart of Vancouver's expensive west side neighbourhoods (City of Vancouver 2021c). Most of the property was purchased in a joint venture between MST and Canada Lands, a Crown corporation, and initial concept plans envisage up to 10,000 housing units. Exclusive holdings of the 1400-person Musqueam Nation (one of the MST partners) also include two golf courses in Vancouver, one on reserve land, and a leased subdivision among its expanding assets; Musqueam are presently developing a nine-hectare village of leased condominium and rental units, adjacent to one of the golf courses.

A radical undermining of prevailing housing regulation is occurring in the development of Senakw by the Squamish Nation, another MST partner, on a waterfront site adjacent to downtown Vancouver (Halliday 2020; Bula and Curry 2022). After lengthy legal battles, the Squamish regained almost five hectares, part of a dispossessed village territory. Because the Court defined the land as a former village site, the Squamish are not subject to municipal planning by-laws. Imagining Senakw consequently evades city planning regulation, and Vancouver's height and density limits are subverted with plans for 6,000 units on this tiny site. Senakw's approximately 10,000 residents will live in towers rising to almost 60 storeys on a sliver of waterfront land following a former railway right of way. Ironically, in by-passing the City's planning regulations, the project will give a huge boost to the Vancouver Housing Strategy's struggling target for purpose-built rental units and affordable dwellings. Senakw appeals as well to the National Housing Strategy, with Prime

Minister Trudeau announcing a long-term loan of $1.4 billion from CMHC to the rental project, the agency's largest pledge ever for a housing development. Partnership marks an expensive entry by the state to the joint pursuit of affordable housing and justice objectives, but the high cost of intervention indicates that its options are limited. Meanwhile land and housing in Vancouver have another weighty project on their ledger, at the front end of the national Truth and Reconciliation call to justice between a settler society and displaced aboriginal peoples.

Notes

1. Ian Egloff is a Vancouver architect, cited in Planner (2017)
2. This section is discussed in more detail in Ley (2010, 2017).
3. 1 CAD = 0.785 USD on 1 January 2021.
4. According to a special tabulation of the 1996 Census, 81% of ethnic Chinese immigrants settling in Vancouver since 1986 were already homeowners in 1996; the level for the entire population in Canada's most expensive metropolitan area was only 59% (Ley 2010).
5. In one of the more egregious cases, Malaysian-owned Holborn Properties bought Little Mountain, a public housing site in Vancouver, in a secretive deal with the BC Liberal government in 2008. Holborn promised to replace 224 public housing dwellings containing 700 tenants, and add substantially more condominium units to a most desirable location. Tenants were speedily evicted, but in mid-2022 only 53 public units and no market units had been built, while the otherwise empty development site had multiplied in value. Persistent freedom of information requests eventually revealed a sweetheart deal. The developer had been offered a mortgage of over $200 million by the Province in 2008, *with no interest due until 2026*, and no timeline for construction (Fumano 2021).
6. Prices are for the third quarter. A benchmark price is derived from a model that is intended to provide a representative value unbiased by extreme cases. For income data, see Statistics Canada (2021b).
7. Like Sydney, local investors were also participants in the inflationary market, though probably not to the same extent in the absence of such generous tax incentives as negative gearing. Nonetheless, 16% of Vancouver resident owners (*ie.* including immigrants but excluding absentee non-residents) owned more than one property in British Columbia in 2018 (including holiday homes). Multiple owners had a median age of 57, and lived in high-value homes (Bekkering et al. 2019). In 2019–2020, multiple property holders held 29% of BC's residential units (Statistics Canada 2022). During the national pandemic boom of 2020–2021, almost a quarter of buyers were investors. dominantly Canadians.

8. I am grateful to Craig Jones who accessed this information in customised tables from federal data bases.

9. The price ripple effect is discussed in more detail for London (Chapter 6).

10. The RBC index is derived by computing the share of a typical household's pre-tax income that would be consumed by servicing the costs of buying a typical family home in the metropolitan area.

11. Compare Chapter 4, footnote 8 for a Sydney comparison.

12. The next two paragraphs are taken from Ley (2017).

13. The composite benchmark price includes apartments, townhouses and detached dwellings. The benchmark excludes extreme cases. Price data are taken from the Real Estate Board of Greater Vancouver (various months/years).

14. Data declared by the government showed $1 billion spent on BC real estate, the large majority in Greater Vancouver, by foreign buyers during a five-week period in June–July 2016.

15. Households in these suburbs face the heaviest proportional mortgage debt loads (Walks 2013).

16. Not to be confused with the BC Liberals, a misnomer for a right of centre party.

17. In the 2015 Federal election, the Liberals rose from a rump of 36 seats to a majority government with 184 seats.

18. The next three paragraphs draw from the discussion in Ley (2021)

19. Similar practices are evident in London's new-build flat market (Chapter 6).

20. In an incisive analysis, Gordon (2022) demonstrated the existence of housing market-labour market decoupling in Vancouver and Toronto municipalities, and showed a very strong relationship (r^2 = 0.92) between the share of low-income, working-age homeowners in single-family dwellings and the share of non-resident ownership of single-family dwellings in Vancouver municipalities. Because the low-income, working-age groups were paradoxically associated with higher house prices an inference of tax avoidance by non-resident homeowners was drawn.

21. When first announced in November 2017, the NHS treasure chest was listed at $40 billion. It had swollen to over $70 billion in a document in May 2018. Critics have stated that these are not all new funds. The figure did include over $7 billion in provincial and territorial cost-matched contributions.

22. Following their joint revelation, one Vision councillor told me, 'We had no idea the off-shore business was this big'. The lack of official data permitted ignorance of inconvenient truths.

23. Only in November 2021 did the Bank of Canada publicly acknowledge the distorting effects of investors in the housing market, shortly after similar illumination was voiced by the Reserve Bank of Australia.

24. Current 1-bedroom monthly rents in Vancouver (October 2022) are $2500, typically more for new units. In a low-wage city, this would require an annual income of $100,000 with rental costs at 30% of gross income.

25. The gross debt service ratio describes housing expenses (mortgage payments, taxes, and heat) as a ratio of gross annual household income. For the rising multiple of mortgage borrowing power to household income from 1986 (2.5) to 2020 (6–7), see Expert Panel (2021, Figure 4). This growing debt load permitted by rock-bottom interest rates introduces serious risk for less qualified borrowers.

26. At least four of the six panelists represented the business community. In this respect, recommendations for a larger role for non-profit housing and tax reform to bring more equity to tenants are quite surprising.

27. BC's 2018 Housing Plan had called for a renter's grant to match the long-established homeowner's grant. This policy has not yet been implemented.

28. In addition to rented condominiums, there is a significant secondary rental supply from informal units, notably basement conversions in detached homes that are rented out as 'mortgage helpers' and have been a critical component of the affordability budget of new homeowners (Mendez 2017).

29. The city's intent was to recoup at least 70% of the land value lift from rezoning for public purposes like social housing, parks, and community centres (CACs), as well as roads and utilities (DCLs).

30. These were primarily rental units, though a small equity-sharing, provincial affordable homeownership programme was announced in 2019.

31. The COVID boom brought some unique features with national price growth exceeding metropolitan growth. Indeed, with the virtual absence of immigration and air travel, globalisation impulses were much reduced. Available evidence identifies national factors as uppermost in Canada's runaway COVID market.

32. In assessing outcomes, it is often difficult to harmonise numbers in Government of Canada (2021) and CMHC (2021) reports. Consequently, I have reproduced few statistics from the reports and emphasised only major trends.

33. Separate initiatives address homelessness and indigenous and northern housing.

34. For the first time in 15 years, a centre-right majority was returned in Vancouver's 2022 civic election.

35. New data on ownership liberated by the NHS and analysed by Andy Yan showed the scale of residential investment, with almost a half of condominiums and a fifth of detached houses in the City of Vancouver *not* occupied by their owners in 2018. The condominium share is particularly high, considering that some strata corporations restrict or forbid tenanted units. For the metropolitan area, the proportions were 37% and 15% (Mackie 2019).

CHAPTER 6

London 2012: The Best of Times, the Worst of Times

The British are not a nation of shopkeepers, as Napoleon said, but rather one of property speculators

(Wolf 2013)

London … is experiencing an acute, pervasive and socially explosive housing crisis so severe and polarising that it has become the city's number one political issue.

(Beswick et al. 2016)

In London we see in sharper profile trends already apparent in Sydney, Vancouver, and Hong Kong. Real estate investment from near and far, despatched by family punters, institutional investors, and property developers, has exacerbated the benefits and losses of an unequal society, where for many affordability is dire, rentals are scarce and expensive, and waiting lists for non-market housing are lengthy. State-induced austerity has sharpened the divisions between housing classes, with the dismantling of public housing and the marketisation of housing associations contrasting with such tags as right-to-buy, buy-to-let, and help-to-buy, each of them advancing neoliberal objectives to promote owner-occupier or landlord property ownership. In London, and the UK generally, housing has been a leading edge, a tool in an ideological project to invoke an enterprise culture where market provision replaces state provision. Homeownership and landlordism generate assets for self-motivated entrepreneurs, as residents transition from clients to 'modern investor subjects', while a welfare state transitions to an asset state. Private investment and public dispossession starkly reveal two sides of deepening housing inequality. These trends in an asset-based society assumed particular visibility in the summer of 2012, a season of excesses.

In a supplement dedicated to London in June 2012, *The Economist's* headline framed the capital as 'On a High' (The Economist 2012c). The central weekend of Queen Elizabeth's Diamond Jubilee was celebrated before large

Housing Booms in Gateway Cities, First Edition. David Ley.
© 2023 John Wiley & Sons Ltd. Published 2023 by John Wiley & Sons Ltd.

London crowds, and the anticipation of the Summer Olympics, to follow the next month, provided a second window on London for a national and international audience. Both the Jubilee and the Olympics were spectacles lauding British memories and successes. Film maker Danny Boyle's artistic pageantry in the Olympic opening ceremony presented a fantastical celebration of national achievement and make believe. 'I'm just a story teller' Boyle declared (McVeigh and Gibson 2012), and his visual narrative, absorbed by 27 million British television viewers, was, to paraphrase Clifford Geertz, a British reading of British experience, 'a story they tell themselves about themselves' (Geertz 1973, p. 448). The Olympic combination of celebrity, athleticism, showmanship, and vivid sensation provided a liminal circus milieu where other realities could be suspended. Beneath the Big Top of the Olympic Stadium, the opening ceremony's portrayal of Britain's long history of accomplishment might temporarily obscure the continuing scars from the Global Financial Crisis (GFC), including soaring public and private debt, a ravaged banking sector, low wages, degraded public services, and a continuing crisis of housing availability and affordability. Perhaps, too, there would be opportunity to forget the riots, the burning, looting, and deaths that had ricocheted through London's deprived neighbourhoods barely a year earlier. Spectacle and animation, effervescence and buzz, while not limited to a neoliberal dream world, fit comfortably there.

London was on a second high in the summer of 2012 with its real estate also visible on domestic and foreign radars. Its property markets were once again racing ahead, with capital rushing into commercial and residential opportunities. Commercial property investment in London in 2012 accounted for a third of all European transactions by value, and exceeded any non-UK *national* total (Germany came second to London), an extraordinary testimony to the advantages of the City of London confirmed in investor behaviour (Hammond 2012a). Following the 2008 crash, and the pound's significant loss of value, investors, both national and global, saw London property as a secure and undervalued asset. In up-market prime Central London, three-quarters of new-build homes were purchased by foreign buyers during the Olympic year. Cheap interest rates and the liquidity created by quantitative easing provided investment opportunities for those with strong credit ratings and robust currencies. Anonymous cash rolled in from tax havens, notably the British Virgin Islands and the Channel Isles.[1] Talk was beginning of an emerging new asset bubble in the London property market. The exuberance of the real estate market matched the ebullience of the summer cultural celebrations. House price losses from the GFC were already recouped in most boroughs, and in the 12 months following the Jubilee, prices would rise by double digits. Yolande Barnes, Director of Research at the Savills property consultancy, had caught the vibe: 'There has been quite a party in London house prices since 2009' (Polakova 2014).

Meanwhile, an austerity regime had bitten deeply into public services, with cuts to local authorities of 50% in real funding between 2010 and 2015 (Penny 2017; Gray and Barford 2018). London's unemployment rate was 7%, but a still larger number was underemployed (Trust for London and New Policy Institute 2013). The waiting list for council housing had reached 380,000 in the Olympic year, comprising more than 10% of London's households (MHCLG 2021a). Converted garages and garden sheds were appearing as informal housing, beds in sheds, in the East End and elsewhere (Dorling 2014; Minton 2017).[2] Confounding Olympic dazzle, the 16 most unaffordable local authorities in England for private rental units in 2012 were all London boroughs. The excess of the Olympics (priced variously between £9 billion and £15 billion) contrasted profoundly with the everyday life of London's East End, site of the Games.[3] The Olympic Stadium was inserted in the borough of Newham, which had the second highest share of housing benefit recipients among local authorities in Great Britain, and the longest housing waiting list among London boroughs. No wonder that a response towards Games-based redevelopment among poorly housed young people in Newham was that 'It's not for us' (Watt 2013). For them, the focus was bread, not circus.

London's position atop the world city hierarchy underscores themes identified in earlier chapters: property markets commodified and financialised as an asset class for local and foreign investors, affordability and availability crises for home seekers, growing inequality in wealth accumulation, sluggish wage rates, and downsized welfare services. To promote marketisation, a national plan had been launched by the Thatcher government during the 1980s, an audacious and sustained *putsch* to undermine the welfare state and showcase an asset-based economy. Homeownership was to be a chosen path to individual wealth accumulation and responsible self-help. With assistance from property investors, housing would also offer a counter-cyclical stimulus in the macro-economy. Advancing this vision, an unrelenting austerity regime followed the GFC, continuing an earlier ground campaign to accelerate marketisation of public housing. Financial discipline was meted out to the poor, wealth accumulation from property ownership was a reward for others. The median net household property wealth of London homeowners had almost doubled since the GFC, and at over £400,000 was twice the median for England as a whole in 2018 (Cosh and Gleeson 2020). This chapter will highlight the inequality accompanying an asset-based society in London, as the housing market–labour market relationship is severed by national and global investor capital working within a neoliberal ideology to liberate markets and downsize welfare state services – especially in housing.

London's House Prices

London's house prices disclose an expensive and unequal city. It is also a city that has dominated the price-lines of its national hinterland, with London home costs consistently exceeding those in the rest of the UK (Hamnett and Reades 2019). In real terms that differential has been steadily rising since 1970, from about a third above the median price in England in the booms of the early 1970s and late 1980s, to double the English price-line in 2016, during the boom following the GFC (Figure 6.1). Overall London prices have risen well over five-fold in real terms in 50 years.

From a peak in 2016, they retreated under the weight of additional stamp duties and the unwelcome prospect of Brexit. In general, prices converge most between London and the rest of England during downturns in the housing cycle; recoveries in contrast typically occur earlier in London, with prices accelerating faster than in the rest of the country. This tendency was pronounced in the early period following the GFC, with the London premium rising steadily; between December 2009 and December 2010, London prices added 15%, and 46% by the end of 2014, almost three times the increase in England as a whole (ONS 2021b). House price indices reveal an accentuation of the division between two nations during the post-GFC austerity period (Martin 2011). The research director at Knight Frank property consultancy identified 'the complete separation between London's economic trajectory and that of the rest of the

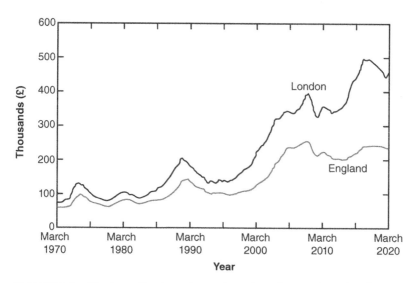

FIGURE 6.1   Real median housing prices, London and England, 1970–2020. (Source: Cosh et al, 2020 / Greater London Authority)

UK. [The housing market in] London has more in common with New York and Hong Kong than with Birmingham or Manchester' (Hammond 2012b).[4]

A second feature of London's dominance in the national housing market is its role as an epicentre of price waves that disseminate outwards to other regions in a ripple effect (Meen 1999; Cook and Watson 2016). These observations are sharpened by data from the Office of National Statistics (ONS) showing house price behaviour for regions in England and Wales from the pre-GFC peak in the first half of 2008 to September 2020 (Table 6.1).[5] The primacy of London in these relationships is emphatic, with trend lines in other regions showing marked subordination to the capital. Prices decline with distance from London, the time lengthens to regain the pre-GFC price peak, and the percentage size of the gain over that peak is diminished. London has by far the highest prices, and the steepest growth curve since the GFC, having made up the ground lost in the 2008 bust by June 2010. The South East and East of England, regions within London's commuter shed, followed six months later, while much of England and Wales did not regain the post-GFC high for a further four years.[6] The clear signal from Table 6.1 is London's growth pole effect in influencing the price trajectories of other regions. With some consistency, the closer a region in England and Wales is to London the more likely it is to exhibit similar house price behaviour. In contrast to the South East region with a trajectory that most resembles the capital's, Wales

TABLE 6.1 Regional house prices in England and Wales, by region, September 2020

Region	Median price, 9.2020 (£ '000s)	% above pre-GFC peak	Months to exceed pre-GFC peak
London	483	79	24
South East	328	47	30
East	292	51	30
South West	260	35	72
West Midlands	200	35	69
East Midlands	197	36	78
North West	170	21	78
Yorkshire	168	24	75
Wales	165	18	87
North East	140	14	69

Source: author from data in ONS (2021b)

and the northern regions had least in common with the exuberant post-GFC recovery of London's housing market.[7]

Property market confidence was re-established earliest in London and spread slowly to restore depressed prices elsewhere. 'As London's market begins to overheat, the rest of the country is warming' (The Economist 2013b). In addition, the London market shows greater volatility than the national profile with somewhat more pronounced price oscillations during housing cycles. It is typically in reference to London that there is concern about the inflation of housing bubbles. London is also dominant as a source of property transaction taxes. Receipts from residential stamp duty rose from less than £250 million in the mid-1990s, or 25% of the English total, to $3.3 billion in 2019–2020, 40% of the English total (HMRC 2020), a weighty addition to the national exchequer. This manifold primacy gives the capital a particularly significant reputational role in the UK property landscape, and in its broader economic geography (Hamnett and Reades 2019).

But a serious deficiency mars the gloss of London's price exuberance. Like other gateway cities we have examined – with the important exception of Singapore – earnings have fallen far behind dwelling prices (Figure 6.2), creating major challenges of affordability (ONS 2020, 2021e). An affordability index, derived from median house prices as a multiple of annual earnings, surged from a ratio of 4.00 in 1997 to 11.72 in 2020 (ONS 2021e).[8] The affordability burden to achieve ownership had almost tripled over this 24-year period. This relationship is a fundamental source of the sweat and tears that shape the emotional world of London's housing ownership crisis. In contrast, the slow growth of

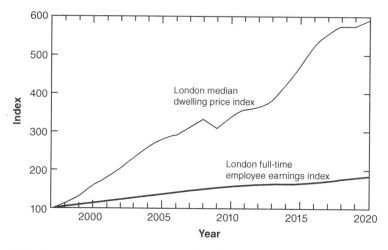

FIGURE 6.2   Median nominal dwelling price and full-time earnings indices, London, 1997–2020. (Source: author from data in ONS 2020, ONS 2021b)

employment earnings has more closely tracked (though still falling behind) the private rental market, a relationship also repeated in other cities (ONS 2021d). It is the ownership market that is once again emphatically decoupled from the regional wage-earning economy, revealing the presence of surplus demand, residential capital sources divorced from the local labour market.

The Significance of Prime London

London's small area statistics permit a fine-grained analysis of price patterns in its 33 local authorities. The city's social geography shows a band of class privilege, including wealthy immigrants and British-born, extending along western and northern sectors from the City of London (Davidson and Wyly 2012). These sectors coincide with the highest dwelling prices, southwest from the City of London along the alignment of the Thames (comprising the boroughs of Westminster, Kensington and Chelsea, Hammersmith and Fulham, Wandsworth, and Richmond), and also north through parts of Camden and Islington (Figure 6.3, Table 6.2, column a). These seven boroughs plus the City include the districts often identified as 'prime London' by the real estate industry, and as London's 'alpha territories' by Atkinson (2020).[9] Half of all residential properties in England valued at above £2 million were found in the two central boroughs of Westminster and Kensington and Chelsea, and a full 90% were located within London itself (Giles 2014). Since 2001, gentrification has pushed eastwards from prime London through poorer neighbourhoods in Camden, Islington, Hackney, and Tower Hamlets, and south into Southwark and Lambeth, with more distant outposts, for example, the Olympic redevelopment site in Newham, part of the long-established immigrant and working-class sector of East London.

To this west–east social class distinction, the centralisation of residential price growth observed in other gateway cities is repeated in Inner London, with steep gains in the central boroughs, while Outer London districts have experienced lesser but still substantial price increases. The outer boroughs include some of London's more affordable suburbs, such as Croydon and Sutton to the south and Barking-Dagenham, Bexley and Havering to the east. It is in some of these outer boroughs that Davidson and Wyly (2012) located a suburbanised white working class, while concentrations of Caribbean, African, and South Asian immigrants together with British-born are found in a middle ring of boroughs.

Analysing nominal dwelling price data (Table 6.2, column b), the Inner London boroughs experienced average price gains of 673% between December 1995, when London was still recovering from the property bust of

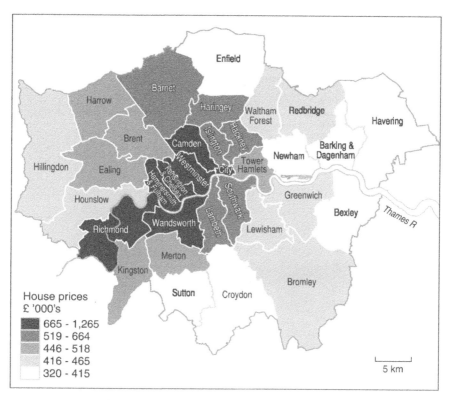

FIGURE 6.3   Median dwelling prices for London boroughs and the City of London, September 2020. (Source: author from data in ONS 2021b)

TABLE 6.2   Dwelling price characteristics in London boroughs

Borough	(a) Median dwelling price, 9/2020 (£'000s)	(b) % Nominal dwelling price growth, 12/95-9/20	(c) Months to exceed pre-GFC price peak	(d) Price volatility 12/95-12/18
London	483	562	24	
Inner London	676	673	26.5	0.54
Kensington/ Chelsea	1265	633	18	0.59
Westminster	980	666	15	0.59

(Continued)

TABLE 6.2 (Continued)

Borough	(a) Median dwelling price, 9/2020 (£'000s)	(b) % Nominal dwelling price growth, 12/95-9/20	(c) Months to exceed pre-GFC price peak	(d) Price volatility 12/95-12/18
Camden	800	602	24	0.52
City of London	782	645	27	0.61
Hammersmith/ Fulham	765	595	18	0.53
Wandsworth	665	673	24	0.53
Islington	650	584	24	0.50
Hackney	626	910	21	0.57
Lambeth	550	733	24	0.53
Southwark	529	645	21	0.54
Haringey	519	675	27	0.55
Tower Hamlets	508	647	27	0.47
Lewisham	430	668	27	0.54
Newham	400	751	75	0.54
Outer London	452	541	41.2	0.48
Richmond	675	525	24	0.47
Barnet	558	556	21	0.48
Brent	498	632	33	0.50
Kingston	492	507	30	0.47
Merton	485	547	24	0.49
Ealing	480	540	39	0.49
Harrow	480	500	30	0.47
Waltham Forest	465	745	60	0.57
Bromley	455	491	27	0.46
Greenwich	440	610	21	0.53
Redbridge	430	532	51	0.48
Hillingdon	430	506	27	0.47
Hounslow	427	485	48	0.45
Enfield	415	529	42	0.48
Sutton	404	503	57	0.46

TABLE 6.2   (Continued)

Borough	(a) Median dwelling price, 9/2020 (£'000s)	(b) % Nominal dwelling price growth, 12/95-9/20	(c) Months to exceed pre-GFC price peak	(d) Price volatility 12/95-12/18
Croydon	390	550	54	0.47
Havering	375	468	66	0.45
Bexley	370	497	60	0.46
Barking/ Dagenham	320	553	69	0.50

Source: author from data in ONS (2021b)

the early 1990s, and September 2020 during a period of continuing austerity, the COVID pandemic, and when some of the lustre had been lost in prime London with the spectre of Brexit.[10] Leading the pack, residential properties in Kensington and Chelsea still recorded an extraordinary median gain of over £1 million during this period, while in the adjacent borough of Westminster, the increment was over £850,000; in percentage terms the leader was Hackney, where gentrification brought an astonishing nominal gain of over 900% in just 25 years. In contrast, Outer London boroughs had lower gains, while still showing price rises of almost 550% on average. Pre-existing patterns of value have been reinforced, as more expensive central boroughs experienced high gains despite their elevated base values in 1995. Wealth deepening in existing elite boroughs is evident, with even higher percentage gains in adjacent boroughs like Hackney and Lambeth where ongoing gentrification is transforming lower-income districts.[11]

In inflation-adjusted real terms, only six high-priced central London boroughs saw price growth from 2007 to 2012 across the GFC, while several poorer boroughs saw losses of 20% or more (Hudson 2012). Column (c) of Table 6.2 shows that the nominal prices of prime central boroughs recovered fastest from the shock of the GFC, recouping lost house value in 15–24 months, while recovery times were typically much slower in Outer London, with losses in some cases continuing for five years or more. The prime districts of west-central London are matching, within the capital, the role of London within England (Webb et al. 2021). The highest prices occur there, with a speedy recovery after downturns. A persuasive negative correlation ($r_s = -0.70$) confirms that the more expensive a borough's housing, the shorter the post-GFC recovery time. Price recovery has then advanced wave-like outwards in subsequent months from prime boroughs in a spatial diffusion process (Figure 6.4). From 1996 to 2018, 74% of boroughs each year that ranked in the top three for annual house price gains were adjacent to one or more top three boroughs from the previous year.[12] It is possible to map the spatial channels followed by this price ripple, and also identify diffusion barriers where delays of at least 12 months occurred between neighbouring boroughs in market recovery (Figure 6.4). Price recovery moved freely between most boroughs in Inner London, but barriers existed around a number of suburbs, indicating a delayed market recovery of several years in Outer London. A comparison of maps of £1 million homes in 2003, 2008, and 2013 revealed a similar spatial diffusion process, with outward wave-like advances from a major initial cluster of expensive properties encircling Hyde Park and a northern spur to Hampstead (Savills 2014).

Price gains spread outwards due both to the spatial *displacement* of demand from outbid potential residents and investors, and also due to *replacement*, profit-taking permitting existing owners to move to larger and/or newer

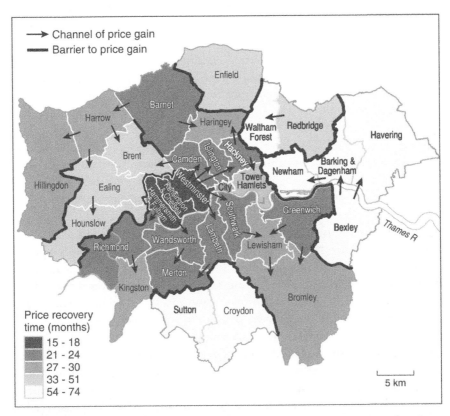

FIGURE 6.4 Ripple effect of dwelling price gains through London boroughs. (Source: author from data in ONS 2021b)

properties in cheaper districts, carrying price inflation with them. Giving substance to Figure 6.4, research by Savills showed that 44,000 people moved in 2013 from addresses in prime London boroughs with high price growth to 10 nearby but cheaper boroughs, including Hackney, Lambeth, Haringey, and Southwark, all of which in turn registered strong percentage price gains (Cook 2014). Selling households who move several stations down the railway line transfer their home equity from Central London to cheaper inner suburban opportunities, with ownership costs falling on average by over £3000 with each additional minute spent in the rail commute to Central London (Savills 2016, p. 10). Sellers from prime London also show up in greater numbers at accessible nodes in the commuter shed around the capital (Chi et al. 2020), and push up prices there, 'taking the capital's housing wealth to more affordable and spacious locations' (Savills 2017, p. 19).

The peak of house price growth in Central London had passed by the end of 2014 and price gains were diffusing to secondary markets; among London boroughs, Barking and Dagenham in the East End, with the cheapest housing market of all, registered among the highest 12-month percentage gains (15%) to September 2014, while in the two years prior to December 2016, prices for its neighbour Newham, no doubt inflated by post-Olympic redevelopment, surged by over 40%. This spatial pattern had been noted in earlier housing cycles as the sharp price rises of Central London cooled. From 2000–2006, '[t]here was a clear diffusion of price increases outwards from the expensive central boroughs to cheaper boroughs, particularly those in East London' (Hamnett 2009, p. 307). Like London in the UK, it is during downturns that prices begin to converge between price leaders and the rest.

A related feature of the London housing market that mimics the national pattern is the spatial pattern of price volatility, defined here as the coefficient of variation of the median annual residential prices for each borough from 1995 to 2018 (Table 6.2, column d). There was a modest decline in price volatility with distance from the City of London.[13] The most volatile values were in the most expensive administrative units, the City of London, Westminster, and Kensington and Chelsea; the lowest volatility in contrast was in the Outer London boroughs. Marked volatility in housing markets may be the result of speculative investment, as investors pile onto opportunities in good times but quickly cut their losses as prices decline.

Another indicator of the pervasive presence of non-local capital is the variable affordability of residential property across boroughs, defined as the ratio of a borough's median house prices to its gross annual workplace earnings (ONS 2021e). Affordability has deteriorated markedly in recent years, with Barking and Dagenham, the most affordable borough in 2020 (with a price-earnings ratio of 9.75), scoring higher (or less affordable) than the ratios of all 33 authorities in 1997, bar Kensington and Chelsea. While chronic across all of London, there is clear geographical differentiation in the afford-ability burden. The East End and outer suburbs are more affordable relative to the earnings of employees working in those boroughs, but the most strik-ing trend is the exceedingly high price-earnings ratios among the prime London boroughs. Six of them score over 18, led by Kensington and Chelsea with the massive price-earnings ratio of over 36, pointing to house prices totally mismatched with local wage earnings. The gap between earnings and housing costs has become a barrier to job recruitment in London; once hous-ing costs are factored into household budgets, incomes in London are lower than those in South West England (Resolution Foundation 2017).

In summary, prime London is the most expensive, the least affordable, the most inflationary, the most volatile, the fastest to recover from down-turns, and the epicentre of new price signals. The resurgence of the Central London housing market was one of the earliest 'green shoots' following the GFC, a consumer-led economic recovery, re-charging first the London and then more slowly, the national economy. Neither industrial production, nor GDP per capita, nor real wages had returned to the 2007 peak by the end of 2013; indeed, real earnings for London residents in 2012 had fallen back to the level reached in 2002 (ONS 2013).[14] But so strong was the rebound of the residential market led by Central London that by 2014, Mark Carney, Governor of the Bank of England, targeted housing as endangering the fragile national economic recovery: 'When we look at domestic risk, the biggest risk to financial stability and therefore to the durability of the expansion (of the economy), those risks centre in the housing market and that's why we are focused on that' (Carney 2014). The housing market was centrally implicated in the GFC bust, subsequent recovery, and, by its exuberance, with threats to that recovery.

'The World Capital for Property Investment'

To understand the source of those green shoots in Central London's housing, among the first indicators of post-GFC economic revival, we need to shift scales to consider London's status as a top-ranked global city, with far-reach-ing economic networks. In addition to the city's well-known economic advan-tages, currency movements can provide a powerful incentive to foreign investors, particularly when a depressed housing market and a weak pound move in tandem, offering significant benefits to holders of non-sterling cur-rency. Compared to its value in 2006, by 2010 the Euro was trading at a premium of almost 20% against the pound, while the US dollar advantage (to which the Hong Kong dollar is pegged) was even higher. As in previous economic recoveries, aided by foreign investor interest, the well-proven prime market could be expected to bounce back, and did so, with gains of around 10% a year from 2010 to 2014. Part of that investor behaviour could be conducted remotely.

In Hong Kong, the Olympic year of 2012 was a busy period for the 5-star Mandarin Oriental Hotel. On weekends the buzz in the hotel was heightened by hundreds of investors arriving to view property exhibitions for new condominium developments, on sale off-plan in gateway cities like Sydney, Vancouver, and especially London. International real estate companies, who curated these open houses, had alerted their lists of investors. On 10 November a full-page ad appeared in the *South China Morning Press* for Fitzroy Place – 'the most significant development in W1 for over 50 years' – marketed in Hong Kong by Savills and CBRE. Another full page in the same issue was dedicated to Stratford Plaza, 'Overlooking the 2012 Olympic Park', marketed by Jones Lang LaSalle, who were offering the project's 'First Worldwide Launch'. Separate half-page ads the same day in the *SCMP* presented two Thames-side projects by the Berkeley Group, the largest British residential builder in prime London. Riverlight (curated by Colliers) was among the first fruits of the vast Nine Elms/Battersea regeneration, while Royal Arsenal Riverside (Knight Frank) offered a 'Unique Investment Opportunity at London's Most Exciting Riverside Address'. On the weekend of 10–11 November 2012, from 11am to 7pm, all four London condominium projects were on sale at the same time in the same hotel, allowing comparative shopping among motivated investors shuttling from room to room, with all the convenience of adjacent vegetable stalls at a Saturday farmers' market. Catering to varied purchasing motives, advertisements featured, besides details of on-site amenities, access times via airports and the Underground, proximity to (world-class) universities, shopping, and in the case of Stratford Plaza, to a casino, and most important to investors, expected rental yields.

This sales model of transnational residential shopping has been well proven. In 2020, during the COVID-19 pandemic, a Malaysian developer sold new London flats valued at £20 million during three weekends of Hong Kong hotel exhibitions. With several active London projects to market, the developer considered London to be 'the world capital for property investment' (Chew 2020). As we saw in Chapter 3, the middle and upper-middle class in Hong Kong (and China) regard property as the most favoured investment, and typically own overseas residential property (Ho and Atkinson 2018). Clients would have been numbered among the 69,000 Hong Kong residents with liquid assets over HK$10 million who between them owned 90,000 residential units overseas (Bray 2019). After the GFC, Hong Kong and Singapore were awash with capital from quantitative easing in the US and elsewhere.[15] Simultaneously the flood of hot money from China into Hong Kong's luxury market was driving prices unattractively high. In contrast, London property was well-priced for 'ordinary' Chinese and Hong Kong buyers, purchasing at variable price points (Brill and Raco 2020; Ho 2020). A property title search revealed that Hong Kong residents led the ranks of registered foreign owners in half the London boroughs (Benham and Reeves 2022).

Singapore was another stop in the sales circuit of London new-build condominiums, and also a destination for a flood of stimulus capital in the post-GFC period, with high property prices leading investors to look at better opportunities overseas (Chapter 2). In the Olympic month of July 2012, the Berkeley Group presented its elite Abell & Cleland 'collection' of luxury, concierge-serviced apartments in a launch through Knight Frank's Singapore office. The apartment building is located in Westminster, at 'one of London's premier addresses … within walking distance of Downing Street and St. James's Park'. The Director of International Marketing at Knight Frank's Singapore office effused: 'This is a fantastic opportunity. Berkeley Homes has decided to offer Asian buyers the first bite of the cake … The project was very well received during our Hong Kong road show. As for the Singapore leg, we will be releasing more choice units. Prior to this weekend's launch, interest levels are high…' (Knight Frank Singapore 2012). The Singapore office had a mailing list of 8,000 subscribers who were alerted to this opportunity; typically, they were successful business and professional households.[16]

Property in the right location is an asset class that has given good returns to footloose capital in an era when other investments offer inferior and unpredictable returns, and in 2012 London was the most favoured global selection for both commercial and residential real estate. Among London's multiple advantages, an asset of particular interest to Asia Pacific investors has been its highly regarded educational sector with private schools and universities that trump competing global cities and have led to flat purchases while children pursue their studies, with rental options before and after.[17] Global purchasers have focussed on the prime London boroughs where they amassed a remarkable 46% of sales in 2012, and 75% of new-build dwellings, led by Hong Kong/Mainland China and Singaporean/Malaysian buyers, while Europeans preferred the resale market (Table 6.3). The following year, over 1800 new-build units were sold in Hong Kong and Singapore, ten percent of *all* London private completions that year (CBRE 2014). Many were investment properties. In the next three years, less than 60% of new-build purchases across all of London included a resident owner; in prime London[18] the share fell to one-third (Wallace et al. 2017). International buyers were concentrated in

TABLE 6.3 Nationality of buyers of prime London housing, by total transactions, 2012

Nationality	Percent prime London sales (all sales)	Percent prime London resales (of all sales)	Percent prime London new-build sales (of all sales)
United Kingdom	53.7	48.0	5.7
Western and N Europe	13.6	12.4	1.2
Hong Kong & China	7.4	1.6	5.8
SE Asia & Australasia	6.4	2.4	4.0
Middle East & N Africa	5.4	2.8	2.6
Eastern Europe & CIS	5.1	3.2	1.9
South Asia	3.4	3.1	<0.5
North America	3.3	3.0	<0.5
Africa	1.7	1.5	<0.5
Latin America	<0.5	<0.5	<0.5
Total	100	78	22

Source: adapted from data in Barnes (2013)

Inner London, while the Outer London boroughs were selected by 55% of London's UK buyers. The six leading boroughs for foreign buyers all included Thames-side frontage, the ribbon of new development favoured by Asian development companies. While almost half of overseas new-build sales went to owners with addresses in Hong Kong/China and South-east Asia, the international 'road shows' were more dispersed. Phase 3 of the Battersea Power Station redevelopment, featuring condominiums by starchitects Norman Foster and Frank Gehry, was launched simultaneously in 13 world cities, with locations in Europe (London, Paris, Milan), the United States (New York, Los Angeles), the Middle East (Dubai, Doha) and Asia (Hong Kong, Shanghai, Beijing, Singapore, Kuala Lumpur, Tokyo). The emphasis on Asian property exhibitions recognises the importance of Asian buyers for new-build condominiums as investment instruments.[19]

In contrast, Western European and North American buyers are more active in the resale market, and purchase is normally associated with work and residence in London (Barnes 2013). Middle Eastern and South Asian purchasers seek second homes, including expensive detached homes, to escape hot regional summers. Russian and Eastern European buyers include some very wealthy households who may purchase both a townhouse and a larger greenbelt property. Among wealthier buyers, the desire to shelter income in sterling-denominated assets may lead to the purchase of several expensive properties. Not surprisingly, then, foreign buyers are more likely to rent out their properties than British buyers. In total Savills estimated that international capital brought some £7 billion to the prime London residential market in the Olympic year alone (Barnes 2013).

Overseas purchasers are varied in both their capacity and their intentions (Glucksberg 2016); some buy as present or future immigrants, others as active investors, and a third group, buy-and-leave investors, are seeking a safe haven for their assets (Chung and Carpenter 2022). New-build homes bought by overseas buyers are primarily (60–70%) bought as rental investments, thereby growing the rental stock (Scanlon et al. 2017).[20] Buy-and-leave investors have considerable capital and have preferred the luxury apartment towers recently built along the Thames and at other amenity locations (Rees 2015; Fernandez et al. 2016; Atkinson 2019). An early precedent was the Candy brothers' Knightsbridge building, One Hyde Park, which for some years contained the most expensive low-rise flats in London and claimed to house 30 nationalities in 62 units, though few were in residence at any one time. One function of a safe haven is to provide security for capital when there is political instability in a foreign jurisdiction. Capital outflows overseas associated with political risk and economic uncertainty lead to investment in London real estate, often in districts where there is a concentration of home country residents. Such flights to safety of economic assets may anticipate later immigration, as asset-holders follow their assets: 'we find economically large, statistically significant, and robust effects of foreign risk on house prices in locations in which the shares of foreign-origin London residents are high' (Badarinza and Ramadorai 2018, p. 554).

Hong Kong has provided a striking case of the movement of crisis capital to London since the 2019–2020 conflicts. Following the Mainland's imposition of a National Security Law on 30 June 2020, Britain assured up to three million Hong Kong residents access to a British National (Overseas) Passport, with applications opening in January 2021. In the first two years of the BN(O) scheme over 160,00 applications were received and 105,000 Hongkongers moved to Britain (Westbrook 2023). With surveys showing that almost 80% of Hong Kong respondents were not optimistic about the city's future (Li, S. 2020), between July 2020 and March 2021, residents of Hong Kong bought almost 2000 dwelling units in London at a cost of close to £1 billion (Arcibal 2021). The combination of Brexit and the COVID-19 pandemic had left sterling weak on foreign exchanges, and Hong Kong buyers, benefitting from currency exchange and a depressed market, were cultivating the next green shoots of economic recovery in London real estate.[21]

In general, overseas residential investment is concentrated in Central London and declines towards the suburbs. For resales, foreign numbers are lower. In Savills' definition of prime London – which includes expensive districts from Canary Wharf westwards to suburban Richmond – only 26% of new-build sales but 62% of resales were bought by people of 'British nationality' in 2012 (Barnes 2013; Table 6.3). The resale market is also much larger comprising close to four out of every five purchases in prime London, so that UK nationals comprised 54% of the entire market. But that still leaves a very large share to overseas buyers. In London where supply consistently falls short of demand, and vacancies are typically low, external capital has significant marginal effects on availability and pricing. The prime market matters beyond its sheer numbers because its high-priced units provide an epicentre, as we saw earlier, for new price signals to be transmitted to a larger market.

Housing transactions originating with companies registered offshore have been a controversial aspect of foreign investment (Sa 2016). Because they are typically based in tax havens, and names of beneficial owners are concealed, it is not possible to allocate companies to an originating nation other than the tax haven.[22] But what does emerge is a strong relationship in England and Wales between local authority house prices and the value and volume of transactions involving offshore companies. A one percent increase in the share of transactions to a local municipality by a company registered offshore is linked to a two percent gain in house prices. The two Central London boroughs of Westminster and Kensington and Chelsea recorded by far the highest share of housing transactions from overseas companies; indeed, seven of the top ten local authorities (by volume) and six (by value) were in London.

Opaque Investment and Money Laundering

Concealing the identity of the beneficial owner of a property has been one of the advantages of company purchase from tax havens. Linked to it has been the opportunity for tax avoidance, notably capital gains tax, inheritance tax, and (until 2012) stamp duty. Within the London residential market, company purchases are concentrated in the highest-priced boroughs of prime London. Some companies are UK-based, some are tied to offshore tax havens, notably the British Virgin Islands (BVI), where financial services are available to support profitable international investment free of scrutiny. Investigative journalism has lifted the lid of some of these capital flows (Leigh et al. 2012; O'Murchu 2014). Land Registry filings showed a significant rise in capital flows to the British market from BVI investment vehicles, from £1.8 billion in 2009 to £3.8 billion in 2012, coinciding with the accelerated take-off of the Central London housing market. At least 30 of the 62 expensive flats owned by British and foreign high net-worth individuals at One Hyde Park in Knightsbridge, completed in 2009, were held by companies with BVI registration (Boffey 2011).[23] Almost 100,000 commercial and residential properties in England and Wales were purchased by offshore companies between 1999 and 2014 (O'Murchu 2014). Half of them were in Greater London, notably in the prime Central London boroughs; Westminster included *over 11,000* residential and commercial properties with an obscure 'beneficial owner' and Kensington and Chelsea almost 6,000. The purchase value of properties held by offshore companies in these two boroughs alone amounted to almost £45 billion.[24] An extraordinary dump of capital reached Central London, and in response property prices soared. Symptomatic of the purely commodified nature of property, the 2011 Census showed that vacancies 'with no usual resident' in these two boroughs reached 10.5% in Kensington and Chelsea and 13.5% in Westminster, indicative of a high share of buy-and-leave and scarcely occupied second home properties (McKenzie and Atkinson 2021). The buy-and-leave ownership model anticipates significant capital gains from a pristine asset.

While these tax sheltering vehicles were legal in themselves, the advantages of anonymity provided opportunity for both tax-avoidance and money-laundering. McKenzie and Atkinson (2021) find that 'the use of offshore investment vehicles and the concealment of wealth from national tax agencies have become key mechanisms by which housing resources have been exploited by the wealthy'. Transparency International (TI 2015) warned that Britain's lightly monitored Tier 1 investor visas had provided another channel for corrupt funds to enter the UK. While the British investor immigration programme is much smaller than related vehicles in Australia, Canada, and the US,[25] its capital requirement of £2 million attracted very wealthy applicants. TI noted that successful applications, primarily from China and Russia, originated in countries with a recent history of illicit outgoing capital flows. Between 2008, when the scheme started, and 2015 almost £2 billion had been invested in the UK by golden visa nationals from these two countries. Transparency International (2015) expressed concern that Britain's visa programme was being used for money laundering. Its report contained no evidence for corruption but established strong levels of plausibility. Like Canada, the investor visa stream received limited oversight or due diligence in the management of the immigration-capital-real estate nexus, making it an attractive potential vehicle for money-laundering. Recognising the weakness of its existing oversight, and noting greater European concern over money laundering (Surak 2022), the visa programme was suspended and has been subject to repeated reviews.

Central London has been the hub of money laundering and associated criminal charges. Transparency International estimated that £4.2 billion in 'suspicious wealth' had been invested in the London property market, highlighting expensive homes (TI 2017). Homeowners implicated in corruption charges lived in property valued at £6 million on average, while homes owned by companies registered in tax havens were priced at almost £2 million. A flurry of activity followed David Cameron's declaration in 2015 to weed out 'dirty cash' from the property market. Regulators began to enforce money-laundering compliance rules, leading to fines for banks and real estate agencies, though they are small relative to the capital assets of the companies; penalties charged to real estate agencies by HM Revenue and Customs were a puny £2.3 million in 2017–2018 (Beioley 2019). But tax reform has removed some of the advantages of offshore companies, including exemptions for non-residents from capital gains tax on second homes, and has established a public registry of beneficial owners challenging anonymity. Checks on the source of wealth are now required for buyers, sellers, tenants, and landlords of luxury rentals (Brooker 2020). Living arrangements that cannot be explained by apparent income sources may lead to issuance of an 'unexplained wealth order' that can be used to freeze assets bought with suspicious funds. But while some regulatory heft has been added to counter dirty money, the test of strengthened policy will be the effectiveness of enforcement (The Economist 2018).

Extraordinary wealth is stored in Central London's 'alpha territories' (Forrest et al. 2017; Atkinson 2020). John Lanchester (2012) observed that London 'has one of the world's largest concentrations of the super-rich, and the reason for that is that we have chosen to have them here.' The annual billionaire count by real estate and wealth management firms underlines the desire of British and global elites to occupy London for at least part of the year. In 2014, the capital's maladroit mayor, Boris Johnson, offered his own assessment: 'London is to billionaires what the jungles of Sumatra are to the orangutan. It is their natural habitat.'[26] Even during the COVID pandemic the very wealthy continued to invest in Central London. Knight Frank reported sales of almost $4 billion on super-prime properties, each valued at over $10 million, in London in 2020, a higher total than in any other metropolis among top global cities (Harley 2021). In a weak sterling market, and with a 20% discount over 2014 prices in prime London, Russian, French, and Chinese/Hong Kong buyers were most active, while a third of buyers were British. The UK complement had risen from just 12% in 2019 due, Knight Frank posited, to impaired travel and transactions for foreign buyers during the COVID-19 pandemic.

Global Property Developers

As we saw in Sydney and Vancouver, the creation of a transnational sales market has been joined by the arrival of global property development companies, primarily from Asia Pacific. There is a reciprocal relationship between builder and buyer for, as in Sydney, overseas investors have an affinity for home-country developers. These companies have undertaken some of the largest regeneration projects on substantial brownfield waterfront sites and council house estates. Large projects on opposite banks of the Thames include the waterfront redevelopment of the Lot's Road power station in Chelsea by Hong Kong's CK Asset Holdings with over 800 flats, and the nearby Battersea/ Nine Elms redevelopment, a vast £8 billion mixed use project undertaken by a Malaysian partnership. The scale of some of these projects requires deep financial resources and resilience to transcend a lengthy and complex development process: CK Asset's Convoy Wharf project, a plan for 3,500 homes on Henry VIII's royal dockyard, took 15 years to gain final planning approval. There are several large Qatari residential projects, including the redevelopment of London's Olympic site and the US Embassy in Grosvenor Square. Meanwhile a 10,000-unit residential project on the Greenwich Peninsula is being built by a subsidiary of Hong Kong's New World Development. In 2013–2014, several large Chinese property companies made their landfall in London, to achieve portfolio diversification in light of a deflating property bubble in China,[27] while the Lodha Group, India's largest developer by sales, announced a £5 billion spending spree, intending by 2018 to become one of London's top house builders (Crabtree and Allen 2014). The large Australian developer, Lendlease, has a major £15 billion development pipeline in the UK, with a focus on London regeneration projects.

Together, Hong Kong/Chinese, Singaporean, Malaysian, and Qatari developers had planning permission to build 33,000 dwellings in London (CBRE 2014). Four years later Savills (2018) recorded an incomplete list of 31 projects under construction by developers from China/Hong Kong, Malaysia, and Singapore. The Asian market prefers mid- and high-rise new build condominiums: Hong Kong's CK Asset is planning three 40-storey towers as part of Convoy's Wharf; China's Greenland Group has half-built Spire London, which at 67 storeys is planned to be Western Europe's tallest residential building. The post-GFC boom is reconfiguring the city's skyline, with over 200 towers of over 20 storeys, the large majority residential. While accelerating the rate of residential construction, the high-priced luxury units have saturated their niche market, and are not addressing London's affordability problem; construction has been halted on the Spire London. Critics claim buy-to-leave, second home, and unsold units create unoccupied lifeless towers in the sky (Atkinson 2019).

British developers may not have pockets as deep as some of these global players. Hong Kong's CK Asset, for example, bought its dockland site in 2005 for £100 million but the site gave no return on that investment until planning permission for phase 1 was finally committed by Lewisham Council in 2020 (Liu and Li 2020).[28] The Berkeley Group, the most active British competition for this luxury apartment market, operates a much tighter ship with pre-sales of 60–70% usually required by banks for project financing. Pre-sale or off-plan purchasing is a more familiar model in Asia Pacific which is one reason why Berkeley projects have depended so heavily on that region for sales. As we saw in Vancouver (Chapter 5), a secondary market has arisen exchanging off-plan contracts before construction is complete, sales are finalised, and stamp duty must be paid. This process of assignment prior to completion typically leads to the inflation of final prices. The Berkeley Group's Riverlight project, which we noted during its marketing in Hong Kong in 2012, was not completed until 2017, allowing opportunity for multiple speculative exchanges of contracts. According to selling agents, some purchasers who bought off-plan near the launch were able to sell on their assignment for a two-bedroom unit a few years later, with profits of up to £500,000 (Hammond 2019). Of course, in a declining market such flipping could equally lead to losses, and significant risk for highly leveraged traders. Either way the secondary market in assignments is a game of commodity trading, property as investment writ large.

The Supply–Demand Imbalance

Quite aside from substantial international investment, the fundamentals of London's economic and demographic growth would support a vibrant housing market. For almost fifty years after its peak in the late 1930s, London lost population. Though economic transition was already underway, financial deregulation in 1986 is widely identified as the iconic event that triggered the globalisation of banking and financial services, the expansion of the advanced services economy, and, in the housing market, the accelerated gentrification of the central boroughs. Since then, London has experienced a population surge, adding close to a million people between 2001 and 2011, and another 750,000 to 2020 to reach nine million, with a projection to exceed ten million during the 2030s (Cosh and Gleeson 2020). This population growth is a fundamental contributor to domestic housing demand. But a globalising, post-industrial economy has left London with a fundamental mismatch: since 1997, job growth (46%) has exceeded population growth (28%), and population growth has exceeded net construction of new dwellings (19%) (Cosh and Gleeson 2020). The under-performance of home construction has been an abiding dilemma for housing London's permanent population.

Like other gateway cities, London displays a net population loss through internal migration which is more than compensated for by net immigration, consolidating the city's stature as a global population hub. Greater London retains its classic role as an escalator region, where young adults with ambition follow the legendary precedent of Dick Whittington and move to the capital, if not to make their fortune, then at least to complete university education and make early career advancement (Fielding 1992). The age group from 20–29 is the only cohort where London collects a net annual population surplus from the rest of the United Kingdom, some 30,000–40,000 students and young professionals in recent years (pre-pandemic). Encountering unaffordable housing costs, they have provided the front line in the gentrification of cheaper neighbourhoods. For all other age groups there is a net outflow, summing to an annual net loss through internal migration of 40,000–50,000 adult Londoners (Cosh and Gleeson 2020). More than compensating for this internal migration deficit has been a net annual average increase of about 100,000 international migrants (pre-Brexit) over the past decade. Contributing to the 'superdiversity' of the metropolis, some 18 nationalities numbered over 50,000 residents each in 2011; indicative of London's global attraction, each continent was represented among these national groups. In addition, natural increase has added around 75,000 Londoners a year; benefitting from immigrant family formation, the total fertility rate, around 1.7 in recent years, is not much less than the level for England and Wales (ONS 2019b).

The resilience of London's global economic status has supported population growth, with the addition of almost two million jobs since 1997 (Hutton 2022). In terms of occupations, 37% of all workers were managers, senior administrators, or professionals in 2011 and this trend is projected to continue into the future, reaching 45% of all jobs by 2041 (GLA Economics 2016). Already the largest economic group in 2011, a third of job growth up to 2041 is expected to be in the professional, real estate, scientific and technical sectors. Manufacturing will continue its precipitous decline, and there will be ongoing shrinkage in clerical and secretarial positions. Financial services, a dominant growth sector up to the GFC, while remaining significant, is expected to grow only modestly.

While there has been disagreement about the emerging class composition of post-industrial London, recent census trends and employment projections seem to point to the continuing professionalisation of the labour force as a dominant narrative, with jobs that require lower human capital declining as a share of London's workers, with the notable exception of the immigrant-heavy hospitality and personal service sectors (GLA Economics 2016). The continuing substantial growth of a well-educated white-collar work force consolidates effective housing demand, and presents a strong incentive for residential investment. In addition to international investors, British and foreign financial and legal professionals in London have propelled the expensive end of the housing market, through high pay and a generous bonus structure. Expansion of the financial and legal sector required not only a new business centre in Canary Wharf but also prompted a new round of housing construction in brownfield waterfront sites, a model that rapidly swept up and downstream in a continuing wave of Thames-side flats (Davidson and Lees 2005). But at the same time there has also been a significant unemployed and economically inactive population, amounting to about a third of Londoners aged 16–64 years (Watt 2008; GLA Economics 2016). Growing inequality indicates substantial housing difficulties for at least a third of the population; as we shall see, housing challenges reach further, and into London's middle classes.

The conventional fundamentals of demand, population growth and an expanding, well-paid employee base, would predict house price increases. But demand does not only comprise a local population and wage economy. Surplus investor demand, both national and international, for London housing vastly expands pressures beyond conventional fundamentals (Gallent et al. 2017). Whitehead (2016) estimated that in England such extraneous demand should inflate estimates of necessary annual new-build supply by around 60%. In London, hub of international property capital, we should expect considerably higher demand inflation.

Dramatic recent population growth has, then, been accompanied by substantial investment by national as well as global buyers with deep pockets. This upswing in demand should have been accompanied by a parallel supply response by the building sector – but that response has not occurred. Like other gateway cities, housing supply in the London market has proven highly inelastic in responding to market signals. Construction peaks of over 30,000 units a year in the 1965–1975 period were achieved through a substantial surge of local authority (council) housing. The abrupt termination of that policy by the Thatcher government in 1980 together with public rental housing's absorption in a preferred ownership model through the right-to-buy policy, was followed by a precipitous decline in new housing supply, and it was almost 40 years before annual completions again reached 30,000 units (Cosh and Gleeson 2020), despite population gains of almost two million people. Estimates identified the need for 49,000 net new units a year over 20 years to meet growing demand and clear the existing backlog (GLA 2014). But the supply backlog intensified; only three years later, the annual target was reassessed at 66,000 new units, with 65% affordable (GLA 2017).[29]

There are competing explanations for this supply failure. A familiar explanation in gateway cities, endorsed by the building industry, lays the blame squarely with excess regulation: the development no-go land of London's green belt, the tardiness of the planning process, an inordinate weight given to protest groups in planning decisions (London First 2014; Cheshire 2018). Pro-regulation groups in contrast hone in on the housing industry and highlight its tendencies to land banking with slow development release to maintain residential scarcity and enhance the advantage of rising land prices (Griffith 2011). While there is always room for efficiency improvements in planning bureaucracies like any other, it is notable that planning permission for an average of 60–65,000 units was granted in London each year from 2010 to 2014, and 80–85,000 from 2015–2019; the completed dwellings during this period were only 20–25,000 units and 30–35,000 units per year respectively (Cosh and Gleeson 2020). Despite loosening planning regulations and government programmes to boost home sales by enhancing access to mortgage credit (notably through help-to-buy), most large builders in the post-2008 environment have been using their capital to extend their land banks.[30]

In a meeting with Treasury officials, the major building companies asserted they could only ramp up production by 5–10% a year, but not higher: 'We are an inelastic industry. Where are we supposed to find that sort of growth?' (Hammond and Pickard 2013). Griffith (2011) sees such inelasticity as a comment not only on sluggish public planning, but also a clue to the housing industry's underperformance and its preference to hoard land rather than build additional houses. Lack of competition, with the top 10 builders providing almost two-thirds of new supply in the UK, introduces oligopolistic inefficiencies (Halligan 2020). Interviews with London housing specialists underscored a tendency among London house-builders to modest 'satisficing' behaviour in unit production. 'Builders want to keep sales volume down, small outputs per year, 90th percentile pricing, rationing product to maximise revenue' (a senior real estate consultant); 'Returns are heavily bonus-driven for managers in the building sector: they don't outperform expectations. It's a huge blockage' (a mortgage professional). While acknowledging 'a sclerotic planning system', a high-ranking GLA manager regarded London house-builders like the Berkeley Group as 'having a large vested interest in constraining supply. Modest volumes and high margins, working at the top end of the market. They are a very happy bunch today'. Consistent with this portrayal, in an interview, the managing director of the Berkeley Group raised a pertinent question: 'The majors aren't going to build a lot more, so who is going to deliver these [additional] homes?' (Sharman 2014).[31]

This failure to scale up has been a key limitation in housing production. With such private and public housing delivery failures, the contributions of international developers have been welcomed, with their deep capital reserves and experience with long and complex large redevelopments, often on difficult brownfield sites.

Public Policy and the Transformation of Housing Supply

Despite the free market mantra of globalisation, public policy runs deeply through London's housing market trends. We have already noted the abrupt slowdown in the prime market with the introduction of stamp duty increases in 2012 and 2014. The potential market leverage of residential taxes was revealed again by the Conservative government's stamp duty holiday introduced as an economic stimulus during the pandemic-induced recession in 2020–2021. The tax saving of £10–15,000 for homes valued above £500,000 contributed significantly to an unanticipated surge in the housing market.

But government policy has reached far deeper than stamp duty over an extended period. These effects can be observed from the changing composition of tenure types in London from 1981 to 2019 (Figure 6.5). A steep rise in mortgaged homeownership occurred during the 1980s following the right-to-buy policy and the continued gentrification of former private flat rentals. By the early 1990s, mortgage holders accounted for 40% of all households; with another 18% outright owners, the market was well on the way to the Conservative goal of homeownership. But subsequent affordability problems and tighter post-GFC bank lending protocols contributed to a sharp retreat of mortgaged homeowners to 26% of households by 2019. This substantial decline points to the precarious status of 'generation rent', young adults increasingly divorced from the prospect of homeownership (Ronald 2018; McKee et al. 2020). In 1990, 57% of London households with a head aged 25–34 were homeowners, but by 2019, this level had fallen precipitously to 29% (Cosh and Gleeson 2020), scarcely surprising when the average London deposit for first-time buyers had more than tripled between 2005 and 2020 to reach £150,000. If somewhat smaller, still unexpectedly large ownership reductions occurred among all age cohorts up to 55, but the pattern was reversed dramatically for those aged 65 and above where ownership rose from 49% to 69%. The elderly are well-represented in the population who enjoy outright ownership (Figure 6.5). These shifts represent extraordinary changes in generational life chances over a very short period, with the property wealth of London homeowners (net of mortgage debt) almost doubling from 2008 to 2018 to a median value of £410,000 (Cosh and Gleeson 2020).[32] Benefitting from favourable tax structures, these owners have been gifted with windfall gains totally inaccessible to the other half of London's households in various rental tenures.

By 2019, London households were almost equally split between ownership and rental status. The ownership share would be even smaller without

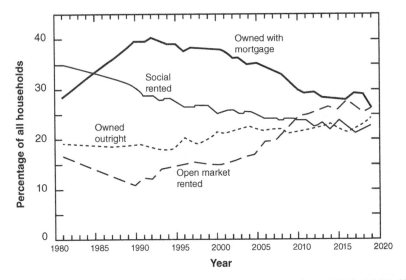

FIGURE 6.5   Changing household tenures in London, 1981–2019. (Source: Cosh et al, 2020 / Greater London Authority)

the help-to-buy policy introduced by the Coalition in 2013 as a new vehicle for advancing homeownership.[33] No less than £12 billion in public funds were allocated to undergird this substantial stimulus to boost homeownership and the private sector actors who produce it. By 2019, help-to-buy house sales peaked at over 6,000 new dwellings in London, principally in the cheaper outer boroughs, with almost all purchases by first-time homebuyers (Cosh and Gleeson 2020). The scheme has been a major stimulus for home builders, accounting for up to a third of sales, and inflating profitability.[34] But like other policies swelling demand, help-to-buy has also inflated prices, introducing an unwelcome additional barrier for present and future aspiring homeowners who do not qualify for the scheme. Critics of this inflationary policy included conservative economists from the IMF, the European Commission, and the UK's Office for Budget Responsibility. An additional objection to help-to-buy is that it is a demand-side policy that does not guarantee additional construction; this task is seconded to the private sector that has been unable to ramp up supply. In its expensive aid to the homeownership lobby, overriding the advice of conservative institutions, help-to-buy is an ambitious effort to advance Mrs. Thatcher's vision of a property-owning democracy. Help-to-buy clearly shares the same family tree as right-to-buy. The determination to propping up homeownership despite criticism from more cautious economists reveals the tenacity and centrality of the ideology of ownership in government circles.

The astonishing reversed status of social and private rentals is a forceful reminder of the power of public policy (Figure 6.5). Social rentals, a major achievement of the welfare state, were the leading tenure form in London in 1981, but in last place in 2019; in contrast private rentals were a declining, bottom rank tenure in 1981, but by 2019 had just overtaken mortgaged ownership to become the leading tenure in contemporary London. The erosion of social rentals was instigated by the radical conservatism of 1980s Thatcherism, with its commitment to whittle down the welfare state and replace it by the marketised values and products of individual responsibility. Right-to-buy, enabling sitting tenants to purchase council flats at steep discounts, was a significant ideological project to privatise the housing stock, and in some boroughs to consolidate Conservative political majorities (Hamnett 2003a). To neoliberal politicians, council housing was profligate and a visible and vulnerable product of the welfare state. From this perspective, it exemplified the failure of a collective view of society that was dismissive of individual responsibility. In contrast the homeowner, and homeownership, should be an emblem of responsible citizenry, liberating an asset-pursuing, self-reliant society of individual households.

After the 1980 Housing Act, some 300,000 London council house units were sold to sitting tenants during the next 40 years, and sales continued through Labour as well as Conservative governments (MHCLG 2021b). Thatcher's reforms also cut central government funding for new local authority housing construction by over 80% (Brownill and Sharp 1992). Substantial council house rent increases between 1985 and 1990 provided the stick to accompany the carrot of deep purchasing discounts. Local authorities lost control of a public asset not only through tenant purchases but also through the transfer of existing council stock to non-profit housing associations. With budget cuts impairing the ability of local authorities to maintain and repair their buildings, there was a considerable incentive to sell off properties in a stock transfer to housing associations. Across the UK the share of local authority rental housing fell from 31% of all dwellings in 1980 to 16% percent in 2008 (Lowe 2011). Remaining and new tenants were poorer and more marginal to the labour market, while rapid turnover compromised stability and the development of bonding social capital. But a 10% increase in national homeownership was achieved in short order.

Housing associations have become the major provider of social housing in the UK; at two million units, their numbers exceeded the dwindling council stock by 2008 (Lowe 2011; Dorling 2014). In London the almost 800,000 affordable homes in 2019 were shared equally by local authorities and housing associations (Cosh and Gleeson 2020). But this total was some 5% lower than the 1997 stock total. In a policy context dominated by market solutions, the non-profit housing associations have faced a challenging borrowing and building environment, with a 60% cut in their budget by the Coalition government in 2010, and substantial withdrawal of the banks from property loans. They have been obliged to secure loans from private lenders and investors, including pension funds and insurance companies (Tang et al. 2017). Housing associations have moved into the capital markets to fund new housing projects with some success, though their business model now moves closer to private sector norms, with affordable rents rising to 80% of market levels. There are also internal resources from rental and other revenues and, more controversially, from the sale of housing assets (Morrison 2017).[35] With the need for cross-subsidies, it is difficult to see capacity for major expansion of production in the current political and fiscal environment, certainly at the low end of the market where social housing has historically been focussed.

In this respect, a promising development was central government's funding of the London Affordable Homes Programme, with a grant to the Greater London Authority of almost £5 billion over seven years. Mayor Sadiq Khan envisaged construction of 116,000 affordable homes by 2022 during the life of the grant, including over 50,000 units with social rent levels (GLA 2018). The emergence of GLA production has coincided with a decline in affordable production from other sources including housing associations. Moreover, with funding pressures, in recent years the share of social rentals from other providers has declined while affordable units, with shallower subsidies, have prevailed.

The private rental market, historically London's dominant sector, has followed a remarkable trajectory of changing fortunes (Figure 6.5). In 1961, 45% of London households lived in private rentals. But the sector dwindled dramatically, as owner occupancy and social housing expanded. Hamnett and Randolph (1984) recorded one aspect of change, the 'flat breakup market' in Central London in the 1970s, when landlords divested low-value rentals to gentrifiers who, through renovation, would add value to the property (Hamnett 2003b). By 1991, the private rental share of the market had fallen below 14%, while owner-occupancy peaked at 57%. But private rentals have moved with some alacrity from last place to leading tenure type in 2019. In part the sector has benefitted from right-to-buy policy, for a quarter of purchased council units have, with resales, become private rentals (Murie 2018). But more rental stock was needed to provide market solutions for lower-income groups stranded by the contraction of council housing. The Conservative government deregulated the private rental sector in the 1988 Housing Act. In this new landlord-friendly environment, a new class of investors was speedily created by the mid-1990s among middle-aged Britons who usually bought a single dwelling with the intent to buy to let, producing a secondary rental income stream, and with a view to a retirement nest egg from eventual capital gains at sale (Leyshon and French 2009; Ronald and Kadi 2018).[36] Buy-to-let development was compatible with the nurturing of investor subjectivities, the Thatcherite view of the self-sufficient citizen using property as asset to cover any shortfall in wage or pension income. Substantial tax concessions boosted the sector. Private landlords received tax breaks as private businesses worth £14 billion in 2012–2013; buy-to-let was so profitable that landlord numbers grew by a third to 2.1 million in the UK over just six years (Pegg 2015). The scheme has been popular in London where past price trends indicated that capital gains could be relied upon. In desirable but not yet top prime districts, like Maida Vale, real estate agents estimated that three-quarters of home sales in 2014 and 2015 were to buy-to-let investors, outbidding first home buyers (Lawford 2018). New as well as resale properties were bought; on London building sites of above 20 units, 45% of purchases in 2013 were buy-to-let investments (Cosh and Gleeson 2020).

But by 2019, the buy-to-let share on these sites had halved. In another indication of the power of public policy in general, and taxation in particular, to direct the housing market, buy-to-let became less profitable as stamp duty was introduced in 2016 on second properties, and tax relief on mortgage interest began to be phased out. Shaping policy was public concern about competition from buy-to-let landlords pre-empting first-time buyers, about unregulated rent and maintenance of properties, and about insecurity of tenure. Diminished yields are leading to a professionalisation of the rental sector with the phased withdrawal of the 'amateur landlord' with a single property. Britain has never had a significant stock of purpose-built rental apartments along North American lines. Much smaller in scale than the buy-to-let stock, so-called build to rent accounts for only one percent of UK dwellings, compared to 45% in the US (Savills 2020b). But large investors see capacity for significant up-scaling. Lloyd's Bank has set up its own home rental subsidiary with plans to build 50,000 units by 2030, or about half the present total stock, and other banks including Goldman Sachs have established rental investment funds (Hammond 2021). Large UK property companies including British Land and the Grosvenor Group, have launched build-to-rent projects in London to diversify their portfolios away from more problematic retail and office holdings.[37] With this weighty support, build-to-rent projects are expanding rapidly, reaching a fifth of residential completions in London in 2020 (BPF 2021).

Austerity: The Metanarrative

These tenure trends must be contextualised against a far-reaching ideology and comprehensive policy direction since 2010, the government-driven metanarrative of public austerity. Only six weeks after a governing Conservative-Liberal Democrat Coalition was formed following the 2010 General Election, a budget was tabled announcing a period of deep austerity to bring Britain's sizable GFC debt under control. An autumn comprehensive spending review battened down the hatches even more tightly. While cuts were expected to address the public debt, their extent was not anticipated if the target was debt reduction alone. But the cuts also continued the theme declared by Conservatives in the 1980s and sustained by New Labour, to rein in government and turn to market solutions. That policy paradigm is evident in the differential fortunes of housing tenures in London, with the decline of social housing, the revival of the private rental sector, and the continuing effort to stimulate homeownership. A decline of homeownership levels was evidently not part of the plan, but became collateral damage in the failure of public policy to address London's housing affordability crisis and the structural inequality that lay behind it (Edwards 2016). While a home owning democracy achieved through privatisation may have been the goal, the market was increasingly unable to deliver that outcome. From a right-to-buy induced peak of 73% in 2008, homeownership steadily fell in the UK to a low of 63% in 2017. In London the 1990s peak of 58% fell to 51% in 2019. It was left to Prime Minister Theresa May to acknowledge that failure by stating the obvious: 'Our broken housing market is one of the greatest barriers to progress in Britain today' (DCLG 2017, p. 5).

Public debt was incurred by a massive transfer of wealth to private institutions; the IMF calculated that for the eight countries most impacted by the GFC, the cost of direct support to the banks alone exceeded $1.5 trillion (Kitson et al. 2011). The Coalition's solution to the debt mountain was to make rapid repayment through deep cuts, including massive layoffs of almost half a million civil servants. Conservative re-election in 2015 carried the programme forward. The most severe cuts were to the local government budget of the Department of Communities and Local Government, a grant reduction of over one half during the 2010–2011 to 2015–2016 budget period (Gray and Barford 2018). This targeting of local government repeated the same practice of downloading cuts to a junior level of government that took place in North America (Peck 2012). Some critics saw in addition a disciplinary, even a punitive intent. The greater the dependence of local authorities on the central government grants compared to their own council taxes and local assets, the greater was the total budget loss. Clearly wealthier (Conservative) councils would ride out this cost-cutting storm much more securely than those in deprived areas, especially as a flat rate reduction across the board would impact richer councils less severely. The outcome was both painful and regressive. Spending cuts to the most deprived tenth of local authorities averaged 31% compared with 16% to the least deprived tenth (Harris et al. 2019).

While the longer-term political project was to shrink the state and introduce market disciplines to its service delivery models, Gray and Barford

(2018, p. 543) identify three consequences of austerity policies that aggravated inequality and spatial injustice: '(i) a shrinking capacity of the local state to address inequality, (ii) increasing inequality between local governments themselves, and (iii) intensifying issues of territorial injustice.' Moreover, welfare cuts to households added to the overall misery of have-not councils and their residents. London local authorities suffered a one-third funding reduction in real terms in the first four years of the Coalition. Councils showed some resilience in absorbing the shocks mainly through greater efficiencies, including much use of volunteer services (Fitzgerald and Lupton 2015). But the continuing accumulation of cuts into the 2015 Conservative government and the legal necessity to provide mandatory services threatened discretionary services like parks and libraries, with frequent contestation about their closure or marketisation (Penny 2017; Smith 2019). Increasingly, marketable assets were sold to cover the costs of mandatory services – and the most marketable and valuable asset was land, notably the land on which council estates were built.

Austerity Vs. Social Housing

Austerity severely compromised social housing and penalised social and private renters. Housing welfare support was cut by almost a half during the tenure of the Coalition government (Perry 2014). Housing benefits, subsidies to low-income social and private renters, were highest in London because it had the highest rents. Five London boroughs, Hackney, Newham, Haringey, Islington, and Tower Hamlets, received the largest housing benefits per capita in England in 2009–2010, while the top 20 local authorities by size of average weekly subsidies were *all* London boroughs (Hamnett 2010). Introduced by the Thatcher Government in 1982 to replace social housing subsidies, the costs of housing benefits to eligible tenants had risen precipitously with social and private rental costs, and were draining the Exchequer by £23 billion in 2011–2012 (Hamnett 2014). Housing critics have pointed to the folly of this payment to (mainly) private landlords, helping to keep rent prices high, instead of applying funds to construct or maintain social housing.

Housing benefits were slashed by the Coalition Government by reducing eligibility and also introducing caps to the size of the benefit for private tenants. Separate cut-backs were extended to tenants in social rentals. The result was significant reduction of affordable private rentals for poorer households, especially in Central and Inner London (Hamnett 2010). Dire projections followed of forced displacement and loss of permanent housing. Sure enough, reports appeared in the next several years of the beginning of re-location of tenants from inner to outer London (DWP 2015). As vacancies disappeared, some local authorities sent homeless families to temporary accommodation outside London. The housing benefit case load peaked at 850,000 in 2013, and has edged downwards since, though it has been re-inflated by COVID-19.[38] Tenants left more exposed and vulnerable by benefit cuts and freezes are disproportionately racial minorities, women, and the disabled (Dorling 2014). For some, dwelling space has reached the bottom rung on the housing ladder, placement in temporary accommodation by London boroughs of otherwise homeless households, amounting to over 60,000 households in 2020, two-thirds of the total for the whole of England (Cosh and Gleeson 2020). The overall outcome has been to displace the poor and extend the concentration of 'alpha territories' in Central and Inner London (Atkinson 2020), a process that then Mayor, Boris Johnson, once denounced as 'Kosovo-style social cleansing' (Dorling 2014, p. 126). Disciplining the poor is seen as a way to incentivise the transition from welfare to the labour market – although a high proportion of housing benefit recipients have jobs, but are members of the working poor. Rising housing costs, principally in the private rental sector, have been the key driver of working poverty (Trust for London and WPI Economics 2020; McNeil et al. 2021). This is an entirely predictable consequence of the reduction of housing benefits and social housing in a tight rental market. Even before the COVID pandemic, 28% of Londoners lived in poverty, a figure far higher than the national average.[39]

The disciplining of the welfare state has been conducted as methodically against properties as it has against tenants. Hundreds of council housing estates in London were a legacy of the post-1945 welfare state and, as Murie has observed, when new they were higher quality housing and offered more tenure security than the private rental units that were the dominant source of supply in the 1950s and beyond: '[Council housing] was supported across party boundaries because the private sector failed to build enough new housing or maintain the existing stock. … It formed a high-quality sector providing the housing of choice for many affluent workers while excluding the poorest households' (Murie 2018, pp. 477–478). But properties aged, maintenance funds were increasingly insufficient, and the status of the estates declined. They became, however, a significant land asset, particularly if located with good access to Central London. The severe cutbacks to local authorities and the legal requirement they provide mandatory services, caused boroughs to sell off assets, and their most valuable asset is land. So began the process of state-led gentrification, what Loretta Lees saw as 'the final frontier' of the displacement-reinvestment cycle as it invaded council estates (Lees 2014).

The story of this uncompromising privatisation of a welfare state legacy has been well told: on the everyday experience of housing estate dispossession in London (Lees and White 2020; Elliott-Cooper et al. 2020b); on the democratic deficit in the redevelopment planning process (Lees 2014; Flynn 2016); on the injustice faced by leaseholders who had followed right-to-buy promises but now found themselves facing a buy-out at devalued prices (Hodkinson and Essen 2015; Elliott-Cooper et al. 2020a); on resistance by estate residents (Watt and Minton 2016; Hubbard and Lees 2018). The estate regeneration policy is displacing poor families from Central London, as council estates are demolished and replaced by a mix of market condominiums and affordable housing, typically with shallow subsidies. The original promise to tenants was commonly better-quality housing in a socially mixed redevelopment, with deep-subsidy social housing interspersed with market rentals and condominiums. The private developer was obligated to honour the borough's affordable housing quota in redevelopment plans according to the Section 106 agreement of the 1990 Town and Country Planning Act, which required developer contributions to meet established public goals. A standard Section 106 objective of local authorities was the inclusion of affordable housing in the rebuilt estate, and many affordable housing units had been completed by housing associations through Section 106 agreements before the GFC; in addition, intermediate units which offered a partial ownership model were part of the mix (Cosh and Gleeson 2020).

But while social rentals had deep subsidies, the Coalition introduced a different concept of affordable housing closer to market rentals in 2010, and this shallow subsidy choice became dominant during the Conservative government that came to office in 2015.[40] This redefinition of affordability penalised the poorest who could not make the jump from a deep (50%) social subsidy to a shallow (20%) affordable subsidy.

Estate regeneration was facilitated by what Tom Slater (2014) called the myth of 'broken Britain'. Representations of local authority estates as dysfunctional in design, in quality of life, or in contributions to society, whether portrayed in the media (especially television and film), in policy pronouncements ('sink estates') and even in academic accounts ('residualisation') together have constructed a stigmatised identity. Loretta Lees (2014) has carefully shown the political process of misinformation and unkept promises to existing tenants and lease-holders on the large Aylesbury Estate in Southwark, and the creation of an overwhelming message of brokenness to rationalise the destruction of 2700 units of social housing, and their planned replacement by 5200 new-build units, 60% market units and 40% affordable dwellings built by a housing association. While displaced residents may be offered the right to return to renewed estates, many cannot afford to do so with higher rents (and far fewer social units).

This is the conundrum at the nearby Heygate Estate (Lees and Ferreri 2016). In an interview a senior GLA housing manager told me: 'The Heygate was expensive to manage, with a heavy concentration of poor, disadvantaged people. It was poorly built and not using the land efficiently. Intensification with mixed tenures will re-provide affordable housing and give local economic development.' But the weasel word is affordable, which can hide a multitude of meanings, for new units may not be affordable to former tenants or lease-holders who were evicted; indeed, on some estates they might not even have the right of return. Reading the blogs and testimonies of former occupants, it is hard to avoid the conclusion that residents were treated shabbily, regarded as obstacles to remove so that state-led gentrification could begin:

> This regeneration scheme was conceived on the premise of creating a more 'mixed community'. In reality what we are seeing is state-spon-sored segregation: the large-scale displacement of those on lower in-comes by high earners and overseas buy-to-let investors. The new homes provided by the development will be available only to those who are wealthy enough to buy, or if there are any new 'affordable homes' on the site then they will only be available to those who qualify for full state housing benefits.
>
> (Southwark Notes 2013)

On the Heygate Estate there were 1200 social rented units, which were to be replaced by 2535 dwellings, mainly market-oriented, about a quarter of them affordable, but only 79 of which would be rented at existing social rates. In 2013, the Sydney-based developer, Lendlease, was advertising one-bedroom flats from £350,000; Heygate residents were offered on average £95,000 for their leased one-bedroom units originally purchased through right-to-buy. A poster on the former residents' notice board at the Estate enlarged Lendlease's off-plan sales advertisement in Chinese characters, reflecting its off-shore marketing. Even before the last eviction, flats at the re-named 'Tribeca Square' were being marketed in East and Southeast Asia. The Heygate was erased and any record of its tenants forgotten, as new market units in South London assumed a global identity: built by an Australian developer and marketed with a New York name to a Chinese market.[41]

In Southwark, the borough with the largest stock of council housing, the required share of affordable housing set by the council in regeneration proj-ects was 35%. Like other savvy developers, Lendlease was able to revise that figure downwards in private negotiations, presenting a viability assessment arguing that compliance to Southwark's affordability threshold would make the project uneconomic according to their profit target (Flynn 2016). The final irony of the Heygate regeneration was that, planned by the borough as a revenue-generating asset sale, site clearance and other costs to the Council actually exceeded the sale price earlier agreed with Lendlease. The Heygate redevelopment was a social and an economic blunder; 1200 social units were lost and the sale was a net drain to the public purse.

Failures like the regeneration of the Heygate Estate have led local authorities to consider other approaches to housing redevelopment. Beswick and Penny (2018) discuss the innovative use of a special purpose vehicle (SPV) by Lambeth Council, a model shared by others. The state became an arm's length developer itself through its wholly owned SPV, Homes for Lambeth, aiming to secure the land value lift as public gain rather than private profit. In so doing the borough assumed the risks and the responsibilities of the marketplace, undertaking a speculative mixed-tenure development by commodifying a public asset. While exercising entrepreneurial agency with a view to turning profit into affordable housing through cross-subsidies, the Lambeth scheme, and similar models in other boroughs, have, like housing associations, become enmeshed in the logic and the circuits of the market in all but their non-profit objectives. Risks and vulnerabilities exist with unanticipated economic and political uncertainties; unsettling Lambeth's model, in 2017 the Conservative government unhelpfully declared that special purpose vehicle schemes should be liable to right-to-buy provisions, potentially depressing the value of the asset (Beswick and Penny 2018).

Evocative terms like 'social cleansing', 'the clearances' (Elmer and Dening 2016), and 'the enclosure of the urban commons' (Hodkinson 2012) introduce a broader historic canvas to portray the injustice and even the violence of housing dispossession (Lees 2014; Elliott-Cooper et al. 2020b; Ferreri 2020; Lees and Hubbard 2021). Austerity has left Councils vulnerable before shrunken revenue and unforeseen exigencies. But innovative local authorities that assumed debt for income-generating investments, commonly in property, are running aground. COVID-19 following Brexit provided the perfect storm of unanticipated consequences. In November 2020, Croydon, a suburban borough, announced it could not meet its legal obligation to balance its budget, as its property earnings had under-performed during the pandemic (Ford 2020). Croydon was not alone. From 2017 to 2020, local authorities had borrowed £6.6 billion from central government for property investment to finance services (Hammond 2020). By early 2021, at least a dozen councils were facing bankruptcy; Newham's Olympic legacies had not deflected a borough budget deficit of £30 million for the fiscal year.

For the neoliberal imagination, the desire to marketise is never assuaged, and in summer 2020, the London Tenants Federation stated on their Estate Watch site that over 35,000 homes on London council estates were still awaiting demolition. The confluence of housing stresses led to an intensification of rhetoric. Shelter, the housing charity, escalated the language of housing crisis to one of an English housing emergency: '17.5 million people are trapped by the housing emergency … Unaffordable. Unfit. Unstable. This is our housing system' (Shelter 2021, p. 4). Noting that the incidence of homelessness in Britain has doubled since the Coalition government came to office in 2010, Shelter proposed building 90,000 social housing units a year. But this is the paradigm that the austerity project firmly rejected. However, austerity received a robust and unexpected rebuff from the UN Rapporteur on extreme poverty and human rights following a visit to Britain. His report to the UN Human Rights Council was scathing (Alston 2019, pp. 4–5):

> …austerity policies have deliberately gutted local authorities and thereby effectively eliminated many social services … much of the glue that has held British society together since the Second World War has been deliberately removed and replaced with a harsh and uncaring ethos … In the face of these problems, the Government has remained determinedly in a state of denial … in the area of poverty-related policy, the evidence suggests that the driving force has not been economic but rather a commitment to achieving radical social re-engineering … to change the value system to focus more on individual responsibility, to place major limits on government support and to pursue a single-minded focus on getting people into employment … British compassion has been replaced by a punitive, mean-spirited and often callous approach apparently designed to impose a rigid order on the lives of those least capable of coping …

Conclusion

London was a city of starkly unequal realities in the summer of 2012. Its most observant Victorian critic had observed a similar dichotomy 150 years earlier, 'It was the best of times, it was the worst of times … it was the season of Light, it was the season of Darkness, it was the spring of hope, it was the winter of despair' (Dickens 1859, p. 1). The hopeful luminosity of the Queen's Jubilee followed quickly by the London Olympics presented uplifting public events. The celebratory spirit was sustained by the frothy real estate in Central London, fuelled in 2012 by national and international investors. But if the spring of hope blossomed notably for the top 10% of Londoners holding 42.5% of the capital's total household wealth, life was more fraught for Londoners in the bottom half of the population holding just 6.8% (Trust for London and WPI Economics 2020, p. 23). The UN Rapporteur on extreme poverty and human rights found a winter of despair in the homes and neighbourhoods of deprived Britain, not least London, where housing availability and affordability were most precarious. East of the Olympic Park in Newham, *The Economist* located tiny shed homes in back gardens in June 2012; in one garden, two sheds, one without electricity, housed between seven and nine immigrants from South Asia, paying a combined rent of £1200 a month (The Economist, 2012d; Minton 2017). A decade later 150,000 homeless Londoners were housed by their local borough in temporary private accommodation (London Councils 2022). Housing has been thrust into the poverty debate, because it is the disproportionate cost of rental housing, together with the reduction of housing benefits, that are central to the expansion of poverty, including poverty among London's working poor (Shelter 2021). The structural inequality of Dickens' London is replayed in the present, with the city both a 'wealth machine and poverty machine ... in an accelerated and violent form' (Edwards 2016, p. 234).

It was hoped that the creation of an Olympic growth pole in London's East End might regenerate districts of deprivation and landscapes of disinvestment. But regeneration is a murky term, opaque and sometimes deceitful in process and unjust in outcome, for displacement and dispossession have become the signature of state-led gentrification. Regeneration encourages the view that 'the state is making a steady switch from a remedial to a *generative* force in respect of marginality, inequality and precarity.' (Slater 2014, p. 964). Though advanced with greater determination by central government since 2010, regeneration represents the ongoing mission announced in Margaret Thatcher's 1980 Housing Act, to subdue an existing housing landscape and way of living. Visible now, over 40 years on, is the evolution of this paradigm change through successive Conservative and Labour governments, with its intent the transition from a welfare-based to an asset-based society (Lowe 2011).

Homeownership is the centrepiece of an asset-based society, the Englishman's castle against ill winds. Household responsibility for household welfare is facilitated by ownership-friendly policies like low interest rates, right-to-buy, help-to-buy, First Homes,[42] stamp duty holidays, and an enticing range of tax concessions. The housing sector is also projected to an important role in the macro-economy as a counter-cyclical stimulus to revive economic growth. Prices are fuelled by the opportunistic eye of the investor: the homeowner, the buy-to-let small investor, and the more substantial investments of national and global high net-worth individuals, pension funds, sovereign funds, private investment funds, and the international property development industry, notably in the central and inner districts of gateway cities. International investment in prime neighbourhoods, especially when prices and currencies are depressed, restores business confidence, encourages other investors to pile on, and inaugurates a new cycle of price gains that diffuses outwards in a largely contagious price ripple effect. A new boom gathers strength and asset-holding homeowners benefit.

An under-appreciated advantage of this paradigm is that homeownership gains across a majority of households do permit some dispersal of wealth creation (Hamnett 1999; Lowe et al. 2012). But this paradigm also contains built-in contradictions. The more successful is its intent of asset inflation, the more dangerous is the prospect that a boom becomes a bubble, whose bursting will play havoc among asset-holders, particularly those encumbered with high mortgage debt. This is a fine balance, and successful management requires the constant interventions of the state with meticulous powers of calibration – as is so evidently apparent in Singapore (Chapter 2) and so obviously lacking in Hong Kong (Chapter 3). Moreover, the larger the constituency of asset-holders, the more electorally compelling is unhindered asset inflation. A second contradiction is that property inflation excludes newcomers from the market without costly interventions like help-to-buy, which perversely further inflate prices for future entrants while boosting profit margins in the building industry. In London, where land inflation has been excessive, homeownership is a fading dream of young adults, and is attained only by substantial family gifts and loans and the acceptance of heavy debt. By default, the outcome is an expensive deregulated private rental market, with limited tenure security and a growing gap between dwelling cost and quality. For poorer households even this default option remains too expensive for tenants and too costly for government with the high bill of housing benefits. 'The broader view, in the context of globalised housing consumption, is that market-led systems appear incapable of delivering for both investment and need' (Gallent et al. 2018, p. 127). Here is the broken housing market Prime Minister May lamented.

If rental housing is the default model for growing numbers, subsidised rental housing is becoming the residual option in the asset-based society. It has been subject to repeated assault in the aggressive moves of right-to-buy and estate regeneration, and a thousand cuts and niggling interventions shifting the compass to market-based solutions and away from equity or justice considerations. The loaded dice aiding developer viability assessments to beat down affordability standards contrasts with the disciplinary intent to make housing constructed by local authorities through innovative special purpose vehicles subject to right-to-buy terms (Beswick and Penny 2018). It is such actions that the UN Rapporteur found punitive and mean-spirited in their impacts on the most vulnerable members of society, including disproportionate numbers of families of colour and single-parent women (Dorling 2014; Shelter 2021).

The marketisation of social housing, the reduction of benefits, regeneration clearances, unregulated and insecure private tenure, and grinding affordability gaps might well lead to a condition of residential alienation (Madden and Marcuse 2016). The polarised world of *A Tale of Two Cities* was in part a meditation on class politics, and this language is commonly employed by critical authors on London's current housing relations. Hodkinson and Robbins (2013, p. 71) wrote of the 'overt class politics' in the housing policy of 'class war conservatives'; Watt (2013, p. 115) observed that 'accumulation by dispossession is producing increasingly antagonistic class relations', and again, that 'London's contemporary class politics … increasingly operate on the housing terrain' (Watt 2016, p. 302). The theoretical significance of such language – we return to this in the Conclusion – is made explicit by Watt and Minton (2016, p. 206): 'what is different now from Victorian days is that housing itself is today at the core of [the] capitalist project'. While authors document many examples of spirited local resistance to residential alienation (Minton 2017), that resistance is 'embryonic but fragmented', 'slow to emerge' (Edwards 2016, pp. 222, 234); 'Nor is there much evidence that a radical, mass-based housing movement is on the horizon' (Hodkinson et al. 2013, p. 11).[43] In London, profound residential inequality, provocative housing policy, and council estate skirmishes, have not yet led to substantial political re-alignment. Indeed, paradoxically, where a Conservative blue wave bulldozed Labour's red wall, recent elections showed English cities with multiply-deprived populations to be moving, at least for now, in the opposite political direction.

Notes

1. By the end of 2009, and benefitting from generous tax loopholes, British banks had outstanding loans of over £14 billion to entities in the BVI and other tax havens (Leigh et al. 2012).
2. Such informal housing reached some outer suburbs. Minton (2017, p. 100) references many beds in sheds in Slough.
3. 1 GBP = 1.36 USD on 1 January 2021.
4. Besides New York and Hong Kong, note the synchronisation of this housing cycle with those discussed in Sydney and Vancouver, gateway cities in four countries on three continents. See IMF (2018b, Chapter 3) for the synchronicity of global city house prices.
5. The ONS defines 'house' inclusively to include all dwellings sold and registered in a given year.
6. The North-East presents an anomaly. While *average* prices identify the North-East as the slowest region to retain its pre-GFC peak, not until December 2020 (ONS 2021c), a temporary blip in 2010 took the *median* price briefly above the June 2008 peak. However, sustained growth above the peak did not begin until 2014, and that is the figure that appears on Table 6.1.

7   Finer spatial disaggregation would show variation to the geographical simplicity of price diffusion at the scale of these ten large regions (Cooper et al. 2013).

8   The ONS affordability index is the ratio of median dwelling price to median gross annual workplace-based earnings by local authority district. Earnings are assessed by place of work, not of residence. To provide comparability with earlier chapters, London ranked 15th in *Demographia's* affordability index for 309 cities in 2019, while Hong Kong ranked 1st, Vancouver 2nd, Sydney 3rd and Singapore 104th (Cox and Pavletich 2020).

9   Davidson and Wyly's maps and discussion emphasise that even the alpha city is not homogenous but includes lower income groups in public and private rentals. Grenfell Tower in blue-blood Kensington and Chelsea provides a poignant example. Nonetheless, rising land values hasten the backfilling of gentrification in lower income blocks of prime London, notably through council estate regeneration.

10 Savills' (2020a) data show a price loss of 20% for prime Central London from the 2014 peak to 2020. Successive stamp duty increases in 2014 and 2016 and greater tax exposure had weakened investor interest, while Brexit was an additional disincentive. With graduated stamp duties, the high-value market declined most. Finally in 2020–2021 COVID-19 led to significant domestic flight from the central London flat market and deterred international investors.

11 Some districts are in a second or third cycle of gentrification. See Butler and Lees (2006) on the 'super gentrification' of Barnsbury in Islington.

12 A formal probit model confirmed a high level of significance for spatial proximity in the price ripple effect. I am grateful to Idaliya Grigoryeva for this analysis.

13 The r^2 value for the variation of price volatility in boroughs against distance from the City of London was 0.62.

14 GDP, not adjusted for population numbers, finally reached its pre-GFC peak in the second quarter of 2014. However, real wages remained 8% below the peak.

15 It is important to note the dynamics of both sending and receiving regions in the flows of investment capital, flows that can be triggered or arrested by economic or political shifts at either end (Raco et al. 2020).

16 A 43-year-old Singaporean doctor, for example, made his first investment, a two-bedroom Chelsea flat, in 2011 for £600,000. He next bought off-plan a one-bedroom unit in the Battersea Power Station site, developed by Malaysian interests (Grant and Allen 2014).

17 In the 2014 QS world ranking of universities, London had five institutions in the top 100 (and three in the top 20), compared with three for Boston and Hong Kong, and only two for New York, Paris, and Tokyo.

18 In this study, Prime London was restricted to the City of London, Westminster, and Kensington and Chelsea.

19   In addition to these exhibitions for sales of private property, Minton (2017) includes a telling account of the London Real Estate Forum, where regeneration sites are brought to market by local authorities.

20.   Several surveys have confirmed that rental investment is the primary motive for overseas buyers of off-plan, new-build units. Knight Frank (2013) identified investment as leading motive for 65%, while family educational use, often followed (or sometimes preceded) by investment, was declared by 33%.

21.   With residential prices down 20% in prime London in 2020, a cheap pound offered a total premium of 27–30% for euro- and dollar-denominated buyers over pre-referendum values in 2016, leading to French, Italian, Swiss, Hong Kong, Chinese, Indian, and American buyers all claiming more than 5% of prime London sales in 2020 (Knight Frank 2020). With the pound's further collapse in autumn 2022, US dollar savings of almost 50% existed for prime London prices over 2014 values. At least four Singapore blogs/newsletters were promptly lauding prime London investment.

22.   Some of these companies would have British beneficial owners. An attempt was made to control for British ownership by removing companies registered in the Channel Isles or the Isle of Man.

23.   Designed by Richard Rogers and built by the Candy Brothers with a Qatari development company owned by a former prime minister, One Hyde Park is an iconic expression of global London in the post-GFC period. Its flats were reputed to be the most expensive in the capital; a penthouse changed hands for £136 million in 2011, and another for £140 million in spring 2014. An offshore company purchased the former penthouse mortgage-free, with the deal consummated by lawyers in Ukraine and Russia (Thomas 2011). Ukraine's wealthiest oligarch, Rinat Akhmetov, owned the property.

24.   A 15% stamp duty was imposed on such properties in 2012 to challenge tax avoidance, with an additional annual tax charge in 2013. It was estimated this second tax would bring in £35 million a year to the Treasury, but it raised almost £200 million in its first 10 months, proving that the scale of company-held properties is much greater than anticipated, and that the 'beneficiary owners' remain willing to conceal their identities despite significant tax penalties to do so – though these penalties are less than the capital gains tax and inheritance tax that could be chargeable with full disclosure (O'Murchu and Houlder 2014).

25.   3048 visas were released from 2008–June 2015, a period with minimal oversight, what TI (2015) calls the 'blind faith' period, 60% awarded to Chinese and Russian nationals. Government depended on the banks to raise red flags about suspicious transactions involving visa applicants, but independent assessments showed limited bank compliance. Reporting of suspicious activity from banking, accounting, and legal firms was 'low to negligible' (TI 2015, p. 17). Parallels with oversight failures in Vancouver (Chapter 5) are striking. Amazingly, 'almost all of

the private sector (anti money-laundering) supervisors are actually lobby groups for the sectors that they supervise, and are funded by the firms that they are obliged to investigate.' (TI 2015, p. 17).

26. The oft-cited statement was from an interview in a Freakonomics podcast in 2014.

27. In the first half of 2014 London received over 40% of all Chinese overseas real estate investment (Cole 2014). In January 2014 the state-owned Greenland Group invested $1.2 billion in two London projects, while Dalian Wanda, China's largest developer, announced an investment of £2–3 billion in UK regeneration including Nine Oaks (China Daily 2014). These numbers have not been sustained.

28. CK Asset's very favourable net gearing, its total debt relative to total shareholder equity, stood at less than 5%, in marked contrast to heavily indebted Mainland developers. The extreme case, Evergrande, had a gearing of over 150% in early 2021.

29. A recent re-assessment boosted the required figure to 90–100,000 new units annually; actual production cranked up to 42,000 in 2019–2020 (London Councils 2021). Completions of non-market units, however, has been running at less than 20% of projected need.

30. Profits for the top seven listed British housebuilders were £1.3 billion in 2013. Concentrating on prime London, Berkeley, one of the seven, declared pre-tax profits of 24% for 2013–2014 on revenue of £1.6 billion (Sharman 2013).

31. The failure of an oligopolistic industry to scale up was acknowledged even by a Conservative government. One of the three problems of 'our broken housing market' was 'a construction industry that is too reliant on a small number of big players' (DCLG 2017, p, 9).

32. In 2015 the average London home inflated in value by more than £22 an hour during the working week, considerably more than the average hourly wage (DCLG 2017, p. 9). This impressive asset return contrasted with sluggish wage growth (Edwards 2016).

33. Help-to-buy is an equity loan scheme with price caps, decreasing the necessary deposit on a new home to 5%.

34. In 2014 Barratt reported help-to-buy was playing a role in 29% of dwelling completions, while at Taylor Wimpey the figure reached 42% (Gregori 2014).

35. For example the case made to me for asset sales by the chief executive of a large housing association as a need to be 'both market-responsible and trying to make the world a better place'. Among the association's inventory of 25,000 units in 2014, 29% were market units.

36. The revival of rental tenure was not specific to the UK. For very similar Dutch trends, see Aalbers et al. (2021), who also extend their findings to other 'financialized homeowner societies'.

37. British Land was heavily exposed to Central London office and retail markets. In the two days following the 2016 Brexit vote, its shares fell by 28%. With the almost complete closure of business in Central London in the first 12 months of the COVID pandemic, British Land's property valuation fell by over a billion pounds.

38. Housing benefits are transitioning into an omnibus universal credit scheme, rolled out at great expense, to incorporate six types of existing benefits. Since 2016, recipients might be funded either by housing benefits or universal credit.

39. For a troubling portrait of the added depredation of the pandemic on the deprived immigrant populations of East London, see Raval (2021). Housing costs consume 56% of the net income of London households in poverty (Trust for London and WPI Economics 2020).

40. This affordable housing inventory produced by housing associations and other providers does not include the separate GLA-funded housing programme, which began in 2012/13. GLA production is presently considerably higher and is trending towards a larger share of 'genuinely affordable' social units while the affordable inventory retains a shallower subsidy of around 20%. Both programmes have a substantial share of intermediate or shared ownership housing, a rent to own model for middle-income households.

41. There was an attempt by local activists to rename Tribeca Square. These are compromises developers are willing to make.

42. First Homes, announced in 2021, is a public scheme to introduce discounts of at least 30% for middle-income, first-time buyers purchasing a new home. At least 10,000 dwellings a year should enter the scheme from 2022.

43. This does suspend judgment on the London riots in 2011. Levitas (2012) observed that 40% of the first 1100 arrests brought to trial lived in the 10% most deprived places in England.

CHAPTER 7

Conclusion: The Place of Housing

Credit markets and housing markets play far more important economic roles at the macro level, as well as at the micro and spatial levels, than will be found in most economics textbooks.

(Muellbauer and Murphy 2008)

Income differences matter and they have also widened but it is asset wealth which has become the novel and sharply differentiating feature of contemporary social structures. For the vast majority of households this asset wealth is in the form of residential property.

(Forrest et al. 2018)

The preceding chapters have examined housing markets in five gateway cities in their distinctive geographical and historical settings, observing the political, economic, and social contexts that give each residential market its recognisable character. The housing experiences of the 30 million residents in these cities are significant in their own right, but this final chapter aims to make explicit what has often been implicit in the case studies, how each of them can speak to broader issues. The argument will proceed in three steps of increasing abstraction.

First, when Michael Goldberg read Maurice Daly's study of housing bubbles in Sydney, he was surprised how processes and outcomes could be transferred so directly to Vancouver and Toronto. We begin this chapter by discussing some of the generalisations observable across the five gateway cities. Second, these trends have unfolded beneath the conceptual thesis of an asset-based society in which homeownership is the centrepiece. While repeated connections were made with this thesis, and inter-city parallels and contrasts were drawn, I was cautious to avoid the all-too-familiar suppression of relevant local specificity by overly intrusive pre-existing theoretical structures. In this final chapter, those broader conceptual concerns become more prominent. Third, the chapter concludes with reflections on the place of

Housing Booms in Gateway Cities, First Edition. David Ley.
© 2023 John Wiley & Sons Ltd. Published 2023 by John Wiley & Sons Ltd.

housing in contemporary society and social theory, arguing that housing and real estate have a largely unacknowledged centrality in mainstream social science in the functioning of post-Fordist capitalist societies.

Intercity Generalisations

Gateways and Nations

Through their airports, seaports, financial hubs, and media centres, gateway cities act as portals between nation states and global flows of migrants, capital, trade, and ideas. They have flourished during accelerated globalisation, with population growth driven by immigration, while the native-born population has declined relatively and often absolutely (Frey 1999). A study of the gateways of Sydney and Toronto showed that immigration pulses were correlated positively with house price growth and negatively with domestic out-migration; in turn, domestic out-migration coincided with low levels of housing affordability (Ley 2007). Immigration and its global networks have become one of the house price fundamentals – 42% of metropolitan Vancouver residents were immigrants in 2021 – in an era when international barriers to capital flows are reduced, and the resilient economies and growth prospects of gateway cities have attracted international property investment, both by individual households and large development companies. Transnational investment has been facilitated by the cultural resources, real estate services, and information networks provided by the presence of co-ethnic immigrants in gateway cities (Anderson et al. 2019; Li Z. et al. 2020).

At the interface between national and international economies, these cities have experienced extraordinary rates of price escalation. London provides a dramatic example, losing two million people in the half-century to 1988, but more than regaining that population in a period of rapid growth since, with real London house prices rising two and a half times in 30 years. In many developed economies there was an annual return of 5–8% on housing assets from 1950 to 2015 (IMF 2018b). National growth rates, however, did not match the rate of price inflation in gateway cities. They show greater price oscillations between peaks and valleys than national trends, and display propensities to form housing bubbles. Such tendencies reflect the quick adjustments of local and global investors following price cycles and are less a feature of those residents who favour use value with a longer-term horizon.

These on–off investment switches re-focus attention to the global scale and the existence of price synchronicity between gateway cities across national borders. Global investors contribute to international house price synchronicity, especially for higher-priced housing, accentuating the risk of price contagion between jurisdictions. Since the 1980s, and especially in open economies, 'house prices have become increasingly synchronized across countries, especially among major cities. Thus, policymakers cannot ignore the possibility that shocks to house prices elsewhere may affect domestic markets' (IMF 2018b, p. 109). A prime example was the role of the Asian Financial Crisis that introduced a simultaneous bust in both Singapore's and Hong Kong's 1990s housing bubbles. London shared a housing meltdown in 2008–2009 with other western gateways, notably in the US, Ireland, and Spain. Sydney and Vancouver, however, like Singapore and Hong Kong, experienced only mild corrections in 2008–2009, sharing a Pacific Basin growth region. Indeed, Vancouver's price-line correlated more closely with the growth of China's GDP, especially after 2002 when Mainland networks replaced Hong Kong in trans-Pacific flows of business migrants and residential investment (Kolet and Quinn 2013).

Synchronicity suggests that gateway cities belong to a global category more or less detached from national trends. But a gateway city is doubly embedded, engaged with the global market but also networked into its hinterland (Scholvin et al. 2019). As such gateways may act as an innovation fulcrum from which international impulses move through hinterlands. Home price diffusion through England and Wales from London as epicentre is a case in point, with house price waves rippling in remarkably regular succession through other regions from a London origin. This price inflation has been carried in part by the net annual population migration of 50–90,000 Londoners, 30 years and older, to the rest of the UK in recent years (Cosh and Gleeson 2020). London leads with the highest prices and the earliest price rises in each housing cycle, but it is not detached from house price trends throughout the UK.

Housing Booms in Time and Space

Boom and bust real estate cycles are not new. Daly (1982) followed volatile property price cycles in Sydney back to the nineteenth century. Stapledon (2012) constructed Sydney's price trajectory to 1880, and his data show that real prices did not increase until the 1960s, with each earlier boom followed by a bust that cancelled speculative price gains. But in the past five decades, real prices quadrupled in value, an extraordinary epochal break in a lengthy historical record. In London, the recent 50-year trend (1970–2020) has shown an almost six-fold increase in real prices, as values rose episodically through booms in the early 1970s, the late 1980s, the long run-up from the late 1990s to the GFC, and then the post-GFC boom to 2016 (Cosh and Gleeson 2020). Aside from the early 1970s, each boom showed a stepped increase in prices, with down-cycle deflation weaker than the up-cycle gain. A somewhat different regional chronology was at play in Asia Pacific. After strong gains in the late 1980s and 1990s, Hong Kong and Singapore were profoundly impacted by the Asian Financial Crisis in 1997, when their real estate bubbles burst, and real Hong Kong prices collapsed 60%, only bottoming out in 2003. Both cities regained price momentum, with a small decline through the GFC, and rapid recovery from 2009, beaten back in Singapore by a proliferation of cooling measures. In Hong Kong, however, local demand together with extravagant capital flows entering the territory both from China and the West overrode financial defences, leading to an astonishing rise of almost 450% in real prices from a nadir in 2003 to a peak in 2019, with the GFC one of several minor deviations. Vancouver's price profile shares features with both the Asia Pacific and Sydney profiles. Real prices rose over four-fold from 1986 to 2020, by-passing the GFC shock, but disrupted by irregular oscillations with the onset of cooling measures in 2016 until the COVID advance in 2020–2021.

In Vancouver and London intra-metropolitan trends in house prices showed that highest absolute gains occurred in neighbourhoods that were already the most expensive in the region, indicating a process of wealth deepening in these elite areas. In Vancouver, these pre-existing blue-chip neighbourhoods also featured high location quotients for wealthy business immigrants. From these favoured sites, price diffusion occurred outwards in a spatially contiguous manner, like the ripples in a pool, with prices declining in a surprisingly regular pattern with distance from the primary epicentre of westside Vancouver (Grigoryeva and Ley 2019). A more detailed examination of the ripple effect in London showed the pivotal role of prime London, a region of contiguous west-central boroughs with an extraordinary concentration of housing wealth and offshore investment; two of the boroughs, Westminster and Kensington-Chelsea, contained half of all properties in England valued at over £2 million in 2014. Prime central boroughs recovered fastest from the price shock of the GFC, and price recovery then advanced wave-like outwards, again displaying the strength of contagious spatial diffusion.

Price gains spread outwards due both to the spatial displacement of demand from out-bid potential buyers, and also due to replacement, profit-taking permitting existing owners to move to larger and/or newer properties in cheaper districts, carrying price inflation with them. The prime central London boroughs, epicentre of price signals, also showed greater volatility with stronger swings between the peaks and troughs of price cycles. In

Vancouver the high-priced central neighbourhoods, hub of price inflation, also reveal higher price oscillations. Singapore's 'core central region', with its expensive private apartments favoured by investors and 'foreign talents', is the entry point for global price signals, and shows more price volatility than the suburban estates of heartlanders (Liao et al. 2015). In each instance, expensive central districts most open to international investment show exaggerated price movements.

During the COVID pandemic, house prices fuelled by cheap credit and government stimulus proved unexpectedly resilient despite ravaged economies. Overall prices in the 37 OECD countries rose by 7% in real terms in 2020, with interest rates in euro-denominated states falling to 1.3% early in 2021 (Ziady 2021). The locational pre-eminence of residential price growth in gateway cities was abruptly reversed by the shock of pandemic. In the UK, the year-over-year house price increase was 13% to June 2021, despite recession, but London's increment was only 6% (ONS 2021b). With many white-collar employees working from home, and lockdowns limiting movement, demand for larger home and garden spaces was created. Suburban and satellite communities were favoured while small central city homes, whether rental or owner-occupied, were at a disadvantage. Further penalising gateway cities, defined by their international connections, was the suspension of temporary and permanent immigration and heavily curtailed airline traffic, limiting access for international tourists and investors. These spatial trends are unravelling as immigration, international travel, and overseas investment flows have resumed, mortgage rates rise, and market corrections are concentrated in suburban and satellite areas. The re-opening of globalisation brings renewed prominence to gateway cities.

The Globalisation of Residential Markets

Earlier chapters demonstrated how gateway cities show abundant evidence of the globalisation of residential real estate (Logan 1992; Rogers and Koh 2018). Upward house price trajectories provide a proven asset for local and international profit-seekers, and transnational institutions – financial entities, investment companies, property developers, and real estate consultancies – are active in investment, development, and marketing. London, with the most extensive global reach, attracted the widest international attention, with development companies from four continents active in housing projects. Even a smaller gateway city like Vancouver saw investment from the four largest development companies in Hong Kong after Expo 86, with additional developers arriving from Japan, Taiwan, China, India, and the UK, among others. Besides the development sector, international holders of large capital funds, including pension funds, national sovereign funds, private equity funds, and REITs are drawn to the investment opportunities in gateway cities. The financing team of the large waterfront redevelopment project of Barangaroo in Central Sydney has included a Canadian pension fund, an Australian pension fund, Singapore, Hong Kong, and Qatar sovereign funds, an Australian corporate fund, and Australian and Chinese developers.

The global reach of banks and other financial institutions permits cross-border borrowing and lending for building projects, while global marketing, especially for larger residential developments, is aided by transnational real estate agencies, allowing, for example, apartment sales from London's Battersea redevelopment to be launched simultaneously in 12 world cities.

Web-based viewing and selling on international platforms like Juwai and through international agencies like Savills allow private investors to go global in residential investment. At the release of units for Barangaroo's first condominium tower, a third of buyers were from outside Australia, while a majority of buyers of new-build flats in prime London are commonly from outside the UK. The London market includes a globally diverse range of private investors with particular market niches, including buyers from Russia and Eastern Europe, the Middle East, Africa, and Asia Pacific, as well as ex-pat buyers from Western Europe and the US working in Central London. In all, over 85,000 property titles in London are registered by individuals with international addresses (Centre for Public Data 2021). Hong Kong residents lead the pack, accounting for over 23,000 titles in England and Wales as a whole in 2021 (a tenfold increase over 2010), and almost 60,000 are registered by individuals in Hong Kong, Singapore, Malaysia, and China. Although the separate category of company registrations is not included, the tax havens of the Channel Islands, Isle of Man, and the British Virgin Islands amount to over 43,000 individually held titles (Centre for Public Data 2021). Investment capital has arrived in pulses, influenced by currency exchange rates, and political instability overseas which brings waves of crisis capital to London's safe haven. Hong Kong is a current example. Following the declaration of the National Security Law by the PRC in 2020, Britain announced passport privileges for up to three million Hong Kong residents.[1] In the next nine months, Hong Kong buyers spent close to an estimated £1 billion on London residential real estate.

The annual reports of development companies chart their decision to go global. Australia's Lendlease has intentionally targeted 15 'gateway cities', which 'relative to their national average, typically experience higher population growth, have the most appealing employment prospects, are more resilient through property and economic cycles, and attract more global investment capital' (Lendlease 2019). CapitaLand, one of Asia's largest developers, already very active in China and Asia Pacific, and financially undergirded through its majority owner, one of Singapore's sovereign investment funds, has declared its intent 'to transform our company from an Asia-focused real estate player to a global one' (CapitaLand 2019a, p. 16). Chinese development companies became large and wealthy through the rapid urbanisation and marketisation of property in China, and sought overseas portfolio diversification once regulatory liberalisation in 2012–2013 permitted large-scale foreign direct investment in less *dirigiste* nations.

Indeed, a theme running through each of the gateway cities is the role of residential investment from Asia Pacific in the post-GFC period. This region has a strong concentration of the world's largest property development companies, notably in China, Hong Kong, and Singapore. The tiny territory of Hong Kong is the base for six of the world's 20 wealthiest real estate billionaires (Carlyle 2016). These companies have swelled rapidly since the 1980s in the world's major economic growth region of Asia Pacific, in particular from participation in China's spectacular urbanisation. Chinese outbound real estate investment accelerated from $5 billion in 2010 to $120 billion in 2017, with another $36 billion from Singapore and Hong Kong combined (Juwai 2018). Chinese companies sought property investment in states honouring the rule of law, removing the prospect of arbitrary state intervention. Following permissive deregulation in the PRC in 2012–2013 they purchased sites in gateway cities in the West, ideally taking advantage of favourable currency exchange. London was an early destination. At its peak, in the first half of 2014, London received 40% of all Chinese overseas commercial and residential property investment (Cole 2014).[2] Asia Pacific invariably comprised the largest purchasing segment for new-build London flats. Aside from its investment value, apartment purchase in London, Sydney, Vancouver, and Singapore might also accommodate an adult child studying at a local university, and sometimes offer a *pied-à-terre* for eventual family migration. A well-developed marketing road show catering to these investors exhibits prime new-build properties from gateway cities at luxury hotels in Hong Kong, Singapore, Shanghai, and other principal cities of Asia Pacific.

There is commonly a preference among Asian buyers for home-country builders. The Asia Pacific buyers in London have a choice of local product from East and Southeast Asian developers whose reputations they value. When the Chinese developer, Greenland, released the first phase of its large Greenland Centre project in Sydney, 80% of units were sold in the first few hours, almost all to Chinese buyers, half of them off-shore investors (Wong 2017). Chinese purchasers have been drawn disproportionately to gateway cities with pre-existing co-ethnic districts. In the US, a huge increase in purchases by Chinese nationals has occurred since the GFC, notably in districts already home to ethnic Chinese. House prices rose substantially in these districts, producing something of 'a China shock' in the residential market (Li et al. 2020; Sakong 2021). Similar booms transformed the residential markets in Sydney where detached home prices accelerated 70% from June 2013–June 2017, and in Vancouver, where prices rose by 52% from June 2013–June 2016, before a foreign buyer's tax temporarily cooled investor desire (Ley 2017; Liu and Gurran 2017). While the boom was short-lived, with the PRC reinstating capital controls, the investment surge in each gateway city was accompanied by a significant long-term decline of affordability.

Housing Inequality

Homeownership is an exuberant, wealth-creating asset for some households in gateway cities, a debilitating, poverty-confirming lack for others, while the ensuing inequality in life chances blocks any comparable right to the city for all (Harvey 2008). Housing is a central, dynamic component of the human geography of gateway cities, occupying a multifaceted position in their economy, politics, and daily life.

There has been some variation among the five cities in housing's place in metropolitan life. At one extreme, in Singapore, housing remains a nexus for national unity, providing affordable homeownership for 90% of citizens and permanent residents in flats built and subsidised on long leases by the national Housing Development Board. Elsewhere, housing affordability has been a *cri de coeur* in Hong Kong, Sydney, Vancouver, and London. The situation for young adults in Hong Kong has been grim, with the housing purchasing power of 20–24 year-olds in 2018 only a quarter of the capacity of their peers 30 years earlier (Zhao 2019), as flat prices boomed while wages fell in real terms. Vancouver has for years been the least affordable city in North America, and has alternated with Sydney for second rank behind Hong Kong in the *Demographia* survey of unaffordability. London, too, is a frequent top 20 entrant. The affordability problem in each city is chronic, often acute. It is also cumulative as renters fail to share increases in real estate value and housing wealth.

The profile of housing inequality is not only generational. Immigrants, especially immigrants of colour, the demographic energy behind the recent growth of gateway cities, feature prominently among the list of vulnerable households who are newcomers to an inflated housing market. The working poor in an unequal post-industrial labour market are also victims of excessive rent increases, inadequate social housing policy, and an increasingly miserly welfare state. Household responses to unaffordability fall within Hirschman's (1970) trilogy of exit, voice, and loyalty. Exit involves out-migration from unaffordable housing markets, an option practised by the poor and the young, among others. Low-income exit from Sydney was noted during and following the late 1980s boom primarily for housing affordability reasons (Burnley and Murphy 2004), and as prices rose, skilled workers joined the flow. By 2015, there were warnings in Vancouver about the imminent loss of such essential workers as police and general practitioners due to unaffordable homeownership (Vancity 2015). For the voice or protest strategy, residential alienation in Vancouver was strong enough to generate an electoral reaction at the ballot box. Hong Kong's young adults were significantly excluded from the asset of ownership, the path to middle-class status, and their marginality predisposed them to political activism. In London there have been many local protests but not (yet) a unified political response. Recent election results in Australia, in contrast, have shown defeat for the Labor Party's plan to rein in the commodification of housing as asset through tax reform. Hirschman's loyalty option may be equated with a large number of quiescent adjustment strategies by residents, most of them inconvenient and undesirable, including a longer commute, reduced housing aspirations in terms of size, location, tenure, and amenities, assuming a heavy debt load, partitioning the home informally to include an additional rent-paying household, and shrinking desired family size, as the need for multiple household incomes may postpone (even cancel) pregnancies (Flynn 2017). These are heavy burdens to bear.

Housing Booms: Market-Based Causes

For analytic convenience the causes of housing booms are separated into market-based and state-based factors, admittedly a crude distinction. The empirical chapters have revealed the sometimes-denied effect of global investment, or demand surplus to user needs, on local markets in gateway cities, but of course not all speculative investors are foreign. We saw in Sydney the role of Australian investors as well as foreign buyers during the 2013–2017 boom, the former incentivised by highly favourable tax concessions. In London too while foreign investors play a major role in the surplus demand for new housing in prime London, British buyers prevail in the resale market. For international investors, the changing balance of currency exchange triggers the timing of investment; the depressed pound and Australian dollar have periodically stimulated inward flows of property capital. Economic conditions at home also prompt investors to look overseas, with Hong Kong, Singapore and PRC investors withdrawing from their own over-heated markets in the years following the GFC to the then cheaper markets in western gateway cities.

Underscoring this mobility of international capital was the liberalisation of financial markets since the 1980s, and the efforts of banking institutions to financialise property in a wave of more flexible and accessible lending instruments. Credit has been cheap with financial policy driving down interest rates, and lending institutions, increasingly drawn to the mortgage market, competing for borrowers. Following the GFC, rounds of quantitative easing and stimulus financing created highly liquid conditions, encouraging the rush to credible assets by both institutional and private investors. Housing in gateway cities has been, so far, a proven asset with reliable medium- and long-term returns. At the same time there is no inevitable linkage between cheap credit and residential price gains. During the 1980s house prices still rose while mortgage rates climbed to double digits in cities including Sydney and Vancouver. So too interest rates may be low, but credit unavailable with tightening stress tests for perceived high-risk borrowers, a growing population in expensive markets, and inciting (notably in Hong Kong) declining real estate transactions. Once booms are underway, behavioural economists have pointed to inflationary traits like imitation and the fear of missing out in a rising market. Investors share a herd instinct, piling on quality housing assets and sometimes producing unstable price bubbles. More abstractly, Shiller (2000, p. 67) has identified frenzied booms as 'speculative feedback loops … in effect naturally occurring Ponzi schemes.' Booms and busts are inherently social events, a form of social contagion launched by instinct as well as reflection.

To address the crisis of housing affordability and availability the default response of the real estate industry and conservative politicians has been to blame impeded supply on complex and tardy planning processes (Phibbs and Gurran 2021). There is an attractive simplicity to this proposition, but it overlooks significant counterfactuals (Gallent et al. 2017, 2018). Housing supply is inelastic, producing too few affordable dwellings even as prices rise, as we saw convincingly in Hong Kong, Sydney, and London. Demand surges are capitalised not in greater supply but in higher prices (Burke et al. 2020). Undoubtedly, planning delays occur, but detailed research in Sydney on the construction timelines of hundreds of apartment plans revealed that the planning process occupied only 13% of the total development period from land purchase to building completion (City Futures Research Centre 2021).

Moreover, as evidence from London and Hong Kong indicated, in an inflating market the developer's profit margin is enhanced by limiting supply from a land bank, typically expanded during down-cycles; indeed, in Hong Kong, developers normally released a new project in phased batches, increasing the price in successive phases. Restricting supply, even with growing demand, has a business logic. Supply-side arguments overlook the fundamental difference between exchange- and use-value. Evidence from Vancouver indicates that the favoured supply response by builders, high-priced condominiums, aggravates affordability problems. Land values are lifted through redevelopment of older apartment buildings or detached houses that had often been converted to include at least one affordable rental unit (Mendez 2017). In contrast, when condominium units are bought as investments, high purchase prices mean that subsequent rental costs are also high, while a ripple effect carries high land prices from one development to adjacent sites, in response to the inflated expectations of landowners.

Nor is demand the self-evident causal factor in booms that conventional theory might prefer. Affordability is aggravated by the decoupling of housing markets from labour markets (Gordon 2020, 2022). While jobs remain local as economic theory prescribes, housing markets in gateway cities are global, with the buyer's wealth accumulated anywhere in the world. The housing stock has to satisfy both local purchasers, buying in general for household use, and the surplus demand of local and global investors. Though rarely considered, some demand is also opaque. Two less desirable aspects of overseas demand are tax avoidance and money laundering that release inflationary impacts on housing markets. Some immigrants arriving as business investors to Canada, and buying expensive Vancouver houses, have declared very low average global incomes in their tax returns, lower than the average figure declared by refugees landing in Canada the same year (Ley 2010). Subsequent detailed research has confirmed this relationship, raising the probability of widespread tax evasion and/or tax avoidance (Gordon 2022). Tax avoidance has also been a publicised feature of off-shore investment from tax havens in London's most expensive boroughs (Atkinson 2020). While tax-sheltering instruments are legal, they can conceal criminal tax avoidance and money laundering both of which help sustain high-priced housing markets.

The State's Role in Incentivising and Cooling Housing Booms

In each of the five cities the state's role has been pivotal in shaping housing booms, not only by their defensive responses once booms threaten household wellbeing, but also through pro-growth initiatives of deregulation and enabling financial policy. Central government facilitates private housing development by stimulating capital flows and a pro-growth regime, while metropolitan governments may complement the real estate industry in a growth coalition. But there is a danger here of over-reach, for too much capital, too many investors, may create a crisis of housing affordability that rankles the public and raises re-election anxieties for politicians. Not even the effectively one-party state in Singapore is complacent about voter dissatisfaction at election time. As the electorate's frustrations escalate, demand management and the introduction of cooling measures become the state's response, usually (but not always) too little and too late.

On isolated occasions, usually following a public crisis of confidence, the state may backtrack, and attempt to reregulate the housing market, trying to restore use value as a criterion in its revamped interventions.

However, the state's instinctive orientation is to population and economic growth, so that it is invariably sympathetic to investment flows, growth coalitions, homeownership, and asset-based accumulation. An active housing market is seen by government to offer a macro-economic lever to stimulate a sluggish regional or national economy. This was the plan of the British Columbia government when they sold the large Expo site in Vancouver to a consortium of Hong Kong's largest development companies in 1988, inaugurating a substantial capital inflow from Asia Pacific to Vancouver real estate in the following decades. Sydney's housing market has been used more than once recently to offset an economic slowdown. The 2013–2017 residential boom was exacerbated by declining interest rates and the falling exchange value of the dollar, conditions which fuelled, as they were intended to, capital inflows during a period when new foreign investment for mineral production was likely to decline. Inflationary effects to the housing market were recognised, but regarded as an acceptable risk. At the global scale this scenario is replicated in low-interest policy with quantitative easing, or other economic stimulus including China's liberalisation of capital controls, providing external shocks inflating housing booms in gateway cities. Hong Kong's supercharged housing market was unable to tame inflationary capital from both China and the US, with whom it has a currency peg, leaving local real interest rates negative and highly inflationary.

Among other instruments, favourable taxation policy has incentivised investment in residential real estate. Hong Kong and Singapore are famously low-tax jurisdictions. But whereas first-time Singapore buyers are protected by subsidy from excessive residential price gains, in Hong Kong there is no such shelter, and residents complain of a hidden tax in their exposure to the territory's excessive price inflation, while tycoons enjoy generous tax exemptions. In London a regressive approach to investment from tax havens allowed avoidance of capital gains tax and inheritance tax by wealthy beneficiary owners whose identities were concealed in company house purchases. British tax policy helped to create another segment of the housing market, buy-to-let rental properties that attracted small, primarily amateur landlords facilitated by the classification of rental properties as private businesses eligible for tax concessions. Perhaps the most celebrated tax policy incentivising investment is the negative gearing permitted by Australian authorities. Like buy-to-let in the UK, these concessions are directed at resident investors. It seems as if 15–20 percent of Australian taxpayers own rental property, often several units, taking advantage of tax code benefits that include partial exemption from capital gains payments and negative gearing, where losses on rental investments can offset taxable income from other sources. With efficient accountants, many landlords are able to register a rental tax loss. The regressive effects of negative gearing have been challenged by the IMF (2020), but the benefit has been endorsed in elections by Australian voters.

The excesses of price inflation, unaffordability, and inequality eventually require intervention by even conservative governments committed primarily to homeownership fortunes. Earlier chapters provide abundant examples of attempts to manage the housing market by re-regulation, or de-financialisation in the broad sense of the term (Wijburg 2021). In Vancouver contestation comprised a range of policies by different levels of government including various taxes on housing investors, macro-prudential controls, renewed commitment to social housing, and tightening institutional loopholes in checking market opportunism. Cooling measures were applied with various degrees of enthusiasm by governments in each of the five gateway cities. Remarkably the strongest macro-prudential interventions were made by Singapore and Hong Kong, normally scoring in the top rankings of free market economies. A sustained sequence of cooling measures in Hong Kong addressed demand management, following two familiar paths, macroprudential policies shrinking credit availability, and tax increases in the form of rising stamp duty on real estate transactions. Taxes were directed against hot money from post-GFC stimulus funds in China and the West that were fuelling rampant residential price inflation. But a 15% tax on flipping in 2010, soon raised to 20%, followed by a transaction tax that rose in stages to 15%, were not enough to bolster the defences. Recognising the strength of non-local property investment, an additional 15% tax was levied against buyers who were not residents of Hong Kong, primarily Mainland purchasers. Macro-prudential measures, the IMF's preferred intervention (IMF 2019c), were applied diligently to withhold mortgage credit from marginal buyers. Eight rounds of credit tightening were applied between 2009 and 2017 to check excessive leverage by purchasers – but the boom raged on.

Some of the demand management measures had a short-term effect, but the most long-lasting effect seemed to be the choking of the secondary (resale) market, where strict limits on credit availability as well as higher stamp duties led to a serious decline in sales volumes. These limits were felt strongly by Hong Kong residents, frustrating aspiring flat purchasers. Many were denied access to mortgage funds, while flat prices continued to rise, leaving them ever further behind the runaway train of price escalation.

Singapore offers a salutary lesson here. Like Hong Kong it faced enormous instability from its openness to the flood of cross-border capital flows, documented by the IMF as a 'huge increase of cross-border assets (outward capital flows) and liabilities (inward capital flows) from 200% of GDP in the 1980s to 1600% in 2010' (IMF 2017b, p. 51). Like Hong Kong, these flows contributed to marked price volatility, and a substantial boom-bust housing cycle in the 1990s and a smaller boom from 2006 to 2010. With the central role played by the residential market in nation-building and political legitimacy (Chua 1997), the Singapore government has been fastidious in its attempts to control prices in both the private market and public Housing and Development Board (HDB) flats. Unlike Hong Kong, government land sales and public supply targets have strong social objectives. Macro-prudential and taxation tools are intended to manage local and foreign investment demand, and to differentiate between first-time and investor purchasers. By force of numbers, Singapore's 17 policy interventions between September 2008 and January 2013 were able to wrestle down powerful inflationary impulses following the GFC crash. As in Hong Kong, measures were directed against speculators and purchasers by national origin, directed most stringently against non-citizens, then permanent residents, then Singaporean citizens with multiple flat ownership, with the lowest levy on citizens with single ownership and first-time buyers. Foreign buyers who were most highly taxed showed the greatest withdrawal from the market. Their share of core central city private residential purchases fell from 34% in 2011, just before the Additional Buyer's Stamp Duty was introduced, to only 8% in early 2022 after the tax had been raised for the fourth time to 30% (Savills Singapore 2022). In the decade following the GFC, Singaporean authorities could register satisfaction in the ongoing campaign to manage inflationary pressures while achieving some balance between price growth for HDB owners and HDB accessibility for first-time buyers.

Singapore is exceptional also in the critical matter of public supply. The other cities marketised and/or truncated social housing delivery in the 1980s and 1990s leaving the private sector responsible for new supply. Is it a coincidence that house price inflation increased soon after? In Hong Kong competition between private supply and an ambitious public housing programme during a real estate bust following the Asian Financial Crisis led to the severe curtailment of the public programme before the pressure of the property growth machine; after 2003, Hong Kong prices skyrocketed. Singapore in contrast has maintained affordable public supply at a high level, with the increasing quality of flats introducing competition to the smaller private sector. Government's near monopoly status as land owner has permitted flexibility in adjusting building volumes to meet changing market conditions.

No other government has been as persistent, resolute, or successful in its interventions. There were scarcely any barriers to foreign investment in Vancouver, indeed no recognition that a housing problem existed to disrupt the sunny skies of neoliberal policy, until 2016 when a 15% foreign investor's tax was forced on a reluctant provincial government by the strength of public opinion. After the 2017 election the new provincial government introduced a series of demand management policies that included recognition of the inflationary effects of market manipulation, notably speculation, money laundering, and tax fraud. Government raised the foreign buyer's tax and the transfer tax on sales, and introduced a property surtax on higher-priced residences. Supply was to be enhanced primarily through affordable rental policies. This omnibus package of cooling measures subdued the market until late 2020 when the COVID boom drew domestic buyers to distant suburbs and satellite markets leading to substantial price increases there, while the central city markets preferred by international buyers saw smaller gains. Sydney policy-makers were also late converts to demand management. Macro-prudential measures were too timid to impress international rating agencies who downgraded Australian banks for their mortgage exposure in 2017, while taxes on foreign buyers and increased transfer taxes were less than half the level imposed in Vancouver, and merely dented the gains made against a devalued dollar by foreign investors.

Not surprisingly, during a decade of austerity governance, real estate cooling measures have not been a major agenda item in London. Some brakes on price increases were achieved by an increase in stamp duties targeting expensive residences in 2014 and again in 2016. The shock of the Brexit vote in 2016 was still reverberating through prime London when COVID-19 arrived. This sequence of blows led to a decline of 20% in the prime central London market from its high point in 2014, a reminder of the power of unanticipated shocks as well as state direction in shaping the housing market. In mid-2022, prime London prices were finally recovering when recession again stymied the market.

Homeownership and an Asset-Based Society

Asset-based welfare, employing the home as primary fungible asset, grew as homeownership expanded, notably in Anglo-American and Asia Pacific societies (Forrest 2021). The thesis of asset-based welfare has broadened from its first principles, when Kemeny (1980, 2005) linked growing homeownership in some western societies to a trade-off against a reduction of pension funding from private and especially public sources. Indeed, the Australian version of asset-based welfare has placed a high premium on successful aging and retirement through homeownership and financial self-dependence (Power 2017). But financialisation and globalisation 'shift[ed] the debate into a new, higher gear' (Lowe 2011, p. 208). New financial instruments were extending home equity withdrawal beyond a role in retirement insurance to a fund that could be drawn down across the life course as need arose (Smith and Searle 2008; Searle and Smith 2010). As the 'bank of mum and dad' one such need has been aiding adult children with home purchase. In addition, middle-aged homeowners in the UK exemplified the neoliberal enterprise society, withdrawing equity from a principal residence to purchase buy-to-let residential property (Ronald et al. 2017). The home's serviceability as retirement insurance, ATM, and much else point not only to the commodification of the primary dwelling, but also provide further evidence of the multiple purposes of housing in civil society.

The asset-based welfare discussion emerged initially in social policy and welfare studies and addressed a trade-off between homeownership and declining public social services in a neoliberal, enterprise state. But the asset of ownership also has to compensate through capital gains, or investment property revenues, for a structural decline in the growth of real employment income, noted in all of our gateway cities except Singapore. It is the severity of the expanding gap, the decoupling, between incomes and house prices that creates affordability challenges, and this outcome is the result of impaired incomes as well as inflating prices. 'The key data point … is the long-term divergence of wages and asset values, in particular property prices' (Adkins et al. 2020, p. 33). The secular decline of wages *vis-à-vis* profits in western nations has been a feature since the late 1970s suggesting an epochal break that co-exists with the emergence of a post-Fordist, finance-led economy (Bengtsson and Ryner 2015), and the decisive escalation in the long-run price gain of housing (Knoll et al. 2017). In a transition from Fordism to finance-led accumulation, consumer demand is sustained by 'the extension of debt underwritten by the increase of asset values' (Bengtsson and Ryner 2015, p. 415).

Kemeny posited acceptance by households of a future of house price Keynesianism (Watson 2010), growing their personal asset through mortgage debt, enabled by tax concessions and other opportunities for household enterprise. In Australian elections, a party that proposed to withdraw some of these concessions in return for a programme of social housing was rebuffed by the electorate. In contrast, expensive and inflationary programmes to aid homeownership, for example the British government's help-to-buy initiative, elide with voter preferences. Polls show the attraction of homeownership to be widespread, and though its disbursements are unequal, it does represent a broader, more democratic distribution of national wealth than earlier tenure models (Hamnett 1999; Smith et al. 2022). Wealth accumulation through housing has been substantial. It bears repeating that in the UK, the housing stock rose in value by over £5 trillion between 1995 and 2016, comprising three-quarters of the total growth in national wealth (ONS 2017). While housing wealth can be widely distributed in comparison to alternatives, significant variation exists by region, by home value, and of course, by tenure. In Vancouver's booming real estate market, the median net worth of all Vancouver families rose by CAD$130,000 in constant dollars *above* the median worth of other Canadian families between 1999 and 2016; for the wealthiest (top quintile) of families, the premium was $575,000 (Gellatly and Richards 2019).[3] Of course, the population includes not only owners, but also tenants who made no capital gains from their homes and may have been negatively impacted by knock-on price pressures from the ownership to the rental market.

Widespread scepticism remains concerning the efficacy of asset-based welfare to provide housing and financial security (Arundel and Ronald 2021). Japan offers a salutary case of the baneful exposure of investor citizens to asset bubbles. The bursting of the property and stock market bubbles in the early 1990s, following rapid asset inflation, widespread speculation, and easy access to credit, led to continuing asset depreciation, harmful to an ageing and dependent population (Hirayama 2010; Izuhara 2016). The Japanese meltdown anticipated the property collapse among the four tigers in 1997, leading to serious asset loss in Singapore and acute devaluation of private homes in Hong Kong. The Global Financial Crisis provided a further severe test of the asset-based economy and starkly revealed its limits. In the United States over six million households lost their prime asset, their home, to foreclosure, facing the ravages of risk society exactly when they needed emergency support. Household wealth in the US declined by more than a fifth, penalising disproportionately Americans of colour (Pew 2011). Since then, a wide-ranging critique claimed that in England 'homeownership does not (and arguably cannot) deliver welfare provisions in the way envisioned by asset-based welfare initiatives' (Montgomerie and Büdenbender 2015, p. 386). Home equity gains are variable by location, by housing type, and by time of entry to the market. They typically sharpen existing inequalities, notably generational, regional, and tenure-based inequalities,[4] leading to an unjust and putatively unstable society (Arundel 2017), trends that are accentuated when the rate of homeownership declines, as it has done in all but Singapore among our gateway cities.

Housing unaffordability, homeownership decline, and inequality in wealth accumulation have become a coherent bundle of personal misfortunes and market and policy failures prominent in the daily life of gateway cities. Even with high levels of homeownership there is no room for complacency regarding wealth distribution. In Australia, with substantial homeownership, high Gini coefficients show a stark level of inequality in the distribution of household wealth (Berry and Dalton 2010). As homeownership declines, socio-economic polarisation rises, with more residents denied property asset accumulation. More recent data from Australia, the UK, and the US reveal that inequality is almost twice as high for housing wealth as it is for incomes, and the gap has been widening (Smith et al. 2022). It is not surprising that asset-based welfare, an offspring of neoliberal ideology, should be breeding rising societal inequality, and potential political instability. When property wealth accounts for half or more of the wealth of homeowners, exclusion from ownership sharply exacerbates economic stratification. Penalised groups are late entrants to the housing market, including new immigrants and youthful households, as well as the working poor and disadvantaged groups. We have seen repeatedly in earlier chapters the marginalised position of first-time buyers in expensive housing markets. In Vancouver, with lack of affordability (and often availability) Generation Squeeze, a lobby group for young rental households, estimated it would take a price crash of 75% to restore ownership affordability for young workers. The accidents of date of birth or period of immigration can unfairly imprint long-lasting inequalities, searing enough that they may generate a state of residential alienation (Madden and Marcuse 2016).

Despite these limitations, in the post-GFC world there has been little will to abandon homeownership as asset-based welfare. Indeed, in London austerity has accelerated the neoliberal drive to reduce state housing benefits while providing new incentives for private ownership. In this context, household assets, notably homeownership, are still highly valued for financial security (Ronald et al. 2017). Consequently, critical assessment of the limitations of asset-based society remains necessary. This study has continued to build out the political and economic contexts of asset-based welfare which impinge closely upon its practical success or failure as a policy metanarrative.

Early accounts saw homeownership primarily in terms of decision trade-offs for individual households. An important emphasis of this study has been to broaden the cast of players and institutions acting upon booming housing markets beyond the end user. The progression to an asset-based society has occurred, first, under the encouraging eye of the neoliberal state, which often holds a formative long-range strategy in rebalancing exchange and social criteria in housing, becoming an active partner, sometimes an ideological leader, in the path to an asset-based society (Lowe 2011; Adkins et al. 2020, 2021). This trajectory closely fits neoliberal objectives of lower taxes and reduced public services for an increasingly self-reliant citizen in an enterprise culture, a citizen adept at identifying and managing financial and property assets (Doling and Ronald 2010a; Lowe 2011). A view of housing as an economic asset expedites the ongoing marketisation of everyday life (Watson 2009). The role of the state is then to launch people onto the homeownership ladder through ownership incentives, while reallocating the national budget away from new social housing commitments. In a coherent ideological mission, seen most fully in the Thatcherite project in the UK, government may limit social services, including social housing, allow real wages to fall, check tax increases, facilitate access to cheap credit, and promote homeownership. Inflating house prices then provide an asset for families to self-supply their own welfare and capital accumulation.

But the logic of the private market may compromise this policy aspiration. An important emphasis of this study has been to highlight the inflationary role of investment interests in the housing market competing with use-oriented buyers. The globalisation and financialisation of real estate have vastly expanded the stock of individual and institutional investors, producing additional or surplus housing demand beyond local population needs. This trend is particularly marked in gateway cities, where past economic and demographic growth identify a quality asset for individual and institutional investors. The level of speculative local and global investment is critical in determining the degree of decoupling between labour markets and housing markets. The wider this gap becomes, the greater the affordability challenge to local workers and their families, and the more inaccessible is homeownership. Investment capital is usually willing and able to outbid local buyers, inflating land and property prices. As we saw in Sydney's 2013–2017 boom, investment capital is volatile, fleeing a depreciating market, but flocking to a rising price line, displacing first-time buyers during boom conditions. When first-time buyers return to a cooling market, prices have typically moved to a higher plateau following the boom, leaving them facing a larger affordability gap.

Consequently, with the additional surplus demand of investment capital, population growth alone provides an inadequate estimate of purchasers. The investor share among borrowers from Australian financial institutions exceeded 40% in the boom years from 2013–2015, having risen steadily from five percent in 1991 (Burke et al. 2020). This surplus demand must be addressed in housing need projections or else supply will inevitably fall ever further behind demand, as has happened most acutely in London. Supply that has to meet both social (use) and economic (exchange) objectives complicates and invariably compromises any rational housing plan. Housing's strategic role as a stimulus in the macro-economy and its popularity as an investment asset ride roughshod over its essential social function as a dwelling. 'The broader view, in the context of globalised housing consumption, is that market-led systems appear incapable of delivering for both investment and need' (Gallent et al. 2018, p. 127).

Because of investor activity, supply engages an expanded market and adjusts to the new shape of demand. Luxury condominiums are a familiar product, with size and amenities built to suit local and global investors. In the hot markets of gateway cities developers adjust price levels rather than production levels. Supply is inelastic to demand, not primarily because of slow-moving planning bureaucracies, but because drip-feeding supply suits the revenue stream and organisational culture of an oligopolistic development sector. When supply attempts to meet local demand in high-priced markets, the product is a steady shrinkage in unit size to micro-units, pioneered in Hong Kong ('nano flats') and Singapore ('shoe boxes'), and mimicked in less extreme form elsewhere.

The typical political culture of gateway cities exacerbates the market-driven excesses of housing markets, imperilling the assumptions of asset-based homeownership. We saw in Hong Kong and Vancouver how property growth machines of interlocking real estate and political elites were able to shape a housing market to enhance growth and profitability, creating increasingly unequal societies of asset-holders and the asset-deprived. The deregulated ecology of a growth coalition displays an institutional atrophy among key gatekeepers tasked to monitor or police the excesses, irregularities, and criminal activities drawn to a hot real estate market (Ley 2021). A government commission examining money laundering in Greater Vancouver found that 'An enormous volume of illicit funds is laundered through the British Columbia economy each year', while the 'real estate sector is highly vulnerable to money laundering' (Cullen Commission 2022, pp. 2, 16). Its report highlighted an excessive failure of oversight among public and private agencies. Institutional failure includes an under-resourced and eviscerated capacity for monitors or gatekeepers. We saw how the Foreign Investment Review Board in Australia, much cited as a model in less regulated nations, is a paper tiger, rubber stamping applications and rejecting virtually none, the best it can do with minimal resources. Yet in 2018-2019 FIRB approved close to 9,000 investment applications with a value of $231 billion. So too, in Hong Kong, where money-laundering is a major problem, the SAR's anti-money laundering agency receives tens of thousands of Suspicious Transaction Reports each year, but has capacity to process only a few hundred. Deregulation, a central theme of neoliberal governance, serves to diminish oversight, and thereby fuel growth machines and residential property prices.

Continuing price inflation that takes homeownership beyond the reach of even middle-class residents is leading to a precipitous conclusion for asset-based policy: the irrevocable growth of rental tenure as a policy solution. The homeownership share in Australia has declined six percent from its peak, the proportion of first-time buyers is shrinking, and safety nets are thin.

Significant construction of social housing was abandoned years ago. Like Vancouver and London, in Sydney 'ownership as a tenure has burnt itself out and private rental is the growth housing sector' (Burke et al. 2020, p. 71). But how does this square with the promise of wealth accumulation through ownership as the trade-off for diminished services and declining real wages? How will an over-stressed rental market provide more affordable rental units when low interest rates entice investors and inflate land prices? The Sydney trend is repeated elsewhere. Ownership, the mainstay of asset-based welfare, declined in London from 59% of households in 1991 to 50% in 2019, with the exclusion of first-time buyers from unaffordable properties. In its place, rental tenure which had been in decline as a share of dwellings, has been resuscitated with buy-to-let investments and more recently with new purpose-built rentals in North America-style apartment buildings. In the UK as a whole, private landlords almost quadrupled in number between 1991 and 2014 with the advantageous terms of buy-to-let policy (Ronald and Kadi 2018). In Vancouver the consensus of all three levels of government is that the future lies with a massive construction of (ever-smaller) rental units. But while a rental strategy is a practical response to housing needs in an unaffordable ownership market, it will inevitably compromise asset-based policy and amplify inequality.

Despite the inherent and actual failures of asset-based welfare policies, they remain *de facto* policy mandates even after their gruelling testing (Arundel and Ronald 2021). Critics have identified a range of other housing paths than asset-based accumulation, beginning with the renewal and expansion of social housing production, an emphasis upon rental rather than ownership policies, reduction or elimination of tax advantages that promote ownership and residential investment, taxation of housing wealth, establishing a land tax that seeks to capture land value gains for public purposes, demand management to constrain residential speculation, and the ending of austerity and restoration of welfare services (see among others, Minton 2017; Gallent et al. 2018; Burke et al. 2020; Ryan-Collins and Murray 2020).[5]

But recent history in Vancouver is daunting. An unusual measure of agreement between different levels of government around 2018 introduced demand management, attention to market distortions from money laundering, tax fraud, and speculation, taxation of offshore investment, North America's first vacancy tax, taxing the accumulation of property wealth, repair of older social housing units and commitment to new construction, and an emphasis on rental properties not ownership. It is too soon to make a final judgement on a 10-year plan, but while checking speculative transnational investment, the plan was too easily disrupted by the COVID-19 residential boom of local buyers and local investors sustained by a flood of cheap credit.

Progress in Vancouver away from a fraught lack of housing affordability has been limited at best. The inequities of asset-based wealth accumulation are deeply entrenched and appear scarcely assailable without unprecedented political will to implement alternate policy tools.

Such political determination and use of varied management instruments exist only in Singapore among our five cities. For all of its democratic limitations, Singapore offers the most plausible case in support of housing as asset-based welfare. Homeownership is shared by 90% of households who are 'residents' (citizens plus permanent residents), with most dwellings leased from the state Housing and Development Board. Rather than cancelling social housing, Singapore has marketised it, but unlike Margaret Thatcher's right-to-buy council housing in the UK, the HDB provides a continuing stream of subsidised new self-owned leasehold flats and shields units from full market forces. In addition, with an average unemployment rate of only 2.5% this century, Singapore is the only city in our study where wages have kept up with home price growth. Housing deposits and monthly payments are financed in part through a compulsory pension plan, so that in a tight integration of housing and finance the family flat both benefits from and contributes to the family pension. In this integrated model of asset-based welfare, government is obligated to ensure constant returns on housing investments as both an economic and political imperative. But returns must not be too high or first-time buyers will be compromised or require deeper state subsidies to join the HDB ladder. To date and not without wrinkles, Singapore's housing as asset model has been successful, due to the fastidious efforts of government to manage inflationary capital inflows and stabilise flat prices. Ironically, housing as a welfare asset managed by the self-dependent owner-investor can only prosper in the context of strong state regulation of the housing and land markets. In this protected policy environment, household net worth rose by 75% from 2010 to 2019, with property amounting for about 55% of household wealth. No wonder there is a deep-seated culture of property in Singapore. In the words of a local urban economist, 'People only think of real estate as an asset, not just to live in. Here they think about property as an investment. It's all about the real estate ladder and upgrading'.

If the state in Singapore has the largest number of supply and demand levers to manage the housing market, in Australia a steady evolution to asset-based welfare predicated on homeownership has been much less successful (Stebbing and Spies-Butcher 2016; Arundel and Ronald 2021), while the UK's entry into asset-based society and its failure have been dramatic (Arundel and Ronald 2021). The substantial transformation of housing tenure in London after 1980 is testimony to the shock treatment of public policy driven towards housing commodification and asset ownership, but foundering as it restricts ongoing contribution to building social housing. Council houses were the homes of one-third of Londoners in 1981, but an ideological transition of rare resolve privatised 300,000 council flats over the next four decades. For a period after right-to-buy legislation launched a major assault on council housing as a product and a social value, mortgage-holding owners rose rapidly in number, but then steadily fell as rising prices squeezed first-time buyers out of the market and right-to-buy council flats turned over to private rental, even as growth in real wages atrophied and welfare benefits were slashed. By 2019 mortgaged owners had fallen substantially in London as a share of the market, despite expensive policies like help-to-buy directed primarily at first-time buyers. There have been 40 years to evaluate the success of Thatcher's neoliberal revolution in housing, undercutting the social goals of the welfare state and replacing them with the exchange ethos of asset-accumulation and rentierism. The result has been grave, with former Conservative Prime Minister Theresa May, lamenting that 'Our broken housing market is one of the greatest barriers to progress in Britain today' (DCLG 2017, p. 5).

Placing Urban Housing Theoretically

In the quotation heading this chapter, Muellbauer and Murphy (2008) chastise fellow economists for their neglect of the role of housing in contemporary macro- and micro-economics. While there is a vibrant field of housing studies, its importance is not reflected in the major social science disciplines, including my own, human geography. The discordance between the primacy of housing in the economics, politics, and livelihoods of gateway cities and the field's minor status in mainline social science was a significant motivation for this book. In earlier chapters we have seen that house and home occupy a primary place in the economy, society, and daily life of each of the five gateway cities. In Singapore, housing is multi-tasked in its roles in service provision, social engineering, wealth accumulation, and political legitimacy. Hong Kong provides a sombre contrast, where the exclusionary power of a property growth coalition boosting prices for their own benefit has exiled a younger generation from the economic and social benefits of ownership, with dire political consequences. In Sydney, tax privileges enhance the homeownership ideal of a settler society, and contribute to the pursuit of real estate as 'the true national sport.' But the satisfaction of substantial capital gains from property does nothing to advance the case of first-time buyers who are increasingly excluded from holding that asset. Affordable housing in Vancouver is the perennial thorn in the side of government, but concerted attempts at *re*regulation, departing from asset-based assumptions and back to state intervention with greater equality, are finding no easy answers. In London, housing was the iconic centrepiece of a wide-ranging ideological campaign to wrest British society from a welfare state to an entrepreneurial state, leading to grave inequality between those who hold assets and those who do not.

In each city we have seen the massive heft of the housing market, in land value, sunk legacies, and partisan interests. It is a very big ship to turn around. Even in the smallest of our five cities, Vancouver, the residential resale market alone in the territory of the Greater Vancouver Real Estate Board recorded CA$38.6 billion in transactions in 2015, three times the combined sales from the established provincial staples of forestry, oil and gas, and mining (O'Brien 2015). In terms of capital circulation, even excluding sales of new dwellings and rental revenues, the housing market trumps the value of conventional staples. The global value of residential property has been estimated at over $250 trillion, almost 80% of the value of all real estate (Tostevin 2021). Its store of wealth is unmatched, three times greater than global GDP and far larger than the value of all equities and debt securities combined. Homeownership creates mammoth mortgage debt loads, commonly 70% of all household debt, estimated at $10 trillion in the US in 2020. High rates of borrowing occur in the property industry, particularly in China, where heavy leveraging to gain land assets is the norm, leading to the 2021 default of one of the world's largest developers, Evergrande, incapacitated by a debt of over $300 billion.

Of course, such economic might generates significant impact in the macro-economy, bringing to mind earlier work by economists arguing that 'Housing is the business cycle' (Leamer 2007). A follow-up analysis of economic cycles in 18 countries concluded that 'in the long run, real house prices and residential investment lead output, interest rates, and credit unequivocally' (Igan et al. 2011, p. 212). Housing's centrality to the economy, and in economic and social policy is matched by the continuity of the strategy of upholding homeownership to fortify household finances in asset-based accumulation. In the past 20 years residential property owners in Britain have received £3 trillion in largely unearned and untaxed capital gains, with the rich, the elderly, and Londoners the leading beneficiaries in this immense redistribution of wealth (Corlett and Leslie 2021). But substantial weaknesses can accompany this strategy, amounting to a false promise of financial security (Arundel and Ronald 2021; The Economist 2022). Assets may tarnish, for the investor citizen is exposed to losses as well as gains, and entry to the risk society means that debt loads may be savagely exposed during episodic shocks to the market. Moreover, as house prices continue to rise, growing numbers are left behind, for the decoupling of housing markets from local labour markets creates problems of affordability, availability, and frequently of quality. Pressures on rental property grow as the numbers excluded from ownership expand. Inequality becomes sharper, life chances are diminished. Every housing boom accentuates exclusion from ownership and rising inequality in wealth accumulation. Every housing market crash creates grave casualties in business bankruptcies and crippling household losses.

Exclusion from this mainspring of economic activity provokes outcomes that range from disappointment to alienation. Madden and Marcuse (2016) defined residential alienation as the variable impacts of exclusion, displacement, disempowerment, insecurity, eviction, foreclosure, and debilitating stress prevailing among growing numbers of urban dwellers, forcing disabling adjustment strategies. For poor households, and we might add younger and middle-class households in gateway cities, 'the current housing system seems designed specifically to produce residential alienation instead of ontological security' (Madden and Marcuse 2016, p. 68). If a right to the city includes a right to housing, there should be 'an ongoing effort to democratize and decommodify housing, and to end the alienation that the present housing system engenders' (ibid, p. 197). We identified residential alienation among young adults in Hong Kong. With declining real wages, weak social benefits, and spiralling flat prices, many were expelled from the asset society and middle-class status; in desperation some joined the long queue for cramped and aging public housing. Though university educated, many described themselves as lower-class (Lee et al. 2019). Residential alienation predisposed some to join street protests. Exclusion from a property-based, middle-class future supplied a shock that mobilised civil disobedience. In contrast in Vancouver alienation took the form of sharp disapproval with a growth coalition of politicians and the real estate industry that regarded good government as welcoming real estate speculation and running up house prices. Alienation was expressed by abrupt rejection at the ballot box of pro-growth incumbent parties at all three levels of government.

When Marx transformed the Judaeo-Christian doctrine of human alienation from God into alienation around production relations, his class division was between owners and workers. But today some authors see the class divide to be increasingly played out between owners and tenants. In London residential abjection has not yet led to a massive political response. But many skirmishes have occurred, primarily in council estates whose residents are threatened by regeneration and displacement. It is notable how often activist academics define these conflicts in the language of class. 'London's contemporary class politics… increasingly operate on the housing terrain' (Watt 2016, p. 302). This attribution carries some theoretical weight: 'what is different now from Victorian days is that housing itself is today at the core of [the] capitalist project' (Watt and Minton 2016, p. 206). The observation that class politics no longer cohere primarily around workplace conflict, but around accumulation or its absence in the housing market has led Australian scholars to redefine class formation based on the current pre-eminence of housing. Building upon trends since the 1980s in Australia and specifically Sydney, Adkins et al. (2020, 2021) find workplace-based schemes of class structure 'anachronistic' (2021, p. 561) in an era when extended homeownership is the vehicle to propel an aspirational asset-owning democracy. '(I)t is the relationship to assets rather than employment that operates as the key decider and distributor of life chances' (Adkins et al. 2021, p. 567). At the same time, accumulation through inheritance, with generational fund transfers facilitating ownership for many first-home buyers, indicate an additional source of wealth only indirectly related to employment income (Forrest and Murie 1989).

The capacity of housing position to shape social structure, suggested by Rex and Moore's (1967) early work on housing classes, was developed further by a number of authors (Kemeny 1980; Saunders 1990). Adkins et al. (2020) formalised a hierarchy of class divisions derived from contemporary housing status in Sydney. At the apex of their hierarchy is the investor or rentier class; a second Australian study has made the same identification, seeing the nation 'as something of an ideal type with regard to housing market rentierization' (Ryan-Collins and Murray 2020, p. 6). The new-found prevalence of the rentier as asset holder has also been observed in the UK: 'perhaps at no point in the UK's history as a capitalist society has rentierism been as prevalent and economically dominant as it is today. ... the rentier has been relentlessly on the ascendancy during the neoliberal era' (Christophers 2019, p. 30). But it is not just at the top of the class hierarchy that housing-based stratification may be found. The remaining classes – mortgage-free owners, mortgaged owners, tenants, and the homeless – are also defined in relationship to housing asset ownership (Adkins et al. 2020).

The proposed application of the categories of alienation and class, central to Marxian analysis, to housing possession and dispossession in gateway cities brings to mind Henri Lefebvre's revisionist thesis to classical political economy, arguing first, that alienation was not limited to the factory but was practised in everyday life, and, second, that the primary site of current alienation was the modern city, a stage for a culture of disorienting consumption and spectacle.[6] In this perspective, a political economy uncritically wedded to the theoretical primacy of the factory floor – from which all else was derived – was misplaced. In contrast, in his response to the student uprisings in Paris in 1968 – which he had in part inspired – Lefebvre identified 'the importance of a new social, political and cultural sphere, *urban society*' (Lefebvre 1969, p. 101), a formation with political and theoretical significance. It was this shared insight that led Guy Debord, sire of the Situationists and Lefebvre's contemporary, to observe that 'urbanism is the modern accomplishment of the uninterrupted task which safeguards class power' (Debord 1973, para 172). Lefebvre developed his position in other work, arguing that any theoretical sovereignty derived from industrial production had been diminished in practice and should also be diminished in theory. In *The Urban Revolution*, he wrote:

> As the percentage of overall surplus value formed and realized by industry begins to decline, the percentage created and realized by real estate speculation and construction increases. The second circuit supplants the first, becomes essential.
>
> (Lefebvre 2003, p. 160)

This was a prophetic insight in 1970 when Lefebvre was originally writing, but is much more demonstrable by contemporary scholars. Quoting this passage, Anne Haila (2016) developed her thesis of the property state to characterise the economic geography of Singapore and Hong Kong, because so much of their economic activity and corporate and household wealth are bound to the realm of land in general and housing in particular. Current events suggest that China could well be a weightier example of a property state. Real estate, dominated by residential development, has frequently been the locomotive propelling China's investment-driven growth, with recent data suggesting that real estate and construction may have contributed as much as 28–30% to Chinese GDP since 2013, an immense escalation from eight percent in 1997 (Rogoff and Yang 2020).[7] The dysfunctions of this concentration include a development model based on excessive leveraging that leaves corporations exposed to sudden economic shocks, with dangers of contagion to the tightly linked financial sector. Speculation has shaped some of the highest house price-income ratios in the world in major Chinese cities, and rapid (but volatile) price growth has produced acute unaffordability and consumer debt. Housing wealth in this extreme case of asset-based accumulation accounts for over three-quarters of overall household assets and speculative investment is rife; from 2016 to 2018 on average almost 65% of new homebuyers each year already owned at least one other dwelling (Rogoff and Yang 2020). Here, perhaps, is the frenzied consummation of rentier class formation in asset-based accumulation, making the Chinese economy vulnerable to a substantial real estate correction in the early 2020s.

In gateway cities, manufacturing industry has typically been in significant decline; in London and Hong Kong manufacturing now accounts for less than five percent of jobs (Hutton 2022, p. 5).[8] Real estate shapes many aspects of urban life: employment, tax revenues, urban politics, investment and wealth generation, inequality, and the material and emotional crises of affordability and property cycles. An important contribution has discussed the largely unrecognised significance of housing to political economy, where, like mainstream social sciences, the sector has been marginalised, and the reciprocal significance of political economy to housing studies (Aalbers and Christophers 2014). The authors underscore the broader significance of housing in contemporary society, including its role in employment and as an industrial multiplier, as stimulus during economic downturns, as an alternate source of personal capital through homeownership and equity withdrawal, and the more general role of ownership in advancing market ideology and undercutting opposing perspectives. Thomas Piketty (2014, p. 119) has shown the steadily increasing contribution of housing to national wealth since the 1950s. According to his calculations by 2010 national housing wealth exceeded national income by a ratio of around three to one in Britain and France. This evidence amply confirms Gotham's theoretical conclusion that rather than a derivative secondary circuit of capital, 'real estate has a *sui generis* quality that forms an independent sector of the economy' (Gotham 2006, p. 233).

Like Haila (2016), Lees et al. (2016) also launch their argument for the explosive power of real estate from the same extract in Lefebvre (2003). In Western Europe and North America, they observe how neoliberal urbanisation has 'facilitated the hegemonic position of real estate, aided by the financialization of real estate properties, enabling mobile properties to be subject to globalized flexible investment strategies' (Lees et al. 2016, p. 35). From this perspective, 'the ascendancy of the secondary circuit of real estate' (ibid, p. 51) is indicative of 'planetary gentrification'. This argument has substantial traction in the gateway cities we examined, though the spatial claims of gentrification now seem too modest. If classic gentrification was concentrated in inner city neighbourhoods, the housing and real estate trends observed in gateway cities are not so spatially circumscribed. In a sense when it comes to investment patterns, house prices, and displacement in gateway cities, virtually the whole metropolitan area has, albeit unequally, become gentrified.

The close relations between finance and residential development encourage the identification of a finance- and property-led regime of growth in these cities. In addressing the question of what follows Fordism, members of the regulation school proposed that a finance-led accumulation regime had appeared in advanced capitalist societies since the 1980s, and that in the US, the UK, and several other nations, '… the financial regime plays the central role that used to be attributed to the wage-labour nexus under Fordism' (Boyer 2000a, p.112). Hofman and Aalbers (2019, p. 91) have extended this argument, positing the development of 'a finance- and real estate-driven regime [of accumulation] embedded in a neoliberal mode of regulation' in their examination of the British economy, notably in London. But while the prospect of 'a finance-dominated or perhaps property-owning growth regime' is raised (Boyer 2000b, p. 274),[9] its viability is questionable, with dangers of consumer debt exposure and rising inequality from uneven asset ownership (Montgomerie and Büdenbender 2015). Moreover, adding to the loss of welfare state services, the emergence of a finance-led accumulation regime correlates with labour's falling wage share (Bengtsson and Ryner 2015).

Financialisation represents a further abstraction of the commodity form of the home to an item that is bundled with others into a tradeable fund. Mortgage-backed securities rose immensely in popularity and profitability in the decade leading up to the Global Financial Crisis, but weak oversight in assessing the quality of loans led to untenable levels of institutional risk-taking. Though an abstraction, low-quality mortgage coupons were not inert paper, and bit back on the hand that unwisely bundled them, leading to a global banking and housing crisis. Nonetheless, the financialisation process continues apace with the widespread popularity of REITs (real estate investment trusts) and the aggressive movement of equity funds into the rental market post-2008, purchasing foreclosed homes as potential rental stock (Fields 2018). From 2011–2013 institutional investors and hedge funds bought an estimated total of 350,000 bank-owned homes in the US. The securitisation of these rental offerings by large corporate landlords has been associated with higher eviction levels and increasing insecurity among tenant households (Raymond et al. 2018). More recently, private equity firms have discovered low-income rental housing as an investment candidate. Blackstone has committed to a $5 billion purchase of a portfolio of low-income, tax-credit housing in the US, similar trends are anticipated in London (Beswick et al. 2016), while Vancouver and Toronto are seeing the same bundling of apartment rental stock by corporate landlords, with the squeezing of value from the properties heightening the risk of rent increases and tenant evictions.

Today the financial and property sectors are joined at the hip. At the household scale, Smith and Searle (2008) showed that each year a third of mortgaged British homeowners treated their home as a bank, withdrawing equity to cover other costs; ownership confers both insurance *and* banking privileges. At the national and global scales, the GFC displayed speedy contagion between the banks and residential markets. Since the GFC, global investment flows, engorged by serial rounds of quantitative easing, have been seeking high-value assets, including property in gateway cities. In each of the cities we have examined, the mortgage business is a major item in the lending portfolio of banks, sometimes accounting for 50% of loans, and displacing loans to less frothy forms of economic activity. Even as conservative a business hub as Singapore was cautioned by the IMF that its banks were becoming overly exposed to the property market through its mortgage business, and in Sydney the regulator had to intervene as banks became too excited by the opportunities of the 2013–2017 boom. In a crossover of roles Lloyd's Bank plans to enter the property business as landlord in under-served purpose-built rental units in the UK, with Goldman Sachs and other banks also eager to invest in this property sector.

The finance-housing nexus can assemble huge amounts of capital to deploy in property purchase and development, outbidding less-resourced buyers while inflating prices. Moreover, the appearance of unconventional mortgage sources adds to the volatility and risk level of housing booms. Shadow banks originate a higher share of riskier, speculative loans. During the GFC, shadow banks were closely associated with the proportion of investors in the US market – which peaked at over 30% in the 2008–2012 period – and these relations were locationally sensitive: 'areas with a higher penetration of shadow banking mortgage activity are disproportionately affected by non-traditional buyers, particularly second-home buyers and short-term investors' (Alter and Dernaoui 2020, p. 6). The credit supply offered by shadow banks encouraged speculative investment and excessively frothy, high-risk markets characteristic of the amplified price cycle of gateway cities.

Housing's scale and value are reflected in Piketty's macro-economic analysis and the sector's dominant position in personal and national wealth accumulation. The GFC equally revealed its vulnerability to catastrophic failure. It is not surprising that real estate collapses have frequently instigated financial crises, when housing plays such a major role in the macro-economy. Mortgage and corporate debt loads are immense, and risk-taking through heavy leveraging sometimes looks like a game of chance. In challenging the productionist emphasis prevailing in some political economy accounts, Lefebvre's critique undercuts the influential account of capital accumulation that sees the built environment as a *secondary* circuit of capital, where overaccumulation from the primary circuit of industrial production can be parked. In light of the empirical heft and strategic role of the housing sector, including its centrality in financial crises, revision of that theoretical position seems necessary. The post-Fordist primacy of housing as both opportunity and disorder in everyday life, the macro-economy, financial institutions, and policy and political cadres should be matched by equal prominence in social and economic theory.

Notes

1. Over half a million British National (Overseas) passports had been issued to Hong Kong residents from 2019 to mid 2022.
2. With the over-leveraging crisis among Chinese development companies in 2021–2022, a number of these investments have been liquidated, while in some development has been suspended.

3. Vancouver families also bore the heaviest debt in 2016, a debt load of 230% of after-tax income, almost 40% above the Canadian mean. The debt load is shared unequally among income groups, reaching the precarious level of 400% among the lowest income quintile, compared to 220% among the top fifth of family incomes (Gellatly and Richards 2019).

4. Walks (2016) has also identified greater spatial segregation and concentration of wealth in Canadian cities associated with rising homeownership levels and, to a lesser degree, with higher house prices.

5. For a comprehensive reformist policy agenda, see *The Shift Directives* (Farha et al. 2022), presented to the European Parliament by a team headed by Leilani Farha, former UN Special Rapporteur on the right to housing.

6. Today race, post-colonial, and feminist theorists (among others) would identify multiple sites for exploitation and alienation. Are we returning to a world of 'universal alienation' (Harvey 2018)? While the variety of sites where Harvey locates alienation is comprehensive, he chooses to limit its interpretation to classical political economy. Others may also see connections to the original Judaeo-Christian formulation.

7. Using the same methodology, real estate and construction accounted for about 17% of GDP in the US, and just under 20% in the UK (Rogoff and Yang 2020). These figures exceed other estimates.

8. In the UK the gross value added (GVA) of manufacturing to the national economy fell from 28% in 1970 to 10% in 2010; real estate and construction's share grew from 12% to 16%, and the broader FIRE sector (including finance/insurance) from 16% to 25% (Hofman and Aalbers 2019).

9. By 'property-owning', Boyer is primarily concerned with household investment through pension funds, direct stock purchase, and only secondarily though homeownership.

References

Aalbers, M. (2016). *The Financialization of Housing*. London and New York: Routledge.

Aalbers, M. (2019). Financial geography: II financial geographies of housing and real
estate. *Progress in Human Geography* 43 (2): 376–387.

Aalbers, M. and Christophers, B. (2014). Centring housing in political economy.
Housing, Theory and Society 31 (4): 373–394.

Aalbers, M., Hochstenbach, C., Bosma, J., and Fernandez, R. (2021). The death and
life of private landlordism; how financialized homeownership gave birth to the
buy-to-let market. *Housing, Theory and Society* 38 (5): 541–563.

Abelson, P. and Chung, D. (2004). Housing prices in Australia 1970 to 2003. *Mac-
quarie University Economics Research Papers, 2004–09*. http://www.econ.mq.edu.
au/__data/assets/pdf_file/0018/220581/Abelson_9_04.pdf (accessed 28 August
2020).

Abeysinghe, T. (2011). Fewer children when house prices head north, *The Straits
Times*, (1 September), p. 38.

Abeysinghe, T. and Gu, J. (2011). Lifetime income and housing affordability in Singapore. *Urban Studies* 48 (9): 1875–1891.

ABS (Australian Bureau of Statistics) (2019) Overseas arrivals and departures,
Australia, December 2019. *Catalogue 3401.0*. https://www.abs.gov.au/AUS-
STATS/abs@.nsf/DetailsPage/3401.0Dec%202019?OpenDocument (accessed 23
September 2020).

ABS (2020a). *Residential property price indexes: eight capital cities. Catalogue 6416.0*.
https://www.abs.gov.au/AUSSTATS/abs@.nsf/Lookup/6416.0Explanatory%20
Notes1Mar%202020?OpenDocument (accessed 27 August 2020).

ABS (2020b). *International trade in goods and services, Australia. Catalogue 5368.0*.
https://www.abs.gov.au/ausstats/abs@.nsf/Latestproducts/5368.0Feature%20
Article1Jul%202020?opendocument&tabname=Summary&prodno=5368.0&is
sue=Jul%202020&num=&view= (accessed 3 September 2020).

ABS (2020c). *Lending indicators. Catalogue 5601.0*. https://www.abs.gov.au/ausstats/
abs@.nsf/exnote/5601.0 (accessed 15 October 2020).

ABS (2020d). *Wage price index, Australia. Catalogue 6345.0*. https://www.abs.gov.au/
statistics/economy/price-indexes-and-inflation/wage-price-index-australia/latest-
release (accessed 20 September 2020).

Adams, N., Holland, C., Penrose, G., and Schofer, L. (2020). Household wealth pri-
or to COVID-19: evidence from the 2018 HILDA survey. RBA *Bulletin*, June,
61–66. https://www.rba.gov.au/publications/bulletin/2020/jun/pdf/household-

Housing Booms in Gateway Cities, First Edition. David Ley.
© 2023 John Wiley & Sons Ltd. Published 2023 by John Wiley & Sons Ltd.

wealth-prior-to-covid-19-evidence-from-the-2018-hilda-survey.pdf (accessed 10 November 2020).

Adkins, L., Cooper, M., and Konings, M. (2020). *The Asset Economy*. Cambridge: Polity.

Adkins, L., Cooper, M., and Konings, M. (2021). Class in the 21st century: asset inflation and the new logic of inequality. *Environment and Planning A* 53 (3): 548–572.

Adrian, C. and Stimson, R. (1986). Asian investment in Australian capital city property markets. *Environment and Planning A* 18 (3): 323–340.

AHL Investments (2018). *25 years of housing trends*. Sydney: Commonwealth Bank of Australia. https:www.aussie.com/au/content/dam/aussie/documents/home-loans/aussie_25_years_report.pdf (accessed 12 November 2020).

Akerlof, G. and Shiller, R. (2009). *Animal Spirits: How Human Psychology Drives the Economy, and Why It Matters for Global Capitalism*. Princeton, NJ: Princeton University Press.

Allen, K. (2013). Singapore developer buys 'blank canvas' in big East London site. *Financial Times*, 1 November. http://www.ft.com/cms/s/053f74ee-42f9-11e3-9d3c-00144feabdc0.html (accessed 1 November 2013).

Allon, F. (2008). *Renovation Nation: Our Obsession with Home*. Sydney: New South.

Alston, P. (2019). *Report of the special rapporteur on extreme poverty and human rights on his visit to the United Kingdom of Great Britain and Northern Ireland*. Human Rights Council, 41st Session, UN General Assembly. https://digitallibrary.un.org/record/3806308?In=en (accessed 1 June 2021).

Alter, A. and Dernaoui, Z. (2020). *Non-primary home buyers, shadow banking, and the US housing market*. IMF Working Paper WP/20/174.

Anderson, K. (2018). Chinatown disoriented: shifting standpoints in the age of China. *Australian Geographer* 49 (1): 133–148.

Anderson, K., Ang, I., Del Bono, A., McNeill, D., and Wong, A. (2019). *Chinatown Unbound: Trans-Asian Urbanism in the Age of China*. London: Rowman and Littlefield.

Ang, I. (2016). At home in Asia? Sydney's Chinatown and Australia's 'Asian Century'. *International Journal of Cultural Studies* 19 (3): 257–269.

Ang, S. (2018). The 'new Chinatown': the racialization of newly arrived Chinese migrants in Singapore. *Journal of Ethnic and Migration Studies* 44 (7): 1177–1194.

Angus Reid (2015). *Lotusland blues*. Vancouver. http://angusreid.org/vancouver-real-estate (accessed 28 June 2021).

Angus Reid (2018) *Banking on a burst bubble*. Vancouver. https://angusreid.org/metro-vancouver-housing-prices-policy (accessed 29 June 2021).

Angus Reid (2021). *To have and have not*. Vancouver. https://angusreid.org/housing-prices-2021 (accessed 29 June 2021).

Arcibal, C. (2021). Hong Kong residents buy US$1.3 billion worth of homes in London after UK opened path to citizenship in July. *South China Morning Post* (27 April). https://www.scmp.com/business/article/3131263/hong-kong-residents-buy-us13-billion-worth-homes-london-after-uk-opened (accessed 29 April 2021).

Arundel, R. (2017). Equity inequity: housing wealth inequality, inter- and intra-generational divergences, and the rise of private landlordism. *Housing, Theory and Society* 34 (2): 176–200.

Arundel, R. and Ronald, R. (2021). The false promise of homeownership: homeowner societies in an era of declining access and rising inequality. *Urban Studies* 58 (6): 1120–1140.

Asia Times (2019). Engineering marvel taking shape 250 meters up in Chongqing. *Asia Times* (16 January). https://asiatimes.com/2019/01/engineering-marvel-taking-shape-250-meters-up-in-chongqing (accessed 9 February 2021).

Atkin, T. and Connolly, E. (2013). Australian exports: global demand and the high exchange rate. *The Bulletin*, Reserve Bank of Australia, June. https://pdfs.semanticscholar.org/83f9/1e8f9ef8ce7e09bbd86b624fc61c9dcdaef7.pdf?_ga=2.161254005.956964211 (accessed 4 September 2020).

Atkinson, R. (2019). Necrotecture: lifeless dwellings and London's super-rich. *International Journal of Urban and Regional Research* 43 (1): 2–13.

Atkinson, R. (2020). *Alpha City: How London Was Captured by the Super-Rich*. London: Verso.

Au, W.A. (2011). Parties and personalities: staying together (or not) under fire. In: *Voting in Change: Politics of Singapore's 2011 Election* (ed. K.Y.L. Tan and T. Lee), 68–89. Singapore: Ethos Books.

Baark, E. and So, A. (2006). The political economy of Hong Kong's quest for high technology innovation. *Journal of Contemporary Asia* 36 (1): 102–120.

Badarinza, C. and Ramadorai, T. (2018). Home away from home? Foreign demand and London house prices. *Journal of Financial Economics* 130 (3): 532–555.

Badcock, B. (1989). Homeownership and the accumulation of real wealth. *Environment and Planning D* 7 (1): 69–91.

Badcock, B. (1992). Adelaide's heart transplant, 1977-88: 2. The 'transfer' of value within the housing market. *Environment and Planning A* 24: 323–339.

Badcock, B. and Beer, A. (2000). *Home Truths: Property Ownership and Housing Wealth in Australia*. Melbourne: Melbourne University Press.

Bagshaw, R. (ed.) (1996). *No Better Land: The 1860 Diaries of the Anglican Colonial Bishop George Hills*. Victoria, BC: Sono Nis Press.

Bankwest (2011). *Third Bankwest key worker housing affordability report*. www.bankwest.com.au (accessed 6 November 2020).

Barangaroo Delivery Authority (various years) *Annual report*. Sydney: Government of New South Wales. https://resource.barangaroo.com/hc/en-us/categories/115001198747-Publications#annual-reports (accessed 12 September 2020).

Bardhan, A., Edelstein, R., and Kroll, C. (ed.) (2012). *Global Housing Markets*. Hoboken, NJ: John Wiley.

Barnes, T., Edgington, D., Denike, K., and McGee, T. (1992). Vancouver, the province and the Pacific Rim. In: *Vancouver and Its Region* (ed. G. Wynn and T. Oke), 171–199. Vancouver: University of British Columbia Press.

Barnes, Y. (2013). Spotlight: the world in London. *Savills World Research*. https://pdf. euro.savills.co.uk/residential—other/spot-worldlondon-lr.pdf (accessed 23 April 2021).

BBC (2017). *BBC World News* (8 August).

BC Housing (2020). *Annual service plan report 2019/20*. Victoria BC: Province of British Columbia. www.bchousing.org (accessed 2012c 10 July 2021).

Beer, A., Kearins, B., and Pieters, H. (2007). Housing affordability and planning in Australia: the challenge of policy under neoliberalism. *Housing Studies* 22 (1): 11–24.

Beioley, K. (2019). Countrywide fined in probe over anti-money laundering procedures. *Financial Times*, 4 March. https://www.ft.com/content/8e4f05ac-3e88-11e9-b896-fe36ec32aece (accessed 5 May 2021).

Bekkering, E., Desechamps-Laporte, J.P., and Smailes, M. (2019) *Residential property ownership: real estate holdings by multiple-property owners*. Ottawa: Statistics Canada catalogue 46- 28-0001. https://www150.statcan.gc.ca/n1/pub/46-28-0001/2019001/article/00001-eng.htm (accessed 12 April 2022).

Bengtsson, E. and Ryner, M. (2015). The (international) political economy of falling wage shares: situating working-class agency. *New Political Economy* 20 (3): 406–430.

Benham and Reeves (2022). Hong Kong homeowners most prevalent nation in 17 London boroughs. London. https://www.benhams.com/press-release/land lords-investors/hong-kong-homeowners-most-prevalent-nation-in-17-london-boroughs (accessed 12 May 2022).

Berry, M. (2003). Why is it important to boost the supply of affordable housing in Australia—and how can we do it? *Urban Policy and Research* 21 (4): 413–435.

Berry, M. and Dalton, T. (2004). Housing prices and policy dilemmas: a peculiarly Australian problem? *Urban Policy and Research* 22 (1): 69–91.

Berry, M. and Dalton, T. (2010). Trading on housing wealth: political risk in an aging society. In: *The Economics of Housing* (ed. S. Smith and B. Searle), 236–256. Chichester UK: Wiley-Blackwell.

Beswick, J., Alexandri, G., Byrne, M. et al. (2016). Speculating on London's housing future. *City* 20 (2): 321–341.

Beswick, J. and Penny, J. (2018). Demolishing the present to sell off the future? The emergence of 'Financialized Municipal Entrepreneurialism' in London. *International Journal of Urban and Regional Research* 42 (4): 612–632.

Black, S., Chapman, B., and Windsor, C. 2017. Australian capital flows. Reserve Bank of Australia, *Bulletin* (June), 23–33. https://www.rba.gov.au/publications/bulletin/2017/jun/pdf/bu-0617-3-australian-capital-flows.pdf (accessed 2 October 2020).

Blackbox Research (2015). Government satisfaction index. Singapore (July). https://blackbox.com.sg/everyone/category/trends/govt-satisfaction-index (accessed 26 September 2015).

Blackbox Research (2020). Government satisfaction index. Singapore (June). https://blackbox.com.sg/everyone/2020/07/24/government-satisfaction-index-gsi-june-2020 (accessed 5 February 2021).

Bland, B. (2017). Hong Kong average price of new home hits $1.8m. *Financial Times* (19 July). https://www.ft.com/content/9206350c-6c62-11e7-bfeb-33fe0c5b7eaa (accessed 26 February 2020).

Blomley, N. (2004). *Unsettling the City: Urban Land and the Politics of Property*. London: Routledge.

Bloomberg (2012). Singapore's Lee says population, property among challenges faced. *Bloomberg* (28 November). http://www.bloomberg.com/news/2012-11-28/singapore-s-lee-says-population-property-among-challenges-faced.html (accessed 15 January 2013).

Bloomberg (2018). HNA's fire sale gets into full swing from Hong Kong to London. *Bloomberg* (12 February). https://www.bloomberg.com/news/articles/2018-02-12/hna-unit-sells-kai-tak-sites-to-henderson-land-for-hk-16-billion (accessed 7 February 2020).

Blunden, H. (2016). Discourses around negative gearing of investment properties in Australia. *Housing Studies* 31 (3): 340–357.

Boffey, D. (2011). Only nine pay council tax in enclave for super-rich. *The Guardian*, 26 November. http://www.theguardian.com/uk/2011/nov/26/one-hyde-park-council-tax= (accessed 26 November 2011).

Boyer, R. (2000a). Is a finance-led growth regime a viable alternative to Fordism? A preliminary analysis. *Economy and Society* 29 (1): 111–145.

Boyer, R. (2000b). The political in the era of globalization and finance: focus on some *régulation* school research. *International Journal of Urban and Regional Research* 24 (2): 274–322.

BPF (British Property Federation) (2021). UK build-to-rent housing supply grows in 2020 despite COVID-19. *Press release* (8 February). https://bpf.org.uk/media/press-releases/uk-build-to-rent-housing-supply-grows-in-2020-despite-covid-19 (accessed 17 May 2021).

Bray, C. (2019). Hong Kong's dollar millionaires swell at the slowest pace since 2014. *South China Morning Post* (16 April). https://www.scmp.com/business/money/wealth/article/3006314/hong-kongs-dollar-millionaires-swell-slowest-pace-2014-trade (accessed 18 March 2020).

Brill, F. and Raco, M. (2020). Towards a pluralistic understanding of Chinese homeowners: the case of 'ordinary' buyers. *Geoforum* 117 (December): 165–172.

Brooker, N. (2020). Uncovering London's hidden property wealth. *Financial Times* (20 March). https://www.ft.com/content/bd548b0c-6762-11ea-800d-da70cff6e4d3 (accessed 5 May 2021).

Brooks, R. and Waters, J. (2013). *Student Mobilities, Migration and the Internationalisation of Higher Education*. Basingstoke: Palgrave Macmillan.

Brownill, S. and Sharp, C. (1992). London's housing crisis. In: *The Crisis of London* (ed. A. Thornley), 10–24. London: Routledge.

Bula, F. and Curry, B. (2022). CMHC offers largest loan ever to BC First Nation rental project. *Globe and Mail* (7 September), p. A1.

Burghardt, A.F. (1971). A hypothesis about gateway cities. *Annals of the Association of American Geographers* 61 (2): 269–285.

Burgos, J. and Ismail, N. (2015). New York apartments, art top gold as stores of wealth, says Fink. *Bloomberg* (April 21). http://www.bloomberg.com/news/articles/2015-04-21/new-york-apartments-art-top-gold-as-stores-of-wealth-says-fink (accessed 15 September 2017).

Burke, T., Nygord, C., and Ralston, L. (2020). *Australian Homeownership: Past Reflections, Future Directions*. Melbourne: Australian Housing and Urban Research Institute, Final Report No. 328. https://www.ahuri.edu.au/research/final-reports/328 (accessed 17 July 2020).

Burnley, I. (2002). Evolution of Chinese settlement geographies in Sydney, Australia. *Urban Geography* 23 (4): 365–387.

Burnley, I. and Murphy, P. (2004). *Sea Change: Movement from Metropolitan to Arcadian Australia*. Sydney: University of New South Wales Press.

Burnley, I., Murphy, P., and Fagan, R. (1997). *Immigration and Australian Cities*. Sydney: The Federation Press.

Butler, T. and Lees, L. (2006). Super-gentrification in Barnsbury, London. *Transactions of the Institute of British Geographers* 31 (3): 467–487.

Cai, Y. (2017). *The Occupy Movement in Hong Kong: Sustaining Decentralized Protest*. London: Routledge.

Caillavet, C. (2021). Kerry-GIC buys mixed-use site in Shanghai's Pudong district for $930m. *Mingtiandi* (28 February). https://www.mingtiandi.com/real-estate/projects-real-estate/kerry-gic-win-pudong-site-for-930m/?utm (accessed 28 February 2021).

CapitaLand (2019a). *Making an impact: CapitaLand annual report 2019. Singapore.* https://www.capitaland.com/content/dam/capitaland-newsroom/International/2020/april/annual-reports-2019/CL-AR2019.pdf (accessed 30 November 2020).

CapitaLand (2019b). *Making a sustainable impact: CapitaLand global sustainability report.* Singapore. https://www.capitaland.com/content/dam/capitaland-sites/international/about-capitaland/sustainability/sustainability-reports/Capitaland_Integrated_Global_Sustainability_Report_2019.pdf (accessed 22 January 2021).

Carlyle, E. (2016). The 20 richest real estate barons in the world 2016. *Forbes* (14 March). https://www.forbes.com/sites/erincarlyle/2016/03/14/the-20-richest-real-estate-barons-in-the-world-2016/#39c74af66540 (accessed 7 February 2020).

Carney, M. (2014). Bank of England's Mark Carney warns on housing market. *BBC News* (18 May). https://www.bbc.com/news/business-27459663 (accessed 22 May 2014).

Carter, T. (1997). Current practices for procuring affordable housing: the Canadian context. *Housing Policy Debate* 8 (3): 593-631.

Castells, M., Goh, L., and Kwok, R.Y.W. (1990). *The Shek Kip Mei Syndrome: Economic Development and Public Housing in Hong Kong and Singapore*. London: Pion.

CBRE (2014). *Supplying London's Housing Needs; Building to Match Demand*. London.

Census and Statistics Department (2019a). *Women and men in Hong Kong: key statistics*. Hong Kong: Government of Hong Kong SAR. https://www.statistics.gov.hk/pub/B11303032019AN19B0100.pdf (accessed 5 March 2020).

Census and Statistics Department (2019b). *Hong Kong annual digest of statistics*. Hong Kong: Government of Hong Kong SAR. https://www.statistics.gov.hk/pub/B10100032019AN19B0100.pdf (accessed 13 March 2020).

Census and Statistics Department (2019c). *Hong Kong poverty situation report 2018*. Hong Kong: Government of Hong Kong SAR. https://www.statistics.gov.hk/pub/B9XX0005E2018AN18E0100.pdf (accessed 23 March 2020).

Census and Statistics Department (2019d). *Living arrangements and household characteristics*. Hong Kong: Government of Hong Kong SAR. https://www.censtatd.gov.hk/en/EIndexbySubject.html?pcode=D5600619&code=180 (accessed 24 March 2020).

Centre for Communication and Public Opinion Survey (2011). Public evaluation on media credibility. *School of Journalism and Communication, Chinese University of Hong Kong*. http://www.com.cuhk.edu.hk/ccpos/en/surveymethod_1.html (accessed 2 August 2012).

Centre for Public Data (2021). *New data on property in England and Wales owned by overseas investors*. https://www.centreforpublicdata.org/property-data-overseas-individuals (accessed 13 November 2021).

Chancellor, J. (2015). Australian buyer Lola Wang Li emerges with Villa del Mare, the $39 million Point Piper FIRB home. *Property Observer*, 13 May. https://www.propertyobserver.com.au/forward-planning/advice-and-hot-topics/china/42684-lola-wang-li-buys-villa-del-mare-the-39-million-point-piper-firb-home.html (accessed 9 October 2020).

Chancellor, J. (2017). Fears of Chinese exodus from Sydney property market. *The Daily Telegraph* (19 August). https://www.pressreader.com/australia/the-daily-telegraph-sydney/20170819/283497911157977 (accessed 28 October 2020).

Chang, E. (2012). Singles will face restrictions if allowed to buy flats. *Straits Times* (9 September).

Chang, R. (2013). Budget 2013: new HDB flats to become cheaper. *The Straits Times* (9 March).

Chang, R. and Chin, D. (2013). The big housing review. *The Straits Times* (13 April) D2.

Chang, T.C. (1997). Heritage as a tourism commodity: traversing the tourist-local divide. *Singapore Journal of Tropical Geography* 18: 48–68.

Chang, T.C. (2000a). Singapore's Little India: a tourist attraction as a contested landscape. *Urban Studies* 37 (2): 343–366.

Chang, T.C. (2000b). Renaissance revisited: Singapore as a global city for the arts. *International Journal of Urban and Regional Research* 24 (4): 818–831.

Chassany, A.S. (2013). Singapore's GIC agrees £1.7bn Broadgate deal. *Financial Times* (24 December). www.ft.com/intl/cms/s/0/7256a258-6bf5-11e3-85b1-00144feabdc0.html (accessed 24 December 2013).

Chen, H.W., Ng, M.K., Es, M. et al. (2018). Socio-spatial polarization and the (re-) distribution of deprived groups in world cities: a case study of Hong Kong. *Urban Geography* 39 (7): 969–987.

Chen, O. (2016). China's Aqualand buys 9th Sydney site for $105m. *Mingtiandi* (29 July). https://www.mingtiandi.com/real-estate/outbound-investment/chinas-aqualand-buys-9th-sydney-site-for-105m (accessed 9 October 2020).

Cheng, J.Y.S. (2014). The emergence of radical politics in Hong Kong: causes and impact. *China Review* 14 (1): 199–232.

Cheng, R. (2017). Flat buyers in for a rude awakening, Hong Kong officials warn. *South China Morning Post* (5 June). https://www.scmp.com/news/hong-kong/economy/article/2096919/high-risks-ahead-hong-kongs-exuberant-property-market-finance (accessed 6 June 2017).

Cheong, A. (2013a). *Singapore Property Press Digest*. Singapore: Savills. (May).

Cheong, A. (2013b). *Briefing: Residential Sales*. Singapore: Savills. (July).

Cheong, A. (2014). *Briefing: Sales & Investment*. Singapore: Savills. (February).

Cheshire, P. (2018). Broken market or broken policy? The unintended consequences of restrictive planning. *National Institute Economic Review* 245 (1): R9–R19.

Cheung, C. (2018). Was Vision Vancouver 'addicted' to selling rezoning? *The Tyee* (1 October). https://thetyee.ca/News/2018/10/01/Vision-Vancouver-Rezoning-Addiction (accessed 26 August 2021).

Cheung, P. (2013). Income growth and redistribution: issues and challenges. In: *Singapore Inclusive: Bridging Divides* (ed. S.H. Kang and C.H. Leong), 7–22. Singapore: World Scientific Publishing.

Cheung, T. (2015). Tycoon Li Ka-shing joins property magnates calling for Hong Kong to pass political reform. *South China Morning Post* (3 June). https://www.scmp.com/news/hong-kong/politics/article/1815642/tycoon-li-ka-shing-joins-property-magnates-calling-hong-kong (accessed 6 February 2020).

Chew, A. (2020). Hongkongers splash out on London property as Boris Johnson's visa offer, weak pound buoy market. *South China Morning Post* (11 June). https://www.scmp.com/week-asia/economics/article/3088600/hongkongers-splash-out-london-property-boris-johnsons-visa (accessed 6 May 2021).

Chi, B., Dennett, A., Morphet, R., and Hutchinson, C. (2020). *Exploring Local Authority Travel Time to London Effects on the Spatio-Temporal Pattern of Local Authority House Price Variation in England*. UCL, CASA Working Paper 218. https://www.ucl.ac.uk/bartlett/casa/sites/bartlett/files/working_paper_218.pdf (accessed 21 April 2021).

China Daily (2014). Real estate giant invests billions of pounds in UK, 24 January. http://www.chinadaily.com.cn/business/2014-01/24/content_17256044.htm (accessed 27 January 2014).

China Daily (2016). Australia to bring its 'largest ever trade mission' to China: minister (4 April). http://www.chinadaily.com.cn/business/2016-04/05/content_24284581.htm (accessed 9 October 2020).

China Daily Canada (2016). Increasingly elusive underground banking targeted, (19 August) p. 3.

Chiu, P. (2018). Record 1.37 million people living below poverty line in Hong Kong. *South China Morning Post*, 19 November. https://www.scmp.com/news/hong-kong/society/article/2174006/record-13-million-people-living-below-poverty-line-hong-kong (accessed 20 March 2020).

Chiu R. LH. (2007). Planning, land and affordable housing in Hong Kong. *Housing Studies* 22 (1): 63-81.

Chiu, S.W.K. and Lui, T.L. (2004). Testing the global city – social polarisation thesis: Hong Kong since the 1990s. *Urban Studies* 41 (10): 1863–1888.

Chow, K.C. and Xie, T. (2016). Are house prices driven by capital flows? Evidence from Singapore. *Journal of International Commerce, Economics and Policy* 7 (1): 1650006 1–21.

Chow, W. (1997) Petter joins opposition to overseas asset reporting law. *Vancouver Sun* (20 September) p. A3.

Christophers, B. (2019). The rentierization of the United Kingdom economy. *Environment and Planning A*. doi:10.1177/0308518×19873007.

Chu, C. (2010). People power as exception: three controversies of privatisation in post-handover Hong Kong. *Urban Studies* 47 (8): 1773–1792.

Chu, K. (2014). Hong Kong protests as much about dollars as democracy. *Wall Street Journal* (19 October). http://www.wsj.com/articles/hong-kong-protests-as-much-about-dollars-as-democracy-1413754381 (accessed 28 May 2016).

Chua, B.H. (1995). *Communitarian Ideology and Democracy in Singapore*. London: Routledge.

Chua, B.H. (1997). *Political Legitimacy and Housing: Stakeholding in Singapore*. London: Routledge.

Chua, B.H. (2000). Public housing residents as clients of the state. *Housing Studies* 15 (1): 45–60.

Chua, B.H. (2003a). Maintaining housing values under the condition of universal home ownership. *Housing Studies* 18 (5): 765–780.

Chua, B.H. (2003b). *Life Is Not Complete without Shopping: Consumption Culture in Singapore*. Singapore: Singapore University Press.

Chua, B.H. (2014). Navigating between limits: the future of public housing in Singapore. *Housing Studies* 29 (4): 520–533.

Chua, B.H. (2015). Financialising public housing as an asset for retirement in Singapore. *International Journal of Housing Policy* 15 (1): 27–42.

Chua, V. (2009). Ethnic segregation and multiculturalism in Singapore: a relational study. *Asian Journal of Social Science* 37 (4): 677–698.

Chua, Y.L. (2012). *Of Singapore and London residential*. Singapore: Jones, Lang, LaSalle, Research Report, September.

Chung, J.Y. and Carpenter, K. (2022). Safe havens: overseas housing speculation and opportunity zones. *Housing Studies* 37 (8): 1350–1378.

CIC (Citizenship and Immigration Canada) (2014). *Evaluation of the Federal Business Immigration Program*. Ottawa: CIC Evaluation Division. https://www.canada.ca/content/dam/ircc/migration/ircc/english/pdf/pub/e2-2013_fbip.pdf (accessed 14 April 2019).

City Developments (2020). *Get inspired: city developments limited annual report 2019.* Singapore. https://ir.cdl.com.sg/static-files/56287c3d-6020-4fa9-9f46-3e4dd44283f3 (accessed 18 January 2021).

City Futures Research Centre (2021). *Submission to the Parliamentary Inquiry: Housing Affordability and Supply in Australia.* Sydney: University of New South Wales.

City of Vancouver (2017). *Housing Vancouver strategy.* https://council.vancouver.ca/20171128/documents/rr1appendixa.pdf (accessed 6 July 2021).

City of Vancouver (2020). *Empty homes tax: annual report.* https://vancouver.ca/files/cov/vancouver-2020-empty-homes-tax-annual-report.pdf (accessed 10 July 2021).

City of Vancouver (2021a). *2020 Housing Vancouver annual report on approvals + 2021 housing work program update.* https://vancouver.ca/files/cov/housing-policy-housing-vancouver-approvals-memo-update-may-2021.pdf (accessed 9 July 2021).

City of Vancouver (2021b) *Vancouver budget 2022: building the budget.* Available at: https://vancouver.ca/files/cov/2022-budget-building-the-budget.PDF (accessed 19 May 2022).

City of Vancouver (2021c). *Jericho Lands planning program.* https://shapeyourcity.ca/jericho-lands (accessed 8 November 2021).

CK Asset Holdings (2019). *Annual report 2018.* Hong Kong. https://www.ckah.com/uploaded_files/news/1014_e_content.pdf (accessed 16 February 2020).

CK Hutchison (2019) *Annual report, 2018.* Hong Kong. https://doc.irasia.com/listco/hk/ckh/annual/2018/ar2018.pdf (accessed 15 February 2020).

Clark, T. and Heath, A. (2013). *Hard Times: The Divisive Toll of the Economic Slump.* New Haven and London: Yale University Press.

Clayton, R. and Pupazzoni, R. (2020). Reserve Bank cuts interest rates to record low of 0.1 per cent during Covid-19 recession. ABC News (3 November). https://www.abc.net.au/news/2020-11-03/rba-cuts-interest-rates-record-low-coronavirus-pandemic/12838760 (accessed 5 November 2020).

CMHC (Canada Mortgage and Housing Corporation) (2017). *Canada's National Housing Strategy: a place to call home.* https://eppdscrmssa01.blob.core.windows.net/cmhcprodcontainer/sf/project/placetocallhome/pdfs/canada-national-housing-strategy.pdf (accessed 5 July 2021).

CMHC (2021). *Building the future together: 2020 National Housing Strategy progress report.* https://assets.cmhc-schl.gc.ca/sites/place-to-call-home/pdfs/nhs-triennial-report-en.pdf?rev=7619f9f0-9c76-4aa6-a418-366e01ea2832 (accessed 13 July 2021).

CNA (Channel NewsAsia) (2012a). *Public housing must keep up with rising aspirations of people: ex-MM Lee.* (4 November). https://www.youtube.com/watch?v=7b4XuKr27NI (accessed 15 January 2013).

CNA (2012b). *Enough HDB flats to meet rising demand: Khaw Boon Wan.* (25 November). https://news.smu.edu.sg/news.smu.edu.sg/files/smu_in_the_news/2012/sources/CNA_20121125_1.pdf (accessed 21 January 2013).

CNA (2013a). *Enough homes for all, says Khaw* (18 January).

CNA (2013b). *Singapore unveils SG$2 billion package to boost fertility rate*. (21 January).

CNA (2019). *Dyson to move global headquarters to St James Power Station in Singapore*. (28 November).

Cole, M. (2013). Greenland sells RMB 1.5 Bil in Sydney homes in first weekend. *Mingtiandi* (3 March). https://www.mingtiandi.com/real-estate/outbound-investment/greenland-sells-rmb-1-5-bil-in-sydney-homes-in-first-weekend (accessed 20 November 2020).

Cole, M. (2014). London biggest draw as China's outbound real estate investment jumps 17 percent. *Mingtiandi* (29 July). http://www.mingtiandi.com/real-estate/outbound-investment/london-biggest-draw-as-chinas-outbound-real-estate-investment-jumps-17 (accessed 6 August 2014).

Cole, M. (2015). Chinese pour $1.23B into Sydney real estate in last two months - more on the way. *Mingtiandi* (4 January). https://www.mingtiandi.com/real-estate/outbound-investment/chinese-pour-1-23b-into-sydney-real-estate-in-nov-dec-more-on-the-way (accessed 9 October 2020).

Cole, M. (2016). Are capital controls clamping down on Chinese purchases of Aussie homes? *Mingtiandi* (2 June). https://www.mingtiandi.com/real-estate/outbound-investment/are-capital-controls-clamping-down-on-chinese-purchases-of-aussie-homes (accessed 28 October 2020).

Cook, L. (2014). Wealth flows: migration patterns. *Residential property focus Q3*. 10. London: Savills World Research. https://pdf.euro.savills.co.uk/residential-property-focus-uk/residential-property-focus-q3-14.pdf (accessed 16 April 2021).

Cook, S. and Watson, D. (2016). A new perspective on the ripple effect in the UK housing market: co-movement, cyclical subsamples and alternative indices. *Urban Studies* 53 (14): 3048–3062.

Cooper, C., Orford, S., Webster, C., and Jones, C. (2013). Exploring the ripple effect and spatial volatility in house prices in England and Wales. *Environment and Planning B* 40 (5): 763–782.

Cooper, S. (2016 13 April). BC watchdog reads riot act to realtors. *Vancouver Sun*. A4.

Corlett, A. and Leslie, J. (2021). *Home county: options for taxing main residence capital gains*. London: Resolution Foundation. https://www.resolutionfoundation.org/app/uploads/2021/12/Home-county.pdf (Accessed 8 January 2022).

Cosh, G. and Gleeson, J. (2020) *Housing in London 2020: the evidence base for the London Housing Strategy*. London: Greater London Authority. https://www.london.gov.uk/sites/default/files/housing_in_london_2020.pdf (accessed 28 April 2021).

Cox, W. and Pavletich, H. (2013). *9th Annual Demographia international housing affordability survey*. http://www.demographia.com/dhi2013.pdf (accessed 28 March 2013).

Cox, W. and Pavletich, H. (2015). *11th Annual Demographia international housing affordability survey*. http://demographia.com/dhi2015.pdf (accessed 5 October 2015).

Cox, W. and Pavletich, H. (2020). *16th Annual Demographia international housing affordability survey*. http://www.demographia.com/dhi2020.pdf (accessed 13 March 2020).

Crabtree, J. and Allen, K. (2014). India's Lhoda Group homes in on London property market. *Financial Times* (21 September). http://www.ft.com/intl/cms/s/0/5814dc2a-3f26-11e4-a861-00144feabdc0.html (accessed 22 September 2014).

Cranston, M. (2020 4 August). China hits 48.8pc of Australian exports. *Australian Financial Review*. https://www.afr.com/policy/economy/china-hits-48-8pc-of-australian-exports-20200804-p55i9d (accessed 7 September 2020).

Cranston, M. and Thistleton, R. (2013). The great Chinese takeaway. *Australian Financial Review, Weekend Fin* (20-26 December). 46–48.

CTV (2015). One-third of Vancouver house units scooped up by foreign buyers. *CTV News Vancouver* (6 May). http://bc.ctvnews.ca/one-third-of-vancouver-house-units-scooped-up-by-foreign-buyers-1.2364478 (accessed 25 June 2015).

Cullen Commission (2022). *Commission of enquiry into money laundering in British Columbia*. https://cullencommission.ca/files/reports/CullenCommission-Final-Report-Full.pdf (accessed 25 June 2022).

Daly, M. (1982). *Sydney Boom, Sydney Bust: The City and Its Property Market, 1850-1981*. Sydney: George Allen & Unwin.

Data.gov.sg (2020a). *Private residential property price index*. https://data.gov.sg/dataset/private-residential-property-price-index-by-type-of-property (accessed 15 June 2020).

Data.gov.sg (2020b). *HDB resale price index*. https://data.gov.sg/dataset/hdb-resale-price-index (accessed 20 July 2020).

Davidson, M. and Lees, L. (2005). New build 'gentrification' and London's riverside renaissance. *Environment and Planning A* 37 (7): 1165–1190.

Davidson, M. and Wyly, E. (2012). Class-ifying London. *City* 16 (4): 395–421.

Davies, P. (2012). Hong Kong harbours 'hot money' misgivings. *Financial Times* (31 October). https://www.ft.com/content/39944cb0-2315-11e2-8edf-00144feabdc0 (accessed 20 February 2020).

DCJ (Department of Communities and Justice) (2020). *Previous rent and sales reports*. Sydney: Government of New South Wales. https://www.facs.nsw.gov.au/resources/statistics/rent-and-sales/back-issues?result_536530_result (accessed 11 November 2020).

DCLG (Department for Communities and Local Government) (2017). *Fixing our broken housing market*. https://assets.publishing.service.gov.uk/government/uploads/system/uploads/attachment_data/file/590464/Fixing_our_broken_housing_market_-_print_ready_version.pdf (accessed 21 May 2021).

De Decker, P. and Dewilde, C. (2010). Homeownership and asset-based welfare: the case of Belgium. *Journal of Housing and the Built Environment* 25 (2): 243–262.

Debelle, G. (2018). Assessing the effects of housing lending policy measures. *Speech to the FINSIA Signature Event in Melbourne* (15 November 2018). https://www.rba.gov.au/speeches/2018/sp-dg-2018-11-15.html (accessed 23 October 2020).

Debord, G. (1973). *Society of the Spectacle*. Detroit: Black and Red.

DeGolyer, M. (2016). *Asian urban wellbeing indicators: Hong Kong report*. Hong Kong: Civic Exchange. https://civic-exchange.org/wp-content/uploads/2016/10/590C-201612WEL_wellbeing_HK_en_updated.pdf (accessed 9 April 2020).

Delfani, N., De Deken, J., and Dewilde, C. (2014). Home-ownership and pensions: negative correlation, but no trade-off. *Housing Studies* 29 (5): 657–676.

Deng, Y.H., Gyourko, J., and Li, T. (2019). Singapore's cooling measures and its housing market. *Journal of Housing Economics* 45: 101573.

Department of Industry (2020a). *Resources and energy quarterly*. Canberra: Government of Australia (March). https:/webarchive.nla.gov.ca/awa/20220604124955/https://www.industry.gov.au/data-and-publications/resources-and-energy-quarterly-march-2020 (accessed 24 September 2020).

Department of Industry (2020b). *Resources and energy quarterly*. Canberra: Government of Australia (June). https:/webarchive.nla.gov.au/awa/20220603091557/https://www.industry.gov.au/data-and-publications/resources-and-energy-quarterly-june-2020 (accessed 4 September 2020).

DFAT (Department of Foreign Affairs and Trade) (2019). *Trade and investment at a glance 2019*. Canberra: Government of Australia. https://www.dfat.gov.au/sites/default/files/trade-and-investment-at-a-glance-2019.pdf (accessed 3 September 2020).

DHA (Department of Home Affairs) (2019). *Country profiles – China*. Canberra: Government of Australia.

DHA (2020). *Significant investor visa statistics*. Canberra: Government of Australia. https://www.homeaffairs.gov.au/research-and-statistics/statistics/visa-statistics/work/significant-investor-visa. (accessed 9 October 2020).

Dickens, C. (1859). *A Tale of Two Cities*. London: Chapman and Hall.

Dieleman, F., Clark, W., and Deurloo, M. (2000). The geography of residential turn-over in 27 large US metropolitan housing markets, 1985–95. *Urban Studies* 37 (2): 223–245.

Doling, J. and Ronald, R. (2010a). Home ownership and asset-based welfare. *Journal of Housing and the Built Environment* 25 (2): 165–173.

Doling, J. and Ronald, R. (2010b). Property-based welfare and European homeowners: how would housing perform as a pension? *Journal of Housing and the Built Environment* 25 (2): 227–241.

Doling, J. and Ronald, R. (ed.) (2014). *Housing East Asia: Socioeconomic and Demographic Challenges*. Basingstoke UK: Palgrave Macmillan.

Donaldson, J. (2019). *Land of Destiny: A History of Vancouver Real Estate*. Vancouver: Anvil Press.

Dorling, D. (2014). *All that Is Solid: The Great Housing Disaster*. London: Allen Lane.

Dunkley, E. (2019). The Hong Kong property bubble that won't burst. *Financial Times* (14 February). https://www.ft.com/content/a854a4f0-2dbe-11e9-8744-e7016697f225 (accessed 2 March 2020).

DWP (Department for Work and Pensions). (2015). *Housing benefit claimants, borough*. https://data.london.gov.uk/dataset/housing-benefit-claimants–borough (accessed 27 May 2021).

Easthope, H. (2019). *The Politics and Practices of Apartment Living*. Cheltenham, UK: Edward Elgar.

The Economist (2005). *In come the waves: special report on the global housing boom* (16 June). https://www.economist.com/special-report/2005/06/16/in-come-the-waves (accessed 24 November 2020).

The Economist (2012a). *Singapore politics: falling on their wallets* (7 January). 34.

The Economist (2012b) *Mid-levels they ain't* (28 April). 78–79.

The Economist (2012c). *On a high: special report on London* (30 June). https://www. economist.com/special-report/2012/06/28/on-a-high (accessed 14 July 2014).

The Economist (2012d). *Home is where the money is* (30 June). https://www.econo mist.com/special-report/2012/06/28/home-is-where-the-money-is (accessed 3 June 2021).

The Economist (2013a). *Singapore banks: the perils of a gilded age* (3 August). 62.

The Economist (2013b). *London property: live and let buy* (9 November). 61–62.

The Economist (2018). *Awash: money-laundering in London* (13 October). 74.

The Economist (2022). *House-price horror show* (28 October). 11.

Edwards, M. (2016). The housing crisis and London. *City* 20 (2): 222–237.

Egan, P.D. and Soos, P. (2014). *Bubble Economics: Australian Land Speculation 1830-2013*. UK: World Economics Association. http://citeseerx.ist.psu.edu/viewdoc/ download?doi=10.1.1.570.2800&rep=rep1&type=pdf (accessed 1 September 2020).

Elliott Cooper, A., Hubbard, P., and Lees, L. (2020a). Sold out? The right-to-buy, gentrification and working-class displacements in London. *Sociological Review* 68 (6): 1354–1369.

Elliott-Cooper, A., Hubbard, P., and Lees, L. (2020b). Moving beyond Marcuse: gentrification, displacement and the violence of un-homing. *Progress in Human Geography* 44 (3): 492–509.

Elmer, S. and Dening, G. (2016). The London clearances. *City* 20 (2): 271–277.

Emmerson, D. (1995). Singapore and the 'Asian values' debate. *Journal of Democracy* 6 (4): 95–105.

Engels, B. (1994). Capital flows, redlining and gentrification: the pattern of mortgage lending and social change in Glebe, Sydney, 1960–1984. *International Journal of Urban and Regional Research* 18 (4): 628–657.

Expert Panel (2021). *Opening Doors: unlocking Housing Supply for Affordability*. Victoria BC: Canada-British Columbia Expert Panel on the future of housing supply and affordability. https://engage.gov.bc.ca/app/uploads/sites/121/2021/06/Opening-Doors_BC-Expert-Panel_Final-Report_Jun16.pdf (accessed 9 July 2021).

Farha, L., Freeman, S., and Gabarre, D.S. (2022) *The Shift Directives*. https:// make-the-shift.org/wp-content/uploads/2022/05/The-Directives-Formatted-DRAFT4.pdf (accessed 5 June 2022).

Farlow, A. (2013). *Crash and Beyond*. Oxford: Oxford University Press.

Fernandez, R., Hofman, A., and Aalbers, M. (2016). London and New York as a safe deposit box for the transnational wealth elite. *Environment and Planning A* 48 (12): 2443–2461.

Ferreri, M. (2020). Painted bullet holes and broken promises: understanding and challenging municipal dispossession in London's public housing 'decanting'. *International Journal of Urban and Regional Research* 44 (6): 1007–1022.

Fielding, A. (1992). Migration and social mobility: South East England as an escalator region. *Regional Studies* 26 (1): 1–15.

Fields, D. (2018). Constructing a new asset class: property-led financial accumulation after the crisis. *Economic Geography* 94 (2): 118–140.

Forrest, R. and Yip, N.M. (ed.) (2011). *Housing Markets and the Global Financial Crisis*. Cheltenham, UK: Edward Elgar.

Forrest, R. and Yip, N.M. (2015). What young people really think about housing in Hong Kong. *South China Morning Post* (6 February). https://www.scmp.com/comment/insight-opinion/article/1704617/what-young-people-really-think-about-housing-hong-kong (accessed 8 April 2020).

Frasers Property (2020). *Agility and tenacity: annual report 2020*. Singapore. https://www.annualreports.com/HostedData/AnnualReportArchive/f/OTC_FSR-PF_2020.pdf (accessed 23 January 2021).

Frey, W. (1999). Immigration and demographic balkanization: toward one America or two? In: *America's Demographic Tapestry* (ed. J. Hughes and J. Seneca), 78–97. New Brunswick, NJ: Rutgers University Press.

FT (Financial Times) (2016). China's capital controls fail to curb outbound investment. *Financial Times* (10 August). https://www.ft.com/content/6a5433a2-5efc-11e6-ae3f-77baadeb1c93 (accessed 3 October 2017).

Fumano, D. (2017a). Offshore money hit real estate in Metro 'like a ton of bricks'. *Vancouver Sun* (28 November). A1.

Fumano, D. (2017b). B.C. real estate regulator ends 'dual agency'. *Vancouver Sun* (16 November). A9.

Fumano, D. (2021). Sweetheart deal for Little Mountain developer sparks public outrage. *Vancouver Sun* (1 September). A1.

Fumano, D. and Culbert, L. (2022) Grow big. Grow together. *Vancouver Sun* (16 July). A12–A13.

Fun, Y. (2015). *Cloaking White-Collar Crime in Hong Kong's Property Sector*. Basingstoke, UK: Palgrave Macmillan.

Fung, J. (2016). An open letter to those who play the race card in the Vancouver housing affordability debate. *Georgia Straight* (11 July). https://www.straight.com/news/734326/justin-fung-open-letter-those-who-play-race-card-vancouver-housing-affordability-debate (accessed 14 June 2017).

Furnivall, J.S. (1956). *Colonial Policy and Practice*. New York: New York University Press.

Gallent, N., Durrant, D., and May, N. (2017). Housing supply, investment demand and money creation: a comment on the drivers of London's housing crisis. *Urban Studies* 54 (10): 2204–2216.

Gallent, N., Durrant, D., and Stirling, P. (2018). Between the unimaginable and the unthinkable: pathways to and from England's housing crisis. *Town Planning Review* 89 (2): 125–144.

Gauder, M., Houssard, C., and Orsmond, D. (2014). Foreign investment in residential real estate. Reserve Bank of Australia. *Bulletin*, June 11-18. https://www.rba.gov.au/publications/bulletin/2014/jun/pdf/bu-0614-2.pdf (accessed 8 October 2020).

Geertz, C. (1973). *The Interpretation of Cultures*. New York: Basic Books.

Gellatly, G. and Morissette, R. (2017). *Non-resident ownership of residential properties in Toronto and Vancouver*. Ottawa: Statistics Canada, Catalogue 11-626-X, No.

Fields, D. and Uffer, S. (2016). The financialisation of rental housing: a con analysis of New York City and Berlin. *Urban Studies* 53 (7): 1486–1502

Fincher, R. and Shaw, K. (2009). The unintended segregation of transnatic dents in central Melbourne. *Environment and Planning A* 41 (8): 1884–

FINTRAC (Financial Transactions and Reports Analysis Centre of Canada) *Indicators of money laundering in financial transactions related to real estate* fintrac-canafe.canada.ca/intel/operation/real-eng (accessed 5 January 20

FIRB (Foreign Investment Review Board) (2012). Annual report 2011-20 *ernment of Australia*. https://firb.gov.au/sites/firb.gov.au/files/2015/11/F nual-Report-2011-12_v4.pdf (accessed 22 September 2020).

FIRB (2020). Annual report 2018-2019. *Government of Australia*. https:// au/sites/firb.gov.au/files/2020-05/FIRB-AR-2018-19.pdf (accessed 24 ber 2020).

Fitzgerald, A. and Lupton, R. (2015). The limits to resilience? The impact government spending cuts in London. *Local Government Studies* 41 (4): 5

Florida, R. (2022). Real estate's role in urban development: Patrice Derr *Built Up. EPA: Economy and Space* 54 (5): 1029–1032.

Flynn, J. (2016). Complete control: developers, financial viability and rege at the Elephant and Castle. *City* 20 (2): 278–286.

Flynn, L. (2017). Delayed and depressed: from expensive housing to smaller *International Journal of Housing Policy* 17 (3): 374–395.

Fong, B.C.H. (2014). The partnership between the Chinese government an Kong's capitalist class. *The China Quarterly* 217: 195–220.

Forbes (2019). *Global 2000: the world's largest public companies*. https://www com/global2000/#7f94e1ea335d (accessed 8 February 2020).

Ford, J. (2020). Local authorities need to be weaned off their debt addiction *cial Times* (21 November). https://www.ft.com/content/168ae76c-5cd! 80f2-0eb5d49a9a6b (accessed 31 May 2021).

Forrest, R. (2018). Housing and asset-based stratification in the enrichment my. *Critical Housing Studies* 5 (2): 4–13.

Forrest, R. (2021). Housing wealth, social structures and changing narrative *national Journal of Urban Sciences* 25 (1): 1–15.

Forrest, R. and Hirayama, Y. (2015). The financialisation of the social proje bedded liberalism, neoliberalism and home ownership. *Urban Studies* 233–244.

Forrest, R., Koh, S.Y., and Wissink, B. (ed.) (2017). *Cities and the Super-Ric Estate, Elite Practices, and Urban Political Economy*. London: Palgrave Mac

Forrest, R., La Grange, A., and Yip, N.M. (2004). Hong Kong as a global city distance and spatial differentiation. *Urban Studies* 41 (1): 207–227.

Forrest, R. and Lee, J. (2004). Cohort effects, differential accumulation and Kong's volatile housing market. *Urban Studies* 41 (11): 2181–2196.

Forrest, R. and Murie, A. (1989). Differential accumulation, wealth, inheritan housing policy reconsidered. *Policy and Politics* 17 (1): 25–39.

Forrest, R. and Xian, S. (2018). Accommodating discontent: youth, conflict a housing question in Hong Kong. *Housing Studies* 33 (1): 1–17.

78. https://www150.statcan.gc.ca/n1/pub/11-626-x/11-626-x2017078-eng.htm (accessed 15 January 2018).

Gellatly, G. and Morissette, R. (2019). *Immigrant ownership of residential properties in Toronto and Vancouver*. Ottawa: Statistics Canada, Catalogue 11-626-X No. 87. https://www150.statcan.gc.ca/n1/pub/11-626-x/11-626-x2019001-eng.htm (accessed 25 November 2020).

Gellatly, G. and Richards, E. (2019). *Indebtedness and wealth among Canadian households*. Ottawa: Statistics Canada, Catalogue 11-626-X No. 89. https://www150.statcan.gc.ca/n1/pub/11-626-x/11-626-x2019003-eng.htm (accessed 25 November 2020).

Generation Squeeze (2020). *Straddling the gap: 3 indicators of BC's ongoing housing affordability crisis*. https://d3n8a8pro7vhmx.cloudfront.net/gensqueeze/pages/6279/attachments/original/1602189949/Straddling_the_Gap_Oct_2020_%281%29.pdf?1602189949 (accessed 20 July 2021).

Giles, C. (2014). ONS data weaken case against mansion tax. *Financial Times* (3 July). http://www.ft.com/cms/s/0/2701e860-0297-11e4-a68d-00144feab7de.html (accessed 4 July 2014).

GLA (Greater London Authority) (2014). *Homes for London: the London housing strategy*. https://www.london.gov.uk/sites/default/files/housing_strategy_2014_report_lowresfa.pdf (accessed 10 July 2014).

GLA (2017). *The 2017 London strategic housing market assessment*. https://www.london.gov.uk/sites/default/files/london_shma_2017.pdf (accessed 11 May 2021).

GLA (2018). *London housing strategy*. https://www.london.gov.uk/sites/default/files/2018_lhs_london_housing_strategy.pdf (accessed 18 May 2021).

GLA Economics (2016). *London labour market projections 2016*. https://www.london.gov.uk/sites/default/files/llmp-2016.pdf (accessed 7 May 2021).

Glass, M. and Salvador, A. (2018). Remaking Singapore's heartland: sustaining public housing through home and neighbourhood upgrade programmes. *International Journal of Housing Policy* 18 (3): 479–490.

Glucksberg, L. (2016). A view from the top: unpacking capital flows and foreign investment in prime London. *City* 20 (2): 238–255.

Goh, R. (2005). *Contours of Culture: Space and Social Difference in Singapore*. Hong Kong: Hong Kong University Press.

Gold, K. (2015). First step: accept there's a problem. *Globe and Mail* (26 September) p. S6.

Gold, K. (2017). The 'Wild West' in condo presales. *Globe and Mail* (22 April), p. S4.

Gold, K. (2022). Truly affordable housing being lost. *Globe and Mail*. (16 September) p. H5.

Goldberg, M. (1984). Review of *Sydney Boom, Sydney Bust*. *Annals of Regional Science* 18 (3): 102–105.

Goldberg, M. (1985). *The Chinese Connection: Getting Plugged in to Pacific Rim Real Estate, Trade and Capital Markets*. Vancouver: UBC Press.

Goodstadt, L. (2013). *Poverty in the Midst of Affluence*. Hong Kong: Hong Kong University Press.

Goodstadt, L. (2018). *A City Mismanaged: Hong Kong's Struggle for Survival*. Hong Kong: Hong Kong University Press.

Gordon, J. (2020). Reconnecting the housing market to the labour market: foreign ownership and housing affordability in urban Canada. *Canadian Public Policy* 46 (1): 1–22.

Gordon, J. (2022). Solving puzzles in the Canadian housing market: foreign ownership and de-coupling in Toronto and Vancouver. *Housing Studies* 37 (7): 1250–1273.

Gotham, K.F. (2006). The secondary circuit of capital reconsidered: globalization and the US real estate sector. *American Journal of Sociology* 112 (1): 231–275.

Gottliebsen, R. (2016). Dramatic shifts herald a new era in residential property. *The Australian* (12 May). https://www.smats.net/news-insight/news-insight/dramatic-shifts-herald-a-new-era-in-residential-property (accessed 26 October 2020).

Government of Canada (2021). *Progress on the national housing strategy.* https://www.placetocallhome.ca/progress-on-the-national-housing-strategy (accessed 13 July 2021).

Government of Hong Kong SAR (2018). *Hong Kong money laundering and terrorist financing risk assessment report.* https://www.cr.gov.hk/en/amlctf/report.htm (accessed 2 April 2020).

Government of Singapore (2013). *A sustainable population for a dynamic Singapore: population white paper.* Singapore: National Population and Talent Division. https://www.strategygroup.gov.sg/media-centre/population-white-paper-a-sustainable-population-for-a-dynamic-singapore (accessed 15 November 2013).

Grant, J. (2013a). Singapore's Temasek warns of Fed disruption amid slowdown. *Financial Times* (5 July). https://www.ft.com/content/d2dcb2fe-e485-11e2-a74d-00144feabdc0 (accessed 22 July 2013).

Grant, J. (2013b). Moody's sounds concern on Singapore banking. *Financial Times* (15 July). https://www.ft.com/content/06bed692-ed2d-11e2-8d7c-00144feabdc0 (accessed 22 July 2013).

Grant, J. (2013c). Singapore loosens Switzerland's grip on wealth management. *Financial Times* (23 July). https://www.ft.com/content/048c3630-f39f-11e2-942f-00144feabdc0. (accessed 19 November 2013).

Grant, J. (2014). Singapore leads the pack in sovereign wealth deals. *Financial Times* (3 November). http://www.ft.com/intl/cms/s/0/3d018fde-6350-11e4-9a79-00144feabdc0.html (accessed 3 November 2014).

Grant, J. and Allen, K. (2014). Singapore buyers pile into London's prime property market. *Financial Times* (7 February). http://www.ft.com/intl/cms/s/0/fdb24120-8fa6-11e3-be85-00144feab7de.html (accessed 7 February 2014).

Grant, J., Walks, A., and Ramos, H. (ed.) (2020). *Changing Neighbourhoods: Social and Spatial Polarization in Canadian Cities.* Vancouver: UBC Press.

Gray, M. and Barford, A. (2018). The depth of the cuts: the uneven geography of local government austerity. *Cambridge Journal of Regions, Economy and Society* 11 (3): 541–563.

Gregori, N. (2014). *What next after help to buy?* London: Savills. https://www.savills.co.uk/research_articles/229130/178188-0 (accessed 14 November 2014).

Griffith, M. (2011) *We must fix it: delivering reform of the building sector to meet the UK's housing and economic challenges.* Institute for Public Policy Research.

https://www.ippr.org/files/images/media/files/publication/2012/02/we-must-fix-it_Dec2011_8421.pdf (accessed 18 June 2014).

Grigoryeva, I. and Ley, D. (2019). The price ripple effect in the Vancouver housing market. *Urban Geography* 40 (8): 1168–1190.

Gu, W. (2014). Hong Kong protests also fueled by widening wealth gap. *Wall Street Journal* (9 October). http://www.wsj.com/articles/hong-kong-protests-also-fueled-by-widening-wealth-gap-1412860304 (accessed 28 May 2016).

Gurran, N., Gallent, N., and Chiu, R. (2016). *Politics, Planning and Housing Supply in Australia, England and Hong Kong*. London: Routledge.

Gurran, N., Maalsen, S., and Shrestha, P. (2022). Is 'informal' housing an affordability solution for expensive cities? Evidence from Sydney, Australia. *International Journal of Housing Policy* 22 (1): 10–33.

Gurstein, P. and Yan, A. (2019). Beyond the dreams of avarice: the past, present and future of housing in Vancouver's planning legacy. In: *Planning on the Edge* (ed. P. Gurstein and T. Hutton), 215–246. Vancouver: UBC Press.

Gutstein, D. (1975). *Vancouver Limited*. Toronto: James Lorimer.

Hage, G. (1998). *White Nation: Fantasies of White Supremacy in a Multicultural Society*. Annandale, NSW: Pluto Press.

Hager, M. (2016). BC releases first set of data on foreign home ownership in Vancouver. *Globe and Mail* (8 July), p. A1.

Haila, A. (2000). Real estate in global cities: Singapore and Hong Kong as property states. *Urban Studies* 37 (12): 2241–2256.

Haila, A. (2016). *Urban Land Rent: Singapore as a Property State*. Chichester, UK: Wiley Blackwell.

Hajdu, J. (1994). Recent cycles of foreign property investment in central Sydney and Melbourne. *Urban Geography* 15 (3): 246–257.

Halliday, M. (2020), The bold plan for an indigenous-led development in Vancouver. *The Guardian* (3 January). https://www.theguardian.com/cities/2020/jan/03/the-bold-new-plan-for-an-indigenous-led-development-in-vancouver (accessed 15 July 2021).

Halligan, L. (2020). How to fix Britain's housebuilding problem. *Financial Times* (14 February). https://www.ft.com/content/a63013ea-4da1-11ea-95a0-43d18ec715f5 (accessed 13 May 2021).

Hamilton, C. (2018). *Silent Invasion: China's Influence in Australia*. Melbourne: Hardie Grant Books.

Hammond, E. (2012a). Foreign money seeks London property. *Financial Times* (17 October). http://www.ft.com/cms/s/0/6e206aa0-185b-11e2-80af-00144feabdc0.html (accessed 22 November 2012).

Hammond, E. (2012b). London house prices soar above regions. *Financial Times* (9 November). http://www.ft.com/cms/s/0/c93abf18-2a7f-11e2-99bb-00144feabdc0.html (accessed 14 December 2012).

Hammond, E. (2013). Singapore underwrites Laxfield's £1bn fund. *Financial Times* (28 January). https://www.ft.com/content/aa32ebf4-66ed-11e2-a83f-00144feab49a (accessed 3 February 2013).

Hammond, E. and Pickford, J. (2013). Builders attack Ed Miliband's 'wild' plan for 200,000 new homes. *Financial Times* (25 September). http://www.ft.com/cms/s/0/dfac3eba-25e8-11e3-8ef6-00144feab7de.html (accessed 25 September 2013).

Hammond, G. (2019). London's property flippers forced to sell at a loss. *Financial Times* (19 February). https://www.ft.com/content/a8e529e4-307a-11e9-8744-e7016697f225 (accessed 7 May 2021).

Hammond, G. (2020). UK local councils banned from making risky property bets. *Financial Times* (25 November). https://www.ft.com/content/be8db50e-04c8-4ce3-aece-b5f4d92277ba (accessed 31 May 2021).

Hammond, G. (2021) Banks to become landlords in growing build-to-rent sector. *Financial Times* (30 August). https://www.ft.com/content/662d3839-2c58-4b88-8df8-71d8f0af85d5 (accessed 31 August 2021).

Hamnett, C. (1999). *Winners and Losers: Home Ownership in Modern Britain*. London: UCL Press.

Hamnett, C. (2003a). *Unequal City: London in the Global Arena*. London: Routledge.

Hamnett, C. (2003b). Gentrification and the middle-class remaking of Central London, 1961-2001. *Urban Studies* 40 (12): 2401–2426.

Hamnett, C. (2009). Spatially displaced demand and the changing geography of house prices in London, 1995–2006. *Housing Studies* 24 (3): 301–320.

Hamnett, C. (2010). Moving the poor out of Central London? The implications of the Coalition Government 2010 cuts to housing benefits. *Environment and Planning A* 42 (12): 2809–2819.

Hamnett, C. (2014). Shrinking the welfare state: the structure, geography and impact of British government benefit cuts. *Transactions of the Institute of British Geographers* 39 (4): 490–503.

Hamnett, C. and Randolph, W. (1984). The role of landlord disinvestment in housing market transformation: an analysis of the flat break-up market in central London. *Transactions of the Institute of British Geographers* 9 (3): 259–279.

Hamnett, C. and Reades, J. (2019). Mind the gap: implications of overseas investment for regional house price divergence in Britain. *Housing Studies* 34 (3): 388–406.

Hansard (2015). Coleman to Eby. *House in Committee, Legislature of British Columbia*. 26 (6) (14 May), p. 8541–8542. http://www.leg.bc.ca/hansard/40th4th/20150514am-Hansard-v26n6.htm# (accessed 15 July 2015).

Harley, F. (2021). *Super-prime sales resilient in 2020 due to domestic demand and the search for space*. London: Knight Frank, The Intelligence Lab. https://www.knightfrank.com/wealthreport/2021-04-12-superprime-sales-resilient-in-2020-due-to-domestic-demand-and-the-search-for-space (accessed 6 May 2021).

Harris, R. (1986). Boom and bust: the effects of house price inflation on homeownership rates in Montreal, Toronto, and Vancouver. *The Canadian Geographer* 30 (4): 302–315.

Harris, R.C. (1997). *The Resettlement of British Columbia*. Vancouver: UBC Press.

Harris, T., Hodge, L., and Phillips, D. (2019). *English local government funding: trends and challenges in 2019 and beyond*. London: The Institute for Fiscal Studies. https://www.econstor.eu/bitstream/10419/235055/1/R166.pdf (accessed 25 May 2021).

Harvey, D. (2008). The right to the city. *New Left Review* 53 (Sept.): 23–40.

Harvey, D. (2018). Universal alienation. *Journal for Cultural Research* 22 (2): 137–150.

Hasson, S. and Ley, D. (1994). *Neighbourhood Organizations and the Welfare State*. Toronto: University of Toronto Press.

Hay, I. (2013). Establishing geographies of the super-rich: axes for analysis of abundance. In: *Geographies of the Super-Rich* (ed. I. Hay), 1–25. Cheltenham: Edward Elgar.

HDB (Housing and Development Board) (2012a). *Heartland beat*. HDB InfoWEB. http://www.hdb.gov.sg/fi10/fi10333p.nsf/w/CNOverview?OpenDocument (accessed 14 December 2012).

HDB (2012b). Buying a new flat. *HDB InfoWEB*. http://www.hdb.gov.sg/fi10/fi10321p.nsf/w/BuyingNewFlatModeEC?OpenDocument (accessed 18 December 2012).

He, D. (2012). Property prices, inflation, and policy challenges in Hong Kong. *Proceedings of the Workshop on Globalization and Inflation Dynamics in Asia and the Pacific, Hong Kong*. Basel: Bank for International Settlements, Papers No. 70.

Heng, J. (2013). Supply of new HDB flats to taper off from 2014. *AsiaOne Business* (2 December). https://www.asiaone.com/supply-new-hdb-flats-taper-2014 (accessed 7 December 2013).

Henry, K., Drysdale, P., Livingstone, C. et al. (2012). *Australia in the Asian Century White Paper*. Canberra: Commonwealth of Australia.

HIA (2018). *Affordability report*. https://www.internationalhousingassociation.org/fileUpload_details.aspx?contentTypeID=3&contentID=254954 (accessed 12 November 2020).

Hiebert, D. (2017). Immigrants and refugees in the housing markets of Montreal, Toronto and Vancouver, 2011. *Canadian Journal of Urban Research* 26 (2): 52–78.

Hirayama, Y. (2010). The role of home ownership in Japan's aged society. *Journal of Housing and the Built Environment* 25 (2): 175–191.

Hirschman, A. (1970). *Exit, Voice and Loyalty*. Cambridge, MA.: Harvard University Press.

HKCSS (Hong Kong Council of Social Service) (2014). *Social development index 2014*. Hong Kong: HKCSS and the Community Chest. http://socialindicators.org.hk/sites/default/files/shares/files/SDI%202014_press_release_final_eng.pdf (accessed 31 March 2020).

HKCSS (2018). *Social development index 2018. Hong Kong: HKCSS and the Community Chest*. https://www.socialindicators.org.hk/sites/default/files/2020-11/SDI2018_PPT_chi.pdf (accessed 31 March 2020).

HKHA (Hong Kong Housing Authority) (2019) *Housing in Figures 2019*. Hong Kong: Government of Hong Kong SAR. https://www.thb.gov.hk/eng/psp/publications/housing/HIF2019.pdf (accessed 13 March 2020).

HKHA (2022) *Number of applications and average waiting time for public rental housing*. Hong Kong: Government of Hong Kong SAR. https://www.housingau thority.gov.hk/en/about-us/publications-and-statistics/prh-applications-average-waiting-time/index.html (accessed 26 May 2022).

HKIC (Hong Kong Ideas Centre) (2015). Situations and aspirations of youths in Hong Kong. https://www.ideascentre.hk/wordpress/wp-content/uploads/2009/02/Youth-study-Report-final.pdf (Chinese) (accessed 8 April 2020).

HKMA (Hong Kong Monetary Authority) (2017). Hong Kong's property market and macroprudential measures. In: *Macroprudential Policy Frameworks, Implementation and Relationships with Other Policies*, 94 (ed. Bank for International Settlements), 141–152. Basel: Bank for International Settlements.

HKUPOP (Hong Kong University Public Opinion Programme) (2017). *Survey on Hong Kong population and housing issues*.

HKUPOP (2019). *People's trust in the Hong Kong Government, 1992–2019*.

HMRC (HM Revenue and Customs) (2020). *UK stamp tax statistics*. https://www.gov.uk/government/statistics/uk-stamp-tax-statistics (accessed 27 May 2021).

Ho, K.C. and Chua, V. (2018). The neighbourhood roots of social cohesion: notes on an exceptional case of Singapore. *Environment and Planning C* 36 (2): 290–312.

Ho, K.H. (2020). Inside the world of middle-class Hong Kong transnational property investors: '5980 miles to my second home'. *International Journal of Housing Policy* 20 (1): 75–99.

Ho, K.H. and Atkinson, R. (2018). Looking for big 'fry': the motives and methods of middle-class international property investors. *Urban Studies* 55 (9): 2040–2056.

Hodal, K. (2013). Singapore protest: 'Unfamiliar faces are crowding our land'. *The Guardian* (15 February). https://www.theguardian.com/world/2013/feb/15/sin gapore-crisis-immigration-financial-crisis (accessed 28 January 2021).

Hodkinson, S. (2012). The new *urban* enclosure. *City* 16 (5): 500–518.

Hodkinson, S. and Essen, C. (2015). Grounding accumulation by dispossession in everyday life. *International Journal of Law in the Built Environment* 7 (1): 72–91.

Hodkinson, S. and Robbins, G. (2013). The return of class war Conservatism? Housing under the UK Coalition Government. *Critical Social Policy* 33 (1): 57–77.

Hodkinson, S., Watt, P. and Mooney, G. (2013). Neoliberal housing policy -- time for a critical re-appraisal. *Critical Social Policy* 33 (1): 3-16.

Hoekstra, G. (2017). For BC liberals, it's all about big donors. *Vancouver Sun* (13 January), A16.

Hofman, A. and Aalbers, M. (2019). A finance- and real estate-driven regime in the United Kingdom. *Geoforum* 100: 89–100.

Holdsworth, D. (1977). House and home in Vancouver: images of West Coast urbanism, 1886-1929. In: *The Canadian City: Essays in Urban History* (ed. A. Artibise and G. Stelter), 186–211. Toronto: McClelland and Stewart.

HSR (2012a). *Chinese participation in the local real estate sector*. Singapore: HSR Real Estate Company, special report (August).

HSR (2012b). *The rise (and rise) of small format homes*. Singapore: HSR Real Estate Company, special report (April/May).

Hubbard, P. and Lees, L. (2018). The right to community: legal geographies of resistance on London's final gentrification frontier. *City* 22 (1): 8–25.

Hudson, N. (2012). A property nation divided. *Residential Property Focus* Q4, 7. https://pdf.euro.savills.co.uk/residential—other/rpf-q412-lr.pdf (accessed 16 April 2021).

Hugo, G., and Bell, M. (1998). The hypothesis of welfare-led migration to rural areas: the Australian case. In: *Migration into Rural Areas: Theories and Issues* (ed. P. Boyle and K. Halfacree), 107–133. Chichester, UK: Wiley.

Hugo, G. and Harris, K. (2011). *Population distribution effects of migration in Australia*. Canberra: Department of Immigration and Citizenship, Government of Australia. https://apo.org.au/node/160676 (accessed 14 August 2020).

Hui, E.C.M., Ho, V., and Ho, D. (2004). Land value capture mechanisms in Hong Kong and Singapore. *Journal of Property Investment and Finance* 22 (1): 76–100.

Hui, E.C.M. and Yu, K.H. (2012). Assisted homeownership, investment and their roles in private property price dynamics in Hong Kong. *Habitat International* 36 (2): 219–225.

Hulchanski, D. (2004). What factors shape Canadian housing policy? The intergovernmental role in Canada's housing system. In: *Canada, State of the Federation 2004: Municipal-Federal-Provincial Relations* (ed. R. Young and C. Leuprecht), 221–247. Montreal and Kingston: McGill-Queens University Press.

Hulse, K., Reynolds, M., and Martin, C. (2020). The Everyman archetype: discursive reframing of private landlords in the financialization of rental housing. *Housing Studies* 35 (6): 981–1003.

Hutton, T. (2019). City on the edge: Vancouver and circuits of capital, control and culture. In: *Planning on the Edge* (ed. P. Gurstein and T. Hutton), 47–74. Vancouver: UBC Press.

Hutton, T. (2022). *Millennial Metropolis: Space, Place and Territory in the Remaking of London*. London: Routledge.

Igan, D. (2012). *Dealing with real estate booms and busts*. Basel: Bank for International Settlements, BIS Paper No. 64J. https://ssrn.com/abstract=2075576 (accessed 9 March 2020).

Igan, D., Kabundi, A., Nadal De Simone, F. et al. (2011). Housing, credit, and real activity cycles: characteristics and comovement. *Journal of Housing Economics* 20 (3): 210–231.

IIF (Institute of International Finance) (2016). *Capital Flows to Emerging Markets*. Washington, D.C.: https://images.magnetmail.net/images/clients/IIF_2/attach/CF_0116_Press(3).pdf (accessed 3 August 2019).

IMF (International Monetary Fund) (2012). *Singapore: 2012 Article IV consultation*. Washington, DC: IMF Country Report No. 12/248. https://www.imf.org/external/pubs/ft/scr/2012/cr12248.pdf (accessed 15 October 2013).

IMF (2016). *Global Housing Watch*. Washington DC. http://www.imf.org/external/research/housing/report/pdf/1116.pdf (accessed 23 December 2020).

IMF (2017a). *Singapore: 2017 Article IV consultation*. Washington, DC: IMF Country Report No. 17/240. https://www.imf.org/en/Publications/CR/Issues/2017/07/28/Singapore-2017-Article-IV-Consultation-Press-Release-Staff-Report-45144 (accessed 29 January 2021).

IMF (2017b). *Singapore selected issues*. Washington, DC: IMF Country Report No. 17/241. https://www.imf.org/en/Publications/CR/Issues/2017/07/28/Singapore-Selected-Issues-45148 (accessed 1 February 2021).

IMF (2018a). *Australia 2017 Article IV consultation*. Washington, DC: IMF Country Report No. 18/44. https://www.imf.org/en/Publications/CR/Issues/2018/02/20/Australia-2017-Article-IV-Consultation-Press-Release-Staff-Report-and-Statement-by-the-45631 (accessed 27 October 2020).

IMF (2018b). *Global financial stability report*. Washington DC: https://www.imf.org/en/Publications/GFSR/Issues/2018/04/02/Global-Financial-Stability-Report-April-2018 (accessed 21 December 2020).

IMF (2019a). *Singapore: 2019 Article IV consultation*. Washington, DC: IMF Country Report No. 19/233. https://www.imf.org/en/Publications/CR/Issues/2019/07/15/Singapore-2019-Article-IV-Consultation-Press-Release-Staff-Report-and-Statement-by-the-47119 (accessed 26 January 2021).

IMF (2019b). *People's Republic of China–Hong Kong SAR*. Washington, DC: IMF Country Report No. 19/394. https://www.imf.org/en/Publications/CR/Issues/2019/12/26/People-s-Republic-of-China-Hong-Kong-Special-Administrative-Region-2019-Article-IV-48919 (accessed 11 March 2020).

IMF (2019c). *Global financial stability report*. Washington DC: https://www.imf.org/en/Publications/GFSR/Issues/2019/03/27/Global-Financial-Stability-Report-April-2019 (accessed 21 December 2020).

IMF (2020). *Australia 2019 Article IV consultation*. Washington DC: IMF Country Report No. 20/68. https://www.imf.org/en/Publications/CR/Issues/2020/03/03/Australia-2019-Article-IV-Consultation-Press-Release-Staff-Report-and-Statement-by-the-49241 (accessed 21 October 2020).

Insights West (2021). Approval levels for Dr Bonnie Henry remain sky-high but cracks appearing for John Horgan as perception of performance overall and on housing, crime and opioid crisis deteriorates (28 June) [online].

Ip, I.C. (2018). State, class and capital: gentrification and new urban developmentalism in Hong Kong. *Critical Sociology* 44 (3): 547–562.

Ip, I.C. (2019). The fall of the Hong Kong dream: new paths of urban gentrification in Hong Kong. In: *Developmentalist Cities?* (ed. J. Doucette and B.G. Park), 271–291. Leiden: Brill.

Izuhara, M. (2016). Reconsidering the housing asset-based welfare approach: reflection from East Asian experiences. *Social Policy and Society* 15 (2): 177–188.

Jacobs, J. and Cairns, S. (2008). The modern touch: interior design and modernisation in post-independence Singapore. *Environment and Planning A* 40 (3): 572–595.

Janda, M. (2014). Chinese buyers to invest $44b in Australian real estate: analysts. *ABC News* (4 March). https://www.abc.net.au/news/2014-03-05/chinese-buyers-to-invest-44-billion-dollars-in-australian-real-/5300494 (accessed 8 October 2020).

Janda, M. (2017). Real estate: overseas buyers account for up to a quarter of new home sales. *ABC News* (10 October). https://www.abc.net.au/news/2017-10-11/foreign-buyers-not-deterred-by-rising-stamp-duty/9038014 (accessed 28 October 2020).

Jang, B. (2016). Luxury tax casts wide net. *Globe and Mail* (18 February), B1, B2.

Jardines (2019). *Annual report 2018*. Hamilton, Bermuda. https://www.jardines.com/assets/files/Investors/Reports/matheson/jm-ar2018.pdf (accessed 22 April 2020).

Jericho, G. (2017). The latest tax data proves it: negative gearing benefits the rich the most. *The Guardian* (12 April). https://www.theguardian.com/business/grogonomics/2017/apr/13/the-latest-tax-data-proves-it-negative-gearing-benefits-the-rich-the-most (accessed 20 October 2020).

JFIU (Joint Financial Intelligence Unit) (2019). *No. of STRs Received*. Hong Kong: Government of Hong Kong SAR. https://www.jfiu.gov.hk/en/statistics_str.html (accessed 18 February 2020).

Johnston, R.J. (1983). Review of *Sydney Boom, Sydney Bust*. *Environment and Planning A* 15 (4): 561.

Jones, C. and Ley, D. (2016). Transit-oriented development and gentrification along Metro Vancouver's low-income corridor. *The Canadian Geographer* 60 (1): 9–22.

Jones, G., Straughn, P., and Chan, A. (ed.) (2009). *Ultra-low Fertility in Pacific Asia: Trends, Causes and Policy Issues*. London: Routledge.

Jupp, J. (1995). From 'White Australia' to 'part of Asia': recent shifts in Australian immigration policy towards the region. *International Migration Review* 29 (1): 207–228.

Jupp, J. (2004). *The English in Australia*. Cambridge: Cambridge University Press.

Juwai (2017). Chinese global property investment report. https://list.juwai.com/news/2017/07/juwai-releases-chinese-global-property-investment-report (accessed 3 May 2019).

Juwai (2018). *Chinese global property investment report*. http://www.sonjapedersen.com/juwai/chinese-global-property-investment-report-2018.pdf (accessed 10 September 2021).

Juwai (2020). *Juwai's mission*. https://list.juwai.com/about (accessed 7 January 2021).

Karp, P. (2016). No changes to negative gearing or capital gains tax in budget says Malcolm Turnbull. *The Guardian* (24 April). https://www.theguardian.com/australia-news/2016/apr/24/michaelia-cash-confirms-government-wont-change-negative-gearing (accessed 21 October 2020).

Kemeny, J. (1980). Home ownership and privatisation. *International Journal of Urban and Regional Research* 4 (3): 372–388.

Kemeny, J. (2005). 'The really big trade-off' between home ownership and welfare: Castles' evaluation of the 1980 thesis, and a reformulation 25 years on. *Housing, Theory and Society* 22 (2): 59–75.

Keppel Corporation (2019). *Forward together: report to shareholders 2019*. Singapore. https://www.kepcorp.com/annualreport2019 (accessed 18 January 2021).

Khadem, N. (2020). Australian property bubble hasn't yet burst, but can house prices keep rising amid the pandemic? *ABC News* (5 November). https://www.abc.net.

au/news/2020-11-06/property-bubble-burst-coronavirus-pandemic-house-pric es/12852854 (accessed 20 November 2020).

Khaw, B.W. (2015). Interview. *Urban Solutions No 7*: 4–11. (Centre for Liveable Cities, Singapore).

Kitson, M., Martin, R., and Tyler, P. (2011). The geographies of austerity. *Cambridge Journal of Regions, Economy and Society* 4 (3): 289–302.

Knight Frank (2013). *International residential investment in London*. https://content. knightfrank.com/research/503/documents/en/2013-1217.pdf (accessed 30 April 2021).

Knight Frank (2020). *UK property market outlook: week beginning 19 October*. https:// www.knightfrank.com/research/article/2020-10-19-uk-property-market-out look-week-beginning-19-october (accessed 29 April 2021).

Knight Frank Singapore (2012). *Berkeley launches new iconic development in the heart of Westminster*. Press release (18 July).

Knight Frank Singapore (2013a). A new wave of cooling measures in Asia. *Asia Pacific Residential Review* (April).

Knight Frank Singapore (2013b). MAS rules on total debt servicing ratio and refinement of LTV rules: possible reduction in investor demand for private homes. *Newsletter* (July).

Knight Frank Sydney (2015). *Chinese outward real estate investment globally and into Australia*. (April). https://content.knightfrank.com/news/6972/852-article-1.pdf (accessed 6 October 2020).

Knight Frank Sydney (2017). *Foreign investment in Australian residential property*. (June). https://content.knightfrank.com/research/825/documents/en/foreign-investment- in-australian-residential-june-2017-4727.pdf (accessed 26 October 2020).

Knoll, K., Schularick, M., and Steger, T. (2017). No price like home: global house prices, 1870-2012. *American Economic Review* 107 (2): 331–353.

Kolet, I. and Quinn, G. (2013). China growth sets Vancouver home prices. *Bloomberg* (20 January). http://www.bloomberg.com/news/articles/2013-01-20/china- growth-sets-vancouver-home-prices-chart-of-the-day (accessed 30 June 2015).

Kong, L. (2011). *Conserving the Past, Creating the Future: Urban Heritage in Singapore*. Singapore: Straits Times Press.

Kong, L. and Yeoh, B.S.A. (2003). *The Politics of Landscape in Singapore: Constructions of "Nation"*. Syracuse: Syracuse University Press.

Kotkin, J., Shroff, A., Modarres, A. et al. (2012). *The Rise of Post-Familialism: Humanity's Future?* Singapore: Centre for Governance and Leadership, Civil Service College.

Kuttner, K. and Shim, I. (2013). Can non-interest rate policies stabilise housing markets? Evidence from a panel of 57 economies. Basel: BIS Working Papers No. 433. https://www.bis.org/publ/work433.pdf (accessed 21 August 2017).

Kwan, S. and Kwan, N. (2009). *The Dragon and the Crown: Hong Kong Memoirs*. Hong Kong: Hong Kong University Press.

Kwang, H.F. (2012). Avoid feast and famine in housing. *The Straits Times* (4 November), p. 43.

La Grange, A. (2007). Housing 1997-2007. In: *The Hong Kong Special Administrative Region in Its First Decade* (ed. J. Cheng), 669–728. Hong Kong: City University of Hong Kong Press.

La Grange, A. and Pretorius, F. (2005). Shifts along the decommodification-commodification continuum: housing delivery and state accumulation in Hong Kong. *Urban Studies* 42 (13): 2471–2488.

La Grange, A. and Pretorius, F. (2014). State-led gentrification in Hong Kong. *Urban Studies* 53 (3): 506–523.

Lai, K.P.Y. (2013). The Lehman Minibonds crisis and financialisation of investor subjects in Singapore. *Area* 45 (3): 273–282.

Lai, C. and Liu, Y. (2010). How the Masterpiece came to feature in a changing landscape. *South China Morning Post* (17 February). http://www.scmp.com/article/706288/how-masterpiece-came-feature-changing-landscape (accessed 1 April 2012).

Lam, K.S. (2018). Sun Hung Kai wraps up biggest weekend launch with a sell-out in Yuen Long as vacancy tax bites. *South China Morning Post* (5 August). https://www.scmp.com/property/hong-kong-china/article/2158289/sun-hung-kai-wraps-biggest-weekend-launch-sell-out-yuen (accessed 2 March 2020).

Lanchester, J. (2012). Why the super-rich love the UK. *The Guardian* (24 February). http://www.theguardian.com/society/2012/feb/24/why-super-rich-love-uk (accessed 25 February 2012).

Lau, M. (2016). Underground banks siphon HK$245 billion out of Chinese province in a single year. *South China Morning Post* (13 January). https://www.scmp.com/news/china/policies-politics/article/1900494/underground-banks-siphon-hk245-billion-out-chinese (accessed 18 February 2020).

Lauster, N. (2016). *The Death and Life of the Single-Family House*. Philadelphia: Temple University Press.

Lawford, M. 2018. Sound of silence sweeps through Maida Vale's housing market. *Financial Times* (12 April). https://www.ft.com/content/413181c2-399e-11e8-8b98-2f31af407cc8 (accessed 17 May 2021).

Leamer, E. (2007). Housing is the business cycle. National Bureau of Economic Research Working Paper *13428*, Cambridge MA.

Lee, C., Ma, L., and Zhou, Y.S. (2017). The changing dynamics of policy experiment in Singapore: does the 2011 general election make a difference? *Asian Journal of Political Science* 25 (3): 287–306.

Lee, F.L.F., Yuen, S., Tang, G., and Cheng, E.W. (2019). Hong Kong's summer of uprising: from anti-extradition to anti-authoritarian protests. *China Review* 19 (4): 1–32.

Lee, J. (2014). Integrating economic and social policy through the Singapore housing system. In: *Housing East Asia* (ed. J. Doling and R. Ronald), 162–179. Basingstoke, UK: Palgrave Macmillan.

Lee, J. (2015). Christy Clark say no to tax on housing investors. *Vancouver Sun* (6 May), p. A1.

Lee, J.W.Y. and Tang, W.S. (2016). The hegemony of the real estate industry. *Urban Studies* 54 (15): 3403–3422.

Lees, L. (2012). The geography of gentrification: thinking through comparative urbanism. *Progress in Human Geography* 36 (2): 155–171.

Lees, L. (2014). The urban injustices of New Labour's 'new urban renewal': the case of the Aylesbury Estate in London. *Antipode* 46 (4): 921–947.

Lees, L. and Ferreri, M. (2016). Resisting gentrification on its final frontiers: lessons from the Heygate Estate in London (1974-2013). *Cities* 57 (1): 14–24.

Lees, L. and Hubbard, P. (2021). ""So, you don't want us here no more?" Slow violence, frustrated hope, and racialized struggle on London's Council estates. *Housing, Theory and Society*. doi:https://doi.org/10.1080/14036096.2021.1959392.

Lees, L., Shin, H.B., and Lopez-Morales, E. (2016). *Planetary Gentrification*. Cambridge, UK: Polity Press.

Lees, L. and White, H. (2020). The social cleansing of London council estates: everyday experiences of 'accumulative dispossession'. *Housing Studies* 35 (10): 1701–1722.

Lee-Young, J. (2020). Corporate landlords boost stake in rentals. *Vancouver Sun* (4 December), p. A8.

Lefebvre, H. (1969). *The Explosion*. New York: Monthly Review Press.

Lefebvre, H. (2003). *The Urban Revolution*. Minneapolis: University of Minnesota Press.

Leigh, D., Frayman, H., and Ball, J. (2012). How secret offshore firms feed London's property boom. *The Guardian* (26 November). https://www.theguardian.com/uk/2012/nov/26/secret-offshore-firms-fuel-london-property (accessed 4 February 2014).

Lendlease (2019). *As the world reinvents itself: annual report 2019*. Sydney: Lendlease. https://www.annualreports.com/HostedData/AnnualReportArchive/l/OTC_LLESF_2019.pdf (accessed 30 November 2019).

Levitas, R. (2012). The just's umbrella: austerity and the Big Society in Coalition policy and beyond. *Critical Social Policy* 32 (3): 320–342.

Lex (2013). Singapore property: seventh time lucky? *Financial Times* (14 January). https://www.ft.com/content/0b4a3284-5e1b-11e2-a771-00144feab49a (accessed 15 March 2014).

Ley, D. (1995). Between Europe and Asia: the case of the missing sequoias. *Ecumene* 2 (2): 187–212.

Ley, D. (1996). *The New Middle Class and the Remaking of the Central City*. Oxford: Oxford University Press.

Ley, D. (2003). Seeking *homo economicus*: the strange story of Canada's Business Immigration Program. *Annals, Association of American Geographers* 93 (2): 426–441.

Ley, D. (2007). Countervailing immigration and domestic migration in gateway cities: Australian and Canadian variations on an American theme. *Economic Geography* 83 (3): 231–254.

Ley, D. (2010). *Millionaire Migrants: Trans-Pacific Life Lines*. Chichester UK: Wiley-Blackwell.

Ley, D. (2013). Does transnationalism trump immigrant integration? Evidence from Canada's links with East Asia. *Journal of Ethnic and Migration Studies* 39 (6): 921–938.

Ley, D. (2017). Global China and the making of Vancouver's residential property market. *International Journal of Housing Policy* 17 (1): 15–34.

Ley, D. (2020). Housing Vancouver, 1972–2017: a personal urban geography. *The Canadian Geographer* 64 (4): 441–454.

Ley, D. (2021). A regional growth ecology, a great wall of capital, and a metropolitan housing market. *Urban Studies* 58 (2): 297–315.

Ley, D. and Teo, S.Y. (2014). Gentrification in Hong Kong? Epistemology *vs.* ontology. *International Journal of Urban and Regional Research* 38 (4): 1286–1303.

Ley, D. and Tutchener, J. (2001). Immigration, globalisation and house price movements in Canada's gateway cities. *Housing Studies* 16 (2): 199–223.

Leyshon, A. and French, S. (2009). 'We All Live in a Robbie Fowler House': the geographies of the buy to let market in the UK. *British Journal of Politics and International Relations* 11 (3): 438–460.

Lhatoo, Y. (2016). 61 sq ft flats in Hong Kong? Why not just bury us in coffins and be done with it? *South China Morning Post* (27 October). https://www.scmp.com/comment/insight-opinion/article/2040613/61-sq-ft-flats-hong-kong-why-not-just-bury-us-coffins-and-be (accessed 8 April 2020).

Li, A.J.J. (2020) Singapore's divisions are deepening. *Financial Times* (28 July). https://www.ft.com/content/103cf18e-18c5-4028-8824-52bdd21a8c1a (accessed 5 February 2021).

Li, L.H., Wong, S.K., and Cheung, K.S. (2016). Land supply and housing prices in Hong Kong: the political economy of urban land policy. *Environment and Planning C* 34 (5): 981–998.

Li, S. (2016) Finance firms upend HKMA's lending caps on property, adding fuel to red-hot market. *South China Morning Post*, 29 September. https://www.scmp.com/property/hong-kong-china/article/2023421/finance-firms-upend-hkmas-lending-caps-property-adding-fuel. Last accessed 11 March 2020.

Li, S. (2017). Who buys multiple apartments in Hong Kong when most struggle to own one? Here's a list. *South China Morning Post* (2 May). https://www.scmp.com/property/hong-kong-china/article/2092396/who-buys-multiple-apartments-hong-kong-when-most-struggle (accessed 26 February 2020).

Li, S. (2020). Hongkongers emerge as some of the busiest buyers of UK homes, as they snap up property ahead of exodus by BN(O) passport holders. *South China Morning Post* (18 November). https://www.scmp.com/business/article/3110325/hongkongers-emerge-some-busiest-buyers-uk-homes-they-snap-property-ahead (accessed 29 April 2021).

Li, S. and Arcibal, C. (2019). Hong Kong's property market has 10 more years in its bull run. *South China Morning Post* (9 May). https://www.scmp.com/property/hong-kong-china/article/3009468/hong-kongs-property-market-has-10-more-years-its-bull-run (accessed 2 March 2020).

Li, SM. (1990). The Sino-British Joint Declaration, 1997, and the land market of Hong Kong. *Review of Urban and Regional Development Studies* 2 (1): 84–101.

Li, SM. (2016). Burst of the property bubble and Hong Kong's changing land and housing policies post-1997. *Eurasian Geography and Economics* 57 (2): 228–248.

Li, W. and Hendrischke, H. (2020). Chinese outbound investment in Australia: from state control to entrepreneurship. *The China Quarterly* 243: 701–736.

Li, X., Hui, E.C.M., and Shen, J. (2020). The consequences of Chinese outward real estate investment: evidence from Hong Kong's land market. *Habitat International* 98: 102151.

Li, Z., Shen, L., and Zhang, C. (2020). Capital flows, asset prices, and the real economy: a "China shock" in the US real estate market. *Federal Reserve International Finance Discussion Papers 1286*. https://www.federalreserve.gov/econres/ifdp/files/ifdp1286.pdf (accessed 7 September 2021).

Liao, W.C., Zhao, D., Lim, L.P., and Wong, G.M.W. (2015). Foreign liquidity to real estate market: ripple effect and housing price dynamics. *Urban Studies* 52 (1): 138–158.

Liaw, T. (2011). Tight squeeze. *The Standard* (Hong Kong) (17 February), p. 16.

Lim, T., Leong, C.H., and Suliman, F. (2020). Managing Singapore's residential diversity through Ethnic Integration Policy. *Equality Diversity and Inclusion* 39 (2): 109–125.

Lin, G.C.S. (1997). *Red Capitalism in South China: Growth and Development in the Pearl River Delta*. Vancouver: UBC Press.

Lin, G.C.S. (2009). *Developing China: Land, Politics, and Social Conditions*. London: Routledge.

Liu, P. and Li, S. (2020). Li Ka-shing's US$1.2 billion scheme to build 3,500 homes on former royal dockyard site in London gets green light after 15 years. *South China Morning Post* (10 July). https://www.scmp.com/business/companies/article/3092713/li-ka-shings-ps1-billion-scheme-build-3500-homes-former-royal (accessed 7 May 2021).

Liu, P., Yiu, E., and Liu, Y. (2020). China Evergrande rues speculative attack amid cash woes. *South China Morning Post* (24 September). https://www.scmp.com/business/companies/article/3102929/evergrande-rues-speculative-attack-amid-cash-woes-ahead-january (accessed 25 November 2020).

Liu, S. and Gurran, N. (2017). Chinese investment in Australian housing: push and pull factors and implications for understanding international housing demand. *International Journal of Housing Policy* 17 (4): 489–511.

Lo, W.C. (2005). A review of the housing policy. In: *The July 1 Protest Rally: Interpreting a Historic Event* (ed. J. Cheng), 337–362. Hong Kong: City University of Hong Kong Press.

Logan, J. (1992). Cycles and trends in the globalization of real estate. In: *The Restless Urban Landscape* (ed. P. Knox), 33–54. Englewood Cliffs, N.J.: Prentice Hall.

London Councils (2021) *Delivering on London's housing requirement: interim report*. https://www.londoncouncils.gov.uk/our-key-themes/housing-and-planning/housing-and-planning-reports/delivering-london's-housing (accessed 18 August 2021).

London Councils (2022) *Winter homelessness briefing 2021-22*. https://www.londoncouncils.gov.uk/our-key-themes/housing-and-planning/housing-and-planning-reports/winter-homelessness-briefing-2021 (accessed 8 December 2022).

London First (2014) *Home truths:12 steps to solving London's housing crisis*. https://www.businessldn.co.uk/sites/default/files/documents/2018-05/Homes-Truths.pdf (accessed 17 June 2014).

Low, A. (2017). Targeting Singapore's property market: Chinese developers leave a trail of unease. *South China Morning Post* (6 August). https://www.scmp.com/week-asia/business/article/2105294/targeting-singapores-property-market-chinese-developers-leave (accessed 29 January 2021).

Lowe, S. (2011). *The Housing Debate*. Bristol: Policy Press.

Lowe, S., Searle, B., and Smith, S. (2012). From housing wealth to mortgage debt: the emergence of Britain's asset-shaped welfare state. *Social Policy and Society* 11 (1): 105–116.

LPI (Land and Property Information) NSW (2012). *Blue Book*. Sydney: Land and Property Information Division, Department of Finance and Services, Government of New South Wales.

Lum, S.K. (2012). Government policy, housing finance, and housing production in Singapore. In: *Global Housing Markets: Crises, Policies, and Institutions* (ed. A. Bardhan, R. Edelstein, and C. Kroll), 421–446. Hoboken, NJ: Wiley.

Lum, S.K. and Zhou, X. (2019). Urban housing affordability: assessing the effectiveness of policy interventions in the Singapore public housing sector. *International Real Estate Review* 22 (4): 597–625.

Ma, N. (2011). Values change and legitimacy crisis in post-industrial Hong Kong. *Asian Survey* 51 (4): 683–712.

Ma, X. (2021). Chinese housing policy, capital switching and the foreign real estate investment 'boom and bust' in Australia. *International Journal of Housing Policy* 21 (3): 451–463.

Macfarlane, L. (2017). It's time to call the housing crisis what it really is: the largest transfer of wealth in living memory. *Open Democracy* (13 November). https://www.neweconomics.opendemocracy.net/time-call-housing-crisis-really-largest-transfer-wealth-living-memory (accessed 25 November 2020).

Mackie, J. (2019). Not-owner-occupied property skyrockets in Vancouver. *Vancouver Sun* (14 June). https://vancouversun.com/news/local-news/not-owner-occupied-property-skyrockets-in-vancouver (accessed 14 July 2021).

MacLeod, A. (2021). BC and Ottawa reject changes to reduce inequality between renters and homeowners. *The Tyee* (18 June). https://thetyee.ca/News/2021/06/18/BC-Ottawa-Say-No-Changes-Reduce-Inequality-Renters (accessed 9 July 2021).

MacQueen, K. (2015). Vancouver: flight of the young. *Maclean's* 128 (15 June), p. 50–51.

Madden, D. and Marcuse, P. (2016). *In Defense of Housing: The Politics of Crisis*. New York: Verso.

Maher, C. (1994). Housing prices and geographical scale: Australian cities in the 1980s. *Urban Studies* 31 (1): 5–27.

Mai, J. (2016). Hong Kong was busiest office of Panama Papers law firm. *South China Morning Post* (7 April). https://www.scmp.com/news/hong-kong/article/1934566/hong-kong-was-busiest-office-panama-papers-law-firm (accessed 20 February 2020).

Mak, A. (2001). *Relocating Careers: Hong Kong Professionals and Managers in Australia*. Hong Kong: University of Hong Kong, Centre of Asian Studies.

Makhtar, F. and Amin, H. (2020). Easing property curbs isn't on Singapore's radar, Deputy PM says. *Bloomberg* (18 February). https://www.bloomberg.com/news/articles/2020-02-19/easing-property-curbs-isn-t-on-singapore-s-radar-heng-says (accessed 5 February 2021).

Marlow, I. (2020). Singapore's Lee says Hong Kong's leaders must act on grievances. *Bloomberg* (23 January). https://www.bloomberg.com/news/articles/2020-01-24/singapore-s-lee-says-hong-kong-s-leaders-must-act-on-grievances (accessed 10 April 2020).

Martin, R. (2011). The local geographies of the financial crisis: from the housing bubble to economic recession and beyond. *Journal of Economic Geography* 11 (4): 587–618.

McCarthy, W. (2016). Vested interests will prevent cleanup of BC's housing mess. *Globe and Mail* (22 July), p. S3.

McKee, K., Soaita, A.M., and Hoolachan, J. (2020). 'Generation rent' and the emotions of private renting: self-worth, status and insecurity amongst low-income renters. *Housing Studies* 35 (8): 1468–1487.

McKenzie, R. and Atkinson, R. (2021). Anchoring capital in place: the grounded impact of international wealth chains on housing markets in London. *Urban Studies* 57 (1): 21–38.

McLennan, D. and Long, J. (2020). *Extending economic cases for housing policies: rents, ownership and assets*. Sydney: City Futures Research Centre, UNSW. https://cityfutures.ada.unsw.edu.au/research/projects/extending-economic-cases-housing-policies-rents-ownership-and-assets (accessed 20 November 2020).

McMartin, P. (2015). Why don't we have real estate data? *Vancouver Sun* (20 June), p. A4.

McNeil, C., Parkes, H., With Garthwaite, K., and Patrick, R. (2021). *No Longer 'Managing': the Rise of Working Poverty and Fixing Britain's Broken Social Settlement*. London: Institute for Public Policy Research. https://www.ippr.org/files/2021-05/no-longer-managing-may21.pdf (accessed 31 May 2021).

McVeigh, T. and Gibson, O. (2012). London 2012: Danny Boyle thrills audiences with inventive Olympics opening ceremony. *The Observer* (28 July). https://www.theguardian.com/sport/2012/jul/28/london-2012-boyle-olympics-opening-ceremony (accessed 30 March 2021).

Meen, G. (1999). Regional house prices and the ripple effect: a new interpretation. *Housing Studies* 14 (6): 733–753.

Mendez, P. (2017). Linkages between the formal and informal sectors in a Canadian housing market: Vancouver and its secondary suite rentals. *The Canadian Geographer* 61 (4): 550–563.

MHCLG (Ministry of Housing, Communities and Local Government) (2021a). *Households on local authority waiting list, borough*. https://data.london.gov.uk/dataset/households-local-authority-waiting-list-borough (accessed 13 May 2021).

MHCLG (2021b). *Live tables on social housing sales, tables 670, 691*. https://www.gov.uk/government/statistical-data-sets/live-tables-on-social-housing-sales#local-authority-housing-statistics-data (accessed 28 May 2021).

Phang, S.Y. (2001). Housing policy, wealth formation and the Singapore economy. *Housing Studies* 16 (1): 443–459.

Phang, S.Y. (2015). Singapore's housing policies: responding to the challenges of economic transitions. *Singapore Economic Review* 60 (3): 1550036, 1–21.

Phang, S.Y., Lee, D., Cheong, A. et al. (2014). Housing policies in Singapore: evaluation of recent proposals and recommendations for reform. *Singapore Economic Review* 59 (3): 1450025, 1–14.

Phibbs, P. and Gurran, N. (2015). Are governments really interested in fixing the housing problem? Policy capture and busy work in Australia. *Housing Studies* 30 (5): 711–729.

Phibbs, P. and Gurran, N. (2021). The role and significance of planning in the determination of house prices in Australia: recent policy debates. *Environment and Planning A* 53 (3): 457–479.

Pickford, J. (2013). Overseas buyers hungry for London new-build. *Financial Times* (16 January). https://www.ft.com/content/39742b02-5f28-11e2-9f18-00144feab49a#axzz2IJLXS39Z (accessed 5 February 2013).

Piketty, T. (2014). *Capital in the Twenty-First Century*. Cambridge, MA: Belknap Press.

Piketty, T. and Yang, L. (2021). Income and Wealth Inequality in Hong Kong, 1981–2020: the Rise of Pluto-Communism? *World Inequality Lab, WP 2021-18*. https://wid.world/document/income-and-wealth-inequality-in-hong-kong-1981-2020-the-rise-of-pluto-communism-world-inequality-lab-working-paper-2021-18 (accessed 18 December 2021).

Planner, S. (2017). There goes neighbourhood commercial: the story of 33rd Avenue and Mackenzie Street. *Viewpoint Vancouver* (27 November). https://viewpointvancouver.ca/2017/11/27/there-goes-neighbourhood-commercialthe-story-of-33rd-avenue-and-mackenzie-street (accessed 13 December 2022).

Polakova, S.W. (2014). Foreign demand fuels London surge. *South China Morning Post* (3 September). http://www.scmp.com/property/international/article/1583769/foreign-demand-fuels-london-surge (accessed 3 September 2014).

Poon, A. (2006). *Land and the Ruling Class in Hong Kong*. Richmond, BC: privately published. (Chinese edition 2010).

Porter, L. (2018). From an urban country to urban Country: confronting the cult of denial in Australian cities. *Australian Geographer* 49 (2): 239–246.

Pow, C.P. (2011). Living it up: super-rich enclave and transnational elite urbanism in Singapore. *Geoforum* 42 (3): 382–393.

Pow, C.P. (2017). Courting the 'rich and restless': globalisation of real estate and the new spatial fixities of the super-rich in Singapore. *International Journal of Housing Policy* 17 (1): 56–74.

Power, E. (2017). Housing, home ownership and the governance of ageing. *Geographical Journal* 183 (3): 233–246.

Province of British Columbia (2018) *Homes for B.C.: a 30-point plan for housing affordability in British Columbia*. https://www.bcbudget.gov.bc.ca/2018/homesbc/2018_homes_for_bc.pdf (accessed 1 July 2021).

Raco, M., Sun, Y., and Brill, F. (2020). Relational regulation and Chinese real estate investment in London: moving beyond the territorial trap, *Territory, Politics, Governance*. https://doi.org/10.1080/21622671.2020.1837224 (accessed 3 March 2021).

Ramdas, K. (2012). Women in waiting? Singlehood, marriage, and family in Singapore. *Environment and Planning A* 44 (4): 832–848.

Randolph, B. (2020). Foreword, to Pawson, H., Milligan, V. and Yates, J. *Housing Policy in Australia: A Case for System Reform*. Singapore: Palgrave Macmillan, vi.

Randolph, B. and Holloway, D. (2002). The anatomy of housing stress in Sydney. *Urban Policy and Research* 20 (4): 329–355.

Randolph, B. and Holloway, D. (2005). The suburbanisation of disadvantage in Sydney: new problems, new policies. *Opolis* 1: 49–65.

Randolph, B., Pinnegar, S., and Tice, A. (2013). The first home owner boost in Australia: a case study of outcomes in the Sydney housing market. *Urban Policy and Research* 31 (1): 55–73.

Randolph, B. and Tice, A. (2014). Suburbanizing disadvantage in Australian cities: socio-spatial change in an era of neoliberalism. *Journal of Urban Affairs* 36 (S1): 384–399.

Rating and Valuation Department (2020). *Property market statistics*. Hong Kong: Government of Hong Kong SAR. https://www.rvd.gov.hk/en/publications/property_market_statistics.html (accessed 20 May 2020).

Raval, A. (2021). Inside the 'covid triangle': a catastrophe years in the making. *Financial Times Magazine* (4 March). https://www.ft.com/content/0e63541a-8b6d-4bec-8b59-b391bf44a492 (accessed 5 March 2021).

Raymond, E., Duckworth, R., Miller, B. et al. (2018). From foreclosure to eviction: housing insecurity in corporate-owned single-family rentals. *Cityscape* 20 (3): 159–188.

RBA (Reserve Bank of Australia) (2020a). RBA says low rates will help the economy, but tourism and education will drop 10%. *The New Daily* (11 March). https://thenewdaily.com.au/finance/finance-news/2020/03/11/coronavirus-economy-rba (accessed 4 September 2020).

RBA (2020b). Bank lending classified by sector. *Statistical Tables D5*. https://www.rba.gov.au/statistics/tables (accessed 23 October 2020).

RBA (2020c). Household debt – distribution. *Statistical Tables E7*. https://www.rba.gov.au/statistics/tables (accessed 13 November 2020).

RBC Economics (2015). *Housing trends and affordability*. June. http://www.rbc.com/newsroom/_assets-custom/pdf/20150622-HA.pdf (accessed 30 June 2015).

REBGV (Real Estate Board of Greater Vancouver) (2015). *Monthly market report*. https://www.rebgv.org/market-watch/monthly-market-report/december-2015.html (accessed 1 July 2021).

RECBC (Real Estate Council of BC) (2017). *Annual report 2017: focus forward*. http://issuu.com/realestatecouncilofbc/docs/recbc_annual_report_2017_final_copy_391b8b9790a9a8?e=26447547 (accessed 5 December 2017).

Rees, P. (2015). London needs homes, not towers of 'safe-deposit boxes'. *The Guardian* (25 January). https://www.theguardian.com/commentisfree/2015/jan/25/planners-must-take-back-control-of-london (accessed 29 April 2021).

Ren, S. (2021). Beijing once again warns investors against betting on China's red-hot residential property market. *South China Morning Post* (10 June). https://www.scmp.com/business/banking-finance/article/3136804/beijing-once-again-warns-investors-against-betting-chinas (accessed 13 June 2021).

Resolution Foundation (2017). The RF earnings outlook. *Quarterly Briefing Q4 2017.* https://www.resolutionfoundation.org/app/uploads/2018/03/Earnings-outlook-Q4-2017.pdf (accessed 21 April 2021).

Reuters (2013). Chinese buyers flee Hong Kong for overseas property markets. *South China Morning Post* (25 June). https://www.scmp.com/property/hong-kong-china/article/1268575/chinese-buyers-flee-hong-kong-overseas-property-markets (accessed 26 October 2020).

Reuters (2014). Australia set to tighten rules for foreign property buyers. *South China Morning Post* (28 November). https://www.scmp.com/property/international/article/1650320/australia-set-tighten-rules-foreign-property-buyers (accessed 9 October 2020).

Reuters (2019). Chinese millionaires propel Singapore's luxury home sales to 11-year high. *South China Morning Post* (20 September). https://www.scmp.com/news/asia/southeast-asia/article/3029734/chinese-millionaires-propel-singapores-luxury-home-sales (accessed 8 February 2021).

Rex, J. and Moore, R. (1967). *Race Community and Conflict; a Study of Sparkbrook.* London: Oxford University Press.

Riordan, P., Chan, H.M., and Lim, A. (2021). Hong Kong's high-end property sales boom despite protests and pandemic. *Financial Times* (12 November). https://www.ft.com/content/6fadc070-f0d3-4554-8aab-c1acbb744324? (accessed 13 November 2021).

Robertson, J. and Farrell, P. (2016). How a Hong Kong corruption scandal sparked strife at Mossack Fonseca. *The Guardian* (4 April). https://www.theguardian.com/news/2016/apr/04/how-a-hong-kong-corruption-scandal-sparked-strife-at-mossack-fonseca (accessed 20 February 2020).

Robertson, S. (2013). *Transnational Student-Migrants and the State: The Education-Migration Nexus.* Basingstoke, UK: Palgrave Macmillan.

Robertson, S. and Rogers, D. (2017). Education, real estate, immigration: brokerage assemblages and Asian mobilities. *Journal of Ethnic and Migration Studies* 43 (14): 2393–2407.

Robinson, J. (2011). Cities in a world of cities: the comparative gesture. *International Journal of Urban and Regional Research* 35 (1): 1–23.

Robinson, J. (2016). Comparative urbanism: new geographies and cultures of theorizing the urban. *International Journal of Urban and Regional Research* 40 (1): 187–199.

Rofe, M. (2003). 'I want to be global': theorising the gentrifying class as an emergent elite global community. *Urban Studies* 40 (12): 2511–2526.

Rogers, D. (2016). Uploading real estate: home as a digital, global commodity. In: *Housing and Home Unbound: Intersections in Economics, Environment and Politics in Australia* (ed. N.T. Cook, A. Davison, and L. Crabtree), 23–28. Abingdon UK: Routledge.

Rogers, D. and Gibson, C. (2021). Unsolicited urbanism: development monopolies, regulatory-technical fixes and planning as deal-making. *EPA: Economy and Space* 53 (3): 525–547.

Rogers, D. and Koh, S.Y. (ed.) (2018). *The Globalisation of Real Estate*. London: Routledge.

Rogers, D., Lee, C.L., and Yan, D. (2015). The politics of foreign investment in Australian housing: Chinese investors, translocal sales agents and local resistance. *Housing Studies* 30 (5): 730–748.

Rogers, D., Nelson, J., and Wong, A. (2018). Geographies of hyper-commodified housing: foreign capital, market activity, and housing stress. *Geographical Research* 56 (4): 434–446.

Rogers, D., Wong, A., and Nelson, J. (2017). Public perceptions of foreign and Chinese real estate investment: intercultural relations in Global Sydney. *Australian Geographer* 48 (4): 437–455.

Rogoff, K. and Yang, Y. (2020). *Peak China Housing*. Cambridge, MA: National Bureau of Economic Research, Working Paper 27697. https://www.nber.org/papers/w27697 (accessed 4 October 2021).

Ronald, R. (2008). *The Ideology of Homeownership*. London: Palgrave Macmillan.

Ronald, R. (2018). 'Generation rent' and intergenerational relations in the era of housing financialization. *Critical Housing Analysis* 5 (2): 14–26.

Ronald, R. and Dewilde, C. (2017). Why housing wealth and welfare? In: *Housing Wealth and Welfare* (ed. C. Dewilde and R. Ronald), 1–34. Cheltenham UK: Elgar.

Ronald, R. and Doling, J. (2010). Shifting East Asian approaches to home ownership and the housing welfare pillar. *International Journal of Housing Policy* 10 (3): 233–254.

Ronald, R. and Kadi, J. (2018). The revival of private landlords in Britain's post-homeownership society. *New Political Economy* 23 (6): 786–803.

Ronald, R., Lennartz, C., and Kadi, J. (2017). Whatever happened to asset-based welfare? Shifting approaches to housing wealth and welfare security. *Policy & Politics* 45 (2): 173–193.

Roney, T. (2017). GIC makes third student housing deal of 2017 with $302M Sydney buy. *Mingtiandi* (27 April). https://www.mingtiandi.com/real-estate/outbound-investment/gic-makes-third-student-housing-deal-of-2017-with-302m-sydney-buy (accessed 28 April 2017).

Rosewall, T. and Shoory, M. (2017). Houses and apartments in Australia. Reserve Bank of Australia, *Bulletin* (June, 1-11). https://www.rba.gov.au/publications/bulletin/2017/jun/pdf/bu-0617-1-houses-and-apartments-in-australia.pdf (accessed 1 October 2020).

Royal Pacific Realty (2015). *Record breaking year for Royal Pacific Realty Group*. Vancouver, BC.

Ruehl, M. (2015). 581 units sell in 5 hours at Lendlease's Darling Square. *Financial Review* (24 May). https://www.afr.com/property/581-units-sell-in-five-hours-at-lend-leases-darling-square-20150524-gh8cwo (accessed 9 October 2020).

Ryan-Collins, J. and Murray, C. (2020). When homes earn more than jobs: the rentierization of the Australian housing market. *UCL Institute for Innovation and Public Purpose, WP 2020-08.* https://www.ucl.ac.uk/bartlett/public-purpose/wp2020-08 (accessed 1 November 2020).

Sa, F. 2016. *The Effect of Foreign Investors on Local Housing Markets: Evidence from the UK.* London: King's College, Centre for Macroeconomics, Discussion Papers 2016-39. http://www.centreformacroeconomics.ac.uk/Discussion-Papers/2016/CFMDP2016-39-Paper.pdf (accessed 30 April 2021).

Sa, H. and Haila, A. (2021). Urban villagers as real estate developers: embracing property mind through 'planting' housing in North-east China. *Housing Studies.* doi:https://doi.org/10.1080/02673037.2021.1888889.

Sakong, J. (2021). Effect of Ownership Composition on Property Prices and Rents: evidence from Chinese Investment Boom in US Housing Markets. *WP-2021-12 Federal Reserve Bank of Chicago.* https://doi.org/10.21033/wp-2021-12 (accessed 7 September 2021).

Sandercock, L. (2003). *Cosmopolis II: Mongrel Cities of the 21st Century.* London: Continuum.

Saunders, P. (1990). *A Nation of Homeowners.* London: Unwin Hyman.

Savills (2014). Market dynamics: the evolution of prime London. *Spotlight: Prime London Residential Market* Autumn 9-11. https://pdf.euro.savills.co.uk/residential—other/spotlight-prime-london-autumn-2014.pdf (accessed 7 January 2015).

Savills (2016). *Spotlight: prime country residential markets.* April. https://pdf.euro.savills.co.uk/uk/residential—other/spotlight-prime-country-residential-markets.pdf (accessed 15 November 2017).

Savills (2017). *Prime London and country.* Autumn. http://pdf.euro.savills.co.uk/uk/spotlight-on/prime-london-and-country-autumn-2017.pdf (accessed 15 November 2017).

Savills (2018). London still calling for Asian developers. *Prospects: Asia Pacific Real Estate Intelligence.* https://www.savills.com/prospects/themes-london-still-calling-for-asian-developers.html (accessed 7 May 2021).

Savills (2020a). Prime London recovery put on hold. *Prime London Residential.* Q1. https://www.savills.co.uk/research_articles/229130/298813-0 (accessed 20 April 2021).

Savills (2020b). Changing drivers of tenure. *Spotlight: UK Residential Research.* April. https://www.savills.com/research_articles/255800/299497-0 (accessed 17 May 2021).

Savills Hong Kong (2018a). *Briefing: residential sales.* June 2018. http://pdf.savills.asia/asia-pacific-research/hong-kong-research/hong-kong-residential/ress06-2018.pdf (accessed 29 February 2020).

Savills Hong Kong (2018b). *Briefing: residential sales.* October 2018.

Savills Hong Kong (2018c) *Property press digest.* August. http://pdf.savills.asia/asia-pacific-research/hong-kong-research/hong-kong-residential/ress10-2018.pdf (accessed 2 March 2020).

Savills Hong Kong (2020a). *Residential sales*. February 2020. https://pdf.savills.asia/asia-pacific-research/hong-kong-research/hong-kong-residential/ress01-2020.pdf (accessed 20 February 2020).

Savills Hong Kong (2020b). Investment quarterly, *Asia Pacific Report, Q4*. http://pdf.savills.asia/asia-pacific-research/asia-pacific-research/apiq-q4-2019.pdf (accessed 16 March 2020).

Savills Singapore (2015a). *Property press digest* (2 January). http://view.email.savills.info/?j=fe9215757c61077f71&m (accessed 2 January 2015).

Savills Singapore (2015b). *Briefing: residential sales*. November. http://pdf.savills.asia/asia-pacific-research/singapore-research/singapore-residential/singapore-residential-sales-briefing-q3-2015.pdf (accessed 4 November 2015).

Savills Singapore (2016). *Property press digest* (10 March). http://view.email.savills.info/?qs=43f770261efc7c6f8562be551b04f0b20fabfa41075c52e4c1d91 (accessed 12 March 2016).

Savills Singapore (2018). *Briefing: residential sales* (December). https://pdf.savills.asia/asia-pacific-research/singapore-research/singapore-residential/singapore-residential-sales-briefing-q3-2018.pdf (accessed 28 November 2021).

Savills Singapore (2022) *Residential sales* (March). https://pdf.savills.asia/asia-pacific-research/singapore-research/singapore-residential/singapore-residential-sales-briefing-q4-2021.pdf?utm. (Accessed 3 March 2022).

Scanlon, K., Whitehead, C., and Blanc, F. (2017). *The role of overseas investors in the London new-build residential market*. London: London School of Economics. https://www.lse.ac.uk/business-and-consultancy/consulting/assets/documents/the-role-of-overseas-investors-in-the-london-new-build-residential-market.pdf (accessed 30 April 2021).

Scholvin, S., Breul, M., and Diez, J.R. (2019). Revisiting gateway cities: connecting hubs in global networks to their hinterlands. *Urban Geography* 40 (9): 1291–1309.

Schwartz, H. and Seabrooke, L. (2008). Varieties of residential capitalism in the international political economy. *Comparative European Politics* 6 (3): 237–261.

SDS (Singapore Department of Statistics) (2010). *Census of population 2010: advance census release*. https://www.singstat.gov.sg/-/media/files/publications/cop2010/census_2010_advance_census_release/c2010acr.pdf(accessed 5 January 2014).

SDS (2012). *Population trends 2012*. http://costofhealthyliving.com/wp-content/uploads/2013/11/population2012.pdf (accessed 5 January 2014).

SDS (2019). *Yearbook of statistics Singapore*. https://seadelt.net/Asset/Source/Document_ID-455_No-01.pdf (accessed 19 January 2021).

SDS (2020). *Population and population structure*. https://www.singstat.gov.sg/find-data/search-by-theme/population/population-and-population-structure/latest-data (accessed 25 January 2021).

SDS (2021). *Marital status, marriages and divorces*. https://tablebuilder.singstat.gov.sg/publicfacing/createDataTable.action?refId=12092 (accessed 3 February 2021).

Searle, B. and Smith, S. (2010). Housing wealth as insurance: insights from the UK. In: *The Blackwell Companion to the Economics of Housing: The Housing Wealth of Nations* (ed. S. Smith and B. Searle), 339–360. Chichester, UK: Wiley-Blackwell.

Shanghai Daily (2016). Pace of home foreclosures in HK to worsen (21 June). https://archive.shine.cn/business/biz-special/Pace-of-home-foreclosures-in-HK-to-worsen/ (accessed 27 March 2020).

Sharman, A. (2013). Housebuilders seek to nail down profits. *Financial Times* (6 November). http://www.ft.com/cms/s/0/c366900a-4624-11e3-9487-00144fe abdc0.html (accessed 7 November 2013).

Sharman, A. (2014). Caution from big UK housebuilders curbs growth. *Financial Times*(28 July). http://www.ft.com/intl/cms/s/0/e695e61e-1416-11e4-b46f-00144fe abdc0.html (accessed 11 August 2014).

Shaw, W. (2007). *Cities of Whiteness*. Oxford: Blackwell.

Shelter (2021). Denied the right to a safe home: exposing the housing emergency. London. https://assets.ctfassets.net/6sxvmndnpn0s/Shelter_Denied_the_right_to_a_safe_home_Report.pdf (accessed 1 June 2021).

Shiller, R. (2000). *Irrational Exuberance*. Princeton: Princeton University Press.

Shoory, M. (2016). The growth of apartment construction in Australia. Reserve Bank of Australia, *Bulletin* (June, 19-26). https://www.rba.gov.au/publications/bulle tin/2016/jun/pdf/bu-0616-3.pdf (accessed 2 October 2020).

Siddall, E. (2019). Our goal: achieving housing affordability for all. *The Housing Observer* (7 February). https://www.cmhc-schl.gc.ca/en/blog/2019-housing-observer/president-ceo-evan-siddall-announces-ambitious-housing-target-2030 (accessed 13 July 2021).

Sidhu, R., Chong, H.K., and Yeoh, B. (2011). The global schoolhouse: governing Singapore's knowledge economy aspirations. In: *Higher Education in the Asia-Pacific* (ed. S. Marginson, S. Kaur, and E. Sawir), 255–271. London: Springer.

Sin, C.H. (2003). The politics of ethnic integration in Singapore: Malay 'regrouping' as an ideological construct. *International Journal of Urban and Regional Research* 27 (3): 527–544.

Sing, T.F., Tsai, I.C., and Chen, M.C. (2006). Price dynamics in public and private housing markets in Singapore. *Journal of Housing Economics* 15 (4): 305–320.

Singapore Economic Development Board (2009). *Singapore: a global hydrohub*. http://www.edbsingapore.jp/edb/sg/en_uk/index/news/articles/Singapore_The_Global_Hydrohub.html (accessed 9 January 2013).

Sisson, A., Rogers, D., and Gibson, C. (2019). Property speculation, global capital, urban planning and financialisation: *Sydney Boom, Sydney Bust* redux. *Australian Geographer* 50 (1): 1–9.

SITE Economics (2017). *Low incomes and high house prices in metro Vancouver*. http://siteeconomics.com/wp-content/uploads/2017/04/High-House-Prices-and-Low-Incomes-April-2017.pdf (accessed 12 July 2018).

Sito, P. (2013). Hong Kong real estate agents hit as policies to cool property prices dent deal volume. *South China Morning Post* (5 July). https://www.scmp.com/property/hong-kong-china/article/1275552/hong-kong-real-estate-agents-hit-policies-cool-property (accessed 16 March 2020).

Sito, P. and Li, S. (2018). As 209-sq ft Pok Fu Lam flat that sells for $7.86 million, any wonder why one in four Hongkongers can't ever afford a home? *South China Morning Post* (21 March). https://www.scmp.com/property/hong-kong-china/article/2138095/one-four-hongkongers-cant-ever-afford-home-micro-flat-sells (accessed 24 March 2020).

Siu, P. and Li, S. (2015). Hong Kong property cooling measures cloud dreams of young homebuyers. *South China Morning Post* (2 March). https://www.scmp.com/news/hong-kong/article/1727195/hong-kong-property-cooling-measures-cloud-dreams-young-homebuyers (accessed 30 March 2020).

Skaburskis, A. (1988). Speculation and housing prices: a study of Vancouver's boom-bust cycle. *Urban Affairs Quarterly* 23 (4): 556–580.

Slater, T. (2014). The myth of 'broken Britain': welfare reform and the production of ignorance. *Antipode* 46 (4): 948–969.

Smart, A. (1989). Forgotten obstacles, neglected forces: explaining the origins of Hong Kong public housing. *Society and Space* 7 (2): 179–196.

Smart, A. and Lam, K. (2009). Urban conflicts and the policy learning process in Hong Kong: urban conflict and policy change in the 1950s and after 1997. *Journal of Asian Public Policy* 2 (2): 190–208.

Smart, A. and Lee, J. (2003). Financialization and the role of real estate in Hong Kong's regime of accumulation. *Economic Geography* 79 (2): 153–171.

Smith, A. (2019). Justifying and resisting public park commercialisation: the battle for Battersea Park. *European Urban and Regional Studies* 26 (2): 171–185.

Smith, S., Clark, W., Ong Viforj, R. et al. (2022). Housing and economic inequality in the long run: the retreat of owner occupation. *Economy and Society* 51 (2): 161–182.

Smith, S. and Searle, B. (2008). Dematerialising money? Observations on the flow of wealth from housing to other things. *Housing Studies* 23 (1): 21–43.

Smyth, J. (2015). Sydney faces wall of Chinese money. *Financial Times* (30 September). https://www.ft.com/content/6bea60a2-4732-11e5-af2f-4d6e0e5eda22 (accessed 11 September 2020).

Smyth, J. (2017). Shanghai United to invest A$1bn in Australia real estate. *Financial Times* (4 June). https://www.ft.com/content/f89e81d6-4762-11e7-8519-9f94ee97d996 (accessed 8 October 2020).

Smyth, J. (2018). Chinese property investment in Australia plummets. *Financial Times* (28 May). https://www.ft.com/content/0e1e411c-62ed-11e8-90c2-9563a0613e56 (accessed 9 October 2020).

Smyth, J. (2020). China demand for Australian resources soars despite souring ties. *Financial Times* (20 July). https://www.ft.com/content/211918d0-8c65-4b94-a0e7-00cdb5f35f84 (accessed 22 July 2020).

Southwark Notes (2013). *One the Elephant.* http://southwarknotes.wordpress.com/local-development-sites/one-the-elephant (accessed 11 September 2014).

Stapledon, N. (2012). Trends and cycles in Sydney and Melbourne house prices from 1880 to 2011. *Australian Economic History Review* 52 (3): 293–317.

Stapledon, N. (2016). The inexorable rise in house prices in Australia since 1970: unique or not? *Australian Economic Review* 49 (3): 317–327.

Statistics Canada (2020). *Table 36-10-0586-01 Distributions of household economic accounts, wealth, Canada, regions and provinces, annual.* https://doi.org/10.25318/3610058601-eng (accessed 14 June 2021).

Statistics Canada (2021a) National balance sheet and financial flow accounts, first quarter 2021. *The Daily* (11 June). https://www150.statcan.gc.ca/n1/daily-quotidien/210611/dq210611a-eng.htm (accessed 14 June 2021).

Statistics Canada (2021b). Income statistics by economic family type and income source. *Table 11- 10-0191-01*. https://www150.statcan.gc.ca/t1/tbl1/en/tv.action?pid=1110019101 (accessed 13 November 2021).

Statistics Canada (2022). Canadian housing statistics program. *The Daily* (12 April). https://www150.statcan.gc.ca/n1/daily-quotidien/220412/dq220412a-eng.htm (accessed 13 April 2022).

Stebbing, A. and Spies-Butcher, B. (2016). The decline of a homeowning society? Asset-based welfare, retirement and intergenerational equity in Australia. *Housing Studies* 31 (2): 190–207.

Stellinga, B. (2022). Housing financialization as a self-sustaining process: political obstacles to the de-financialization of the Dutch housing market. *Housing Studies*. doi:10.1080/02673037.2022.2091117.

Stephens, M. and Norris, M. (2011). Introduction to special issue: comparative housing research. *International Journal of Housing Policy* 11 (4): 333–336.

Stevenson, A. (2015). A high-end property collapse in Singapore. *New York Times* (17 February) B1.

Story, L. and Saul, S. (2015). Stream of foreign wealth flows to elite New York real estate. *New York Times* (7 February). http://www.nytimes.com/2015/02/08/nyregion/stream-of-foreign-wealth-flows-to-time-warner-condos.html (accessed 14 February 2016).

Strange, C. (2010). The personality of environmental prediction: Griffith Taylor as 'latter-day prophet'. *Historical Record of Australian Science* 21 (2): 133–148.

Strijbosch, K. (2015). Single and the city: state influences on intimate relationships of young, single, well-educated women in Singapore. *Journal of Marriage and Family* 77 (5): 1108–1125.

Sun, S.H.L. (2012a). *Population Policy and Reproduction in Singapore: Making Future Citizens*. Abingdon, UK: Routledge.

Sun, S.H.L. (2012b). Social reproduction and the limits of a neoliberal approach: the case of Singapore. *Citizenship Studies* 16 (2): 223–240.

Surak, K. (2022). Who wants to buy a visa? Comparing the uptake of residence by investment programs in the European Union. *Journal of Contemporary European Studies* 30 (1): 151–169.

Suttor, G. (2016). *Still Renovating: A History of Canadian Social Housing Policy*. Montreal and Kingston: McGill-Queen's University Press.

Tan, E. (2011). Election issues. In: *Voting in Change: Politics of Singapore's 2011 General Election* (ed. K.Y.L. Tan and T. Lee), 27–47. Singapore: Ethos Books.

Tan, K.P. (2012). Singapore in 2011: a 'new normal' in politics? *Asian Survey* 52 (1): 220–226.

Tan, S.L. (2019). Aqualand buys out Oxford Properties at Barangaroo Central. *Financial Review* (1 September). https://www.afr.com/property/residential/aqualand-buys-out-oxford-properties-at-barangaroo-central-20190830-p52mi5 (accessed 9 October 2020).

Tang, C., Oxley, M., and Mekic, D. (2017). Meeting commercial and social goals: institutional investment in the housing association sector. *Housing Studies* 32 (4): 411–427.

Tang, W.S. (2008). Hong Kong under Chinese sovereignty: social development and a land (re)development regime. *Eurasian Geography and Economics* 49 (3): 341–361.

Taylor, G. (ed.) (1953). *Geography in the Twentieth Century*. London: Methuen.

Temasek (2020). *Temasek*. https://www.temasek.com.sg/en/what-we-do/our-portfolio (accessed 18 January 2021).

Terrones, M. (2005). Housing prices and macro-economics. *IMF Research Bulletin* 6 (4): 1–3. https://www.imf.org/External/Pubs/FT/irb/2005/eng/04/index.pdf (accessed 27 November 2020).

Thomas, D. (2011). Flat sold for £135m at UK's dearest address. *Financial Times* (15 April). http://www.ft.com/intl/cms/s/0/68e7aafe-678a-11e0-9138-00144fe ab49a.html (accessed 7 December 2012).

TI (Transparency International) (2015). Gold rush: investment visas and corrupt capital flow into the UK. London. https://www.transparency.org.uk/sites/default/files/pdf/publications/GoldRush-TI-UK.pdf (accessed 3 May 2021).

TI (2016). No reason to hide: unmasking the anonymous owners of Canadian companies and trusts. Toronto. https://transparencycanada.ca/link-to-research-materials/no-reason-to-hide-unmasking-the-anonymous-owners-of-canadian-companies-and-trusts (accessed 5 July 2018).

TI (2017). Faulty towers: understanding the impact of overseas corruption on the London property market. https://issuu.com/transparencyuk/docs/tiuk_faulty_towers_april_web (accessed 4 May 2021).

Todd, D. (2021). Liberals simple-minded when it comes to housing. *Vancouver Sun* (10 July), p. B3.

Todd, D. (2022) City has 'created a monster' by taking cash for upzoning. *Vancouver Sun* (21 June), p. A1.

Tomlinson, K. (2016a). Dozens of real estate firms run afoul of money-laundering law. *Globe and Mail* (18 March), p. A1.

Tomlinson, K. (2016b). Shadow flipping. *Globe and Mail* (6 February), p. A8.

Tomlinson, K., (2018). Flipping of condo units by insiders fuels hot Vancouver market. *Globe and Mail* (30 April), p. A1.

Tostevin, P. (2021). The total value of global real estate. *Impacts* (September). https://www.savills.com/impacts/market-trends/the-total-value-of-global-real-estate.html (accessed 6 October 2021).

Troy, L., Randolph, B., Pinnegar, S. et al. (2020). Vertical sprawl in the Australian city: Sydney's high-rise residential development boom. *Urban Policy and Research* 38 (1): 18–36.

Troy, P. (ed.) (2000). *A History of European Housing in Australia*. Cambridge: Cambridge University Press.

Trust for London and New Policy Institute (2013). *London's poverty profile, 2013*. https://www.npi.org.uk/files/3313/8150/0123/Final_full_report.pdf (accessed 31 May 2021).

Trust for London and WPI Economics (2020). *London's poverty profile 2020*. https://trustforlondon.fra1.cdn.digitaloceanspaces.com/media/documents/Londons_Poverty_Profile_2020.pdf (accessed 31 May 2021).

Tsang, D., (2006). Big market, small government. *Press release, Government of Hong Kong SAR.* https://www.ceo.gov.hk/archive/2012/eng/press/oped.htm (accessed 26 November 2021).

Tse, S. (2015). Rethinking graduated citizenship: contemporary public housing in Singapore. *Geoforum* 65: 222–231.

Tsui, E. (2012). Hong Kong warns of assets bubble risk. *Financial Times* (14 September). https://www.ft.com/content/4e4735ac-fe56-11e1-8228-00144feabdc0 (accessed 25 February 2020).

Tsui, E. and Sender, H. (2012). Hong Kong: a majority to accommodate. *Financial Times* (23 April). https://www.ft.com/content/90f19c96-8942-11e1-bed0-00144feab49a (accessed 27 March 2020).

UBS (2018). UBS global real estate bubble index 2018. Zurich. https://www.ubs.com/global/en/media/display-page-ndp/en-20180927-global-real-estate-bubble-index-2018.html (accessed 15 February 2020).

UBS (2019). Billionaire insights 2019. Zurich. https://www.ubs.com/global/en/wealth-management/uhnw/billionaires-report.html (accessed 10 April 2020).

Valuer-General (1986). *New South Wales Real Estate Market.* Sydney: Government of New South Wales.

Vancity (2015). Help wanted: salaries, affordability and the exodus of labour from metro Vancouver. Vancouver City Savings Credit Union. https://www.vancity.com/SharedContent/documents/News/Help_Wanted_May_2015.pdf (accessed 30 June 2015).

Vangrunsven, L. (1992). Integration versus segregation: ethnic minorities and urban politics in Singapore. *Tijdschrift voor Economische en Sociale Geografie* 83 (3): 196–215.

Vogel, R., Ryan, R., Lawrie, A. et al. (2020). Global city Sydney. *Progress in Planning* 136: 100426.

Wake, J. (2020). *17 interactive Case-Shiller home price charts for 20 metros and USA.* https://realestatedecoded.com/case-shiller (accessed 27 November 2020).

Walks, A. (2013). Mapping the urban debtscape. *Urban Geography* 34 (2): 153–187.

Walks, A. (2016). Homeownership, asset-based welfare and the neighbourhood segregation of wealth. *Housing Studies* 31 (7): 755–784.

Walks, A. and Clifford, B. (2015). The political economy of mortgage securitization and the neoliberalization of housing policy in Canada. *Environment and Planning A* 47 (8): 1–19.

Wallace, A., Rhodes, D., and Webber, R. (2017). Overseas investors in London's new build residential housing market. University of York, Centre for Housing Policy. https://www.london.gov.uk/moderngovmb/documents/s58641/pdf (accessed 30 April 2021).

Wang, S.Q., Sigler, T., Liu, Y., and Corcoran, J. (2018). Shifting dynamics of Chinese settlement in Australia: an urban geographic perspective. *Geographical Research* 56 (4): 447–464.

Ware, R., Fortin, P., and Paradis, P.E. (2010). *The economic impact of the immigrant investor program in Canada.* Montreal: Analysis Group. https://www.analysisgroup.com/Insights/publishing/the-economic-impact-of-the-immigrant-investor-program-in-canada-english (accessed 5 March 2015).

Watson, M. (2009). Planning for the future of asset-based welfare? New Labour, financialized economic agency and the housing market. *Planning, Practice and Research* 24 (1): 41–56.

Watson, M. (2010). House price Keynesianism and the contradictions of the modern investor subject. *Housing Studies* 25 (3): 413–426.

Watt, P. (2008). The only class in town? Gentrification and the middle-class colonization of the city and the urban imagination. *International Journal of Urban and Regional Research* 32 (1): 206–211.

Watt, P. (2013). 'It's not for us': regeneration, the 2012 Olympics and the gentrification of East London. *City* 17 (1): 99–118.

Watt, P. (2016). A nomadic war machine in the metropolis. *City* 20 (2): 297–320.

Watt, P. and Minton, A. (2016). London's housing crisis and its activisms. *City* 20 (2): 204–221.

Webb, R., Watson, D., and Cook, S. (2021). Price adjustment in the London housing market. *Urban Studies* 58 (1): 113–130.

Weber, R. (2015). *From Boom to Bubble: How Finance Built the New Chicago*. Chicago: University of Chicago Press.

Westbank (nd). Dialogue with Michael Braun. Vancouver.

Westbrook, L. (2023). 105,000 Hongkongers start new lives in UK since BN(O) visa scheme began 2 years ago. *South China Morning Post* (23 February). https://www.scmp.com/news/hong-kong/society/article/3211282/more-105000-hongkongers-start-new-lives-uk-bno-scheme-began-2-years-ago? (accessed 24 February 2023).

Whitehead, C. (2016). Using projections of household numbers – tensions between planning and economics. *Town and Country Planning* 85 (10): 415–421.

Wijburg, G. (2021). The de-financialization of housing: towards a research agenda. *Housing Studies* 36 (8): 1276–1293.

Wildau, G. (2017). Chinese top official warns economy 'kidnapped' by property bubble. *Financial Times* (10 August). https://www.ft.com/content/3bfea8be-7da2-11e7-9108-edda0bcbc928 (accessed 25 November 2020).

Wineland, D. (2017). Li Ka-shing to sell stake in HK skyscraper for record $5.2 billion, *Financial Times* (2 November). https://www.ft.com/content/32aead4e-bf8e-11e7-9836-b25f8adaa111 (accessed 19 April 2020).

Wissink, B., Koh, S.Y., and Forrest, R. (2017). Tycoon city: political economy, real estate and the super-rich in Hong Kong. In: *Cities and the Super-Rich: Real Estate, Elite Practices, and Urban Political Economy* (ed. R. Forrest, S.Y. Koh, and B. Wissink), 229–252. London: Palgrave Macmillan.

Wokker, C. and Swieringa, J. (2020). The effect of foreign demand on residential property prices: evidence from Australia. *Australian Economic Review* 53 (1): 35–49.

Wolf, M. (2013) Buyers beware of Britain's absurd property trap. *Financial Times* (10 October). https://www.ft.com/content/aa1c9dfa-30ea-11e3-b478-00144fe ab7de (accessed 7 April 2021).

Wong, A. (2017). Transnational real estate in Australia: new Chinese diaspora, media representation and urban transformation in Sydney's Chinatown. *International Journal of Housing Policy* 17 (1): 97–119.

Wong, L. (2003). Chinese business migration to Australia, Canada and the United States: state policy and the global immigration marketplace. *Asian and Pacific Migration Journal* 12 (3): 301–336.

Wong, M. (2018). Why the wealth gap? *South China Morning Post* (27 September). https://www.scmp.com/news/hong-kong/society/article/2165872/why-wealth-gap-hong-kongs-disparity-between-rich-and-poor (accessed 23 March 2020).

Wong, P.Y., Higgins, D., and Wakefield, R. (2017). Chinese investors investment strategies in the Australian residential property market. *Pacific Rim Property Research Journal* 23 (3): 227–247.

Wong, S.HW. (2015). Real estate elite, economic development, and political conflicts in postcolonial Hong Kong. *China Review* 15 (1): 1–28.

Wong, S.HW. (2018). The real estate elite and real estate hegemony. In: *Routledge Handbook of Contemporary Hong Kong* (ed. T.L. Lui, S.W.K. Chiu, and R. Yep), 342–361. London: Routledge.

Wong, S.Y.S., Tsang, W.W.H., Ip, R.M.K. et al. (2018). *Lacunae in land planning: undersized, undersupplied and underestimated*. Hong Kong: Our Hong Kong Foundation, Land and Housing Policy Series. https://www.ourhkfoundation.org.hk/sites/default/files/media/pdf/land_housing_research_report_engv3.pdf (accessed 15 February 2020).

Wong, T., Yeoh, B., Graham, E., and Teo, P. (2004b). Spaces of silence: single parenthood and the 'normal family' in Singapore. *Population, Space and Place* 10 (1): 43–58.

Wong Y.C.R. (2015). *Hong Kong Land for Hong Kong People*. Hong Kong: Hong Kong University Press.

World Bank 2020. *GDP per capita, PPP-Singapore*. Washington DC: World Development Indicators Data Base. https://data.worldbank.org/indicator/NY.GDP.PCAP.PP.CD?end=2019&locations=SG&start=1990&view=chart (accessed 22 January 2021).

Wu, F. (2015). Commodification and housing market cycles in Chinese cities. *International Journal of Housing Policy* 15 (1): 6–26.

Wyly, E., Moos, M., Hammel, D., and Kabahizi, E. (2009). Cartographies of race and class: mapping the class-monopoly rents of American subprime mortgage capital. *International Journal of Urban and Regional Research* 33 (2): 332–354.

Wynn, G. (1992). The rise of Vancouver. In: *Vancouver and Its Region* (ed. G. Wynn and T. Oke), 69–148. Vancouver: UBC Press.

Yao, E. (2014). High rent, low salaries: how young Hongkongers are scheming to secure subsidised housing. *South China Morning Post* (6 November). https://www.scmp.com/lifestyle/article/1633546/high-rent-low-salaries-how-young-hongkongers-are-scheming-secure (accessed 30 March 2020).

Yates, J. (2011). Housing in Australia in the 2000s: on the agenda too late? *Proceedings of The Australian Economy in the 2000s Conference*. Reserve Bank of Australia, Sydney.

Yates, J. (2013). Evaluating social and affordable housing reform in Australia: lessons to be learned from history. *International Journal of Housing Policy* 13 (2): 111–133.

Yates, J. (2016). Why does Australia have an affordable housing problem and what can be done about it? *Australian Economic Review* 49 (3): 328–339.

Ye, J. (2016). *Class Inequality in the Global City: Migrants, Workers and Cosmopolitanism in Singapore*. Basingstoke, UK: Palgrave Macmillan.

Ye, J. (2017). Managing urban diversity through differential inclusion in Singapore. *Society and Space* 35 (6): 1033–1052.

Yeoh, B. (2006). Bifurcated labour: the unequal incorporation of transmigrants in Singapore. *Tijdschrift voor Economische En Sociale Geografie* 97 (1): 26–37.

Yeoh, B. and Lam, T. (2016). Immigration and its (dis)contents: the challenges of highly skilled migration in globalizing Singapore. *American Behavioral Scientist* 60 (5–6): 637–658.

Yeoh, B. and Lin, W. (2012). Rapid growth in Singapore's immigrant population brings policy challenges. *Migration Information Source* (April). http://www.migrationinformation.org/Profiles/display.cfm?id=887 (accessed 19 October 2012).

Yip, N.M. (2014). Housing, crises, and interventions in Hong Kong. In: *Housing East Asia: Socioeconomic and Demographic Challenges* (ed. J. Dorling and R. Ronald), 71–90. Basingstoke, UK: Palgrave Macmillan.

Yip, N.M., Forrest, R., and La Grange, A. (2007). Cohort trajectories in Hong Kong's housing system, 1981-2001. *Housing Studies* 22 (1): 121–136.

Yip, P.S.L. (2019). *From the Global Financial Tsunami to the Property Bubbles in Asia*. Singapore: World Scientific Publishing.

Yiu, C.Y. (2010). Negative real interest rate and housing bubble implosion – an empirical study of Hong Kong. *Journal of Financial Management of Property and Construction* 14 (3): 257–270.

Young, I. (2015). Something is grotesquely wrong with Vancouver's housing market, and the time for denialism is over. *South China Morning Post* (28 May). http://www.scmp.com/comment/blogs/article/1804916/something-grotesquely-wrong-vancouvers-housing-market-and-time (accessed 18 June 2016).

Young, I. (2016a). In Vancouver, house owners made more sitting on their assets than entire population did by actually working last year. *South China Morning Post* (1 June). http://www.scmp.com/comment/blogs/article/1962014/vancouver-house-owners-made-more-sitting-their-assets-entire (accessed 18 June 2016).

Young, I. (2016b). Panama papers: Vancouver is Canada's hotspot for secret tax haven firms, with hundreds of addresses in leaked papers. *South China Morning Post* (25 May). http://www.scmp.com/news/world/united-states-canada/article/1953614/panama-papers-vancouver-canadas-hotspot-secret-tax (accessed 18 June 2016).

Young, I. (2016c). Canada tax chiefs knew foreign money's big role in Vancouver housing 20 years ago, leaked documents show, but they 'ignored' auditors' warning. *South China Morning Post* (20 August). http://www.scmp.com/news/world/united-states-canada/article/2005794/canada-tax-chiefs-knew-foreign-moneys-big-role (accessed 26 August 2016).

Yu, J. and Yu, S. (2014). Hong Kong urged to end property controls. *South China Morning Post* (17 January). https://www.scmp.com/property/hong-kong-china/article/1407261/hong-kong-urged-end-property-controls (accessed 10 March 2020).

Yung, B. (2008). *Hong Kong's Housing Policy: A Case Study in Social Justice*. Hong Kong: Hong Kong University Press.

Zhang, G. and Wang, W.Y. (2019). 'Property talk' among Chinese Australians: WeChat and the production of diasporic space. *Media International Australia* 173 (1): 53–65.

Zhang, J. and Yeoh, B. (2017). The state of fun? Exclusive casino urbanism and its biopolitical borders in Singapore. *Pacific Affairs* 90 (4): 701–723.

Zhao, S. (2017). Does Hong Kong's land sale system need a new lease of life? *South China Morning Post* (18 April). https://www.scmp.com/news/hong-kong/economy/article/2088556/does-hong-kongs-land-sale-system-need-new-lease-life (accessed 16 March 2020).

Zhao, S. (2018). Ramshackle subdivided flats in Hong Kong's old buildings are an 'urban ticking time bomb', researchers warn. *South China Morning Post* (16 July). https://www.scmp.com/news/hong-kong/health-environment/article/2155358/ramshackle-subdivided-flats-hong-kongs-old (accessed 19 March 2020).

Zhao, S. (2019). Property purchasing power of Hong Kong's university graduates only a quarter of those 30 years ago, thanks to high home prices. *South China Morning Post* (31 January). https://www.scmp.com/news/hong-kong/hong-kong-economy/article/2184364/property-purchasing-power-hong-kongs-university (accessed 10 April 2020).

Ziady, H. (2021). People are panic buying homes as prices skyrocket around the world. *CNN Business* (13 May). https://www.cnn.com/2021/05/13/business/global-real-estate-prices/index.html (accessed 14 May 2021).

Index

Note: 'n' after a page number denotes a note number on that page.

Housing Booms in Gateway Cities, First Edition. David Ley.
© 2023 John Wiley & Sons Ltd. Published 2023 by John Wiley & Sons Ltd.